GAINING
WORD POWER

GAINING WORD POWER

Dorothy Rubin
Trenton State College

Macmillan Publishing Co., Inc.
New York
Collier Macmillan Publishers
London

Macmillan Publishing Co., Inc.
866 Third Avenue, New York, New York 10022

Collier Macmillan Canada, Ltd.

ISBN 0-02-404340-0

Printing: 1 2 3 4 5 6 7 8   Year: 8 9 0 1 2 3 4

With love to my understanding and supportive husband Artie, my delightful daughters Carol and Sharon, my precious granddaughter Jennifer, and my dear mother Clara.

PREFACE

Gaining Word Power is an outgrowth of ten years' work ·in helping college students and other adults to build and retain better vocabularies. From that practical experience I have produced a text designed to generate a basic college-level vocabulary quickly, effectively, and pleasantly.

In the book, I develop and apply a number of approaches to vocabulary building based on sound psychological learning principles. Words are presented systematically in graduated levels of difficulty. The learning process in each lesson is stimulated by challenging exercises and puzzles and reinforced by immediate access to the answers and solutions for self-evaluation of progress. Students' individual differences are accommodated not only in the self-contained chapters that permit each student to work at his or her own pace, but also in the extra practice provided for those who need it and in the addition of more difficult words for those who are ready to absorb them. I stress overlearning, the repetition of experiences in different circumstances, because it is essential to the retention of information. A word once introduced will usually recur in many subsequent exercises, for the later exercises build on roots, affixes, and words encountered in the earlier ones.

Although this book has a distinctly pedagogical structure, the structure is diffused for the student among a variety of practices and drills, as well as in crossword puzzles, word scrambles and squares, analogy activities, and cartoons sprinkled through the text. To promote interest, additional, more difficult words are presented in a more challenging approach. Extra practice for those who need or want it occurs in each chapter as a separate section labeled "Additional Practice Sets," in which a variety of alternative exercises covers words introduced in the chapter. Tests and scoring scales are provided so that students may determine how well they are doing.

Gaining Word Power is organized in two parts. Part I emphasizes combining forms and words derived from them; Part II presents words derived less obviously from combining forms. (Combining forms are defined in this text as word parts that join with a word or another word part to form a new word.) Knowledge of combining forms helps students to build new words and to decipher unfamiliar ones. In both parts, words are presented in context, and students are guided in the interpretation of context clues. The two systems, combining forms and context clues, produce an effective gain in an individual's word power.

This book can be used with equal success in a conventional class or by an individual in a learning lab or self-help program.

Acknowledgments

The author wishes to acknowledge her gratitude to Anthony English, for his valuable suggestions, able and creative editing, and support. She also wishes to thank Ron Harris for providing polish and precision to the manuscript. Special thanks must go to her daughter Sharon who not only typed the manuscript and gave of her time but also made helpful and perceptive comments and suggestions.

D. R.

Contents

Appendixes

CHAPTER ONE[1]

This chapter discusses the organization of this book and how one can best go about improving one's vocabulary. Let us begin by considering the importance of vocabulary growth.

THE IMPORTANCE OF VOCABULARY GROWTH

A good vocabulary and good reading go hand in hand. Unless you know the meaning of words, you will have difficulty in understanding what is read. And the more you read, the more words you will add to your vocabulary. Read the following statement:

> The misanthrope was apathetic to the sufferings of those around him.

Do you understand it? Unless you know the meanings of *misanthrope* and *apathetic,* you are not able to read the statement. In order to *read,* you must know the *meanings* of words and the way words are used in sentences.

Acquiring word meanings is an important reading skill. Because of its importance, this skill is being presented in a text by itself.

---

[1]It is very important that you read Chapter One. This chapter introduces you to *Gaining Word Power*. It gives you the information you will need to use this book successfully.

1

THE ORGANIZATION OF THIS BOOK

This book is divided into two parts. Part I deals with vocabulary building through *combining forms*. (The meaning of *combining forms* will be explained to you at the beginning of Part One.) The emphasis is on the *overlearning* of the combining forms so that they can help you to unlock the meanings of many words. (The term *overlearning* is explained later on.) Many words made up from combining forms are presented.

Part II consists of vocabulary words that are not easily made up from combining forms. These words, like the words in Part I, are those that are used very often in lectures, textbooks, and newspapers.

Answers for the exercises are provided at the end of each chapter.

HOW EXERCISES ARE PRESENTED

In Part I the exercises are presented in three steps. The steps are the same for all exercises:

Step I. *Presentation of new combining forms and their meanings.*
  A. Learn new combining forms with their meanings.
  B. Cover the meanings of the combining forms, read the combining forms, and try to recall their meanings. Check the answers immediately.
  C. Cover the combining forms, read the meanings, and try to recall the combining forms. Check the answers immediately.
  D. Cover the meanings of the combining forms again, read the combining forms, and write their meanings in the space provided.

Step II. *Presentation of vocabulary derived[2] from combining forms.*
  Learn words with their meanings and other information as you see the words used in sentences. The words are based on the combining forms learned in Step I. (See the following section.)

Step III. *Practice.*
  Use the words in several different practices to ensure overlearning. After every three exercises, crossword puzzles, word scrambles, and analogies are provided for the given combining forms and words. A multiple-choice vocabulary test and a true-false vocabulary test are supplied for Step II words. Scoring scales are given so that you will know where you stand. If you score below a certain level, you are provided with additional practice sets. In these *additional practice sets,* you are directed to restudy only the combining forms and words you have missed. You are provided with different practice exercises to help you to learn the words you have missed.

---

[2]*Derived* means "made up from."

2

In Part II, Steps II and III are the same as in Part I, but Step I differs. In Step I of Part II, you learn words presented in sentences with context clues for each word. The sentences use many of the words from Part I.

HOW WORDS ARE PRESENTED

The combining forms and words presented are a base from which you can increase your vocabulary quickly and easily. Combining forms and words have been selected on the basis of how often they appear in novels, stories, poems, textbooks, and other nonfiction books, newspapers, and magazines. Words that are commonly used in college lectures are also included.

Words are presented with the following information to help your understanding of the word:

1. Correct spelling and plural (abbreviated *pl.*). Only irregular plurals are shown.

2. Division into syllables. For example: bi · ol · o · gy.

3. Pronunciation. The phonetic (pronunciation) spelling of the word may differ from the regular spelling to describe the pronunciation of the word. For example: **biology** (bī · ol′ o · jē) Usually the syllabication and pronunciation aids are combined in one entry. At times an extra entry is given following the syllabication entry. This extra entry is presented as a further pronunciation aid.

4. Kind of word it is: *v.* for verb, *n.* for noun, *adj.* for adjective, *adv.* for adverb, and *prep.* for preposition.

5. Meaning of the word.[3]

6. Use of the word in a sentence. Only one sentence is given for each word even though the word may have more than one meaning.

Here is an example of the presentation of a word with an extra entry:

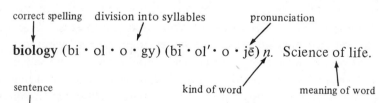

correct spelling   division into syllables   pronunciation

biology (bi · ol · o · gy) (bī · ol′ · o · jē) *n.* Science of life.

sentence   kind of word   meaning of word

Because I intend to be a doctor, I am taking a course in **biology** *to learn about living things.*

---

[3] The meanings of the words are based on *Webster's New Twentieth Century Dictionary*, 2nd ed.; *Webster's Third New International Dictionary*, Unabridged; Funk & Wagnalls *Standard College Dictionary*; *Random House Dictionary of the English Language*; and *The American Heritage Dictionary of the English Language*.

SPECIAL NOTES

A "Special Notes" section includes special information about words that might cause you unusual difficulty.

EXTRA WORD POWER

The combining forms presented in the "Extra Word Power" section are those often used with thousands of words. For this reason they are presented in a special boxed section. The "Extra Word Power" section will give additional help to your vocabulary growth.

ADDITIONAL WORDS

The "Additional Words" section presents some more difficult words. You can unlock their meanings by using combining forms and context clues. To help you still more, a practice activity is provided for these words.

UNDERSTANDING ANALOGIES

Analogy practice is presented after every three exercises. Analogies have to do with relationships. They are relationships between words or ideas. In order to make the best use of analogies, you must know not only the *meanings* of the words, but also the relationship of the words or ideas to one another. For example, "*doctor* is to *hospital* as *minister* is to _____ ." Yes, the answer is *church*. The relationship has to do with specialized persons and the places with which they are associated. Let's try another one: "*beautiful* is to *pretty* as _____ is to *decimate*." Although you know the meanings of *beautiful* and *pretty* and you can figure out that beautiful is more than pretty, you will not be able to arrive at the correct word to complete the analogy if you do not know the meaning of *decimate*. *Decimate* means "to reduce by one tenth" or "to destroy a considerable part of." Because the word that completes the analogy must express the relationship of more or greater than, the answer could be *eradicate* or *annihilate*, because these words mean "to destroy completely."

Some of the relationships that words may have to one another are similar meanings, opposite meanings, classification, going from particular to general, going from general to particular, degree of intensity, specialized labels, characteristics, cause-effect, effect-cause, function, whole-part, ratio, and many more. The preceding relationships do not have to be memorized. You will gain clues to these from the pairs making up the analogies; that is, the words express the relationship. For example: "*pretty* is to *beautiful*"—the relationship is degree of intensity; "*hot* is to *cold*"—the relationship is one of opposites; "*car* is to *vehicle*"—the relationship is classification.

4

PRONUNCIATION KEY

The pronunciation (the way a word sounds) of the words in this book is based on Webster's *New Twentieth Century Dictionary*, 2nd ed., in which a simplified pronunciation key is used. In order to simplify pronunciation further, the author has given only long vowel markings and included only the primary accent mark (').

The accent mark (') is used to show which syllable in a word is stressed. This mark comes right after and slightly above the accented syllable. For example:

pilot (pī ' lot)   biology (bī · ol' o · jē)

In the preceding two words, the syllables *pi'* and *ol'* are sounded with more stress and are called the accented syllables. The dot (·) is used to separate syllables. Note that no dot is used between syllables when the syllable is accented. Also note that the *y* in *biology* has been changed to an $\bar{e}$ and the *g* has been changed to a *j* to aid you in pronunciation.

The long vowel mark (–) also helps to indicate pronunciation. A vowel that has a long vowel mark sounds like its letter name.

A slash through a letter means that the sound it stands for is silent. For example:

bākø nōtø ātø bōat.

As another aid in pronunciation, the following key should be used:

Words ending in *tion, sion,* sound like *shun,* as in *nation.*

Words ending in *cian, tian,* and *sian* sound like *shin,* as in *Martian.*

Words ending in *cious* sound like *shus,* as in *delicious.*

Words having *ph* sound like *f* in *fat, foot,* as in *phone.*

Words ending in *ique* sound like *ēk* in *leøk,* as in *critique, unique.*

Words ending in *le* preceded by a consonant sound like *ul* in *bull,* as in *bubble, candle.*

Words ending in *cial* sound like *shul,* as in *special.*

Words ending in *ce* sound like *s* in *safe, so,* as in *notice, sentence.*

Words beginning in *ce* or *ci* sound like *s* in *safe, so,* as in *cent, cease, citizen.*

Words ending in *c* sound like *k* in *like,* as in *picnic, traffic.*

Words beginning in *c* sound like *k* in *like,* as in *cat, catalog.*

Words beginning in *qu* sound like *kw* as in *queen, quick.*

5

UNDERSTANDING THE TERM *OVERLEARNING*

Although you may have at one time or another met many of the vocabulary words presented in this book, you may not be able to read or use the words because you have not *overlearned* them. Throughout this book, the emphasis is on the overlearning of vocabulary. *Overlearning* is not bad like *overcooking* the roast. Overlearning will help you to hold on to information over a long period of time. To overlearn the material, concentrate on the words to be learned, memorize them, and do all the exercises. Overlearning will take place only if practice is continued even after you think you have learned the information. The additional practice you engage in after you think you have mastered the material is called *overlearning*. As practice is the key to overlearning, you will continue to meet in the practice sets of later exercises many words that you have learned earlier.

SUGGESTIONS ON HOW TO STUDY VOCABULARY

1. You should choose a time best for you so that you do not feel pressured.

2. You should try to find a place free of things that may disturb your studying.

3. You shouldn't try to do all the exercises in one sitting. Studies have shown that you will remember your material better if you space your studying over a period of time. The thing to do is to find and work at a pace that is good for you.

4. *Recall*, which refers to how much you remember, is very important in learning. Recall is used as part of the teaching method in this book. After the presentation of the word and its meaning(s), you are asked to cover the meaning(s) to see if you can recall it (or them).

5. When the entire exercise is completed, go over the words you have learned. In addition, take a few minutes before a new exercise to *review* the previous exercise.

6. To make sure you remember the vocabulary words, try to use them daily in your written work or speech. In addition, see how many times you meet these words in your classroom lectures and readings.

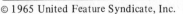
© 1965 United Feature Syndicate, Inc.

6

PART I

COMBINING FORMS AND VOCABULARY DERIVED FROM COMBINING FORMS

Introduction

As a means of helping you to use combining forms to increase your vocabulary, some terms should be defined. There are a great number of words that combine with other words to form new words with different but related meanings, for example, *grandfather* (*grand* + *father*) and *policeman* (*police* + *man*)—both compound words. Many words are combined with additional letters or syllables—either at the beginning (prefix) or at the end (suffix) of the word—to form a new, related word, for example, *replay* (*re* + *play*) and *played* (*play* + *ed*).

In the words *replay* and *played, play* is a root, *re* is a prefix, and *ed* is a suffix. A *root* is the smallest unit of a word that can exist and have meaning. It cannot be divided further. *Replay* is not a root word because it can be divided into *re* and *play*. *Play* is a root word because it cannot be divided further and still keep a meaning related to the root word.

Combining forms are usually defined as roots borrowed from another language that join together or that join with a prefix, a suffix, or both a prefix and a suffix to form a word. Often the English combining forms are derived from Greek and Latin roots. Because the emphasis in this book is on the building of vocabulary meanings rather than on the naming of word parts, prefixes, suffixes, English roots, and combining forms will *all* be referred to as combining forms. *Combining forms in this book are defined as any word part that can join with another word or word part to form a word or a new word.*

The exercises build on previously learned combining forms. Care is taken not to present those that are similar in appearance in the same exercise.

Knowledge of the most common combining forms is valuable in helping you to learn the meaning of an unfamiliar word. For example, knowing that *pseudo* means "false" helps you to "unlock" *pseudoscience*, which means "false science." Knowing that *bi* means "two" and *ped* means "foot" helps you to determine the meaning of *biped* as a two-footed animal.

As an indication of the power of knowing a few combining forms, it has been estimated that with the knowledge of thirty combining forms (which are included in this text), one can unlock the meanings of as many as 14,000 words. Obviously, familiarity with a mere thirty forms is the quickest way to learning the largest number of words. It is also a method that, once learned, helps you to unlock new words all through your life.

CHAPTER TWO

EXERCISE 1

Step I. Combining Forms

A. Directions: A list of combining forms with their meanings follows. Look at the combining forms and their meanings. Concentrate on learning each combining form and its meaning. Cover the meanings, read the combining forms, and state the meanings to yourself. Check to see if you are correct. Now cover the combining forms, read the meanings, and state the combining forms to yourself. Check to see if you are correct.

Combining Forms	*Meanings*
1. anni, annu, enni	year
2. aut, auto	self
3. bio	life
4. bi	two
5. graph	something written; machine

6. ology   the study of; the science of

7. ped,[1] pod   foot

B. Directions: Cover the preceding meanings. Write the meanings of the following combining forms.

Combining Forms	Meanings
1. anni, annu, enni	_____
2. aut, auto	_____
3. bio	_____
4. bi	_____
5. graph	_____
6. ology	_____
7. ped, pod	_____

Step II. Words Derived[2] from Combining Forms

1. **biology** (bi · ol · o · gy) (bī · ol′ o · jē)[3] *n.* The science of life. ***Biology** helps students to learn about living things.*

2. **biography** (bi · og · ra · phy) (bī · og′ ra · fē) *n.* (*pl.* **phies**)[4] An account of a person's life; a person's life story. *I learned all about the life of Martin Luther King, Jr. when I read Coretta King's **biography** of him.*

3. **autobiography** (au · to · bi · og · ra · phy) (au · to · bī · og′ ra · fē) *n.* (*pl.* **phies**) A person's life story written by himself or herself. *Helen Keller, who was deaf, mute, and blind, gives an interesting account of her life in her **autobiography**.*

4. **autograph** (au′ to · graf) *n.* Signature. *adj.* Written by a person's own hand: *an **autograph** letter*; containing autographs: *an **autograph** album*. *v.* To write one's name on or in. *After I get the **autograph** of a famous person, I compare that person's signature with other signatures I have collected.*

---

[1]Only one meaning for the combining form *ped* is presented in Exercise 1. Another meaning will be presented in a later exercise.

[2]*Derived* means "made up from."

[3]When you see two entries in parentheses following the word, the first refers to the syllabication of the word, and the second refers to the phonetic spelling of the word.

[4]*Pl.* is the abbreviation for *plural.*

5. **annual** (an′ n̄u · al) *adj.* Every year; yearly. *At the end of every year the stockholders receive their **annual** report concerning the company's progress.*

6. **anniversary** (an · n̄i · ver′ sar · ē) *n.* (*pl.* **ries**). The yearly return of day or date marking an event or occurrence of some importance. *adj.* Returning or recurring each year. *On August 24 I always celebrate the **anniversary** of my marriage.*

7. **biannual** (bī · an ′ n̄u · al) *adj.* Twice a year; (loosely) occurring every two years. *Our **biannual** block parties, which come twice a year, are lots of fun.*

8. **biennial** (bī · en ′ n̄ē · al) *adj.* Once every two years; lasting for two years. *Our vacation is a **biennial** event because we can afford a vacation only every two years.*

9. **biweekly** (bī · wē̄k ′ lē) *adj.* Every two weeks; twice a week. *My **biweekly** paycheck is always gone at the end of two weeks.*

10. **bimonthly** (bī · month′ lē) *adj.* Every two months; twice a month. *I feel we should change our **bimonthly** meetings to monthly meetings because meeting every two months is not often enough.*

11. **bicycle** (bi · cy · cle) (bī′ si · kul) *n.* A vehicle having two wheels. *You need good balance in order to be able to ride a **bicycle**.*

12. **biped** (bī ′ ped) *n.* A two-footed animal. *Humans, who are **bipeds**, are not the only two-footed animals.*

13. **pedestrian** (pe · des ′ trē · an) *n.* One who goes on foot. ***Pedestrians** as well as motorists should obey traffic laws.*

Special Notes

Note that *biannual* almost always means "twice a year," but when *biannual* is used loosely, it can mean "every two years." *Biennial* means "every two years" or "lasting for two years." In botany, a biennial plant is one that lasts for two years.

Note that the meanings for *biweekly* and *bimonthly* may at times be almost the same, because *biweekly* can mean "every two weeks" and *bimonthly* can mean "twice a month." However, when a word has more than one meaning, *the sentence usually provides clues for the proper meaning.*

1. **bimonthly.** Once every two months; twice a month. *The theater group decided to stop giving **bimonthly** plays because two months did not give them enough time to practice.*

11

2. **biweekly**. Once every two weeks; twice a week. *The **biweekly** newspaper is very large because it comes out only every two weeks.*

Step III. Practice

A. Directions: Using the combining forms that follow, build a word to fit the blank in the sentence.

Combining Forms

bi, anni, auto, bio, graph, ology, ped, pod.

1. You celebrate the _____ of your birth on the same day every year.

2. When you write your _____ , you are writing your own life story.

3. Crossing the street in some cities can be dangerous for the _____ .

4. Can you name an animal, other than man, who is a(n) _____ ?

5. The study of _____ has helped me to learn about living things.

6. One of my assignments is to read a(n) _____ of any president that was written about him after his death.

7. As we have two picnics a year, it is a(n) _____ event.

8. Last year at our _____ Halloween dance, a number of persons developed food poisoning.

9. I have a(n) _____ collection, which includes signatures of some very famous people.

STOP. Check answers at the end of the chapter.

B. Directions: A list of definitions follows. Give the word that *best* fits the definition. Try to relate your definition to the meanings of the combining forms.

Word List

autobiography, bimonthly, biweekly, biology, biannual, biography, anniversary, biennial, bicycle, autograph, biped, annual, pedestrian.

1. A vehicle with two wheels _____

2. Life story written by oneself _____

3. Your signature _____

4. Twice a year _____

5. Life story (written) _____

6. A two-footed or two-legged animal _____

7. The science or study of life _____

8. Every two years _____

9. One who goes on foot _____

10. Once every two months; twice a month _____

11. Once every two weeks; twice a week _____

12. Once a year _____

13. Yearly return of a day or date marking an event of some importance

_____

STOP. Check answers at the end of the chapter.

EXTRA WORD
POWER

> **ar, er, or.** One who; that which. Note the three different spellings. When *ar, er,* or *or* is found at the end of a word, the word concerns a person or thing. For example: *biographer*—a person who writes biographies; *killer*—one who kills; *player*—one who plays; *author*—one who writes; *beggar*—one who begs; *captor*—one who holds someone a prisoner; *prisoner*—one who is kept in prison. How many more words that end in *ar, er,* or *or* can you supply?

Additional Words Derived from Combining Forms

From your knowledge of combining forms, can you define the following words?

1. **graphology** (gra · phol · o · gy) (gra · fol′ o · jē) *n.* *Detectives sometimes use **graphology** to learn about the character of a suspect.*

_____

2. **graphic** (graph · ic) (graf′ ik) *adj.* *His description was so **graphic** that it left nothing to the imagination.*

_____

3. **orthography** (or · thog · ra · phy) (or · thog ′ ra · fē) *n.* (*pl.* **ies**) *Know-ledge of the orthography of words helps in writing.*

---

4. **annuity** (aṇ · nū ′ i · tē) *n.* *He receives a sizable annuity each year from his investment.*

---

5. **bifocals** (bi · fo · cals) (bī · fō′kulz) *n.* (*pl.*) *When my mother's eye doctor recommended bifocals for her, she felt that it was a sure sign that she was getting old.*

---

6. **bilateral** (bī · lat ′ er · al) *adj.* *The two nations began bilateral talks, hoping to conclude a peace treaty between them.*

---

7. **bilingual** (bi · lin · gual) (bī · ling′ gwal) *adj. n.* *A number of schools are providing bilingual programs for students who speak a language other than English.*

---

8. **binary** (bī ′ na · rē) *adj.* *The binary system of numbers is used with digital computers.*

---

9. **biopsy** (bī ′ op · sē) *n.* *In order to determine whether major surgery is necessary, the surgeon usually takes a biopsy of the organ in question.*

---

10. **podium** (pō′ dē · um) *n.* *When the conductor took his position on the podium, all eyes were directed toward him.*

---

11. **pedestal** (ped ′ es · tal) *n.* *The newly acquired statue was placed on a special pedestal for all to view.*

---

12. **automatic** (au · to · mat ′ ik) *adj.* *Automatic washers and dryers have helped to provide more leisure time for persons.*

---

13. **automaton** (au · tom ′ a · ton) *n.* *The goose-stepping soldiers in Hitler's army looked like automatons.*

14

14. **autonomous** (au · ton ′ o · møus) *adj.* *Because education is not mentioned in the Constitution, each state is **autonomous** in this area.*

STOP. Check answers at the end of the chapter.

Practice for Additional Words Derived from Combining Forms

Directions: Match each word with the *best* definition.

_____ 1. annuity   a. consisting of two parts

_____ 2. bifocals   b. the study of handwriting

_____ 3. bilateral   c. the cutting out of a piece of living tissue for examination

_____ 4. graphic   d. using two languages equally well

_____ 5. graphology   e. glasses with two-part lenses

_____ 6. orthography   f. self-governing

_____ 7. podium   g. moving by itself

_____ 8. pedestal   h. two-sided

_____ 9. binary   i. the art of correct spelling

_____ 10. automatic   j. yearly payment of money

_____ 11. automaton   k. a base or bottom support

_____ 12. biopsy   l. a raised platform for an orchestra conductor

_____ 13. bilingual   m. marked by realistic and vivid detail

_____ 14. autonomous   n. a person or animal acting in a mechanical way

STOP. Check answers at the end of the chapter.

EXERCISE 2

Step I. Combining Forms

A. Directions: A list of combining forms with their meanings follows. Look at the combining forms and their meanings. Concentrate on learning each combining form and its meaning. Cover the meanings, read the combining forms, and state the meanings to yourself. Check to see if you are correct. Now cover the combining forms, read the meanings, and state the combining forms to yourself. Check to see if you are correct.

Combining Forms	Meanings
1. tele	from a distance
2. scope	a means for seeing, watching, or viewing
3. geo	earth
4. meter	measure
5. micro	very small
6. scrib, scrip	write
7. phon, phono	sound

B. Directions: Cover the preceding meanings. Write the meanings of the following combining forms.

Combining Forms	Meanings
1. tele	_____
2. scope	_____
3. geo	_____
4. meter	_____
5. micro	_____
6. scrib, scrip	_____
7. phon, phono	_____

Step II. Words Derived from Combining Forms

1. **telegraph** (tel ′ e · graf) *n.* Instrument for sending a message in a code at a distance. *v.* To send a message from a distance. *The **telegraph** is not used as much today as it used to be because there are now faster and simpler ways to send messages from a distance.*

2. **telephone** (tel′ e · fōn¢) *n.* Instrument that sends and receives sound, such as the spoken word, over distance. *v.* To send a message by tele-

16

phone. *I use the **telephone** when my girl friend is away, and I want to hear the sound of her voice.*

3. **telescope** (tel′ e · skōpϵ) *n.* Instrument used to view distant objects. *Standing on the roof of the Empire State Building, he used the **telescope** to view the city.*

4. **microscope** (mi · cro · scope) (mī′ kro · skōpϵ) *n.* Instrument used to make very small things appear larger so that they can be seen. *The **microscope** has helped scientists to observe objects too small to be seen with the naked eye.*

5. **geometry** (ge · om · e · try) (jē · om′ e · trē) *n.* Branch of mathematics dealing with the measurement of points, lines, and planes, among other things. *An engineer uses his knowledge of **geometry** to measure the land for the building of new roads.*

6. **geography** (ge · og · ra · phy) (jē · og′ ra · fē) *n.* Study of the earth's surface and life. *In **geography** you learn about the earth's surface and about the plant and animal life there.*

7. **geology** (ge · ol · o · gy) (jē · ol′ o · gē) *n.* Study of the earth's physical history and makeup. ***Geology** helps people learn about the makeup of the earth, especially as revealed by rocks.*

8. **script** (skript) *n.* Writing that is cursive, printed, or engraved; a piece of writing; a prepared copy of a play for the use of actors. *The actors read from the **script** only for the first rehearsal, but after that they could not depend on any writing to help them.*

9. **scripture** (scrip · ture) (skrip′ chur) *n.* The books of the Old and New Testaments, or either of them; a text or passage from the Bible. *There are some lawyers who quote from the Holy **Scriptures** because they feel a reference to the Bible will gain the jury's sympathy.*

10. **description** (de · scrip · tion) (de · skrip′ shun) *n.* An account that gives a picture of something in words. *Carol's **description** of the college was so graphic that I could actually picture it in my mind.*

Special Notes

1. Note that in the words *telescope* and *microscope* the meaning of the words includes the term *instrument*. A telescope is an instrument used to view distant objects. A microscope is an instrument used to make small objects appear larger so that they can be seen.

2. The word *script* can refer to typed or printed matter and also to a piece of writing, especially a prepared copy of a play or dramatic role for the use of actors. For example:
   a. *This sentence is in **script**.*
   b. *The researchers were looking for the original ancient **script**.*
   c. *The **script** for the new play was not ready.*

3. *The term **Scripture** is used chiefly in the plural with* the *(and often* Holy*) and has a capital letter because it refers to the books of the Old and New Testaments or of either of them—in short, the Bible.*

Step III. Practice

A. Directions: Following are a number of sentences with missing words. Choose the word that *best* fits the sentence from the following words, and write it in the blank. (Some words are from Exercise 1.)

Word List

microscope, telescope, geology, geography, autobiography, biographer, telegraph, script, Scripture, telephone, geometry, description.

1. Because I am interested in becoming a biologist, I should learn how to use the _____ , which helps one to view plant and animal cells.

2. I took _____ in high school because a good mathematics background is important for the career I want.

3. However, I found that I enjoyed _____ more because I like to learn about the earth's surface.

4. With the invention of machines that can also send messages in ordinary language or letters at a distance very rapidly, the _____ is not used as much as it used to be.

5. I enjoy looking through the _____ because it helps me to view such a large part of the city.

6. A course that I am taking next semester in college is _____ because I like to study rocks and rock formation.

7. I use the _____ when I become lonely for the sound of my friend's voice.

8. In church, reading from _____ is always part of the service.

9. Presidents have many _____ (s) because people are interested in presidents' lives.

18

10. Helen Keller, who was deaf, mute, and blind, tells in her _____ how she learned about language.

11. If I do not learn my _____ by tomorrow, I will not be in the play.

12. From your _____ of that teacher, I can imagine what takes place in class.

STOP. Check answers at the end of the chapter.

B. Directions: A list of definitions follows. In the space provided, insert the letter for the word that *best* fits the definition.

_____ 1. Instrument used to view distant objects
   a. telegraph   c. telescope
   b. telephone   d. microscope

_____ 2. Instrument used for sending coded messages
   a. telephone   c. telegraph
   b. telescope   d. microscope

_____ 3. Branch of mathematics dealing with measurements
   a. geology   c. geography
   b. biology   d. geometry

_____ 4. Study of the earth's physical history and makeup
   a. geography   c. biology
   b. geology   d. biography

_____ 5. Instrument used to make very small objects appear larger
   a. telegraph   c. microscope
   b. telescope   d. telephone

_____ 6. Printed matter; a piece of writing
   a. Scripture   c. biographer
   b. pedestrian   d. script

_____ 7. Instrument that sends sound at a distance
   a. telephone   c. telescope
   b. telegraph   d. microscope

_____ 8. Study of the earth's surface
   a. biology   c. geometry
   b. geology   d. geography

_____ 9. Writings from the Bible
   a. script   c. Scripture
   b. autobiography   d. biography

_____ 10. An account that gives a picture of something in words
   a. Scripture   c. description
   b. script   d. autobiography

STOP. Check answers at the end of the chapter.

> **re** Again; back. *Re* is found at the beginning of
> many words. For example: *rewrite*—to write
> again; *redo*—to do again; *recomb*—to comb again;
> *rerun*—to run again; *rework*—to work again; *repay*—
> to pay back; *return*—to go back. How many
> more words that begin with *re* can you supply?

Additional Words Derived from Combining Forms

From your knowledge of combining forms, can you define the following words?

1. **meter** (mē′ ter) *n.* *A **meter** is approximately 3.3 feet or 1.1 yards.*

   _____

2. **telemeter** (te · lem′ e · ter) *n.* *The ground crew serving a space station uses a **telemeter** to learn what is happening in the space ship.*

   _____

3. **micrometer** (mī · krom′ e · ter) *n.* *Technicians use a **micrometer** when measuring material because it helps them to be as accurate as possible.*

   _____

4. **microbe** (mī′ krōbė) *n.* *Doctors determine through tests what **microbes** in our bodies are causing our diseases.*

   _____

5. **microorganism** (mi · cro · or · gan · ism) (mī · krō · or′ gan · iz · um) *n.* *A virus is a **microorganism** that cannot be seen by the naked eye.*

   _____

6. **microphone** (mi · cro · phone) (mī′ kro · fōnė) *n.* *The speaker used the **microphone** to make sure that the people in the rear of the large room could hear the speech.*

   _____

7. **microfilm** (mī′ kro · film) *n.* *Many of the older copies of newspapers that I needed for my report were on **microfilm** in the library.*

   _____

8. **scribe** (skrībė) *n.* *In ancient times a **scribe** was held in very high esteem because not many persons were able to read or write then.*

   _____

9. **inscription** (in · scrip · tion) (in · skrip′ shun) *n.* The **inscription** *on the Statue of Liberty beckons all to our shores.*

_____

10. **prescription** (pre · scrip · tion) (pre · skrip′ shun) *n.* Many patients may *endanger their health because they fail to follow their doctor's **prescription**.*

_____

11. **transcript** (tran′ skript) *n.* The lawyer asked for a **transcript** *of a court case to review what had taken place during the trial.*

_____

12. **geocentric** (ge · o · cen · tric) (jē · ō · sen′ trik) *adj.* In ancient times man *thought that the universe was **geocentric**.*

_____

13. **phonics** (phon · ics) (fon′ iks) *n.* Children who are good in **phonics** *are able to figure out many words independently.*

_____

14. **phonetics** (pho · net · ics) (fo · net′ iks) *n.* Many actors and actresses *take courses in **phonetics** to learn how to pronounce words better.*

_____

15. **stethoscope** (steth′ o · skōpe̸) *n.* The doctor used the **stethoscope** *to listen to his patient's heartbeat.*

_____

STOP. Check answers at the end of the chapter.

Practice for Additional Words Derived from Combining Forms

Directions: Match the definition that *best* fits to the word.

_____ 1. telemeter   a. a brief dedication in a book; something written or engraved on some surface

_____ 2. micrometer   b. a writer

_____ 3. microorganism   c. a very small living thing that cannot be seen with the naked eye

_____ 4. microbe	d.	study of the relationship of written symbols to sound symbols
_____ 5. microphone	e.	relating to the earth as the center
_____ 6. microfilm	f.	a copy of an original
_____ 7. transcript	g.	study of speech sounds
_____ 8. scribe	h.	A doctor's instrument used to hear heart, lungs, and so forth
_____ 9. prescription	i.	a device to magnify weak sounds
_____ 10. inscription	j.	an instrument used to measure distance
_____ 11. phonics	k.	film on which printed material is reduced in size
_____ 12. phonetics	l.	a doctor's written directions for medicine
_____ 13. geocentric	m.	an instrument that measures very small distances
_____ 14. stethoscope	n.	a very small living thing that cannot be seen with the naked eye
_____ 15. meter	o.	an instrument that measures the amount of something

STOP. Check answers at the end of the chapter.

EXERCISE 3

Step I. Combining Forms

A. Directions: A list of combining forms with their meanings follows. Look at the combining forms and their meanings. Concentrate on learning each combining form and its meaning. Cover the meanings, read the combining forms, and state the meanings to yourself. Check to see if you are correct. Now cover the combining forms, read the meanings, and state the combining forms to yourself. Check to see if you are correct.

Combining Forms	_Meanings_
1. gram	something written or drawn; a record
2. uni	one

22

3. dic, dict   say; speak

4. contra   against; opposite

5. spect   see; view; observe

6. phob, phobo   fear

B. Directions: Cover the preceding meanings. Write the meanings of the following combining forms.

Combining Forms   *Meanings*

1. gram   _____

2. uni   _____

3. dic, dict   _____

4. contra   _____

5. spect   _____

6. phob, phobo   _____

Step II. Words Derived from Combining Forms

1. **telegram** (tel′ e · gram) *n.* Message sent from a distance. *A telegram is usually sent when the message is important.*

2. **uniform** (ū′ ni · form) *adj.* Being always the same; alike. *n.* A special form of clothing. *Persons in the armed forces wear uniforms that have been specially designed for them.*

3. **unique** (u · nique) (ū′ nēk) *adj.* Being the only one of its kind. *The ancient statue found in a cave was unique because there were no others like it.*

4. **union** (un · ion) (ūn′· yun) *n.* A joining; a putting together; something formed by joining. *A labor union is a group of people who have joined together because they have similar interests and purposes.*

5. **universe** (ū′ ni · versȼ) *n.* Everything that exists; all creation; all mankind. *With space exploration, man has made but a small probe into the vast unknown regions of the universe.*

6. **universal** (ū · ni · ver′ sal) *adj.* Applying to all. *It is very hard to give universal satisfaction to people because not everyone agrees on what is satisfactory.*

7. **unison** (ū′ ni · son) *n.* A harmonious agreement; a saying of something together. **In unison** *adv.* precise and perfect agreement. *Choral groups speak in unison when they recite.*

8. **diction** (dic · tion) (dik′ shun) *n.* Manner of speaking; choice of words. *Mrs. Smith's* **diction** *is so precise that no one has any difficulty in understanding her speech.*

9. **dictation** (dic · ta · tion) (dik · tā′ shun) *n.* The act of speaking or reading aloud to someone who takes down the words. *On Monday Mr. Jones sometimes loses his voice because of the great amount of* **dictation** *he gives his secretary.*

10. **dictionary** (dic · tion · a · ry) (dik′ shun · a · rē) *n.* A book for alphabetically listed words in a language, giving information about their meanings, pronunciations, and so forth. *Whenever I don't know the pronunciation or meaning of a word, I look it up in the* **dictionary.**

11. **dictator** (dik′ tā · tor) *n.* A ruler who has absolute power; a ruler who has complete control and say. *Hitler was a* **dictator** *who had complete control over the German people.*

12. **contrary** (con · trar · y) (kon′ trar · ē) *adj.* Opposite. *We disagree because his opinion is* **contrary** *to ours.*

13. **contradiction** (con · tra · dic · tion) (kon · tra · dik′ shun) *n.* Something (such as a statement) consisting of opposing parts. *If I answer yes and no to the same statement, I am making a* **contradiction.**

14. **contrast** (kon′ trast) *n.* Difference between things; use of opposites for certain results. *The black chair against the white wall makes an interesting* **contrast.**

15. **spectacle** (spec · ta · cle) (spek′ ta · kul) *n.* Something showy that is seen by many (the public); an unwelcome or sad sight. *The drunken man made a terrible* **spectacle** *of himself for the crowd of people.*

16. **spectator** (spek′ tā · tor) *n.* An onlooker; one who views something, such as a spectacle. *There were many* **spectators** *at the fair who enjoyed looking at the sights.*

17. **spectacular** (spec · tac · u · lar) (spek · tak′ ū · lar) *adj.* Relating to something unusual, impressive, exciting, or unexpected. *The* **spectacular** *rescue of the child from the burning house was widely applauded.*

18. **phobia** (pho · bi · a) (fō′ bē · a) *n.* Extreme fear. *My friend, who has a* **phobia** *about cats, is afraid to be in the same room with one.*

Special Notes

1. The term *phobia* is usually used to refer to an extreme fear of something. For example: *The doctors tried to help the man to overcome his* **phobia** *about heights.*

2. The term *Union*, which begins with a capital letter, refers to the United

States as a national unit or to any other nation that is a unit, such as the USSR.

3. The combining form *gram* means *something written; a record.* However, *gram* is also a noun that refers to a measurement of weight in the metric system.

4. The plural of *spectacle* (spectacles) can also refer to eyeglasses.

Step III. Practice

A. Directions: A list of definitions follows. In the space provided, insert the letter for the word that *best* fits the definition.

____ 1. A saying of something together

   a. union   c. unison
   b. universe   d. uniform

____ 2. Refers to the Bible

   a. autobiography   c. autograph
   b. Scripture   d. script

____ 3. An extreme fear

   a. biology   c. phobia
   b. biped   d. pedestrian

____ 4. Being the same

   a. union   c. universe
   b. unique   d. uniform

____ 5. Applying to all

   a. unique   c. unison
   b. union   d. universal

____ 6. A joining together

   a. unique   c. universal
   b. union   d. uniform

____ 7. Something (such as a statement) consisting of opposing parts

   a. unique   c. contradiction
   b. unison   d. uniform

____ 8. The science of life

   a. geology   c. biography
   b. geography   d. biology

____ 9. Being unlike anything else

   a. phobic   c. telegraphic
   b. unique   d. contrasting

____10. Message from a distance

   a. telegraph   c. telescope
   b. telegram   d. autograph

____11. One who views something

   a. spectator   c. spectacular
   b. spectacle   d. script

____12. Relating to something impressive

   a. spectator   c. spectacular
   b. Scripture   d. spectacle

____13. Something showy

   a. spectacular   c. phobia
   b. spectator   d. spectacle

14. A ruler with complete control   a. dictation   c. autobiography
                                          b. diction   d. dictator

15. Manner of speaking   a. dictionary   c. diction
                                          b. dictation   d. dictator

16. The act of speaking to some-   a. dictation   c. diction
     one who takes it down   b. dictionary   d. dictator

STOP. Check answers at the end of the chapter.

B. Directions: Twelve sentences follow. Define the underlined word. Put
                 your answer in the blank.

1. It's a contradiction to be happy and unhappy at the same time.

_____

2. He is making a spectacle of himself by behaving that way in front of so
many people.

_____

3. Although it is a statement contrary to the opinions of other people, I will
stick to it.

_____

4. You have such a unique way of holding your tennis racket.

_____

5. If that is a universal belief, everyone should agree with it.

_____

6. Because I am still afraid to go in the water, my doctor has not cured me of
my phobia.

_____

7. The color of your blouse makes a good contrast to your skirt.

_____

8. The spectators were not able to believe their eyes.

_____

9. If the two of you join in marriage, that will make a good union.

_____

10. Although the trapped men seemed surely doomed, the firemen made a
spectacular rescue at the last minute.

_____

11. John behaves like a dictator in class because he likes to have everyone do
what he wants.

_____

12. Instructors' <u>diction</u> must be excellent if many students are to listen to their lectures.

STOP. Check answers at the end of the chapter.

> **ion, sion, tion.** State of; act of; result of. Note the three spellings. When *ion, sion,* or *tion* is found at the end of a word, it means that the word is a noun. For example: *diction*—the act of speaking in a certain manner; *dictation*—the act of speaking to someone who takes it down; *question*—the act of asking; *description*—the act of describing.

Additional Words Derived from Combining Forms

From your knowledge of combining forms, can you define the following words?

1. **Dictaphone** (dic · ta · phone) (dik′ ta · fōng̸) *n. Sometimes Mr. Jones used a **Dictaphone** to record his letters for his secretary.*

---

2. **dictum** (dik′ tum) *n. The union leaders impressed the strikers with their **dictum** of nonviolence.*

---

3. **indictment** (in · dīȼt′ ment) *n. The jury felt that the prosecutor had enough evidence to warrant an **indictment** against the defendant.*

---

4. **unilateral** (ū · ni · lat′ er · al) *adj. There is a tendency today in corporations toward consensus decisions by management rather than **unilateral** ones by individual executives.*

---

5. **unify** (ū′ ni · fī) *v. After the strike it was difficult to **unify** the different groups because there was still resentment against those who had crossed the picket lines.*

---

6. **acrophobia** (ac · ro · pho · bi · a) (ak · ro · fō′ bē · a) *n. You would not find a person with **acrophobia** at the top of the Empire State Building.*

_____

7. **hydrophobia** (hy · dro · pho · bi · a) (hī · dro · fō′ bē · a) *n. I know someone who developed **hydrophobia** after being thrown in the water as a child.*

_____

8. **claustrophobia** (claus · tro · pho · bi · a) (klaus · tro · fō′ bē · a) *n. How horrible to get stuck in an elevator when you have **claustrophobia**!*

_____

9. **grammar** (gram′ mar) *n. Studies have shown that a knowledge of **grammar** does not help students to speak or write better because grammar merely describes the way an individual speaks.*

_____

10. **speculate** (spec · u · late) (spek′ yu · lāte) *v. I do not like to **speculate** in the stock market because I like only sure things.*

_____

STOP. Check answers at the end of the chapter.

Practice for Additional Words Derived from Combining Forms

Directions: Match each word with the best definition.

_____ 1. Dictaphone   a. a fear of heights

_____ 2. dictum   b. that part of the study of language dealing with structure and word forms

_____ 3. indictment   c. to think about from all sides; take part in any risky venture

_____ 4. unilateral   d. a fear of closed-in places

_____ 5. unify   e. a machine for recording speech

_____ 6. acrophobia   f. a charge

_____ 7. hydrophobia   g. form into one

_____ 8. claustrophobia   h. an authoritative statement

_____ 9. grammar   i. one-sided

_____ 10. speculate   j. a fear of water

STOP. Check answers at the end of the chapter.

CROSSWORD PUZZLE 1

Directions: The meanings of many of the combining forms from Exercises 1–3
follow. Your knowledge of these combining forms will help you to
solve this crossword puzzle. Note that *combining form* is abbreviated as *comb. f.*

Across

1. A word ending meaning "one who"
3. Past tense of the verb *have*
5. Comb. f. for *foot*
7. Comb. f. for *life*
9. Comb. f. for *from a distance*
11. Same as #1 Across
12. Third letter of the alphabet
13. Comb. f. for *something written*
16. Opposite of *night*

Down

1. You make this sound when you
   are surprised
2. To tap; strike
4. That which one owes
6. This happens when you stop
   breathing
8. Comb. f. for *the study of*
10. An error; a mistake
12. You will do this to your lips

18. Sliced pork meat
20. Pronoun
21. Comb. f. for *a means for seeing*
23. A car you can hire to drive you somewhere
26. Opposite of *off*
27. Word meaning "on"; "near"; "by"
28. Comb. f. for *self*
30. Opposite of *out*
31. What you hang clothes on
34. Same as #1 Down

when they are too dry
14. An indefinite article
15. Comb. f. for *sound*
16. Comb. f. for *say*
17. Same as #14 Down
19. A pronoun
21. Nineteenth letter of the alphabet
22. Something to sleep on
24. Same as #14 Down
25. Money that is put up to release an arrested person from jail before his trial
27. Same as #14 Down
29. Comb. f. for *one*
32. Opposite of *yes*
33. A sound that means, "What did you say?"

STOP. Check answers at the end of the chapter.

WORD SCRAMBLE 1

Directions: Word Scramble 1 is based on words from Exercises 1–3. The meanings are your clues to arranging the letters in correct order. Write the correct word in the blank.

Meanings

1. fmniuor   _____   being the same

2. ueqinu   _____   only one of its kind

3. hbaiop   _____   fear

4. yclbeic   _____   two-wheeler

5. rpuotghaa   _____   signature

6. dseerniapt   _____   one who goes on foot; one who walks

7. iewbyelk   _____   every two weeks

8. elooygg   _____   study of the earth's physical history and makeup

9. oghuaaypoitbr   _____   life story written by oneself

10. ebpid   _____ two-footed animal

11. clesetepo   _____ instrument used for viewing distant objects

12. crpits   _____ a piece of writing

13. repicmoocs   _____ instrument used to make very small objects appear larger so that they can be seen

14. luanvirse   _____ referring to all

15. lunnaa   _____ yearly

16. yoeghgrpa   _____ study of the earth's surface and life

17. nitooctnricad   _____ something (such as a statement) consisting of opposite parts

18. roptsacet   _____ one who views something

19. blooyig   _____ the study of living things

20. libeanni   _____ every two years

STOP. Check answers at the end of the chapter.

ANALOGIES 1

Directions: Find the word from the following list that *best* completes each analogy. There are more words in this list than you need. The symbol : means "is to," and the symbol : : means "as."
Example: Brutal is to savage as viewer is to *spectator*.
Brutal: savage : : viewer : *spectator*.

Word List

autograph, spectacle, hydrophobia, podium, biped, annually, bifocals, orthography, biennial, biweekly, prescription, unique, automation, pedestrian, telescope, uniform, transcript, contrast, automatic, contradict, biography, indictment, unite, bicyclist, microbe, phobia, spectator, spectacular, automaton.

1. Riding : walking : : motorist : _____ .

2. Accessory : scarf : : instrument : _____ .

3. Height : acrophobia : : water : _____.

4. Hear : racket : : view : _____.

5. Solo : duet :: weekly : _____.

31

6. Snow : blizzard :: interesting :_____.

7. Groomed : disheveled :: common : _____.

8. Hamper : hinder :: same : _____.

9. Arrest : stop :: dais : _____.

10. Primary : first :: signature : _____.

11. Automobile : vehicle :: robot : _____.

12. Pretty : beautiful :: fear : _____.

13. Smooth : wrinkled :: agree: _____.

14. Dress : gown :: spectacles : _____.

15. Hate : detest :: join : _____.

16. Structure : grammar :: spelling : _____.

17. End : beginning :: original : _____.

18. Advice : counsel :: charge : _____.

19. One : two :: annual : _____.

20. Rule : law :: microorganism : _____.

STOP. Check answers at the end of the chapter.

MULTIPLE-CHOICE VOCABULARY TEST 1

Directions: This is a test on words in Exercises 1–3. Words are presented according to exercises. *Do all exercises before checking answers.* Underline the meaning that *best* fits the word.

Exercise 1

1. bicycle
   a. two-wheeler
   b. two-footed
   c. circles
   d. refers to time

2. biology
   a. study of earth
   b. study of people
   c. study of life
   d. science

3. biography
   a. life story written by oneself
   b. a science
   c. life story
   d. some writing

4. autograph
   a. life story
   b. a machine that writes
   c. some writing
   d. signature

5. annual
   a. money
   b. every year
   c. every two years
   d. twice a year

32

6. biennial   a. every two years   c. celebration of birthday
   b. twice a year   d. once a year

7. autobiography   a. life story   c. writing machine
   b. life story written by oneself   d. science of writing

8. anniversary   a. refers to annual   c. yearly return of a date marking an important event
   b. every two years   d. a celebration

9. biannual   a. lasting for two years   c. twice a year
   b. yearly   d. once a year

10. biweekly   a. every two weeks   c. every four weeks
   b. once a week   d. two weeks every year

11. bimonthly   a. every two months   c. four times yearly
   b. every month   d. two times yearly

12. biped   a. feet   c. two-footed animal
   b. two socks for feet   d. two-footed human

13. pedestrian   a. one who goes on foot   c. a foot doctor
   b. a foot rest   d. refers to two feet

Exercise 2

14. telescope   a. an instrument used to view small objects   c. an instrument used for viewing distant objects
   b. an instrument used to see large objects   d. an instrument used to record sound

15. geology   a. science of life   c. study of the earth's surface and life
   b. study of the earth   d. study of the earth's physical makeup

16. telegraph   a. instrument used to see from a distance   c. a machine that measures distance
   b. a machine used to send messages   d. a message

17. microscope   a. an instrument that makes things appear small   c. an instrument that grows small things
   b. an instrument used to make small objects appear larger   d. something small

18. telephone
   a. a sounding machine
   b. a recording machine
   c. an instrument that sends sound at a distance
   d. an instrument that measures sound at a distance

19. geography
   a. a branch of mathematics
   b. study of the earth
   c. study of the earth's physical makeup
   d. study of the earth's surface and life

20. geometry
   a. study of earth's physical makeup
   b. study of the earth's surface and life
   c. a branch of mathematics
   d. measurement

21. Scripture
   a. refers to any writings
   b. the Bible
   c. refers to a script
   d. refers only to the Old Testament

22. script
   a. a piece of writing
   b. a part in a play
   c. a writer
   d. the Bible

23. description
   a. an account that gives a picture of something in words
   b. some writing
   c. your signature
   d. a play script

Exercise 3

24. telegram
   a. a message sent from a distance
   b. a machine used to send a message
   c. something from a distance
   d. a record

25. phobia
   a. a disease
   b. refers to hate
   c. extreme fear
   d. refers to sound

26. uniform
   a. joining together
   b. clothing
   c. special form of clothing
   d. all

27. unique
   a. only one of its kind
   b. all
   c. the same
   d. joining together

28. union
   a. all
   b. refers to only one
   c. the act of putting together
   d. complete agreement

29. universal
   a. applying to none
   b. putting together
   c. applying to all
   d. only one of a kind

30. universe
- a. complete agreement
- b. similar
- c. everything that exists
- d. together

31. unison
- a. a saying of something together
- b. manner of speaking
- c. similar
- d. all

32. dictionary
- a. study of words
- b. a book on speech
- c. a book for alphabetically listed words in a language
- d. study of speaking

33. dictator
- a. ruler
- b. a ruler without power
- c. a person who speaks
- d. a ruler with absolute power

34. dictation
- a. act of speaking
- b. act of writing
- c. act of speaking to someone who takes down the words
- d. a ruler with absolute power

35. diction
- a. manner of speaking
- b. a ruler
- c. act of writing
- d. act of speaking to someone who takes down the words

36. contrary
- a. no agreement
- b. opposite
- c. use of opposites for effect
- d. against someone

37. contradiction
- a. something (such as a statement) consisting of opposing parts
- b. something not in complete agreement
- c. use of opposites for effect
- d. against

38. contrast
- a. difference between things
- b. against someone
- c. no agreement
- d. against everything

39. spectacle
- a. one who views something
- b. glasses
- c. something showy seen by the public
- d. a place to see things

40. spectator
- a. one who wears glasses
- b. one who views something
- c. a place for seeing
- d. something unusual

41. spectacular   a. a person who sees   c. a shameful sight
                        things   d. refers to something
                   b. one who wears   unusual
                        glasses

TRUE/FALSE TEST 1

Directions: This is a true/false test on Exercises 1–3. Read each sentence carefully. Decide whether it is true or false. Put a *T* for *true* or an *F* for *false* in the blank. The number after the sentence tells you if the word is from Exercise 1, 2, or 3.

_____ 1. When something is done in <u>unison</u>, it is done together.   3

_____ 2. In <u>geology</u> class you learn about plants and animals.   2

_____ 3. When something is a <u>contradiction</u> of something else, it is in agreement with it.   3

_____ 4. A <u>biographer</u> would write your autobiography.   1

_____ 5. A <u>pedestrian</u> is one who goes on a bicycle.   1

_____ 6. When something is <u>unique</u>, it is the same for all persons.   3

_____ 7. If everyone were to agree, there would be a <u>universal</u> agreement.   3

_____ 8. If I receive interest <u>biennially</u>, I receive it twice a year.   1

_____ 9. Not all animals are <u>bipeds</u>.   1

_____ 10. The <u>telescope</u> helped me to get a better view of the one-celled animals.   2

_____ 11. If you had a <u>phobia</u> concerning water, you would fear going into deep water.   3

_____ 12. A <u>spectator</u> is one who watches others.   3

_____ 13. When something is <u>spectacular</u>, it is very exciting to observe.   3

_____ 14. *<u>Scripture</u>* refers to a play script.   2

_____ 15. When you give your <u>autograph</u>, you are giving your life story.   1

_____ 16. Any person who gives <u>dictation</u> is a dictator.   3

STOP. Check answers for both tests at the end of the chapter.

SCORING OF TESTS

Multiple-Choice Vocabulary Test		True/False Test	
Number Wrong	*Score*	*Number Wrong*	*Score*
0–3	Excellent	0–1	Excellent
4–6	Good	2	Good
7–9	Weak	3–4	Weak
Above 9	Poor	Above 4	Poor
Score _____		Score _____	

1. If you scored in the excellent or good range on *both tests*, you are doing well. Go on to Chapter Three.

2. If you scored in the weak or poor range on either test, look below and follow directions for Additional Practice. Note that the words on the tests are arranged so that you can tell in which exercise to find them. This will help you if you need additional practice.

ADDITIONAL PRACTICE SETS

A. Directions: Write the words you missed on the tests from the three exercises in the space provided. Note that the tests are presented so that you can tell to which exercises the words belong.

Exercise 1 Words Missed

1. _____   6. _____

2. _____   7. _____

3. _____   8. _____

4. _____   9. _____

5. _____   10. _____

Exercise 2 Words Missed

1. _____   6. _____

2. _____   7. _____

3. _____   8. _____

4. _____   9. _____

5. _____   10. _____

Exercise 3 Words Missed

1. _____   6. _____

2. _____   7. _____

3. _____   8. _____

4. _____   9. _____

5. _____   10. _____

B. Directions: Restudy the words that you have written on p. 37 and this page. Study the combining forms from which those words are derived. Do Step I and Step II for those you missed. Note that Step I and Step II of the combining forms and vocabulary derived from these combining forms are on the following pages:

Exercise 1–pp. 9–12.

Exercise 2–pp. 15–18.

Exercise 3–pp. 22–25.

C. Directions: Do Additional Practice 1 on this page and the next if you missed words from Exercise 1. Do Additional Practice 2 on pp. 39–40 if you missed words from Exercise 2. Do Additional Practice 3 on pp. 40–41 if you missed words from Exercise 3. Now go on to Chapter Three.

Additional Practice 1 for Exercise 1

A. Directions: Following are the combining forms presented in Exercise 1. Match the combining form with its meaning.

_____ 1. aut, auto   a. the study of or science of

_____ 2. bi   b. something written; machine

_____ 3. bio   c. self

_____ 4. graph   d. life

_____ 5. ology   e. foot

_____ 6. ped, pod   f. two

_____ 7. anni, annu, enni   g. year

STOP. Check answers at the end of the chapter.

38

B. Directions: Following are the words presented in Exercise 1. Match the
word with its meaning.

_____ 1. bicycle   a. every two years

_____ 2. biology   b. yearly

_____ 3. biography   c. life story

_____ 4. autobiography d. two-wheeler

_____ 5. autograph   e. one who goes on foot

_____ 6. bimonthly   f. signature

_____ 7. biweekly   g. yearly return of a date marking
an event

_____ 8. pedestrian   h. two-footed animal

_____ 9. biped   i. every two weeks; twice a week

_____10. annual   j. every two months; twice a
month

_____11. anniversary   k. life story written by oneself

_____12. biannual   l. twice a year

_____13. biennial   m. study or science of life

STOP. Check answers at the end of the chapter.

Additional Practice 2 for Exercise 2

A. Directions: Following are the combining forms presented in Exercise 2.
Match the combining form with its meaning.

_____ 1. tele   a. a means for seeing, watching,
or viewing

_____ 2. scope   b. sound

_____ 3. geo   c. very small

_____ 4. meter   d. earth

_____ 5. micro   e. write

_____ 6. scrib, scrip   f. measure

_____ 7. phon, phono g. from a distance

STOP. Check answers at the end of the chapter.

B. Directions: Following are the words presented in Exercise 2. Match the
word with its meaning.

_____ 1. telescope   a. instrument for sending a message in code at a distance

_____ 2. geology   b. a piece of writing

_____ 3. microscope   c. branch of mathematics dealing with the measurement of points, lines, and planes, among other things.

_____ 4. geography   d. study of the earth's surface and life

_____ 5. geometry   e. instrument that sends sound at a distance

_____ 6. telegraph   f. study of the earth's physical makeup

_____ 7. Scripture   g. instrument used to make very small objects appear larger so that they can be seen

_____ 8. telephone   h. instrument used for viewing distant objects

_____ 9. script   i. Bible

_____10. description   j. an account that gives a picture of something in writing

STOP. Check answers at the end of the chapter.

Additional Practice 3 for Exercise 3

A. Directions: Following are the combining forms presented in Exercise 3.
Match the combining form with its meaning.

_____1. spect   a. against; opposite

_____2. uni   b. say; speak

_____3. phob, phobo   c. one

_____4. gram   d. fear

_____5. contra   e. something written or drawn; a record

_____6. dic, dict   f. see; view; observe

STOP. Check answers at the end of the chapter.

B. Directions: Following are the words presented in Exercise 3. Match the
word with its meaning.

_____ 1. dictionary

a. manner of speaking

_____ 2. spectator

b. being the only one of its kind

_____ 3. telegram

c. the act of putting together

_____ 4. phobia

d. something (such as a statement) consisting of opposing parts

_____ 5. uniform

e. everything that exists

_____ 6. unique

f. applying to all

_____ 7. union

g. message sent from a distance

_____ 8. universe

h. being always the same

_____ 9. universal

i. extreme fear

_____10. unison

j. act of speaking to someone who takes down the words

_____11. contrary

k. a saying of something together

_____12. contradiction

l. book of alphabetically listed words in a language

_____13. contrast

m. one who views something

_____14. dictator

n. referring to something unusual; exciting

_____15. diction

o. opposite

_____16. dictation

p. difference between things

_____17. spectacle

q. something showy

_____18. spectacular

r. a ruler with absolute power

STOP. Check answers at the end of the chapter.

ANSWERS

Exercise 1 (pp. 9-15)

Practice A

(1) anniversary, (2) autobiography, (3) pedestrian, (4) biped, (5) biology,
(6) biography, (7) biannual, (8) annual, (9) autograph.

Practice B

(1) bicycle, (2) autobiography, (3) autograph, (4) biannual, (5) biography,
(6) biped, (7) biology, (8) biennial, (9) pedestrian, (10) bimonthly,
(11) biweekly, (12) annual, (13) anniversary.

Additional Words Derived from Combining Forms (pp. 13–15)

1. **graphology.** The study of handwriting, especially for character analysis.

2. **graphic.** Marked by realistic and vivid detail.

3. **orthography.** The part of language study that deals with correct spelling; the art of writing words with correct spelling.

4. **annuity.** An investment yielding a fixed sum of money, payable yearly, to continue for a given number of years or for life; a yearly payment of money.

5. **bifocals.** A pair of glasses with two-part lenses, with one part helping you see what is near and one part helping you see from a distance.

6. **bilateral.** Involving two sides.

7. **bilingual.** Having or using two languages equally well; a bilingual person.

8. **binary.** Made up of two parts; twofold; relating to base two.

9. **biopsy.** In medicine, the cutting out of a piece of living tissue for examination.

10. **podium.** A low wall serving as a foundation; a raised platform for the conductor of an orchestra; a dais.

11. **pedestal.** A base or bottom support; any foundation or support; to put or set on a pedestal; to regard with great admiration.

12. **automatic.** Moving by itself; performed without thinking about it.

13. **automaton.** Anything that can move or act by itself; a person or animal acting in an automatic or mechanical way.

14. **autonomous.** Self-governing; functioning independently of other parts.

Practice for Additional Words Derived from Combining Forms (p. 15)

(1) j, (2) e, (3) h, (4) m, (5) b, (6) i, (7) l, (8) k, (9) a, (10) g, (11) n, (12) c, (13) d, (14) f.

Exercise 2 (pp. 15–22)

Practice A

(1) microscope, (2) geometry, (3) geography, (4) telegraph, (5) telescope,

(6) geology, (7) telephone, (8) Scripture, (9) biographer, (10) autobiography, (11) script, (12) description.

Practice B

(1) c, (2) c, (3) d, (4) b, (5) c, (6) d, (7) a, (8) d, (9) c, (10) c.

Additional Words Derived from Combining Forms (pp. 20–21)

1. **meter.** In the metric system, a unit of length equal to approximately 39.37 inches; an instrument for measuring the amount of something (as water, gas, electricity); an instrument for measuring and recording distance, time, weight, speed, and so forth; a measure of verse.

2. **telemeter.** An instrument that measures distance; an instrument that sends information to a distant point.

3. **micrometer.** An instrument used to measure accurately very small distances, angles, and diameters.

4. **microbe.** A very small living thing, whether plant or animal; a microorganism.

5. **microorganism.** Any organism that is so small that it can be seen only under a microscope—protozoa, bacteria, viruses, and the like.

6. **microphone.** A device that magnifies weak sounds.

7. **microfilm.** Film on which documents, printed pages, and so forth, are photographed in a reduced size for storage convenience.

8. **scribe.** A writer, author; a public writer or secretary; in Scripture and Jewish history, a man of learning.

9. **inscription.** Something written or engraved (words, symbols) on some surface; a brief or informal dedication in a book to a friend.

10. **prescription.** A doctor's written directions for the preparation and use of medicine; an order; direction; rule.

11. **transcript.** A written or typewritten copy of an original; a copy or reproduction of any kind.

12. **geocentric.** Relating to the earth as the center.

13. **phonics.** Study of the relationship between letter symbols of a written language and the sounds they represent.

14. **phonetics.** A study dealing with speech sounds and their production.

15. **stethoscope.** A hearing instrument used in examining the heart, lungs, and so on.

Practice for Additional Words Derived from Combining Forms (pp. 21–22)

(1) j, (2) m, (3) c or n, (4) c or n, (5) i, (6) k, (7) f, (8) b, (9) l, (10) a, (11) d, (12) g, (13) e, (14) h, (15) o.

Exercise 3 (pp. 22–28)

Practice A

(1) c, (2) b, (3) c, (4) d, (5) d, (6) b, (7) c, (8) d, (9) b, (10) b, (11) a, (12) c, (13) d, (14) d, (15) c, (16) a.

Practice B

(1) something consisting of opposites; (2) something showy; (3) opposite; (4) being the only one of its kind; (5) referring to all; (6) extreme fear; (7) use of opposites for certain results; (8) onlookers; (9) a joining; a putting together; (10) unusual, exciting, impressive; (11) a ruler who has absolute power; (12) manner of speaking.

Additional Words Derived from Combining Forms (pp. 27–28)

1. **Dictaphone.** A machine for recording and reproducing words spoken into its mouthpiece (differs from a tape recorder because it has controls that fit into use in transcription). *Dictaphone* is capitalized because it is a trademark.

2. **dictum.** An authoritative statement; a saying.

3. **indictment.** A charge; an accusation.

4. **unilateral.** Occurring on one side only; done by one only; one-sided.

5. **unify.** To make or form into one.

6. **acrophobia.** An abnormal fear of high places.

7. **hydrophobia.** An abnormal fear of water; an inability to swallow water when rabies is present.

8. **claustrophobia.** An abnormal fear of being confined, as in a room or a small place.

9. **grammar.** That part of the study of language that deals with the forms and structure of words (morphology) and their arrangement in phrases and sentences (syntax); the study or description of the way language is used.

10. **speculate.** To think about something by turning it in the mind and viewing it in all its aspects and relations; to take part in any risky business venture.

Practice for Additional Words Derived from Combining Forms (p. 28)

(1) e, (2) h, (3) f, (4) i, (5) g, (6) a, (7) j, (8) d, (9) b, (10) c.

Crossword Puzzle 1 (pp. 29–30)

Word Scramble 1 (pp. 30–31)

(1) uniform, (2) unique, (3) phobia, (4) bicycle, (5) autograph, (6) pedestrian, (7) biweekly, (8) geology, (9) autobiography, (10) biped, (11) telescope, (12) script, (13) microscope, (14) universal, (15) annual, (16) geography, (17) contradiction, (18) spectator, (19) biology, (20) biennial.

Analogies 1 (pp. 31–32)

(1) pedestrian, (2) telescope, (3) hydrophobia, (4) spectacle, (5) biweekly, (6) spectacular, (7) unique, (8) uniform, (9) podium, (10) autograph, (11) automaton, (12) phobia, (13) contradict, (14) bifocals, (15) unite, (16) orthography, (17) transcript, (18) indictment, (19) biennial, (20) microbe.

Multiple-Choice Vocabulary Test 1 (pp. 32–36)

Exercise 1

(1) a, (2) c, (3) c, (4) d, (5) b, (6) a, (7) b, (8) c, (9) c, (10) a, (11) a, (12) c,[5] (13) a.

Exercise 2

(14) c, (15) d, (16) b, (17) b, (18) c, (19) d, (20) c, (21) b, (22) a, (23) a.

Exercise 3

(24) a, (25) c, (26) c,[6] (27) a, (28) c, (29) c, (30) c, (31) a, (32) c, (33) d,[7] (34) c, (35) a, (36) b, (37) a,[8] (38) a, (39) c, (40) b, (41) d.

True/False Test 1 (p. 36)

(1) T, (2) F, (3) F, (4) F, (5) F, (6) F, (7) T, (8) F, (9) T, (10) F, (11) T, (12) T, (13) T, (14) F, (15) F, (16) F.

STOP. Turn to page 37 for the scoring of the tests.

Additional Practice Sets (pp. 37–41)

Additional Practice 1

A. (1) c, (2) f, (3) d, (4) b, (5) a, (6) e, (7) g.
B. (1) d, (2) m, (3) c, (4) k, (5) f, (6) j, (7) i, (8) e, (9) h, (10) b, (11) g, (12) l, (13) a.

Additional Practice 2

A. (1) g, (2) a, (3) d, (4) f, (5) c, (6) e, (7) b.
B. (1) h, (2) f, (3) g, (4) d, (5) c, (6) a, (7) i, (8) e, (9) b, (10) j.

Additional Practice 3

A. (1) f, (2) c, (3) d, (4) e, (5) a, (6) b.
B. (1) l, (2) m, (3) g, (4) i, (5) h, (6) b, (7) c, (8) e, (9) f, (10) k, (11) o, (12) d, (13) p, (14) r, (15) a, (16) j, (17) q, (18) n.

---

[5] *Two-footed animal* is a better answer than *two-footed human* because there are animals other than humans who are bipeds.

[6] *Special form of clothing* is a better answer than *clothing* because clothing refers to all that you wear. Not all clothing is a uniform; a uniform is a special form of clothing.

[7] *A ruler with absolute power* is a better answer than *a ruler* because not all rulers are dictators.

[8] A contradiction refers to something, such as *two statements about the same thing that are complete opposites*. It is not the use of opposites for effect.

46

CHAPTER THREE

EXERCISE 4

Step I. Combining Forms

A. Directions: A list of combining forms with their meanings follows. Look
at the combining forms and their meanings. Concentrate on
learning each combining form and its meaning. Cover the meanings, read the combining forms, and state the meanings to
yourself. Check to see if you are correct. Now cover the combining forms, read the meanings, and state the combining forms
to yourself. Check to see if you are correct.

Combining Forms	*Meanings*
1. cent, centi	hundred; hundredth part
2. dec, deca	ten
3. milli	thousand; thousandth part
4. port	carry
5. cred	believe

B. Directions: Cover the preceding meanings. Write the meanings of the following combining forms.

Combining Forms   Meanings

1. cent, centi   _____

2. dec, deca   _____

3. milli   _____

4. port   _____

5. cred   _____

Step II. Words Derived from Combining Forms

1. **century** (cen · tu · ry) (sen′ chu · rē) *n.* (*pl.* **ies**) Period of one hundred years. *A man who is 110 years old has lived more than a whole century.*

2. **centennial** (cen · ten · ni · al) (sen · ten′ nē · al) *adj.* Pertaining to a period of one hundred years; lasting one hundred years. *n.* A one-hundredth anniversary. *The centennial celebration for the United States took place in 1876.*

3. **bicentennial** (bi · cen · ten · ni · al) (bī · sen · ten′ nē · al) *adj.* Pertaining to or in honor of a two-hundredth anniversary; consisting of or lasting two hundred years; occurring once in two hundred years. *n.* A two-hundredth anniversary. *The United States celebrated its bicentennial in 1976.*

4. **million** mil · lion (mil′ yun) *n.* One thousand thousands (1,000,000); a very large or indefinitely large number. *adj.* Being one million in number; very many; one thousand thousands. *A million years equals ten thousand centuries.*

5. **millennium** (mil · len′ nē · um) *n.* (*pl.* **niums, nia**) Period of one thousand years; a one-thousandth anniversary; a period of great happiness (the millennium). *When the millennium arrives, there will be great happiness on earth.*

6. **decade** (dek′ ād) *n.* Period of ten years. *I can't believe that ten years have passed and that it's already a decade since I last saw my married brother.*

7. **credible** (cred · i · ble) (kred′ i · bul) *adj.* Believable. *I doubt if anyone will believe you because that is not a credible story.*

8. **credit** (kred′ it) *n.* Belief in something; trust; faith; good name; a recognition by name of a contribution to a performance; something that adds to a person's reputation; in an account, the balance in one's favor; an amount

of goods or money a person receives and pays for in the future; a unit of academic study. *v.* To supply something on credit to. *Because of his strong financial position, he can receive as much **credit** as he needs from the bank.*

9. **credential** (cre · den · tial) (kre · den′ shul) *n.* Something that entitles one to credit or confidence; something that makes others believe in a person; a document such as a degree, diploma, or certificate; *pl.* **credentials:** *testimonials entitling* a person to credit or to exercise official power. *His **credentials** for the job were so good that everyone felt he would do the work very well.*

10. **incredible** (in · cred · ible) (in · kred′ i · bul) *adj.* Not believable. *It is not believable that you could have gotten yourself into such an **incredible** situation.*

11. **porter** (port′ er) *n.* A person who carries things; one who is employed to carry baggage at a hotel or transportation terminal. *At the airport, I always tip the **porter** who carries my luggage.*

12. **reporter** (rē · port′ er) *n.* A person who gathers information and writes reports for newspapers, magazines, and so on. *I have always wanted to be a **reporter** because I like to gather information and write reports.*

13. **port** (port) *n.* Place to or from which ships carry things; place where ships may wait. *When a ship comes to **port**, its cargo is usually unloaded immediately.*

14. **export** (ex · port) (ek · sport′) *v.* To carry away; to transport or send something to another country. *n.* Something that is exported. *The United States **exports** wheat to many nations.*

15. **import** (im · port′) *v.* To carry in; bring in goods from another country. *n.* Something that is imported. *The United States **imports** coffee from South America.*

16. **portable** (port · a · ble) (port′ a · bul) *adj.* Can be carried; easily or conveniently transported. ***Portable** goods are those that you can easily take from one place to another.*

Special Notes

1. The combining form *centi* meaning *hundredth part* is used chiefly in terms belonging to the metric system (*centimeter*).

2. The combining form *deci* means "tenth part."

3. The combining form *kilo* means "thousand."

A. Directions: Underline the word that *best* fits the meaning given for each group of words.

1. A hundredth anniversary
   - a. century
   - b. centennial
   - c. bicentennial
   - d. decade

2. A period of ten years
   - a. centennial
   - b. century
   - c. million
   - d. decade

3. Believable
   - a. credit
   - b. credential
   - c. credible
   - d. incredible

4. Place where ships wait
   - a. port
   - b. porter
   - c. import
   - d. deport

5. A person who gathers information for news-papers
   - a. port
   - b. import
   - c. deport
   - d. reporter

6. A document such as a degree or diploma
   - a. credit
   - b. credential
   - c. credible
   - d. incredible

7. Period of one hundred years
   - a. decade
   - b. century
   - c. bicentennial
   - d. millennium

8. Someone who carries things
   - a. reporter
   - b. port
   - c. porter
   - d. import

9. One thousand thousands
   - a. millennium
   - b. centennial
   - c. bicentennial
   - d. million

10. Period of a thousand years
    - a. century
    - b. millennium
    - c. million
    - d. bicentennial

11. Not believable
    - a. credit
    - b. credential
    - c. incredible
    - d. credible

12. Can be carried
    - a. porter
    - b. import
    - c. deport
    - d. portable

13. Two-hundredth anniversary
    - a. bicentennial
    - b. millennium
    - c. centennial
    - d. century

14. Bring in goods from another country
    - a. import
    - b. export
    - c. portable
    - d. porter

15. Balance in one's favor
    - a. credential
    - b. credit
    - c. credible
    - d. incredible

16. To carry or send something to another country or region
    - a. port
    - b. import
    - c. reporter
    - d. export

STOP. Check answers at the end of the chapter.

B. Directions: A few paragraphs with missing words follow. Fill in the blanks
with the word that *best* fits. Words may be used more than once.

Word List

*million, credential, reporter, decade, incredible, portable, port, export, import,
credible, credit.*

As a 1_____ for a large newspaper, I am always looking for
a good story. Approximately nine and one-half years ago, almost a whole
2_____ ago, a lot of drugs were stolen right under the noses
of the police. Only persons with proper 3_____ s were allowed
to deal with the drugs. It just did not seem possible that the drugs could be
stolen. It seemed 4_____. The amount of money involved was
said to be thousands of thousands of dollars, over a(n) 5_____
dollars.

Recently, 6_____ for this 7_____ robbery was
given to insiders who had proper police 8_____ s. The inform-
er's story about the robbery is a(n) 9_____ one, and everyone
seems to believe it. It seems that persons with 10_____ s were
able to get into the place where the drugs were stored. They were able to place
the drugs on a 11_____ table and calmly walk out with them. They
replaced the drugs with a mixture of sugar and salt. The robbers than took the
drugs to 12_____ , where they had a ship waiting for them. The
drugs were 13_____ ed to another country. When things quiet-
ed down, the drugs were 14_____ ed to the United States and sold
for 15_____ s of dollars.

STOP. Check answers at the end of the chapter.

EXTRA WORD
POWER

> **able, ible.** Can do; able. When *able* or *ible* is found
> at the end of a word, the word is an adjective mean-
> ing "able" or "can do." For example: *portable*—
> able to be carried; *incredible*—not able to be believed;
> *credible*—able to be believed; *manageable*—able to be
> managed; *laughable*—able to be laughed at; *enjoyable*—
> able to be enjoyed. How many more *able* or *ible*
> words can you think of?

Additional Words Derived from Combining Forms

From your knowledge of combining forms, can you define the following words?

1. **decimal** (des′ i · mal) *adj. n. Most of the world's currency uses the
   decimal system, which divides the prime unit of money (such as
   dollars) into tenths or hundredths.*

2. **decimate** (des' i • māt¢) *v.* *If you have to lose a battle, it is better to be* **decimated** *than obliterated because in the former case, nine tenths of your troops will survive.*

_____

3. **decameter** (dek' a • mē • ter) *n.* *Because the United States is converting to the metric system, persons should become familiar with such terms as* **decameter**.

_____

4. **decimeter** (des' i • mē • ter) *n.* *A decimeter is approximately 4 inches, so that it would take about 3* **decimeters** *to equal 1 foot.*

_____

5. **millimeter** (mil' łi • mē • ter) *n.* *Microorganisms are even smaller than a* **millimeter**.

_____

6. **centimeter** (sen' ti • mē • ter) *n.* *I measured the distance in* **centimeters** *because I needed to know it to the nearest hundredth of a meter.*

_____

7. **kilometer** (kil' o • me • ter) *n.* *There are approximately 1.6* **kilometers** *to a mile.*

_____

8. **centipede** (sent' i • pēd¢) *n.* *The* **centipede** *crawled along on its many feet.*

_____

9. **creed** (krē¢d) *n.* *The* **creed** *"All men are created equal" is found in our Constitution.*

_____

10. **accreditation** (ac • cred • i • ta • tion) (ak̸ • kred • i • tā' shun) *n.* *If a college does not have the proper* **accreditation**, *students might have difficulty in getting jobs or getting into graduate schools.*

_____

11. **creditor** (kred' it • or) *n.* *Savings and loan associations are more likely to be large* **creditors** *to the public through home purchase loans than are commercial banks.*

_____

12. **deportment** (dē · port' ment) *n.* *Because his **deportment** has always been above question, everyone is confused by his present behavior.*

STOP. Check answers at the end of the chapter.

Practice for Additional Words Derived from Combining Forms

Directions: Match each word with the *best* definition.

_____ 1. decimal	a. statement of belief	
_____ 2. decimate	b. one to whom something is due	
_____ 3. decameter	c. conduct	
_____ 4. millimeter	d. 1/100 of a meter	
_____ 5. centimeter	e. wormlike animal with many legs	
_____ 6. centipede	f. 1/1,000 of a meter	
_____ 7. accreditation	g. to destroy one tenth of; to destroy but not completely	
_____ 8. creed	h. ten meters	
_____ 9. creditor	i. numbered by ten	
_____10. deportment	j. a giving authority to	
_____11. decimeter	k. 1,000 meters	
_____12. kilometer	l. 1/10 of a meter	

STOP. Check answers at the end of the chapter.

EXERCISE 5

Step I. Combining Forms

A. Directions: A list of combining forms with their meanings follows. Look at the combining forms and their meanings. Concentrate on learning each combining form and its meaning. Cover the meanings, read the combining forms, and state the meanings to yourself. Check to see if you are correct. Now cover the combining forms, read the meanings, and state the combining forms to yourself. Check to see if you are correct.

Combining Forms	Meanings
1. agogue, agog	leading; directing; inciting
2. arch	rule; chief
3. ali	other
4. dem, demo	people
5. mon, mono	one
6. theo	God

B. Directions: Cover the preceding meanings. Write the meanings of the following combining forms.

Combining Forms	Meanings
1. agogue, agog	_____
2. arch	_____
3. ali	_____
4. dem, demo	_____
5. mon, mono	_____
6. theo	_____

Step II. Words Derived from Combining Forms

1. **monarchy** (mon′ ar · kē) *n.* A government or state headed by a single person, who is usually a king, queen, or emperor: called absolute (or despotic) when there is no limitation on the monarch's power and constitutional (or limited) when there is such limitation. *Although England is a **monarchy**, the king or queen does not exercise any power at all.*

2. **autocracy** (au · toc · ra · cy) (au · tok′ ra · sē) *n.* A form of government in which one person possesses unlimited power. *In any **autocracy** the head of government has absolute control of the country.*

3. **autocrat** (au′ to · krat) *n.* A ruler who has absolute control of a country. *The head of government who has absolute control in an autocracy is called an **autocrat**.*

4. **anarchy** (an · ar · chy) (an′ ar · kē) *n.* No rule; disorder; the absence of government; chaos. *In the West, years ago, **anarchy** existed in many towns because there were no laws.*

5. **atheist** (ā′ thē · ist) *n.* One who does not believe in the existence of God. *An atheist does not believe in the existence of God.*

6. **theocracy** (the · oc · ra · cy) (thē · ok′ ra · sē) *n.* Government by a religious group. *A country ruled by clergy (persons allowed to preach the gospel) would be called a theocracy.*

7. **theology** (the · ol · o · gy) (thē · ol′ o · jē) *n.* The study of religion. *Mininsters, priests, and rabbis must take courses in theology to learn about religion.*

8. **democracy** (de · moc · ra · cy) (de · mok′ ra · sē) *n.* A form of government in which there is rule by the people either directly or through elected representatives. *In a democracy the people, through their voting power, have a say in who the leaders of the government will be.*

9. **demagogue** (dem′ a · gogu̸e̸) *n.* A person who stirs up the emotions of people in order to become a leader and achieve selfish ends. *A demagogue is usually a highly persuasive speaker who plays on the emotions of the crowds for his own ends.*

10. **alias** (ā′ lē · as) *n.* *(pl.* **ses)** Another name taken by a person, often a criminal. *A person who uses an alias doesn't want others to know what his real name is.*

11. **alien** (al · ien) (āl′ yun) *n.* A foreigner; a person from another country. *adj.* Foreign. *If aliens in the United States neglect to register as aliens, they may be deported to their country of origin.*

12. **alienate** (al · ien · ate) (āl′ yun · āt¢) *v.* To make others unfriendly to one; to estrange (to remove or keep at a distance). *The politicians try not to alienate any voters.*

Special Notes

1. The word *demagogue* is a little more difficult to define even though you know the meanings of the combining forms. A *demagogue* is a person who stirs the emotions of people to become a leader and gain selfish ends. A *demagogue* appeals usually to popular passion, especially by making extravagant promises or charges. This word is used to refer to leaders who use people for their own ends. *Hitler is probably the most hated demagogue of the twentieth century.*

2. The word *autocrat* means "a ruler in absolute control." An *autocrat* does not have to be a king or a queen. The word *autocracy* means "government by an autocrat." A *monarchy,* which is rule by a monarch, either a king, queen, or emperor, does not have to be an autocracy; that is, a country

can have a king or a queen, but the king or queen does not necessarily have absolute control of the government.

3. When the combining form *arch* is the final element of a word, it means "rule." When *arch* is used at the beginning of a word (such as *archbishop*, *archfiend*), it means "chief."

Step III. Practice

A. Directions: Following are the words presented in Exercise 5. Match the word with its meaning. Put the letter of the meaning in the space before the word.

Words	*Meanings*
_____ 1. theocracy	a. a person who stirs emotions of people in order to become a leader and achieve selfish ends
_____ 2. theology	b. a ruler in absolute control
_____ 3. atheist	c. to make others unfriendly to one
_____ 4. alien	d. another name, usually used by criminals
_____ 5. alienate	e. one who does not believe in God
_____ 6. monarchy	f. a government headed by a king, queen, or emperor
_____ 7. autocrat	g. the study of religion
_____ 8. anarchy	h. a foreigner
_____ 9. democracy	i. the absence of government
_____ 10. autocracy	j. a form of government in which one person possesses unlimited power
_____ 11. demagogue	k. government of a state by a religious group
_____ 12. alias	l. a form of government in which there is rule by the people

STOP. Check answers at the end of the chapter.

B. Directions: A number of sentences with missing words follows. Underline the word that *best* fits the sentence. Two choices are given for each sentence.

1. When there are no laws or government, a state of (autocracy, anarchy) usually exists.

2. Huey Long, a former governor of Louisiana, was known to be a(n) (autocrat, demagogue) because he was able to stir persons' emotions to achieve his own selfish ends.

3. In a (monarchy, democracy) there is rule by the people directly or through elected representatives.

4. A monarchy that is also a(n) (theocracy, autocracy) is one in which the ruler has supreme and unlimited power.

5. A country that is headed by a king, a queen, or an emperor is called an absolute (democracy, monarchy) when there are no limitations on the ruler's powers.

6. A person who does not believe in the existence of God is called an (atheist, anarchist).

7. An (atheist, autocrat) is a ruler who has absolute power in his or her government.

8. John used an (autograph, alias) when he didn't want people at the hotel to recognize his famous name.

9. Every year (autocrats, aliens) living in the United States must register as citizens of another country.

10. I never (alienate, describe) anyone on purpose because I don't like to have enemies.

11. In a(n) (autocracy, theocracy) God is recognized as the ruler.

STOP. Check answers at the end of the chapter.

> **a.** Without; not. *A* is used in front of some words
> and means "without" or "not." For example: *an-*
> *archy*—without rule; *atheist*—one who is without
> belief in God; *amoral*—without morals; without
> being able to tell right from wrong. *Those that*
> *bombed many buildings filled with people are*
> **amoral** *because they do not know right from wrong.*
> The people in this sentence are *amoral.* An amoral
> person does not have a sense of right or wrong. How-
> ever, an *immoral* person does know the difference
> between right and wrong, but he or she chooses to
> do wrong.

Additional Words Derived from Combining Forms

From your knowledge of combining forms, can you define the following words?

1. **apodal** (ap′ o · dal) *adj. The snake is an **apodal** animal.*

   _____

2. **demography** (de · mog · ra · phy) (de · mog′ ra · fē) *n. Demographers study the **demography** of a population to determine the trends of vital statistics.*

   _____

3. **archetype** (ar · che · type) (ar′ ke · tīpe) *n. The architect showed an **archetype** of the building to the interested spectators.*

   _____

4. **monotone** (mon′ o · tōne) *n. v. When a lecturer speaks in a **monotone**, listeners have difficulty paying attention to what is being said.*

   _____

5. **monotonous** (mo · not′ o · nøus) *adj. Doing the same things over and over again is very **monotonous**.*

   _____

6. **monorail** (mon′ o · rāil) *n. When you ride on the **monorail** at Walt Disney World, everything on the ground appears to be so small.*

   _____

7. **monophobia** (mon · o · pho · bi · a) (mon · o · fō′ bē · a) *n. I can't imagine a person who is suffering from **monophobia** living alone in the mountains.*

   _____

8. **monoglot** (mon' o · glot) *n. adj.* *There are probably more **monoglots** in the United States than in Europe because Europe does not have a single dominant language.*

_____

9. **monopoly** (mo · nop' o · lē) *n.* (*pl.* **ies**). *Because the company had a **monopoly** on the grain market, they were able to charge whatever they wanted for grain.*

_____

10. **oligarchy** (ol · i · gar · chy) (ol' i · gar · kē) *n.* (*pl.* **ies**). ***Oligarchy**, as a form of government, usually fails because each of the rulers generally competes with the others to try to gain more power for himself.*

_____

STOP. Check answers at the end of the chapter.

Practice for Additional Words Derived from Combining Forms

Directions: Match each word with the *best* definition.

_____ 1. apodal

_____ 2. demography

_____ 3. archetype

_____ 4. monophobia

_____ 5. monoglot

_____ 6. monorail

_____ 7. monotone

_____ 8. monotonous

_____ 9. monopoly

_____ 10. oligarchy

a. cars suspended from a single rail

b. a form of government in which there is rule by a few

c. dull; changeless

d. speech not having any change in pitch

e. being without feet

f. the exclusive control of something

g. the first of its kind; model

h. study of populations

i. the fear of being alone

j. a person who knows only one language

STOP. Check answers at the end of the chapter.

EXERCISE 6

Step I. Combining Forms

A. Directions: A list of combining forms with their meanings follows. Look at the combining forms and their meanings. Concentrate on learning each combining form and its meaning. Cover the meanings, read the combining forms, and state the meanings to yourself. Check to see if you are correct. Now cover the combining forms, read the meanings, and state the combining forms to yourself. Check to see if you are correct.

Combining Forms	Meanings
1. mis, miso[1]	hate; wrong
2. poly	many
3. gamy	marriage
4. hom, homo[1]	same; man; human
5. gen, geno	race; kind; descent
6. anthrop, anthropo	man; human; mankind
7. leg, legis, lex	law

B. Directions: Cover the preceding meanings. Write the meanings of the following combining forms.

Combining Forms	Meanings
1. mis, miso	_____
2. poly	_____
3. gamy	_____
4. hom, homo	_____
5. gen, geno	_____
6. anthrop, anthropo	_____
7. leg, legis, lex	_____

---

[1] When words combine with *mis* in this exercise, *mis* means "hate." When words combine with *homo* in this exercise, *homo* means "same." You will meet words with the other meanings for *mis* and *homo* in a later exercise.

1. **monogamy** (mo · nog′ a · mē) *n.* Marriage to one spouse at one time. *In the United States, **monogamy** is practiced, so you can be married to only one spouse (husband or wife) at one time.*

2. **bigamy** (big′ a · mē) *n.* Marriage to two spouses at the same time. *Because **bigamy** is not allowed in the United States, you will not find many persons who are married to two spouses at the same time.*

3. **polygamy** (po · lyg · a · my) (po · lig′ a · mē) *n.* Marriage to many spouses at the same time. *Because **polygamy** is allowed in some Middle Eastern countries, you will find some persons with many spouses in such countries.*

4. **anthropology** (an · thro · pol · o · gy) (an · thro · pol′ o · jē) *n.* The study of mankind; the study of the cultures and customs of people. *In **anthropology** we studied about a tribe of people who had an entirely different way of life from ours.*

5. **misanthrope** (mis′ an · thrōpₑ) *n.* Hater of mankind. *Although Jim does not like women, he is not a **misanthrope** because he doesn't hate all people.*

6. **legal** (lē′ gal) *adj.* Referring to law; lawful. *Although the business deal was **legal**, it did not sound lawful to me.*

7. **legislature** (leg · is · la · ture) (lej′ is · lā · chur) *n.* Body of persons responsible for lawmaking. *The **legislature** is the body of persons given the power to write laws for a state or nation.*

8. **homosexual** (ho · mo · sex · u · al) (hō · mo · sek′ shū · al) *adj.* Referring to the same sex or to sexual desire for those of the same sex. *n.* A homosexual individual. *A **homosexual** is one who prefers a relationship with an individual of the same sex.*

9. **homograph** (hom′ o · graf) *n.* A word spelled the same way as another but having a different meaning. *The verb* saw *and the noun* saw *are **homographs**.*

10. **homogeneous** (hō · mo · jē′ nē · ₑus) *adj.* Being the same throughout; being uniform. *It is difficult to have a **homogeneous** group of students because students are not all the same.*

11. **general** (jen′ er · al) *adj.* Referring to all. *n.* In the U.S. Army and Air Force, an officer of the same rank as an admiral in the U.S. Navy. *The statement "All men are equal" is a **general** statement.*

12. **generic** (ge · ner · ic) (je · ner′ ik) *adj.* Referring to all in a group or class. *When one uses the term* man *in the **generic** sense, he or she is referring to both males and females.*

Special Notes

1. **homograph.** A word written the same way as another but having a different meaning. *General* and *general* are two words in this exercise that are *homographs* because they are spelled alike but have different meanings.

2. The term *generic* means "general," "referring to all in a group or class." Persons use the word *generic* in order to make their statements more clear. For example: *I am speaking in the **generic** sense when I use the word* mankind *because* mankind *refers to both males and females.* When the word *chairman* is used, it is used in the *generic* sense; that is, a person can be chairman and be either a man or a woman. Today the word *chairperson* is used more often because it is more general.

Step III. Practice

A. Directions: A number of sentences with missing words follows. Choose the word that *best* fits the sentence. Put the word in the blank. *Not all words fit in.*

Word List

monogamy, alien, alienate, homogeneous, generic, anthropologist, biology, geology, autocracy, atheist, centennial, bicentennial, anthropology, homograph, misogamist, misanthrope, legal, legislature, homosexual, bigamy, decade, incredible, century.

1. Because I am interested in learning about other cultures and the way man lives, I studied _____ in college.

2. The term *man* in sentence 1 is used in the _____ sense because it refers to both men and women.

3. In the year 1976 America celebrated its _____.

4. It is not _____ to practice _____ in the United States.

5. In the United States _____ is practiced because it's not legal to have more than one spouse.

6. The terms *spring* meaning "season" and *spring* meaning "to leap" are _____ s.

7. A person who hates people would be called a(n) _____.

8. We will be entering another _____ in the year 2000.

9. The _____ has voted more rights for women.

62

10. Margaret Mead, who studies about other people around the world, is a famous _____ .

11. Margaret Mead has written about the customs of other people, and these may appear_____ to people in the Western world.

STOP. Check answers at the end of the chapter.

B. Directions: Following is a list of definitions. Choose the word that *best* fits the definition. Try to relate your definition to the meanings of the combining forms. *All the words fit in.*

Word List

misanthrope, monogamy, bigamy, decade, anthropology, anthropologist, legal, legislature, homosexual, century, bicentennial, homogeneous, polygamist, homograph, generic, centennial.

1. hater of mankind _____

2. one who is married to many spouses at the same time _____

3. hundredth anniversary _____

4. being of the same kind _____

5. lawful _____

6. a period of one hundred years _____

7. word written the same as another but having a different meaning _____

8. every two hundred years _____

9. referring to a relationship with the same sex _____

10. the study of mankind or different cultures _____

11. marriage to one spouse at one time _____

12. referring to all in a group or class _____

13. marriage to two spouses at the same time _____

14. one who studies different cultures _____

15. body of persons responsible for lawmaking _____

16. a period of ten years _____

STOP. Check answers at the end of the chapter.

ist. One who. When *ist* is found at the end of a noun, it means "one who" and changes the word to a certain type of person. For example, let's add *ist* to a number of words you have met: *geologist*—one who is in the field of geology; *biologist*—one who is in the field of biology; *anthropologist*—one who is in the field of anthropology; *theologist*—one who is in the field of theology; *bigamist*—one who is married to two spouses at the same time; *polygamist*—one who is married to many spouses at the same time; *monogamist*—one who believes in or practices monogamy; *anarchist*—one who believes that there should be no government. How many more words with *ist* can you add to this list?

Additional Words Derived from Combining Forms

From your knowledge of combining forms, can you define the following words?

1. **polyglot** (pol′ ē · glot) *adj. n. Linguists are generally **polyglots**.*

   _____

2. **polygon** (pol′ ē · gon) *n. In geometry I always had difficulty solving problems involving **polygons** because they have so many angles.*

   _____

3. **podiatrist** (po · dī′ a · trist) *n. After I went on a ten-mile hike, my feet hurt so much that I needed to visit a **podiatrist**.*

   _____

4. **bisexual** (bi · sex · u · al) (bī · sek′ shū · al) *adj. n. Because some plants are **bisexual**, they can fertilize themselves to reproduce the next generation.*

   _____

5. **misogamist** (mi · sog′ a · mist) *n. Although Jim has never married, I do not think he is a **misogamist**.*

   _____

6. **anthropomorphic** (an · thro · pō · mor′ fik) *adj. In Walt Disney films, all of the animals have **anthropomorphic** characteristics.*

   _____

64

7. **anthropoid** (an′ thro • poid) *adj.* *n. The gorilla, orangutan, and chimpanzee are **anthropoids**.*

---

8. **genealogy** (gen • e • al • o • gy) (jē • nē • al′ o • jē) *n. (pl.* **ies**) *Mrs. Smith went to England to acquire certain documents that would help her in tracing the **genealogy** of her family.*

---

9. **genus** (jē′ nus) *n. (pl.* genera) (jen′ er • a) *In biology, when plants or animals are classified according to common characteristics, the name of the **genus** begins with a capital letter.*

---

10. **generate** (jen′ er • āte) *v. Every animal **generates** its own species or kind.*

STOP. Check answers at the end of the chapter.

Practice for Additional Words Derived from Combining Forms

Directions: Match each word with the *best* definition.

_____ 1. polyglot   a. hater of marriage

_____ 2. polygon   b. resembling or suggesting an ape

_____ 3. podiatrist   c. speaking many languages

_____ 4. bisexual   d. class, kind, or group marked by common characteristics

_____ 5. misogamist   e. to produce

_____ 6. anthropomorphic   f. foot doctor

_____ 7. anthropoid   g. described in human terms

_____ 8. genealogy   h. study of one's descent

_____ 9. genus   i. a many-sided plane figure

_____10. generate   j. of both sexes

STOP. Check answers at the end of the chapter.

CROSSWORD PUZZLE 2

Directions: The meanings of many of the combining forms from Exercises 4–6 follow. Your knowledge of these combining forms will help you to solve this crossword puzzle. Note that *combining form* is abbreviated as *comb. f.*

Across

1. A small word that refers to a position
3. A small word that means "in the same manner"
5. Comb. f. for *ten*
8. A monkey
9. A musical syllable
10. In poker, the stake put up before dealing the cards
11. Comb f. for *kind* or *species*
13. Same as #9 Across
15. Refers to yourself
16. Part of a shoe
18. Comb. f. for *mankind*
24. Same as #8 Across

Down

1. Abbreviation for *advertisement*
2. Comb. f. for *from a distance*
3. Abbreviation for *apartment*
4. Meaning of *spect*
6. A container
7. Comb. f. for *without*
8. An indefinite article
10. Same as #7 Down
11. Word meaning *class*; *kind*; *group*
12. Fifteenth letter of the alphabet
13. Supporting yourself against something
14. A high mountain
15. An informal way of referring to mother

26. Twenty-first letter of the alphabet
27. Comb. f. for *one*
28. Opposite of *men*
30. Same as #7 Down
31. A piece of wood that supports a sign
33. Opposite of *gain*
34. Refers to a kind of metal
37. Sound made to quiet someone
38. Comb. f. for *marriage*
41. Twentieth letter of the alphabet
42. Opposite of *yes*
43. Meaning of *uni* and *mono*

16. Comb. f. for *man*; *same*
17. Fifth letter of the alphabet
19. Refers to an explosive
20. A greeting
21. Eighteenth letter of the alphabet
22. Sound made when you are hurt
23. Comb. f. for *many*
25. What you do when you are hungry
26. Opposite of *down* (pl.)
29. The ending of *highest*
32. An exclamation of surprise
35. Opposite of *out*
36. A negative answer
38. Opposite of *stop*
39. Same as #8 Down
40. Same as #15 Across

STOP. Check answers at the end of the chapter.

WORD SCRAMBLE 2

Directions: Word Scramble 2 is based on words from Exercises 4–6. The meanings are your clues to arranging the letters in correct order. Write the correct word in the blank.

Meanings

1. onllmii _____ one thousand thousands

2. eecrildb _____ believable

3. nucteyr _____ period of one hundred years

4. eddace _____ period of ten years

5. primto _____ to bring goods in from another country

6. leraiedtcn _____ something that gives someone authority

7. bropelat _____ able to be carried

8. yrcmnoah _____ government headed by a king, queen, or emperor

9. aanychr _____ no rule

10. seiahtt _____ one who dies not believe in God

11. cttuoaar   _____ absolute ruler

12. nalei   _____ a foreigner

13. ooelytgh   _____ the study of religion

14. saail   _____ another name

15. ooohalgyntrp _____ the study of mankind

16. llgea   _____ lawful

17. reengla   _____ a high-ranking officer in the army

18. ooguhsoenem _____ being of same kind

19. namgoyom   _____ marriage to one at one time

20. magyib   _____ marriage to two spouses at one time

STOP. Check answers at the end of the chapter.

ANALOGIES 2

Directions: Find the word from the following list that *best* completes each
analogy. There are more words listed than you need.

Word List

*physician, polyglot, polygon, cent, deca, podiatrist, anthropoid, milli, century,
decade, anthropology, million, export, anarchy, millennium, penny, archetype,
arch, autocracy, bigamy, alienate, alias, credential, decimate, decimal, alien,
decameter, centimeter, millimeter, credit, incredible, atheist, reporter, creditor.*

1. Scientist : biologist : : doctor :_____.

2. Mono : poly :: monoglot :_____.

3. Millimeter : centimeter :: meter : _____ .

4. Vehicle : automobile :: writer :_____.

5. Pepper : spice : : hexagon :_____.

6. Milli : cent : : cent : _____ .

7. Pedestal : base : : foreigner : _____ .

8. Two : binary : : ten : _____ .

9. Democracy : autocracy : : import : _____ .

10. None : universal :: credible :_____.

11. Decade : century : : century :_____.

68

12. Beautiful : pretty : : obliterate :_____.

13. One : ten : : decade : _____ .

14. Conduct : deportment : : disorder :_____ .

15. Earth : geology : : man :_____.

16. Genus : kind : : model : _____ .

17. Week : fortnight : : monogamy : _____ .

18. Same : unique : : debtor : _____

19. Glasses : spectacles :: separate : _____ .

20. Suit : clothing : : degree : _____.

STOP. Check answers at the end of the chapter.

MULTIPLE-CHOICE VOCABULARY   TEST 2

Directions: This is a test on words in Exercises 4–6. Words are presented according to exercises. *Do all exercises before checking answers.* Underline the meaning that *best* fits the word.

Exercise 4

1. century
   a. a hundredth anniversary
   b. period of one hundred years
   c. period of ten years
   d. period of one thousand years

2. million
   a. one thousand thousands
   b. period of one thousand years
   c. period of one hundred years
   d. period of great happiness

3. millennium
   a. one thousand thousands
   b. period of two thousand years
   c. period of great happiness
   d. a hundredth anniversary

4. centennial
   a. two thousand years
   b. one thousand thousands
   c. one thousand years
   d. a hundredth anniversary

5. decade
   a. period of ten years
   b. one hundred years
   c. twenty years
   d. one thousand years

6. bicentennial
   a. one thousand years
   b. a two-hundredth anniversary
   c. one hundred years
   d. period of great happiness

7. credible
   a. good faith
   b. a balance
   c. good name
   d. believable

8. incredible
   a. believable
   b. not faithful
   c. not a good reputation
   d. not believable

9. porter
   a. a person who gathers information
   b. something that can be carried
   c. one who carries things
   d. place for ships

10. port
    a. to carry out
    b. to carry in
    c. place where ships may wait
    d. able to be carried

11. import
    a. able to be carried
    b. place where ships wait
    c. to carry out goods
    d. to carry in goods from other areas or countries

12. export
    a. carry in goods
    b. carry out goods to other areas or countries
    c. able to be carried
    d. one who carries things

13. reporter
    a. person who carries things
    b. able to be carried
    c. a place where ships wait
    d. a person who gathers information for newspapers

14. portable
    a. carry in goods
    b. able to be carried
    c. carry out goods
    d. one who carries things

15. credit
    a. balance in one's favor in an account
    b. owe money
    c. believable
    d. something that gives someone authority

16. credential
    a. good name
    b. owe money
    c. something that entitles someone to credit or confidence
    d. believable

Exercise 5

17. monarchy
    a. rule by many
    b. rule by a few
    c. rule by king, queen, or emperor
    d. absolute rule

18. autocracy
    a. absolute rule
    b. rule by one
    c. rule by a few
    d. no rule

19. autocrat
    a. one who does not believe in rule
    b. absolute ruler
    c. ruler who shares power
    d. one who does not believe in God

70

20. anarchy
   - a. without belief in God
   - b. no rule
   - c. absolute rule
   - d. rule by one

21. atheist
   - a. one who believes in no rule
   - b. one who believes in absolute rule
   - c. one who believes in rule by a religious group
   - d. one who does not believe in God

22. theocracy
   - a. belief in God
   - b. rule by a religious group
   - c. the study of religion
   - d. absolute rule

23. theology
   - a. rule by a religious group
   - b. belief in God
   - c. absolute rule
   - d. the study of religion

24. democracy
   - a. absolute rule
   - b. leader who influences persons for his own purposes
   - c. rule by the people
   - d. the study of people

25. demagogue
   - a. ruler of people
   - b. rule by the people
   - c. leader who influences persons for his own purposes
   - d. leader of people

26. alias
   - a. a foreigner
   - b. unfriendly
   - c. another name
   - d. turns people away

27. alien
   - a. another name
   - b. a foreigner
   - c. turns people away
   - d. unfriendly

28. alienate
   - a. make others unfriendly
   - b. a foreigner
   - c. another name
   - d. makes friends

Exercise 6

29. monogamy
   - a. hater of marriage
   - b. no belief in marriage
   - c. marriage to one spouse at one time
   - d. the study of marriage

30. bigamy
   - a. something not lawful
   - b. marriage to two spouses at the same time
   - c. having been married twice
   - d. marriage to one spouse at one time

31. polygamy
   - a. marriage to many spouses at one time
   - b. many marriages
   - c. something not legal
   - d. the study of many marriages

| 32. misanthrope | a. hater of marriage | c. hater of mankind |
| | b. married to a man | d. the study of mankind |

| 33. anthropology | a. marriage to men | c. a science |
| | b. the study of mankind | d. hater of mankind |

| 34. legal | a. person responsible for law | c. lawful |
| | b. body of persons responsible for lawmaking | d. a person who defends others |

| 35. legislature | a. lawful | c. body of persons responsible for lawmaking |
| | b. person responsible for laws | d. persons who defend others |

| 36. homosexual | a. same kind | c. one who prefers relationships with the same sex |
| | b. referring to man | d. one who prefers relationships with the opposite sex |

| 37. homogeneous | a. being of the same kind | c. referring to man |
| | b. the same sex | d. one who prefers relationships with the same sex |

| 38. homograph | a. the study of man | c. the same word |
| | b. the study of graphs | d. a word spelled the same as another but having a different meaning |

| 39. general | a. referring to the same | c. referring to a group of people |
| | b. referring to all | d. referring to kinds of people |

| 40. generic | a. referring to all in a group or class | c. referring to a group |
| | b. referring to people | d. referring to generals in the army |

TRUE/FALSE TEST 2

Directions: This is a true/false test on Exercises 4–6. Read each sentence carefully. Decide whether it is true or false. Put a *T* for *true* or an *F* for *false* in the blank. The number after the sentence tells you if the word is from Exercise 4, 5, or 6.

_____ 1. One who hates mankind is called a misanthrope. 6

_____ 2. A misogamist must also be a misanthrope. 6

_____ 3. Ten hundred thousand equals one million. 4

_____ 4. Ten decades do not equal a century. 4

_____ 5. An anthropologist is interested in studying ants. 6

_____ 6. An atheist believes in God. 5

_____ 7. A bachelor must be a misogamist. 6

_____ 8. When you import something, you send it out of the country. 4

_____ 9. A centennial celebration takes place every one thousand years. 4

_____10. If you have a good credit rating, you have a good financial reputation. 4

_____11. Your credentials are what you have that makes persons believe you can do a certain job. 4

_____12. An autocrat is a ruler in a democracy. 5

_____13. An anarchist is one who believes in no government. 5, 6

_____14. An anarchist must be an atheist. 5, 6

_____15. A demagogue uses people for his or her own selfish ends. 5

_____16. An alien is someone who enters another country not legally. 5, 6

_____17. When you use an alias, you are using your given name. 5

_____18. _Saw_ (the past tense of _to see_) and _saw_ (something that you cut with) are examples of homographs. 6

_____19. Persons with homogeneous tastes are persons who must like men. 6

_____20. In the word _mankind, man_ is used in the generic sense because it refers to both men and women. 6

_____21. Someone who commits bigamy may be jailed because this is not legal in the United States. 6

_____22. The legislature is responsible for making laws for the state or federal government. 6

STOP. Check answers for both tests at the end of the chapter.

SCORING OF TESTS

Multiple-Choice Vocabulary Test		True/False Test	
Number Wrong	_Score_	_Number Wrong_	_Score_
0–3	Excellent	0–1	Excellent
4–6	Good	2–3	Good
7–9	Weak	4–5	Weak
Above 9	Poor	Above 5	Poor
Score _____		Score _____	

1. If you scored in the excellent or good range on *both tests*, you are doing well. Go on to Chapter Four.

2. If you scored in the weak or poor range on either test, look below and follow directions for Additional Practice. Note that the words on the test are arranged so that you can tell in which exercise to find them. This will help you if you need additional practice.

ADDITIONAL PRACTICE SETS

A. Directions: Write the words you missed on the tests from the three exercises in the space provided. Note that the tests are presented so that you can tell to which exercises the words belong.

Exercise 4 Words Missed

1. _____   6. _____
2. _____   7. _____
3. _____   8. _____
4. _____   9. _____
5. _____   10. _____

Exercise 5 Words Missed

1. _____   6. _____
2. _____   7. _____
3. _____   8. _____
4. _____   9. _____
5. _____   10. _____

Exercise 6 Words Missed

1. _____   6. _____
2. _____   7. _____
3. _____   8. _____
4. _____   9. _____
5. _____   10. _____

B. Directions: Restudy the words that you have written down on this page. Study the combining forms from which those words are derived. Do Step I and Step II for those you missed. Note that Step I and Step II of the combining forms and vocabulary derived from these combining forms are on the following pages:

Exercise 4—pp. 47–49

Exercise 5—pp. 53–59

Exercise 6—pp. 60–62

C. Directions: Do Additional Practice 1 on this page and the next if you missed words from Exercise 4. Do Additional Practice 2 on pp. 76–77 if you missed words from Exercise 5. Do Additional Practice 3 on pp. 77–78 if you missed words from Exercise 6. Now go on to Chapter Four.

Additional Practice 1 for Exercise 4

A. Directions: Following are the combining forms presented in Exercise 4. Match the combining form with its meaning.

_____ 1. cent, centi   a. carry

_____ 2. dec, deca   b. hundred; hundredth part

_____ 3. milli   c. believe

_____ 4. port   d. thousand; thousandth part

_____ 5. cred   e. ten

STOP. Check answers at the end of the chapter.

B. Directions: Following are sentences containing the meanings of vocabulary presented in Exercise 4. Choose the word that *best* fits the meaning of the word or phrase underlined in the sentence.

Word List

century, centennial, bicentennial, million, millennium, decade, credible, credits, credentials, incredible, porter, reporter, port, export, imports, portable.

_____ 1. It is <u>not believable</u> that you are able to do all that.

_____ 2. In <u>a period of one hundred years</u> many changes have taken place in the United States.

_____ 3. What do you call <u>the place where a ship waits?</u>

_____ 4. <u>The one-hundredth anniversary</u> of the first spaceship's landing on the moon will be in 2069.

_____ 5. When complete peace comes to earth, <u>a period of great happiness</u> will exist.

_____ 6. That is a <u>believable</u> statement.

_____ 7. How many <u>academic units</u> have you earned toward your degree?

_____ 8. <u>One thousand thousands</u> is a large number.

_____ 9. The man's <u>college degree,</u> as well as his <u>work experiences,</u> helped him to get the job.

_____10. The person who <u>carried my baggage</u> was very strong.

_____11. My television set is on a table that <u>can be moved very easily</u> to any part of the room.

_____12. She is a person who <u>gathers information and writes articles</u> for the magazine.

_____13. When will you <u>take the goods out of the country?</u>

_____14. The year 1976 was <u>the two-hundredth anniversary</u> of the United States.

_____15. Every year the United States <u>brings into the country</u> many goods made by foreign countries.

_____16. In <u>a ten-year period</u> clothing styles may change from one extreme to another.

STOP. Check answers at the end of the chapter.

Additional Practice 2 for Exercise 5

A. Directions: Following are the combining forms presented in Exercise 5. Match the combining form with its meaning.

_____ 1. agog, agogue   a. rule; chief

_____ 2, arch   b. other

_____ 3. ali   c. God

_____ 4. dem, demo   d. leading, directing; inciting

_____ 5. mon, mono   e. people

_____ 6. theo   f. one

STOP. Check answers at the end of the chapter.

B. Directions: Following are a number of sentences with missing words. Fill in the blank with the word that *best* fits.

76

Word List

monarchy, autocracy, autocrat, anarchy, atheist, theocracy, theology, democracy, demagogue, alias, alien, alienate.

1. You will _____ a lot of people by the way you are acting.

2. As I did not want to be recognized when I traveled, I wore a disguise and used a(n)_____.

3. A(n) _____ is a person who belongs to another country.

4. In a(n)_____ a king or queen may be at the head of government but not necessarily have any power.

5. A(n) _____ has absolute power in his country.

6. I would not like to live in a(n) _____ because one does not have any freedom to disagree with the ruler.

7. In our_____ all persons over eighteen have the right to vote and the government is ruled by the people through elected representatives.

8. In a state of_____ there is confusion because there are no laws.

9. A(n) _____ would not be a churchgoer because he or she does not believe in the existence of God.

10. _____ does not exist any more, as it did in the Middle Ages, when the Church ruled a large part of Europe.

11. Persons who study_____ are interested in religion.

12. Hitler is a good example of a(n)_____ because he could stir persons' emotions and get them to do what he wanted.

STOP. Check answers at the end of the chapter.

Additional Practice 3 for Exercise 6

A. Directions: Following are the combining forms presented in Exercise 6. Match the combining form with its meaning.

_____ 1. mis, miso   a. law

_____ 2. poly   b. many

_____ 3. gamy   c. kind; race, descent

_____ 4. hom, homo   d. marriage

_____ 5. gen, geno   e. hate; wrong

_____ 6. anthrop, anthropo   f. man; human; mankind

_____ 7. leg, legis, lex   g. same; man; human

STOP. Check answers at the end of the chapter.

B. Directions: Following are the words presented in Exercise 6. Match the word with its meaning.

_____ 1. hater of mankind

_____ 2. a high-ranking office in the army; referring to all

_____ 3. marriage to many spouses at the same time

_____ 4. marriage to one spouse at one time

_____ 5. marriage to two spouses at the same time

_____ 6. referring to all in a group or class

_____ 7. being of the same kind

_____ 8. lawful

_____ 9. body of persons who make laws

_____ 10. referring to the same sex

_____ 11. the study of mankind

_____ 12. a word written in the same way as another but having a different meaning

a. homograph

b. bigamy

c. monogamy

d. legislature

e. legal

f. homogeneous

g. misanthrope

h. homosexual

i. generic

j. anthropology

k. general

l. polygamy

STOP. Check answers at the end of the chapter.

ANSWERS

Exercise 4 (pp. 47–53)

Practice A

(1) b, (2) d, (3) c, (4) a, (5) d, (6) b, (7) b, (8) c, (9) d, (10) b, (11) c, (12) d, (13) a, (14) a, (15) b, (16) d.

Practice B

(1) reporter, (2) decade, (3) credential, (4) incredible, (5) million, (6) credit, (7) incredible, (8) credential, (9) credible, (10) credential, (11) portable, (12) port, (13) export, (14) import, (15) million.

Additional Words Derived from Combining Forms (pp. 51–53)

1. **decimal.** Numbered by tens; based on 10; pertaining to tenths or the number 10; a decimal fraction.

2. **decimate.** To take or destroy a tenth part of; to destroy but not completely; to destroy a great number or proportion of.

3. **decameter.** In the metric system, a measure of length containing 10 meters, equal to 393.70 inches or 32. 81 feet.

4. **decimeter.** In the metric system, a unit of length equal to 1/10 meter.

5. **millimeter.** In the metric system, a unit of length equal to 1/1,000 meter (0.03937 inch).

6. **centimeter.** In the metric system, a unit of measure equal to 1/100 meter (0.3937 inch).

7. **kilometer.** In the metric system, a unit of length equal to 1,000 meters.

8. **centipede.** Wormlike animal with many legs.

9. **creed.** A statement of religious belief; a statement of belief, principles.

10. **accreditation.** The act of bringing into favor; a vouching for; a giving authority to.

11. **creditor.** One to whom a sum of money or other thing is due.

12. **deportment.** The manner of conducting or carrying oneself; behavior; conduct.

Practice for Additional Words Derived from Combining Forms (p. 53)

(1) i, (2) g, (3) h, (4) f, (5) d, (6) e, (7) j, (8) a, (9) b, (10) c, (11) l, (12) k.

Exercise 5 (pp. 53–59)

Practice A

(1) k, (2) g, (3) e, (4) h, (5) c, (6) f, (7) b, (8) i, (9) l, (10) j, (11) a, (12) d.

Practice B

(1) anarchy; (2) demagogue; (3) democracy; (4) autocracy; (5) monarchy; (6) atheist; (7) autocrat; (8) alias; (9) aliens; (10) alienate; (11) theocracy.

Additional Words Derived from Combining Forms (pp. 58–59)

1. **apodal.** Having no feet.

2. **demography.** The statistical study of human populations, including births, deaths, marriages, population movements, and so on.

3. **archetype.** The original pattern or model of a work from which something is made or developed.

4. **monotone.** A single unchanging tone; speech not having any change in pitch; to speak in an unvaried tone.

5. **monotonous.** Changeless; having no variety; uniform; dull

6. **monorail.** A single rail serving as a track for trucks or cars suspended from it or balanced on it.

7. **monophobia.** An abnormal fear of being alone.

8. **monoglot.** A person who knows, speaks, or writes only one language; speaking or writing only one language.

9. **monopoly.** Exclusive control of a commodity or service in a given market; control that makes possible the fixing of prices and the elimination of free competition.

10. **oligarchy.** A form of government in which there is rule by a few (usually a privileged few).

Practice for Additional Words Derived from Combining Forms (p. 59)

(1) e, (2) h, (3) g, (4) i, (5) j, (6) a, (7) d, (8) c, (9) f, (10) b.

Exercise 6 (pp. 60–65)

Practice A

(1) anthropology; (2) generic; (3) bicentennial; (4) legal, bigamy; (5) monogamy; (6) homograph; (7) misanthrope; (8) century; (9) legislature; (10) anthropologist; (11) incredible.

Practice B

(1) misanthrope, (2) polygamist, (3) centennial, (4) homogeneous, (5) legal, (6) century, (7) homograph, (8) bicentennial, (9) homosexual, (10) anthropology, (11) monogamy, (12) generic, (13) bigamy, (14) anthropologist, (15) legislature, (16) decade.

Additional Words Derived from Combining Forms (pp. 64–65)

1. **polyglot.** A person who knows, speaks, or writes many languages; speaking or writing many languages.

2. **polygon.** A closed plane figure with several angles and sides.

3. **podiatrist.** Foot doctor.

4. **bisexual.** Of both sexes; having both male and female organs, as is true of some plants and animals; a person who is sexually attracted by both sexes.

5. **misogamist.** Hater of marriage.

6. **anthropomorphic.** Giving human shape or characteristics to gods, objects, animals, and so on.

7. **anthropoid.** A person resembling an ape either in stature, walk, or intellect; resembling man—used especially of apes such as the gorilla, chimpanzee, and orangutan; resembling or suggesting an ape.

8. **genealogy.** The science or study of one's descent; a tracing of one's ancestors.

9. **genus.** A class, kind, or group marked by shared characteristics or by one shared characteristic.

10. **generate.** To produce; to cause to be; to bring into existence.

Practice for Additional Words Derived from Combining Forms (p. 65)

(1) c, (2) i, (3) f, (4) j, (5) a, (6) g, (7) b, (8) h, (9) d, (10) e.

Crossword Puzzle 2(pp. 66-67)

(1) million, (2) credible, (3) century, (4) decade, (5) import, (6) credential, (7) portable, (8) monarchy, (9) anarchy, (10) atheist, (11) autocrat, (12) alien, (13) theology, (14) alias, (15) anthropology, (16) legal, (17) general, (18) homogeneous, (19) monogamy, (20) bigamy.

Analogies 2 (pp. 68-69)

(1) podiatrist, (2) polyglot, (3) decameter, (4) reporter, (5) polygon, (6) deca, (7) alien, (8) decimal, (9) export, (10) incredible, (11) millennium, (12) decimate, (13) century, (14) anarchy, (15) anthropology, (16) archetype, (17) bigamy, (18) creditor, (19) alienate, (20) credential.

Multiple-Choice Vocabulary Test 2 (pp. 69-72)

Exercise 4

(1) b, (2) a, (3) c, (4) d, (5) a, (6) b, (7) d, (8) d, (9) c, (10) c, (11) d, (12) b, (13) d, (14) b, (15) a, (16) c.

Exercise 5

(17) c, (18) a, (19) b, (20) b, (21) d, (22) b, (23) d, (24) c, (25) c, (26) c, (27) b, (28) a.

Exercise 6

(29) c, (30) b, (31) a, (32) c, (33) b,[2] (34) c, (35) c, (36) c, (37) a, (38) d, (39) b, (40) a.

True/False Test 2 (pp. 72-73)

(1) T, (2) F,[3] (3) T,[4] (4) F, (5) F, (6) F, (7) F,[5] (8) F, (9) F, (10) T, (11) T, (12) F, (13) T, (14) F,[6] (15) T, (16) F,[7] (17) F, (18) T, (19) F, (20) T, (21) T, (22) T.

STOP. Turn to page 73 for the scoring of the tests.

---

[2] Although anthropology is a science, the better answer is *study of mankind,* which describes what kind of science anthropology is and gives more information.

[3] Even if someone hates marriage, it does not mean that he or she must also hate people.

[4] Ten times 100 equals 1,000. One thousand thousands equals 1 million.

[5] Not necessarily.

[6] Not so. Persons who believe in no government rule *may* believe in God.

[7] An *alien* is a foreigner. He or she can legally come to this or any other country. Although there are aliens who enter a country illegally, this is not part of the definition of an alien.

Additional Practice Sets (pp. 74–78)

Additional Practice 1

A. (1) b, (2) e, (3) d, (4) a, (5) c.

B. (1) incredible, (2) century, (3) port, (4) centennial, (5) millennium,
    (6) credible, (7) credits, (8) million, (9) credentials, (10) porter,
    (11) portable, (12) reporter, (13) export, (14) bicentennial, (15) im-
    ports, (16) decade.

Additional Practice 2

A. (1) d, (2) a, (3) b, (4) e, (5) f, (6) c.

B. (1) alienate, (2) alias, (3) alien, (4) monarchy, (5) autocrat, (6) autocracy,
    (7) democracy, (8) anarchy, (9) atheist, (10) theocracy, (11) theology,
    (12) demagogue.

Additional Practice 3

A. (1) e, (2) b, (3) d, (4) g, (5) c, (6) f, (7) a.

B. (1) g, (2) k, (3) l, (4) c, (5) b, (6) i, (7) f, (8) e, (9) d, (10) h, (11) j,
    (12) a.

CHAPTER FOUR

EXERCISE 7

Step I. Combining Forms

A. Directions: A list of combining forms with their meanings follows. Look at the combining forms and their meanings. Concentrate on learning each combining form and its meaning. Cover the meanings, read the combining forms, and state the meanings to yourself. Check to see if you are correct. Now cover the combining forms, read the meanings, and state the combining forms to yourself. Check to see if you are correct.

Combining Forms	Meanings
1. vis, vid	see
2. sci, scio	know
3. poten	powerful
4. omni	all
5. aqua, aqui	water
6. astro	star
7. naut	sailor
8. ven, veni, vent	come

B. Directions: Cover the preceding meanings. Write the meanings of the following combining forms.

Combining Forms	Meanings
1. vis, vid	_____
2. sci, scio	_____
3. poten	_____
4. omni	_____
5. aqua, aqui	_____
6. astro	_____
7. naut	_____
8. ven, veni, vent	_____

Step II. Words Derived from Combining Forms

1. **vision** (vi · sion) (vizh′ un) *n.* The sense of sight. *Because the man's **vision** was blocked by the screen, he could not see what the spectators were looking at.*

2. **visible** (vis · i · ble) (viz′ i · bul) *adj.* Able to be seen; evident; apparent; on hand. *On a clear day the skyline of the city is **visible.***

3. **invisible** (in · vis · i · ble) (in · viz′ i · bul) *adj.* Not able to be seen. *In the film, the **invisible** man was able to appear in many prohibited places because no one was able to see him.*

4. **television** (tel · e · vi · sion) (tel′ e · vizh · un) *n.* An electronic system for the transmission of visual images from a distance; a television receiving set. ***Television** is viewed by so many people all over the country that sponsors pay millions of dollars to advertise their products on it.*

5. **provision** (pro · vi · sion) (pro · vizh′ un) *n.* The act of being prepared beforehand; preparation; something made ready in advance; (*pl.*) needed materials, especially a supply of food for future needs; a part of an agreement referring to a specific thing. *The army was running out of necessary **provisions**, and the men were beginning to complain that they did not have enough supplies to carry on their operations.*

6. **evident** (ev′ i · dent) *adj.* Obvious; clearly seen; plain. *From everything that you have said, it is **evident** that he is lying about where he was on the night of the murder.*

7. **evidence** (ev′ i · dense) *n.* That which serves to prove or disprove something. *The **evidence** was so strong against the defendant that it didn't seem possible that he could prove his innocence.*

8. **science** (sci' ense) *n.* Any area of knowledge in which the facts have been investigated and presented in an orderly manner. *New sciences develop as we learn more and more about the universe.*

9. **astrology** (a · strol · o · gy) (a · strol' o · jē) *n.* The art or practice that claims to tell the future and interpret the influence of the heavenly bodies on the fate of people; a reading of the stars. *There are a large number of people who believe in astrology's ability to predict their futures.*

10. **astronomy** (a · stron' o · mē) *n.* The science that deals with stars, planets, and space. *When I studied astronomy, I used a very high-powered telescope to view the stars and planets.*

11. **astronaut** (as' tro · naut) *n.* One who travels in space, that is, beyond the earth's atmosphere; a person trained to travel in outer space. *The Apollo astronauts shook hands with the Russian astronauts in space during a special space flight in 1975.*

12. **aquanaut** (aq · ua · naut) (ak' wa · naut) *n.* One who travels undersea; a person trained to work in an underwater chamber. *Jacques Cousteau has many aquanauts on his team who explore the wonders under the seas.*

13. **aquatic** (a · quat · ic) (a · kwat' ik) *adj.* Living or growing in or near water; performed on or in water. *The best swimmers performed in our aquatic ballet.*

14. **aquarium** (a · quar · i · um) (a · kwar' ē · um) *n.* A pond, a glass bowl, a tank, or the like, in which aquatic animals and/or plants are kept; a place in which aquatic collections are shown. *The aquatic plants and animals in my aquarium are specially chosen to make sure that they can live together.*

15. **convene** (kon · vēne') *v.* To come together; to assemble. *The assemblymen were waiting for everyone to arrive so that they could convene for their first meeting of the year.*

16. **convention** (con · ven · tion) (kon · ven' shun) *n.* A formal meeting of members for political or professional purposes; accepted custom, rule, or opinion. *The teachers hold their convention annually to exchange professional views and learn about new things.*

17. **convenient** (con · ven · ient) (kon · vēn' yent) *adj.* Well suited to one's purpose, personal comfort, or ease; handy. *The professional and political conventions are held in cities that have convenient hotels and halls to take care of a great number of people.*

18. **potent** (po · tent) (pōt' ent) *adj.* Physically powerful; having great authority; able to influence; strong in chemical effects. *The drug was so potent that it actually knocked out John, who is over 6 feet tall and weighs almost 200 pounds.*

19. **impotent** (im′ po · tent) *adj.* Without power to act; physically weak; incapable of sexual intercourse (said of males). *The monarch in England is politically impotent because he or she has hardly any power in the governing of the country.*

20. **potential** (po · ten · tial) (po · ten′ shul) *n.* The possible ability or power one has. *adj.* Having force or power to develop. *The acorn has the potential to become a tree.*

21. **omnipresent** (om · ni · prez′ ent) *adj.* Being present everywhere at all times. *The omnipresent toothpaste commercial was annoying because it seemed to be on all the channels at the same time.*

Special Notes

1. When the term *potential* is used, it refers to *possible ability*. This means that potential is something that a person may have within him or her, but it may or may not necessarily come out. The following cartoon illustrates this idea very nicely.

Understanding the Term *Potential*

© 1959 United Feature Syndicate, Inc.

2. *Astrology* is concerned with the reading of the stars. Astrologists use the stars to try to predict the future of persons. Do not confuse astrology, which is a false science, with astronomy, which is a science that deals with the study of stars, planets, and space.

Step III. Practice

A. Directions: Following are a number of sentences with missing words. Choose the word that *best* fits the sentence. Put the word in the blank. *Not all words fit in.*

Word List

potent, impotent, evidence, evident, vision, invisible, convention, convenient, astronaut, aquanaut, scientist, aquatic, aquarium, astrology, astronomy, provision, science, omnipresent, television, convene, potential.

1. All _____s must be in top physical shape in order to travel in space.

2. Because I love swimming and diving and I'm very interested in sea life, I want to be a(n) _____ .

3. You find _____ plants in the ocean.

4. Some poisons are so _____ that one-quarter teaspoon will kill you.

5. I enjoy watching the plants in my _____ .

6. The fortune-teller I went to used her knowledge of _____to predict my future.

7. I want to study_____ in college because I enjoy learning about stars and planets.

8. Because the stop sign was not clearly_____, I went right past it.

9. Have you made any special _____ s for yourself for when you retire?

10. Although he is the head of government, he is politically_____because he has no say in anything.

11. The district attorney must have some_____to support his case before he can try to prove the guilt of someone.

12. Astronomy, biology, and geology are all_____s.

13. _____ s are formal meetings, which are usually held annually.

14. With your good_____, you should be able to see the board from where you're sitting.

15. The _____ warriors seemed to be everywhere.

16. If that time is not _____ for you, we'll change it for a better one.

17. It is difficult to talk about my ability level, for I do not know what my _____ is.

18. The judge said that the court would _____ in one hour to continue the trial.

STOP. Check answers at the end of the chapter.

B. Directions: A few paragraphs with missing words follow. Fill in the blanks with the words that *best* fit. *Words may be used more than once.*

Word List

anniversary, visible, convention, evident, omnipresent, decade, television, scientists, reporter, convenient, astrologist, aquanauts, astronauts, evidence, provision, incredible, invisible, aquatic, impotent.

As a(n) 1_____ I get to investigate and write stories. I especially remember one story I wrote about a 2_____ago. I remember it was ten years ago because my wife and I were celebrating our first wedding 3_____ with a special dinner, when the phone rang. It was my boss. His excitement was clearly 4_____. "Joe, did you see what just happened on 5_____?" he asked. "No, we didn't have the 6_____ . . ." Before I could finish answering, he said, "Well, get down here immediately. I want you to cover a special story that just broke." Although it was not a 7_____time for me, I went to meet him.

It seemed that a group of well-known 8_____ , such as biologists, geologists, astronomists, and so on, were meeting at a national 9_____ held in our city. At the 10_____ there were exhibits of materials that 11_____ had brought back from space. There were also special 12_____ plants that 13_____ had found underseas.

At about ten in the morning, a woman phoned the editor in the newspaper office. She said she was a(n) 14_____ who could foretell the future. She told the editor to watch the 15_____ exhibits that were being shown on 16_____ to people all over the country. She knew that something 17_____ was going to take place shortly and that it would be 18_____ to all who were watching. The editor felt that from the way the woman was talking it was 19_____ she was a "crackpot." He receives so many calls from people telling about things that would happen that never did. There are so many crackpots around that they seem to be 20_____.

Well, at eight that night, in plain view of all who had their 21_____s tuned to the channel covering the exhibits, a(n) 22_____ robbery took place. The people watching the robbery must have felt 23_____ because they had no power to do anything about it.

Persons dressed as 24_____ who were going on a space flight and 25_____who were going to explore the ocean, stole the priceless materials on display.

Nobody could figure out how they got into the special room. It was as if they were 26_____ and at the proper moment they materialized and became 27_____ for all to see. They seemed to have had all the 28_____s they needed to carry out the robbery.

It was so well planned that no 29 _____ as to who they were or why they did it has ever been found.

STOP. Check answers at the end of the chapter.

C. Directions: The Combining Form Square contains the combining forms from this exercise as well as many from other exercises. Definitions of combining forms follow. See how many of the combining forms you can find in the square. Fill them in the blanks. If a definition appears more than once, it means that the combining form may have different spellings for the same meaning.

COMBINING FORM SQUARE

V	E	N	A	U	T	O	A
I	S	T	Q	V	A	P	N
S	G	E	O	E	L	O	T
E	R	L	A	N	I	R	H
H	O	E	I	B	D	T	R
O	C	S	C	I	I	R	O
M	O	N	O	O	C	O	P
O	N	U	N	I	T	R	O

1. _____ self

2. _____ see

3. _____ know

4. _____ man

5. _____ one

6. _____ one who

7. _____ one who

8. _____ one who

9. _____ two

10. _____ carry

11. _____ one

12. _____ sailor

13. _____ earth

14. _____ life

15. _____ come

16. _____ without

17. _____ with; together

18. _____ from a distance

19. _____ other

20. _____ say

21. _____ mankind

STOP. Check answers at the end of the chapter.

less. Without. When *less* is placed at the end of a word, it means "without." *Less* changes a noun into an adjective. For example: the word *mother* becomes *motherless*—without a mother; *father* becomes *fatherless*—without a father; *blame* becomes *blameless*—without blame; without fault; *harm* becomes *harmless*—without harm; without hurting. For example: *How lucky you are that you have both a mother and a father. Mary is a **motherless** child.* How many more words with *less* can you supply?

con, co, cor, com, col. Together; with. When *con* is placed at the beginning of some words, the *n* may change to an *l*, *m*, or *r*. The *n* in some words may be left out altogether. However, *con, com, cor, col,* and *co* all mean "together" or "with." Examples: *co-worker*—someone working with you; *convene*—come together; assemble; *convention*—a meeting where persons come together; *combine*—to join together; unite; *collect*—to gather together; *correspond*—to be equivalent; to write letters to one another.

Additional Words Derived from Combining Forms

From your knowledge of combining forms, can you define the following words?

1. **omnipotent** (om · nip' o · tent) *adj. No matter how much wealth, power, and prestige someone has, he or she is not **omnipotent**.*

   _____

2. **omniscient** (om · nis · cient) (om · nish' ent) *adj. With the rapid increase of knowledge, it is not possible for someone to be **omniscient**.*

   _____

3. **omnibus** (om' ni · bus) *n. Because we had a large group, we chartered an **omnibus** to take us to our destination.*

   _____

4. **visage** (vis · age) (viz' ij¢) *n. His wolfish **visage** warned me about what he might be thinking.*

   _____

5. **visor** (vī′ zor) *n.* *Baseball players wear hats with* **visors** *because the game is often played in bright sunlight.*

_____

6. **visa** (vi · sa) (vē′ za) *n.* *We need a* **visa** *to visit Russia.*

_____

7. **envision** (en · vi · sion) (en · vizh′ un) *v.* *The shipwrecked crew, who had been drifting on the raft for two days, deliriously* **envisioned** *a banquet.*

_____

8. **visionary** (vi · sion · ar · y) (vizh′ un · er · ē) *n.* *(pl.* **ies***) The leader of the newly formed religious group claims that he is a* **visionary** *who has seen visions of things to come.*

_____

9. **nautical** (nau′ tik · al) *adj.* *Because John has a* **nautical** *bent, he wants to become a sailor.*

_____

10. **venture** (ven · ture) (ven′ chur) *n.* *Because the business* **venture** *involved a great amount of speculation, I did not want to become a part of it.*

_____

11. **potentate** (pō′ ten · tāt) *n.* *The* **potentate** *of that country is an autocrat whom I would not want as my enemy.*

_____

STOP. Check answers at the end of the chapter.

Practice for Additional Words Derived from Combining Forms

Directions: Match each word with the *best* definition.

_____ 1. omnipotent   a. a risky, dangerous undertaking

_____ 2. omniscient   b. the face

_____ 3. omnibus   c. person possessing great power

_____ 4. visage   d. pertaining to seamen, ships

_____ 5. visa   e. all-powerful

_____ 6. envision   f. large bus

_____ 7. visionary   g. the projecting front brim of a cap

_____ 8. nautical   h. all-knowing

_____ 9. visor	i.	a person who sees visions
_____10. venture	j.	to imagine something
_____11. potentate	k.	something granting entrance to a country

STOP. Check answers at the end of the chapter.

EXERCISE 8

Step I. Combining Forms

A. Directions: A list of combining forms with their meanings follows. Look at the combining forms and their meanings. Concentrate on learning each combining form and its meaning. Cover the meanings, read the combining forms, and state the meanings to yourself. Check to see if you are correct. Now cover the combining forms, read the meanings, and state the combining forms to yourself. Check to see if you are correct.

Combining Forms	*Meanings*
1. cide	murder; kill
2. pathy	feeling; suffering
3. syl, sym, syn	same; with; together; along with
4. frater, fratr	brother
5. mors, mort	death
6. capit	head
7. corp, corpor	body
8. em, en	into; in

B. Directions: Cover the preceding meanings. Write the meanings of the following combining forms.

Combining Forms	*Meanings*
1. cide	_____
2. pathy	_____
3. syl, sym, syn	_____
4. frater, fratr	_____
5. mors, mort	_____

94

6. capit   _____

7. corp, corpor   _____

8. em, en   _____

Step II. Words Derived from Combining Forms

1. **homicide** (hom' i · sīdǿ) *n.* Any killing of one human being by another. *The spectator witnessed a horrible **homicide**, in which the victim was beaten to death.*

2. **suicide** (sū' i · sīdǿ) *n.* The killing of oneself. *I wonder if persons who try to kill themselves know that it is against the law to commit **suicide.***

3. **genocide** (gen · o · cide) (jen' o · sīdǿ) *n.* The systematic and deliberate killing of a whole racial group or a group of people bound together by customs, language, politics, and so on. *During World War II, Hitler attempted to commit **genocide** against the Jewish people because he wanted to wipe them out completely.*

4. **sympathy** (sym · pa · thy) (sim' pa · thē) *n.* (*pl.* **ies**) Sameness of feeling with another; ability to feel pity for another. *When Mary lost both her parents in an automobile accident, we all felt deep **sympathy** for her.*

5. **empathy** (em' pa · thē) *n.* (*pl.* **ies**) The imaginative putting of oneself into another person's personality; ability to understand how another feels because one has experienced it firsthand or otherwise. *I felt **empathy** for the boy with the broken arm because the same thing had happened to me.*

6. **apathy** (ap' a · thē) *n.* Lack of feeling; indifference. *He had such **apathy** regarding the sufferings of persons around him that he didn't care one way or the other what happened to the hurt people.*

7. **fraternity** (fra · ter' ni · tē) *n.* (*pl.* **ies**) A group of men joined together by common interests for fellowship; a brotherhood; a Greek letter college organization. *In college I decided to join a **fraternity** so that I could make a lot of new friends.*

8. **capital punishment** (kap' i · tal pun' ish · ment) *n.* The death penalty. ***Capital punishment** has been outlawed in many countries because it is felt that the death penalty is a punishment that is too extreme.*

9. **capitalism** (cap · i · tal · ism) (kap' i · tal · iz · um) *n.* The economic system in which all or most of the means of production, such as land, factories, and railroads, are privately owned and operated for profit. *Because **capitalism** is practiced in the United States, individuals privately own and operate their businesses for profit.*

10. **capital** (kap′ i · tal) *n.* City or town that is the official seat of government; money or wealth; first letter of a word at the beginning of a sentence. *adj.* Excellent. *The **capital** of the United States is Washington, D.C.*

11. **corpse** (korps¢) *n.* Dead body. *After the detective examined the **corpse**, he was told that there was another dead body in the next room.*

12. **corporation** (cor · po · ra · tion) (kor · po · ra′ shun) *n.* A group of people who get a charter granting them as a body certain of the powers, rights, privileges, and liabilities (legal responsibilities) of an individual, separate from those of the individuals making up the group. *The men formed a **corporation** so that they would not individually be liable (legally responsible) for the others.*

13. **incorporate** (in · kor′ po · rāt¢) *v.* To unite; combine. *The men decided to **incorporate** because by joining together, they could be a more potent company.*

14. **corporal punishment** (kor′ po · ral pun′ ish · ment) *n.* Bodily punishment; a beating. *Because New Jersey is a state that outlaws **corporal punishment** in the schools, it is illegal for teachers to hit students.*

15. **mortal** (mor′ tul) *adj.* Referring to a being who must eventually die; causing death; ending in death; very grave; said of certain sins; to the death, as mortal combat; terrible, as mortal terror. *n.* A human being. *Because he still advanced, after being shot six times, everyone began to wonder whether he was a **mortal**.*

16. **immortal** (im · mor′ tul) *adj.* Referring to a being who never dies; undying. *n.* One who never dies. *Because a human being must eventually die, he or she is not **immortal**.*

17. **mortality** (mor · tal′ i · tē) *n.* The state of having to die eventually; proportion of deaths to the population of the region, nation, and so on; death rate; death on a large scale, as from disease or war. *The **mortality** of children among minority groups is decreasing because the living conditions of such groups are improving.*

18. **mortician** (mor · ti · cian) (mor · ti′ shin) *n.* A funeral director; undertaker. ***Morticians** are accustomed to handling corpses because their job is to prepare the dead for burial.*

19. **mortgage** (mort · gage) (mor′ gij) *n.* The pledging of property to a creditor (one to whom a sum of money is owed) as security for payment. *v.* To put up property as security for payment; to pledge. *Most persons who buy homes obtain a **mortgage** from a bank.*

20. **morgue** (morg¢) *n.* Place where dead bodies (corpses) of accident victims and unknown persons found dead are kept; for reporters it refers to the

reference library of old newspaper articles, pictures, and so on. *The police took the accident victim's body to the **morgue** because they could find no identification on it.*

Special Notes

1. **empathy** and **sympathy**. **empathy**: The imaginative putting of oneself into another in order to better understand him or her; putting oneself into the personality of another. *When people feel **empathy** for another, they know how the other person feels because they have had the same experience or can put themselves into the personality of the other.*
   sympathy: Sameness of feeling with another; ability to feel pity for another. *When you have **sympathy** for someone, you feel pity for him or her. You do not have to go through the same experience as the person.* Empathy is a stronger feeling than sympathy. When you say that you *sympathize* with someone's views, it means that you have the same feeling about the views as the person.

2. **apathy**. Lack of feeling; indifference. *He felt complete **apathy** for the whole situation.* The term *apathy* means that someone has no feeling one way or another. Such a person is indifferent.

3. The term *homicide* is used in the generic sense. You met the term *generic* in an earlier exercise. *Generic* means "referring to all within a group." Therefore, when someone says that *homicide* is used in the generic sense, he or she means that the combining form *homo* (meaning "man" in the word *homocide*) refers to both men and women, not just to males.

4. Remember the term *misanthrope*? *Misanthrope* means "hater of mankind." The word is also used in the generic sense in that *mankind* refers to both men and women, not just to men.

Step III. Practice

A. Directions: Following are a number of sentences with missing words. Choose the word that *best* fits the sentence. Put the word in the blank. *Words may be used in more than one sentence.*

Word List

capital punishment, corporal punishment, capital, corporation, capitalism, fraternity, suicide, mortality, immortal, morgue, mortgage, genocide, sympathy, mortal, empathy, homicide, incorporate, apathy, mortician.

1. The _____ of New York State is Albany, the
_____ of Tennessee is Nashville, and the _____
of California is Sacramento.

2. The five businessmen decided to form a _____ so that each
would not be legally responsible for the debts of the others.

3. Under _____ persons can own their businesses and work
for a profit.

4. In order to start a business, you need _____ because without _____ you cannot purchase the things you need.

5. As most people do not have enough money to pay for a house, they try
to secure a(n) _____ from a bank.

6. We had to go to the _____ to identify a relative who had
been killed in an accident.

7. We went to a(n) _____ to arrange for the funeral of our
relative.

8. The men were happy they had decided to _____, joining in
a business venture, because together they were doing better than they had
alone.

9. The way George drives his car, he must think that he is _____
and that nothing can kill him.

10. Now that women are more involved in careers, they may be more subject
to heart attacks and ulcers, and, as a result, their _____
will increase.

11. On earth only _____ s exist because no one has yet been
able to cheat death.

12. More people are trying to get their legislatures to pass a law to bring back
_____ _____ because people feel that fear
of death will prevent some crimes.

13. When a(n) _____ is committed, the police try to find a suspect who had a motive, the opportunity, and the means to kill the person.

14. Some persons would choose _____ _____
over lesser _____ _____ because they cannot stand beatings.

15. I felt great _____ for the person whose mother died in an
automobile accident because I had experienced the same thing a decade ago.

16. I have no _____ for Alice because I told her beforehand
that she would fail if she didn't do any work.

17. It seems incredible that one man was almost able to commit _____ and wipe out a whole race of people.

18. What seems even more incredible is that some people had such _____ about what was going on that they did not care one way or the other.

19. No one could understand why he committed_____because he seemed to have everything to live for.

20. I joined a(n) _____ in college in order to be with lots of friendly people and to have a place to go.

STOP. Check answers at the end of the chapter.

B. Directions: A list of definitions follows. In the space provided, insert the letter for the meaning that *best* fits the word.

_____ 1. The killing of a whole racial, political, or cultural group
   a. homicide   c. genocide
   b. suicide   d. fratricide

_____ 2. Lack of feeling
   a. sympathy   c. fraternity
   b. empathy   d. apathy

_____ 3. Dead body
   a. mortal   c. mortality
   b. corpse   d. immortal

_____ 4. Death rate
   a. mortal   c. mortality
   b. immortal   d. corpse

_____ 5. Ability to put self into another's personality
   a. empathy   c. fraternity
   b. apathy   d. sympathy

_____ 6. A brotherhood
   a. fraternity   c. capitalism
   b. corporation   d. capital

_____ 7. The feeling of pity for another
   a. empathy   c. apathy
   b. sympathy   d. fraternity

_____ 8. Killing of one person by another
   a. homicide   c. mortality
   b. suicide   d. genocide

_____ 9. Killing of oneself
   a. genocide   c. mortality
   b. homicide   d. suicide

_____10. To unite
   a. incorporate   c. convene
   b. corporation   d. fraternity

_____11. Money or wealth
   a. capitalism   c. capital
   b. corporation   d. incorporate

_____12.	Bodily punishment	a. corporal punishment	c. corpse
		b. capital punishment	d. corp-oration
_____13.	Death penalty	a. capital punishment	c. mortality
		b. corporal punishment	d. capitalism
_____14.	Place where unidentified dead are held	a. mortality	c. corpse
		b. mortal	d. morgue
_____15.	Economic system based on profit	a. capital	c. incorporate
		b. corporation	d. capitalism
_____16.	An undertaker	a. mortician	c. mortality
		b. mortal	d. immortal
_____17.	Referring to one who never dies	a. mortal	c. mortality
		b. immortal	d. corpse
_____18.	One who must die	a. immortal	c. mortal
		b. corpse	d. immortal
_____19.	The pledging of property to a creditor	a. morgue	c. mortician
		b. mortgage	d. mortality

STOP. Check answers at the end of the chapter.

C. Directions: Fifteen sentences follow. Define the underlined word or phrase. Put your answer in the blank.

1. Most homicides are the results of arguments among people who know each other. _____

2. Persons who commit suicide have usually given others around them warnings that they were going to kill themselves. _____

3. Meg's apathy toward the upcoming dance was obvious, and she couldn't have cared less whether she went or not. _____

4. I felt great sympathy for Jack when he had to drop out of college to help support his family after his father died. _____

5. Not everyone likes to join a fraternity because if a person does join one, he tends to spend most of his time with only those fellows in the fraternity.

_____

6. The idea of anyone's attempting genocide to get rid of a whole racial, political, or cultural group seems incredible. _____

100

7. In geography, when we had to list all the capitals of the states, I always listed Washington, D.C., which is, however, the capital of the United States and not a state capital. _____

8. Because I can't stand to look at dead bodies, I did not go to the morgue to help to identify the accident victim._____

9. The mortician made the corpse look lifelike. _____,_____

10. The men incorporated and formed a corporation so that each would not be liable for the others in their business._____,_____

11. Because corporal punishment is allowed in most states, school systems have set up regulations regarding when and how a child can be hit._____

12. Do you feel that capital punishment will stop persons from committing horrible crimes because they will be afraid of being put to death?_____

13. Some works of art are called immortal because it is thought that they will live forever. _____

14. I know of no mortal who has lived over 120 years._____

15. If you stop paying the money you owe on your mortgage, the bank will be able to take away your house, because your house was put up as security for the loan._____

STOP. Check answers at the end of the chapter.

EXTRA WORD
POWER

un. Not. When *un* is placed at the beginning of a word, it means "not." *Un* is used with a very great number of words. Examples: *unwed*—not married; *unaided*—not helped; *unloved*—not loved; *unable*—not able; *uncooked*—not cooked; *unclaimed*—not claimed; *uncaught*—not caught; *uncarpeted*—not carpeted. How many other words can you supply with *un*?

pre. Before. When *pre* is placed in front of a word it means "before in time" or "before in order." *Pre,* like *un,* is used with a very great number of words. Examples: *prehistoric*—referring to time before history was recorded; *pre-Christian*—referring to time before there were Christians; *prerevolutionary*—referring to time before a revolution; *preheat*—to heat before; *prejudge*—to judge or decide before; *prejudice*—an opinion or judgment made beforehand; *preunite*—to join together before; *preset*—to set before;

> *premature*—ripened before; developed before the natural or proper period; *predict*—to say before; to foretell; to forecast, to tell what will happen. See how many more words with *pre* you can supply. Use the dictionary to see the great number of words there are that begin with *un* and *pre*.

Additional Words Derived from Combining Forms

From your knowledge of combining forms, can you define the following words?

1. **fratricide** (frat′ ri · sīdé) *n.* ***Fratricide*** *is an especially horrible crime because it involves the murder of a close relative.*

   _____

2. **corpulent** (kor′ pū · lent) *adj.* ***Corpulent*** *people usually eat a lot.*

   _____

3. **mortify** (mor′ ti · fī) *v.* *The minister was* ***mortified*** *that the people in his church had been involved in the riots.*

   _____

4. **amortize** (am′ or · tīzé) *v.* *The accountant* ***amortized*** *the plant's machinery on a twenty-year schedule.*

   _____

5. **caption** (cap · tion) (kap′ shun) *n.* *By reading chapter* ***captions***, *I am able in a very short time to gain some idea about the chapter.*

   _____

6. **capitulate** (ca · pit · u · late) (ka · pich′ u · lāté) *v.* *With the criminal gang surrounded by the police and having no possible means of escape, they had no choice but to* ***capitulate***.

   _____

7. **symbol** (sym · bol) (sim′ bul) *n.* *The dove is a* ***symbol*** *of peace, the cross is a* ***symbol*** *of Christianity, and the Star of David is a* ***symbol*** *of Judaism.*

   _____

8. **syllable** (syl · la · ble) (sil′ la · bul) *n.* *In the word* pilot *which has two* ***syllables***, pi *is the first* ***syllable***, *and* lot *is the second syllable.*

   _____

9. **monosyllable** (mon · o · syl · la · ble) (mon′ o · sil · la · bul) *n.* *The word* made *is a* ***monosyllable***.

   _____

102

10. **symphony** (sym · pho · ny) (sim′ fo · nē) *n. In the* **symphony** *the instruments blended together in perfect harmony.*

_____

11. **symptom** (symp · tom) (simp′ tum) *n. The doctor said that the rash was a definite* **symptom** *of the disease and that there was a cure for it.*

_____

12. **synthesis** (sin′ the · sis) *n. (pl.* **theses**) *The architect was told that his design must be a* **synthesis** *of everyone's ideas.*

_____

13. **symmetry** (sym · me · try) (sim′ me · trē) *n. (pl.* **ies**) *He disliked the disorganized pattern because it lacked* **symmetry.**

_____

STOP. Check answers at the end of the chapter.

Practice for Additional Words Derived form Combining Forms

Directions: Match each word with the *best* definition.

_____ 1. fratricide

_____ 2. corpulent

_____ 3. mortify

_____ 4. caption

_____ 5. amortize

_____ 6. capitulate

_____ 7. symbol

_____ 8. monosyllable

_____ 9. syllable

_____10. symphony

_____11. symmetry

_____12. synthesis

_____13. symptom

a. heading of a chapter, section, and the like

b. to cause to feel shame

c. something that stands for another thing

d. to cancel a debt by periodic payments

e. a putting together to form a whole

f. a letter or a group of letters with one vowel sound

g. balanced form or arrangement

h. harmony of sound

i. the killing of a brother

j. to surrender

k. a condition that results from a disease

l. word consisting of one syllable

m. fat

STOP. Check answers at the end of the chapter.

103

EXERCISE 9

Step I. Combining Forms

A. Directions: A list of combining forms with their meanings follows. Look at the combining forms and their meanings. Concentrate on learning each combining form and its meaning. Cover the meanings, read the combining forms, and state the meanings to yourself. Check to see if you are correct. Now cover the combining forms, read the meanings, and state the combining forms to yourself. Check to see if you are correct.

Combining Forms	Meanings
1. man, manu	hand
2. fac, fect, fic	make; do
3. loc, loco	place
4. pseudo	false
5. bene	good
6. cura	care
7. aud, audi	hear
8. onym, nomin	name

B. Directions: Cover the preceding meanings. Write the meanings of the following combining forms.

Combining Forms	Meanings
1. man, manu	_____
2. fac, fect, fic	_____
3. loc, loco	_____
4. pseudo	_____
5. bene	_____
6. cura	_____
7. aud, audi	_____
8. onym, nomin	_____

Step II. Words Derived from Combining Forms

1. **manual** (man' ū · al) *adj.* Referring to the hand; made, done, or used by the hands. *n.* A handy book used as a guide or source of information. *Some persons prefer manual labor because they like to work with their hands.*

2. **manicure** (man′ i · kūrǿ) *n.* Care of the hands and fingernails. *v.* To provide care for hands and nails with a manicure; to cut closely and evenly. *Because I like my fingernails to look good, I give myself a **manicure** every week.*

3. **manuscript** (man · u · script) (man′ yu · skript) *adj.* Written by hand or typed; not printed. *n.* A book or document written by hand; a book written by hand and usually sent in for publication; style of penmanship in which letters are not joined together, whereas in cursive writing they are. *When an author sends a **manuscript** to a publisher, he or she hopes that the editor will like it.*

4. **manufacture** (man · u · fac · ture) (man · yu · fak′ chur) *v.* To make goods or articles by hand or by machinery; to make something from raw materials by hand or machinery. *n.* The act of manufacturing. *Some very special and expensive items are still made by hand, but most goods are **manufactured** by machine on a large scale.*

5. **factory** (fac · to · ry) (fak′ to · rē) *n.* (*pl.* **ies**) A building or buildings in which things are manufactured. *My mother and father work in a **factory** where automobiles are made.*

6. **benefactor** (ben′ e · fak · tor) *n.* One who gives help or confers a benefit; a patron. *Many times artists have **benefactors** who help to support them while they are painting.*

7. **beneficiary** (ben · e · fi · ci · ar · y) (ben · e · fish′ ē · er · ē) *n.* (*pl.* **aries**) One who receives benefits or advantages; the one to whom an insurance policy is payable. *Joyce, as the only **beneficiary** of her husband's insurance policy, did not know that she would receive all the money.*

8. **benefit** (ben′ e · fit) *n.* That which is helpful; advantage; a payment; a performance given to raise funds for a worthy cause. *v.* To be helpful or profitable to; to receive benefit; to aid. *The actors gave a **benefit** to collect money for the needy children.*

9. **affect** (aǿ · fekt′) *v.* To act upon or to cause something; to influence; to produce an effect or change in. *Your poor study habits will definitely begin to **affect** your grades and cause them to go down.*

10. **effect** (eǿ · fekt′) *n.* Something brought about by some cause; the result; consequence. *I told you what the **effects** of your not studying would be before the results were in.*

11. **effective** (eǿ · fek′ tivǿ) *adj.* Producing or having the power to bring about an intended result; producing results with the least amount of wasted effort. *His way of doing the job is much more **effective** than yours because it takes him so much less time to do the same amount of work.*

12. **audible** (au · di · ble) (au′ di · bul) *adj.* Capable of being heard. *He spoke so softly that what he had to say was hardly **audible** to anyone.*

13. **auditorium** (au · di · to · ri · um) (au · di · tor′ ē · um) *n.* A building or hall for speeches, concerts, public meetings, and so on; the room in a building occupied by an audience. *The school **auditorium** was so large that it was able to seat the entire graduating class and their parents.*

14. **audience** (au · di · ence) (au′ dē · ens̸) *n.* An assembly of listeners or spectators at a concert, play, speech, and so on. *The **audience** listened to the politicians' speeches to learn what their views were on the income tax.*

15. **audit** (au′ dit) *v.* To examine or check such things as accounts; to attend class as a listener. *n.* An examination of accounts in order to report the financial state of a business. *Every year banks have their accounts **audited** to check if everything is in order.*

16. **audition** (au · di · tion) (au · dish′ un) *n.* A trial hearing, as of an actor or singer; the act of hearing. *v.* To try out for a part in an audition. *Carol's first **audition** for the part in the play was so successful that she was told there was no reason to listen to any other person.*

17. **audiovisual** (au′ di · o · vis · u · al) (au′ dē · ō · vizh′ ū · al) *adj.* Of, pertaining to, involving, or directed at both hearing and sight. *Many teachers use **audiovisual** aids in the classroom because the added senses of seeing and hearing help in learning.*

18. **local** (lō′ kal) *adj.* Referring to a relatively small area, region, or neighborhood; limited. *As a child, I always went to the **local** movie theater because it was close to where I lived.*

19. **location** (lo · ca · tion) (lo · kā′ shun) *n.* A place or site; exact position or place occupied; an area or tract of land; a place used for filming a motion picture or a television program (as in the expression *to be on location*). *The **location** for our picnic was perfect because it was such a scenic place.*

20. **allocate** (al′ ̸o · kāt̸) *v.* To set something apart for a special purpose; to divide up something; to divide and distribute something. *Each person was **allocated** a certain share of the profits according to the amount of time and work he or she had put into the project.*

21. **antonym** (an′ to · nim) *n.* A word opposite in meaning to some other word. *The words* good *and* bad *are **antonyms** because they are opposite in meaning.*

22. **synonym** (syn · o · nym) (sin′ o · nim) *n.* A word having the same meaning as some other word. *The words* vision *and* sight *are **synonyms** because they have the same meaning.*

23. **homonym** (hom′ o · nim) *n.* A word that agrees in pronunciation with some other word but differs in spelling and meaning. *The color* red *and*

106

the verb read *are* **homonyms** *because they sound alike but are spelled differently and have different meanings.*

24. **pseudonym** (p̸s̸u' do · nim) *n.* False name, used by an author to conceal his or her identity; pen name; false name. *Samuel Clemens wrote under the name Mark Twain, his* **pseudonym.**

25. **misnomer** (mis · nō' mer) *n.* A name wrongly applied to someone or something; an error in the naming of a person or place in a legal document. *It is a* **misnomer** *to call a spider an insect.*

26. **anonymous** (a · non' i · m̸us) *adj.* Lacking a name; of unknown authorship. *As it is the policy of the newspaper to publish signed letters only, the* **anonymous** *letter was not published.*

Special Notes

1. Note that *alias* (a word from Exercise 5) and *pseudonym* are basically synonyms. However, the term *alias* is usually used when a criminal uses a name other than his or her own, whereas the term *pseudonym* is usually used when an author uses a name other than his or her own.

   Do not confuse *pseudonym* and *alias* with *misnomer.* The term *misnomer* refers to someone's using a wrong name or word accidentally, that is, *not on purpose.* When someone uses an *alias* or *pseudonym,* he or she is doing it *on purpose* and has not made a mistake.

   The term *anonymous* refers to someone who has not signed his or her name, so that the name of the person is unknown. When you see *anonymous* at the end of a poem or story, it means that the author is unknown.

2. *Affect* and *effect* are terms that are used a great deal. However, they are often used incorrectly. Note the way the words are used in the sentences that follow.
   affect. *v.* To act upon or to cause something; to influence. *You will probably* **affect** *your team's chances to win because you seem to have such a great influence on them.*
   effect. *n.* Something brought about by some cause; the result. *The* **effect** *on the team was that they won the game.*

Step III. Practice

A. Directions: Following is a list of definitions. Choose the word that *best* fits the definition. Try to relate your definition to the meanings of the combining forms. *All the words fit in.*

Word List

manual, manicure, manufacture, manuscript, factory, benefactor, beneficiary, benefit, affect, effect, effective, audible, auditorium, audience, audit, audition, audiovisual, local, location, allocate, antonym, synonym, homonym, pseudonym, misnomer, anonymous.

1. A false name _____
2. A name wrongly applied _____
3. A word opposite in meaning to some other word _____
4. A word similar in meaning to some other word _____
5. Lacking a name _____
6. Made by hand _____
7. Written by hand _____
8. Care of the hands and fingernails _____
9. A building in which things are made _____
10. One who gives help _____
11. One who receives aid _____
12. An advantage; payment _____
13. To make goods by hand or machinery _____
14. To influence _____
15. A result _____
16. Producing results with the least amount of wasted effort _____
17. A building or hall for speeches, meetings, and the like _____
18. An assembly of listeners at a concert, play, and so on _____
19. Capable of being heard _____
20. Involving both hearing and sight _____
21. A trial hearing _____
22. To examine or check accounts _____
23. To set apart for a special purpose _____
24. A place or site _____
25. Referring to a relatively small area, region, or neighborhood _____
26. A word that is pronounced the same as some other word but is spelled differently and has a different meaning _____

STOP. Check answers at the end of the chapter.

B. Directions: Following are a number of sentences with missing words. Fill in the word that *best* fits the sentence. Two choices are given for each sentence.

1. As the _____ of the policy, you will receive everything. (benefactor; beneficiary)

2. In the _____ we are making a large supply of toy trains. (factory; location)

3. The author did not sign his own name, so he used a _____ . (misnomer; pseudonym)

4. I hate to receive_____ letters because then I don't know who sent them. (manual; anonymous)

5. When I write in_____ , my letters are not joined together. (manual; manuscript)

6. The _____ where the people met to listen to the concert was very large. (factory; auditorium)

7. The _____ you are having on your brother is not the one we wanted. (affect; effect)

8. Try not to _____ your brother as much as you do. (affect; effect)

9. *Alias* and *pseudonym* are_____ s. (antonym; synonym)

10. *Happy* and *sad* are _____ s. (antonym; synonym)

11. *Sew* and *so* are _____ s. (synonym; homonym)

12. When something is_____ , it brings about results with the least amount of effort. (effective; anonymous)

13. Each employee of the corporation was_____ a certain share of the profits. (affected; allocated)

14. I was not able to hear it, because it was not _____ . (effective; audible)

15. Because I like to stay close to my home, I shop in_____ places. (audiovisual; local)

16. The company decided to_____ its accounts to check for errors. (allocate; audit)

17. If I don't get a(n) _____ soon for a play, I will give up trying to be an actress. (location; audition)

STOP. Check answers at the end of the chapter.

C. Directions: A few paragraphs with missing words follow. Fill in the blanks
with the word that *best* fits. *Words may be used more than
once.*

Word List

pseudonym, audible, audition, effect, manicure, location, local, effective, audience, benefit, benefactor, factory, manual, manufacture, beneficiary.

Because I enjoy making things and working with my hands, I don't mind
1_____ labor even though I'm a woman. However, my parents
want me to have lots of 2_____ s. They feel that the only way
I can get the advantages they want me to have is by finishing college. In order
to go to college, I work in a 3_____ in which clothing is
4_____d on a large scale. I have no 5_____to
help me, and I am not the 6_____ of any rich old uncle's insurance policy.

This summer they used the 7_____where I am working as the
8_____ for a movie. It was very exciting! Everyday we had a
large 9_____ watch the making of the film. The spectators came
from all over. The movie people were so 10_____ in getting the
11_____s they wanted for the film that very little time was wasted.
When they worked, no outside sounds were 12_____because
they told the spectators to be silent.

They were going to use a number of 13_____ people in some of
the mob scenes. As I lived in the neighborhood, I was chosen for a(n)
14_____. I was told that if they liked what they saw and heard,
they would use me in the movie. Well, I tried to make myself look as glamorous
as possible. I even decided to give my hands a(n)15_____.

When the day for my 16_____ came, I was so excited that I
could hardly talk. By the time I got to the 17_____ for my test,
my voice was not 18_____ .

The director told all of us that we were supposed to be in a scene where we
all fall into mud. Ugh! And for this I made myself glamorous and gave myself
a(n) 19_____. For this role I would probably use a 20_____
_____ rather than my real name.

STOP. Check answers at the end of the chapter.

EXTRA WORD
POWER

anti. Against; opposed to. *Anti,* meaning "against,"
is found at the beginning of a great number of words.
For example: *antiwar*—against war; *antigambling*—
against gambling; *antimachine*—against machines;

antimen—against men; *antiwomen*—against women; *antilabor*—against labor. Note that *anti* changes to *ant* before words that begin with a vowel, as in *antacid*—something that acts against acid; *antonym*— a word opposite in meaning to some other word. As you can see, you can place *anti* at the beginning of a lot of words. Can you think of some words to which you might add *anti*? Use the dictionary to see the great number of words there are with *anti*.

non. Not. When *non* is placed in front of a word, it means a simple negative or the absence of something. The number of words beginning with *non* is so large that the dictionary has them listed in a special section. Check your dictionary to see how many it has. Following are some words with *non*: *nonbeliever*—not a believer; *non-Arab*—not an Arab; *non-Catholic*—not Catholic; *noncapitalist*—not a capitalist; *non-Communist*—not a Communist; *non-efficient*—not efficient; *noncriminal*—not criminal; *non-English*—not English. How many more can you supply?

Additional Words Derived from Combining Forms

From your knowledge of combining forms, can you define the following words?

1. **audiometer** (au · dē · om′ e · ter) *n. The doctor used the **audiometer** to determine if John had a hearing problem.*

_____

2. **audiology** (au · di · ol · o · gy) (au · dē · ol′ o · jē) *n. Sally decided to major in **audiology** in college because she wanted to help children who had hearing problems.*

_____

3. **benediction** (ben · e · dic · tion) (ben · e · dik′ shun) *n. At the end of the church service the minister gave the **benediction**.*

_____

4. **antipathy** (an · tip′ a · thē) *n. Mary had great **antipathy** toward the persons who injured her brother.*

_____

5. **pseudopodium** (p̸s̸ū · do · pō′ dē · um) *n.* (*pl.* dia) *Some one-celled animals have **pseudopodia**, which are used for taking in food and for movement.*

---

6. **curator** (kū · rā′ tor) *n.* *A good **curator** of a museum should know everything that is going on in the museum.*

---

7. **pedicure** (ped′·i · kūr̸) *n.* *I always have a **pedicure** before I wear open sandals.*

---

8. **pseudoscience** (p̸s̸ū · dō · s̸ī′ ens̸) *n.* *Astrology is a **pseudoscience** because it involves only the reading of the stars to foretell the future and is not based on rational principles.*

---

9. **manipulation** (ma · nip · u · la · tion) (ma · nip′ yu · lā · shun) *n.* *By his clever **manipulation** of all those around him, he was able to gain the position he desired.*

---

10. **emancipate** (ē · man′ si · pāt̸) *v.* *After enslaved people have been **emancipated**, they must learn how to live like free people.*

---

11. **personification** (per · son · i · fi · ca · tion) (per · son · i · fi · kā′ shun) *n.* *"The clouds wept a torrent of tears that almost flooded the city," is an example of **personification**.*

---

12. **facsimile** (fak · sim′ i · lē) *n. v.* *The little girl was the **facsimile** of her mother at the same age.*

---

13. **faction** (fac · tion) (fak′ shun) *n.* *There was a special **faction** in the union that was trying to gain power so that its members could further their own desires.*

STOP. Check answers at the end of the chapter.

Practice for Additional Words Derived from Combining Forms

Directions: Match each word with the *best* definition.

_____ 1. audiometer

_____ 2. audiology

_____ 3. benediction

_____ 4. antipathy

_____ 5. pseudopodia

_____ 6. curator

_____ 7. pedicure

_____ 8. pseudoscience

_____ 9. manipulation

_____ 10. emancipate

_____ 11. personification

_____ 12. facsimile

_____ 13. faction

a. a blessing

b. an exact copy

c. to free from servitude or slavery

d. a figure of speech in which human qualities are given to nonliving things

e. a dislike for someone

f. a group in an organization or government, often self-seeking, with common ends

g. one in charge, as of a department in a museum

h. an instrument used to measure hearing

i. the study of hearing

j. a false science

k. the skillful handling of something

l. false feet

m. care or treatment of the feet

STOP. Check answers at the end of the chapter.

Question: When doesn't it pay to increase your vocabulary?

© 1975 by NEA, Inc.

"MY MOTHER JUST DECREASED MY VOCABULARY BY ONE WORD!"

Answer: When the words you use hurt.

CROSSWORD PUZZLE 3

Directions: The meanings of many of the combining forms from Exercises 7–9
follow. Your knowledge of these combining forms will help you to
solve this crossword puzzle. Note that *combining form* is abbreviated as *comb. f.*

Across

3. Comb. f. for *without*
4. A misanthrope is a____of
   mankind
8. Same as # 1 Down
9. Squirrels eat these.
12. Two-wheeler
15. Comb. f. for *place*
16. To be
17. Comb. f. for *in*
18. An artificial waterway
19. Meaning of *vis*; *vid*
20. Comb. f. for *care*
24. Rhymes with *ham*
26. Opposite of *off*
27. Comb. f. for *hand*
30. Same as # 3 Across
31. Word for *strong feeling
    against*
34. Same as # 26 Across
35. Word for *written by hand*
41. Rhymes with *hit*
42. Comb. f. for *wrong; hate*

Down

1. Comb. f. for *make; do*
2. Comb. f. for *come*
3. Comb. f. for *water*
4. A sound you make when you
   laugh
5. A monarch is a____of a monarchy
6. Comb. f. for *see*
7. Comb. f. for *good*
8. You put this around a picture
10. A homonym of *two*
11. Comb. f. for *know*
12. Marriage to two spouses at
    the same time
13. Opposite of *no*
14. Comb. f. for *without*
18. Something to sleep on
20. Comb. f. for *body*
21. Comb. f. for *not; lack of*
22. Word meaning *yearly*
23. Comb. f. for *head*
25. A way of saying *mother*

114

43. Comb. f. for *star*
45. To hand out something a little at a time
46. A period of time
48. Comb. f. for *from a distance*
50. You do this in a chair
51. Abbreviation for *advertisement*
52. A long slippery fish
53. Opposite of *friend*
54. Comb. f. for *sail*
55. Comb. f. for *powerful*
56. Comb. f. for *kill*
59. Comb. f. for *all*

28. Comb. f. for *name*
29. Word meaning *to join*
30. Comb. f. for *hear*
31. Same as # 3 Across
32. Past tense of *eat*
33. A farmer uses this tool
35. Comb. f. for *death*
36. A homonym of *sew*
37. You can do this when you put two hands together
38. When you do something again, you____it
39. A pronoun
40. He is a ____-ager
43. Same as # 3 Across
44. Comb. f. for *same*
47. Comb. f. for *again, back*
49. Same as # 15 Across
50. To be in appearance
57. Same as # 39 Down
58. When you carry out an act, you ____it

STOP. Check answers at the end of the chapter.

WORD SCRAMBLE 3

Directions: Word Scramble 3 is based on words from Exercises 7-9. The meanings are your clues to arranging the letters in correct order. Write the correct word in the blank.

		Meanings
1. siivno	_____	sense of sight
2. eeiilotvns	_____	electronic system for transmitting images from a distance
3. niiibelvs	_____	not able to be seen
4. vrooiisnps	_____	food or supplies
5. cendeive	_____	that which serves to prove or disprove something
6. cciseen	_____	an area of knowledge in which facts have been investigated and presented in an orderly manner

7. taslrygoo   _____   the false science of foretelling the future from the stars

8. tysaromno   _____   the study of stars, planets, and space

9. tnaoaustr   _____   one who travels in space

10. catuaiq   _____   referring to water

11. noecnev   _____   to come together

12. ivnenocnte   _____   well suited to one's purposes

13. tentop   _____   powerful

14. apenotlit   _____   ability or power you might have

15. restennopim   _____   being present everywhere at all times

16. deoiimhc   _____   the killing of one person by another

17. thapya   _____   lack of feeling

18. nodeigce   _____   the killing of a whole racial, political, or cultural group

19. ymethap   _____   putting yourself into the personality of another

20. patcalmisi   _____   economic system based on profit

21. notareorpic   _____   to unite; combine

22. persoc   _____   dead body

23. troaimlm   _____   referring to a being who never dies

24. gtromega   _____   the pledging of property to a creditor

25. luaanm   _____   referring to hands

26. eeaotfbnrc   _____   one who gives help

27. carytfo   _____   a building in which things are manufactured

28. fcteef   _____   a result

29. catffe   _____   to influence

30. eaubild   _____   capable of being heard

31. tiadu   _____   to examine accounts

32. lotaaecl   _____   to divide and distribute something

33. duesypnom   _____   false name

34. yysmonn   _____   a word having the same meaning as another

35. sanyonuom   _____   lacking a name

STOP. Check answers at the end of the chapter.

ANALOGIES 3

Directions: Find the word from the following list that *best* completes each
analogy. There are more words listed than you need.

Word List

*deny, pedestrian, capitulate, capital, convenient, creed, creditor, apathy, stars,
underwater, pseudoscience, facsimile, omnipresent, omniscient, omnipotent,
effect, affect, impotent, potential, convene, convention, anonymous, pseudopodal, mortify, audible, caption, audiometer, audiology, audition, suicide,
homicide, genocide, corpulent, antipathy, love, feel, sympathy, empathy,
visage.*

1. Astronaut : space :: aquanaut :_____.

2. Visible : evident : : everywhere :_____.

3. Incredible : credible : : potent : _____ .

4. Mortal : immortal : : adjourn : _____.

5. Astronomy : science : : astrology :_____.

6. Snake : apodal : : amoeba :_____.

7. Incorporate : unite : : humiliate : _____.

8. Benediction : blessing : : heading : _____.

9. Pseudonym : alias : : face :_____.

10. Autograph : signature : : copy :_____

11. Life : biology : : hearing :_____.

12. Vest : clothing :: fratricide : _____ .

13. Deny : contradict : : fleshy :_____.

14. Symmetry : balance : : dislike :_____.

15. Assembly : meeting : : handy : _____.

16. Benefit : advantage : : indifference :_____.

17. Noise : clamor : : faith : _____.

18. Handbook : manual : : result :_____ .

19. Location : site : : nameless :_____.

20. Anarchy : order : : resist : _____.

STOP. Check answers at the end of the chapter.

MULTIPLE-CHOICE VOCABULARY TEST 3

Directions: This is a test on words in Exercises 7–9. Words are presented according to exercises. *Do all exercises before checking answers.* Underline the meaning that *best* fits the word.

Exercise 7

1. vision
   a. able to be seen
   b. system for the transmission of visual images from a distance
   c. sense of sight
   d. easily recognized

2. visible
   a. sense of sight
   b. system for the transmission of visual images from a distance
   c. able to be seen
   d. not seen

3. television
   a. sense of sight
   b. system for the transmission of visual images from a distance
   c. able to be seen
   d. plain

4. invisible
   a. not able to be seen
   b. in disguise
   c. out of sight
   d. to view from inside

5. provision
   a. something made ready in advance
   b. something to see from a distance
   c. something to see
   d. to see for someone

6. evident
   a. clearly seen
   b. sense of sight
   c. able to see from a distance
   d. to view

7. evidence
   a. that which seems to prove or disaprove something
   b. able to see clearly
   c. that which is seen from a distance
   d. that which shows something

8. science
   a. a knowing person
   b. able to know
   c. the sense of knowing
   d. area of ordered and investigated knowledge

118

9. astrology
   a. the study of heavenly bodies
   b. the reading of the stars to foretell the future
   c. a true science
   d. refers to stars

10. astronomy
   a. the study of stars, planets, and space
   b. the reading of the stars
   c. a true science
   d. refers to stars

11. astronaut
   a. refers to space
   b. refers to stars
   c. one who travels underwater
   d. one who travels in space

12. aquanaut
   a. refers to undersea
   b. one who travels undersea
   c. refers to water
   d. refers to one who travels in space

13. aquatic
   a. referring to a water plant
   b. referring to a water flower
   c. referring to water
   d. referring to undersea plants

14. aquarium
   a. a water bowl
   b. refers to water
   c. a globelike bowl or rectangular container for water plants and animals
   d. an area of study

15. convene
   a. something suitable
   b. a meeting
   c. to come together
   d. to call a special meeting

16. convention
   a. a friendly get-together
   b. a formal meeting of members for professional purposes
   c. something suitable
   d. to come together

17. convenient
   a. suited to one's purpose
   b. a get-together
   c. joining together
   d. a special meeting

18. potent
   a. a drug
   b. a perfume
   c. powerful
   d. refers to money

19. impotent
   a. refers to sex
   b. without power
   c. refers to power
   d. refers to males only

20. potential
   a. the ability or power one may have
   b. refers to sex
   c. refers to males only
   d. refers to feeling

21. omnipresent   a. referring to a gift   c. referring to everyone
                   b. referring to all   d. being present every-
                                                where at all times

Exercise 8

22. homicide   a. killing of a brother   c. killing of one person
                b. killing of oneself   by another
                                           d. killing of a whole group
                                              of people

23. suicide   a. killing of oneself   c. killing of a brother
                b. killing of a whole   d. killing of one person
                   group of people   by another

24. genocide   a. killing of man   c. killing of a brother
                b. killing of a whole racial, d. killing of oneself
                   political, or cultural
                   group

25. sympathy   a. feeling sad   c. self-pity
                b. ability to put oneself d. ability to feel pity
                   into the personality   for another
                   of another

26. empathy   a. ability to feel pity for   c. self-pity
                b. ability to put one-   d. feeling sad
                   self into the person-
                   ality of another

27. apathy   a. refers to pity   c. lack of feeling
                b. self-pity   d. feeling sad

28. fraternity a. a Greek letter college c. killing of a brother
                   organization   d. refers to friends and
                b. a brother   relatives

29. capital punishment a. bodily harm   c. death penalty
                        b. head punishment d. beatings

30. capitalism a. refers to profit   c. an economic system in
                b. an economic system   which all or most of the
                   in which all or most of   means of production are
                   the means of production   not privately owned
                   are privately owned   d. an economic system in
                                              which all or most of the
                                              means of production are
                                              privately owned and op-
                                              erated for profit

31. capital
   a. official seat of government
   b. relevant
   c. refers to an economic system
   d. refers to death

32. corpse
   a. a body
   b. a dead body
   c. a group of people
   d. refers to beatings

33. corporation
   a. men getting together
   b. a business
   c. a group of people with a charter granting them certain powers and making them not legally responsible for each other
   d. a group of people with a charter granting them certain powers to rule

34. incorporate
   a. to unite
   b. to join a club
   c. refers to a body
   d. men getting together

35. corporal punishment
   a. death penalty
   b. a beating
   c. refers to the body
   d. refers to punishment of an officer in the service

36. mortal
   a. referring to death
   b. referring to a dead person
   c. referring to any dead animal
   d. referring to someone who must die

37. immortal
   a. referring to all living persons
   b. referring to all dead persons
   c. referring to death
   d. referring to a being who never dies

38. mortality
   a. dead persons
   b. death rate
   c. one who never dies
   d. one who must die

39. mortician
   a. a dead man
   b. one who must die
   c. a person who counts the dead
   d. an undertaker

40. mortgage
   a. refers to death
   b. pledging property
   c. giving up your property
   d. pledging property to a creditor as security for payment

41. morgue
   a. refers to the dead
   b. place to keep all dead bodies
   c. an undertaker's office
   d. place where unidentified dead bodies are kept

Exercise 9

42. manual
    - a. referring to the hands
    - b. referring to manly work
    - c. referring to men
    - d. referring to help

43. manicure
    - a. refers to cure
    - b. refers to hands
    - c. the curing of hand problems
    - d. the care of the hands and fingernails

44. manuscript
    - a. a newspaper
    - b. a role in a play
    - c. to make by hand or machine from raw material
    - d. a letter

45. manufacture
    - a. to make machinery
    - b. to store in a factory
    - c. to make by hand or machine
    - d. made to sell

46. factory
    - a. a building
    - b. a house
    - c. a place for storing things only
    - d. a place for manufacturing things

47. benefactor
    - a. one who gets help
    - b. one who gives help
    - c. someone good
    - d. a blessing

48. beneficiary
    - a. one who gives help
    - b. one who needs help
    - c. one who gets help
    - d. a blessing

49. benefit
    - a. a performance for some charity or cause
    - b. a blessing
    - c. a performance
    - d. charity

50. affect
    - a. the result
    - b. to bring
    - c. an action
    - d. to influence

51. effect
    - a. to influence
    - b. the result
    - c. the action
    - d. to bring something

52. effective
    - a. producing no results after a while
    - b. producing
    - c. making something do
    - d. producing results in a minimum of time

53. audible
    - a. referring to hearing
    - b. referring to a listener
    - c. capable of being heard
    - d. not heard

54. auditorium
    - a. a building in which things are made
    - b. a special building
    - c. a place for workers
    - d. a place for speeches, concerts, and so on.

55. audience
    - a. a group of listeners or spectators at a play, concert, and so on
    - b. spectacles
    - c. people
    - d. a building

56. audit
   a. to hear
   b. to examine accounts
   c. to examine
   d. to be a spectator

57. audition
   a. an examination of books
   b. an examination
   c. a hearing for a jury trial
   d. a trial hearing for an actor or singer

58. audiovisual
   a. instruction using books
   b. instruction using printed matter
   c. instruction using only television
   d. pertaining to hearing and seeing

59. local
   a. referring to a neighborhood area
   b. referring to a distant place
   c. referring to a place
   d. referring to a situation

60. location
   a. in the neighborhood
   b. a place or site
   c. a situation
   d. any place close

61. allocate
   a. to place
   b. to set
   c. to divide and distribute
   d. to put together

62. antonym
   a. a word similar to another in meaning
   b. a word opposite in meaning to another
   c. a word that is pronounced the same as another
   d. a word that is spelled like another

63. synonym
   a. a word similar in pronounciation to another
   b. a word opposite in meaning to another
   c. a word similar to another in spelling
   d. a word similar to another in meaning

64. homonym
   a. a word similar to another in spelling
   b. a word similar to another in pronunciation
   c. a word different from another in meaning and spelling but similar in pronunciation
   d. a word different in meaning from another

65. pseudonym
   a. wrong name
   b. same name
   c. lacking a name
   d. false name

66. misnomer
   a. false name
   b. lacking a name
   c. same name
   d. wrong name

67. anonymous
   a. wrong name
   b. false name
   c. lacking a name
   d. same name

True/False Test 3

Directions: This is a true/false test on Exercises 7–9. Read each sentence carefully. Decide whether it is true or false. Put a *T* for *true* or an *F*
for *false* in the blank. The number after the sentence tells you if
the word is from Exercise 7, 8, or 9.

_____ 1. A <u>fratricide</u> would also be a <u>homicide.</u> 8

_____ 2. A <u>suicide</u> is also a <u>homicide.</u> 8

_____ 3. <u>Corporal punishment</u> refers to a beating. 8

_____ 4. Some <u>mortals</u> are able to survive forever. 8

_____ 5. If the proportion of minority group children who die is higher,
then the <u>mortality</u> of such children is lower than that for children as a whole. 8

_____ 6. A person who receives <u>capital punishment</u> is not executed. 8

_____ 7. <u>Astrology</u> is a science. 7

_____ 8. <u>Astronauts</u> travel undersea. 7

_____ 9. If something is <u>convenient</u> for you, it occurs at a bad time. 7

_____10. You can hear your <u>potential.</u> 7

_____11. An <u>omnipresent</u> thing is present everywhere all the time. 7

_____12. You can have <u>sympathy</u> for someone even if you can't experience
how he or she feels. 8

_____13. <u>Genocide</u> is a fatal illness. 8

_____14. The words *antipathy* and *apathy* are synonyms. 8, 9

_____15. The words *synonym* and *antonym* are antonyms. 9

_____16. To <u>audit</u> the books means to examine them. 9

_____17. The words *alias* and *pseudonym* are synonyms. 9

_____18. Man is <u>immortal.</u> 8

_____19. A <u>morgue</u> is where all dead bodies are stored. 8

_____20. A <u>manuscript</u> can refer to a book written by hand and sent in for
publication. 9

_____21. Something <u>audible</u> can be heard. 9

_____22. The words *pseudonym* and *misnomer* are synonyms. 9

_____23. The words *bury* and *berry* are <u>synonyms.</u> 9

_____24. The words *fat* and <u>*corpulent*</u> are synonyms. 8, 9

_____25. The words <u>*anonymous*</u> and *alias* are synonyms. 9

STOP. Check answers for both tests at the end of the chapter.

SCORING OF TESTS

Multiple-Choice Vocabulary Test

Number Wrong	Score
0–4	Excellent
5–10	Good
11–14	Weak
Above 14	Poor

Score_____

True/False Test

Number Wrong	Score
0–2	Excellent
3–5	Good
6–7	Weak
Above 7	Poor

Score_____

1. If you scored in the excellent or good range on *both tests,* you are doing well. Go on to Chapter Five.

2. If you scored in the weak or poor range on either test, look below and follow directions for Additional Practice. Note that the words on the tests are arranged so that you can tell in which exercise to find them. This will help you if you need additional practice.

ADDITIONAL PRACTICE SETS

A. Directions: Write the words you missed on the tests from the three exercises in the space provided. Note that the tests are presented so that you can tell to which exercises the words belong.

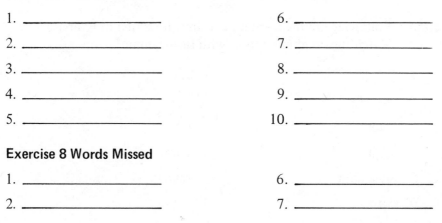

Exercise 7 Words Missed

1. _____   6. _____

2. _____   7. _____

3. _____   8. _____

4. _____   9. _____

5. _____   10. _____

Exercise 8 Words Missed

1. _____   6. _____

2. _____   7. _____

3. _____ 8. _____

4. _____ 9. _____

5. _____ 10. _____

Exercise 9 Words Missed

1. _____ 6. _____

2. _____ 7. _____

3. _____ 8. _____

4. _____ 9. _____

5. _____ 10. _____

B. Directions: Restudy the words that you have written down on p. 125 and this page. Study the combining forms from which those words are derived. Do Step I and Step II for those you missed. Note that Step I and Step II of the combining forms and vocabulary derived from these combining forms are on the following pages:

Exercise 7—pp. 85–88.

Exercise 8—pp. 94–97.

Exercise 9—pp. 104–107.

C. Directions: Do Additional Practice 1 on this page and pp. 127–128 if you missed words from Exercise 7. Do Additional Practice 2 on pp. 128–129 if you missed words from Exercise 8. Do Additional Practice 3 on pp. 130–131 if you missed words from Exercise 9. Now go on to Chapter Five.

Additional Practice 1 for Exercise 7

A. Directions: Following are the combining forms presented in Exercise 7. Match the combining form with its meaning.

_____ 1. vis, vid   a. star

_____ 2. sci, scio   b. all

_____ 3. poten   c. see

_____ 4. omni   d. come

_____ 5. aqua, aqui   e. sailor

_____ 6. astro   f. water

_____ 7. naut   g. powerful

_____ 8. ven, veni, vent   h. know

STOP. Check answers at the end of the chapter.

B. Directions: Following are sentences containing the meanings of vocabulary
                 presented in Exercise 7. Choose the word that *best* fits the
                 meaning of the word or phrase underlined in the sentence. A
                 word may be used only once. Put the word in the blank.

Word List

*potent, convenient, astrology, conventions, astronomy, aquatic, convene, as-
tronauts, aquarium, television, visible, evident, provisions, science, evidence,
invisible, impotent, potential, omnipresent, aquanauts, vision.*

1. If you are blind, you do not have your sense of sight. _____

2. In the film, a man played a ghost who was not able to be seen. _____

3. I enjoy visual image shows that come from New York and California in my
   own home. _____

4. The sign was able to be seen, but I went past it. _____

5. We will take enough supplies for our trip. _____

6. I am studying astronomy, which is a field of organized knowledge concerning
   heavenly bodies. _____

7. The lawyer needed something that would prove that his client was innocent
   of the charges. _____

8. It is plain from the way you are acting that you want me to leave.
   _____

9. Some people believe that a reading of the stars will predict their futures.
   _____

10. What do you call men who travel in space? _____

11. What do you call men who travel undersea? _____

12. My favorite course is the study of stars, planets, and space.
    _____

13. I enjoy studying about water plants and animals. _____

14. I keep my water plants and animals in a large tank where I can watch them.
    _____

15. The judge said that the people in court should come together again at two
    in the afternoon. _____

127

16. I enjoy attending <u>formal professional meetings</u>. _____

17. Attending classes in the afternoon is not <u>suitable</u> for me because I work in the afternoon. _____

18. That is <u>powerful</u> medicine you are taking. _____

19. The person in charge was merely a figurehead who was <u>without power</u>.
_____

20. If I knew what my <u>possible ability</u> was, I would try to do something with it.
_____

21. The bandits seemed to be <u>present everywhere at all times</u>.
_____

STOP. Check answers at the end of the chapter.

Additional Practice 2 for Exercise 8

A. Directions: Following are the combining forms presented in Exercise 8.
Match the combining form with its meaning.

_____ 1. cide	a. into; in
_____ 2. pathy	b. kill; murder
_____ 3. syl, sym, syn	c. death
_____ 4. frater, fratr	d. same; with; together; along with
_____ 5. mors, mort	e. brother
_____ 6. capit	f. feeling; suffering
_____ 7. corp, corpor	g. head
_____ 8. em, en	h. body

STOP. Check answers at the end of the chapter.

B. Directions: Following are sentences containing the meanings of vocabulary presented in Exercise 8. Choose the word that *best* fits the meaning of the word or phrase underlined in the sentence. Put the word in the blank.

Word List

genocide, apathy, empathy, sympathy, suicide, homicide, capitalism, immortals, fraternity, capital, mortals, capital punishment, corporation, incorporate, corporal punishment, corpse, mortality, mortgage, mortician, morgue.

1. More and more persons are involved in <u>the act of killing others</u>.
   _____

2. Only a madman would attempt <u>the destruction of a whole race of people</u>.
   _____

3. I have <u>the ability to understand how you feel</u> because I had the same experience. _____

4. I have <u>no feeling</u> about that. _____

5. I have <u>pity</u> for the child who lost both parents in an accident. _____

6. The man resorted to <u>the act of killing himself</u> when he lost all his money.
   _____

7. I am joining <u>a Greek Letter college organization</u> next semester. _____

8. My father's friends formed <u>an association of a number of businessmen</u>, <u>which took out a special charter granting it certain rights</u>. _____

9. In the United States we have <u>an economic system based on private ownership and profit</u>. _____

10. Are you and the other men going to <u>join together to form a business</u>?
    _____

11. All <u>human beings</u> must eventually die. _____

12. <u>Undying beings</u> do not exist on earth. _____

13. We found <u>a dead body</u> in the woods. _____

14. I wonder if <u>the death penalty</u> will return. _____

15. Many persons believe that children should not be subjected to <u>a beating</u> in school. _____

16. Do you know <u>the death rate</u> of teen-agers involved in automobile accidents?
    _____

17. Because it was unidentified, the body was taken to <u>a special place where unidentified bodies are held</u> until it could be claimed. _____

18. They had difficulty paying off <u>the loan on their property</u> because of other very large unexpected expenses. _____

19. She went to <u>an undertaker</u> to arrange for her father's funeral. _____

20. Do you have enough <u>money</u> to start such a business venture? _____

STOP. Check answers at the end of the chapter.

129

A. Directions: Following are the combining forms presented in Exercise 9. Match the combining form with its meaning.

_____ 1. man, manu a. make; do

_____ 2. fac, fect, fic b. place

_____ 3. loc, loco c. hear

_____ 4. pseudo d. care

_____ 5. bene e. name

_____ 6. aud, audi f. false

_____ 7. cura g. good

_____ 8. onym, nomin h. hand

STOP. Check answers at the end of the chapter.

B. Directions: Following are sentences containing the meanings of vocabulary presented in Exercise 9. Choose the word that *best* fits the meaning or phrase underlined in the sentence. Put the word in the blank.

Word List

manual, beneficiary, benefit, affect, effect, effective, audible, misnomer, anonymous, pseudonyms, allocate, antonyms, synonyms, auditorium, audience, audit, audition, manufacture, audiovisual, location, local, homonyms, benefactor, factory, manicure, manuscript.

1. She goes to the beauty shop for the care of her fingernails. _____

2. We learned the style of writing our letters without joining them together. _____

3. My husband works in a building that makes furniture. _____

4. Many artists have a person who supports them so that they do not have to worry about money. _____

5. Hand labor does not bother me. _____

6. The speaker was just capable of being heard. _____

7. When they examine the accounts, they had better balance, or you will be in trouble. _____

8. There will be a tryout for the new play next week. _____

9. In my school we use a lot of television, radio, records, and picture aids. _____

10. The method you have for studying is really <u>productive in getting results</u> for you. _____

11. The concert is being held in <u>a large special room</u> used for such performances in the school._____

12. In this day and age we <u>make goods by machinery</u> on a large scale in order to have enough available for so many people. _____

13. What <u>result,</u> if any, did you find?_____

14. I just found out that I am <u>the receiver of a large amount of money</u> that was left to me by an old uncle who recently died. _____

15. What is the major <u>advantage</u> of going to college?_____

16. <u>The group of listeners at the concert</u> was so quiet that you could hear a pin drop. _____

17. I am not going to <u>influence</u> your brother in any way. _____

18. *Bear* and *bare* are <u>words that sound alike but are spelled differently and have different meanings.</u> _____

19. *Corpulent* and *fat* are <u>words similar in meaning.</u> _____

20. *Antonym* and *synonym* are <u>words opposite in meaning.</u> _____

21. Some authors use <u>pen names or names other than their own names.</u>

_____

22. When I used the term *misanthrope* to mean a hater of marriage, I was using <u>a wrong word.</u>_____

23. The poem was <u>without an author's name.</u> _____

24. I shop only in <u>neighborhood</u> stores. _____

25. The men will <u>set aside</u> a certain number of tickets for us. _____

26. Our house is in a lovely <u>place.</u> _____

STOP. Check answers at the end of the chapter.

ANSWERS

Exercise 7 (pp. 85-94)

Practice A

(1) astronaut, (2) aquanaut, (3) aquatic, (4) potent, (5) aquarium, (6) astrology, (7) astronomy, (8) evident, (9) provision, (10) impotent, (11) evidence, (12) science, (13) convention, (14) vision, (15) omnipresent, (16) convenient, (17) potential, (18) convene.

Practice B

(1) reporter, (2) decade, (3) anniversary, (4) evident[1], (5) television, (6) television, (7) convenient, (8) scientists, (9) convention, (10) convention, (11) astronauts, (12) aquatic, (13) aquanauts, (14) astrologist, (15) convention, (16) television, (17) incredible, (18) visible,[1] (19) evident, (20) omnipresent, (21) television, (22) incredible, (23) impotent, (24) astronauts, (25) aquanauts, (26) invisible, (27) visible, (28) provision, (29) evidence.

Practice C

(1) auto, (2) vis, (3) sci, (4) homo, (5) mono, (6) er, (7) ist, (8) or, (9) bi, (10) port, (11) uni, (12) naut, (13) geo, (14) bio, (15) ven, (16) a, (17) con, (18) tele, (19) ali, (20) dict, (21) anthropo.

Combining Form Square

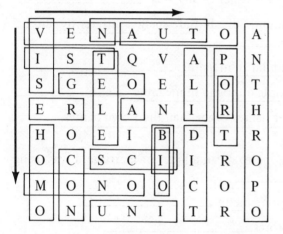

Additional Words Derived from Combining Forms (pp. 92-93)

1. **omnipotent.** All-powerful.

2. **omniscient.** All-knowing.

3. **omnibus.** A large bus designed to carry a number of people as passengers, An *omnibus* bill is a legislative bill that carries a mixture of provisions.

4. **visage.** The face; the appearance of the face or its expression.

5. **visor.** The projecting front brim of a cap for shading the eyes.

6. **visa.** Something stamped or written on a passport that grants an individual entry to a country.

---

[1] Answer can be either *evident* or *visible*.

7. **envision.** To imagine something; to picture in the mind.

8. **visionary.** A person who sees visions.

9. **nautical.** Pertaining to seamen, ships, or navigation.

10. **venture.** A risky or dangerous undertaking, especially a business enterprise in which there is a danger of loss as well as a chance for profit.

11. **potentate.** A person possessing great power; a ruler; a monarch.

Practice for Additional Words Derived from Combining Forms (pp. 93-94)

(1) e, (2) h, (3) f, (4) b, (5) k, (6) j, (7) i, (8) d, (9) g, (10) a, (11) c.

Exercise 8 (pp. 94-103)

Practice A

(1) capital, (2) corporation, (3) capitalism, (4) capital, (5) mortgage, (6) morgue, (7) mortician, (8) incorporate, (9) immortal, (10) mortality, (11) mortal, (12) capital punishment, (13) homicide, (14) capital punishment, corporal punishment, (15) empathy, (16) sympathy, (17) genocide, (18) apathy, (19) suicide, (20) fraternity.

Practice B

(1) c, (2) d, (3) b, (4) c, (5) a, (6) a, (7) b, (8) a, (9) d, (10) a, (11) c, (12) a, (13) a, (14) d, (15) d, (16) a, (17) b, (18) c, (19) b.

Practice C

(1) killing of one person by another; (2) killing of oneself; (3) lack of feeling; (4) ability to feel sorry for; (5) a men's organization at college; (6) the killing of a whole group of people; (7) city or town that is the official seat of government; (8) place where unidentified dead are kept; (9) undertaker; (10) joined together; group of people who get a charter granting them certain rights as a body; (11) a beating; (12) death penalty; (13) that which never dies; (14) person who must die or human being; (15) pledge of property as security with a creditor.

Additional Words Derived from Combining Forms (pp. 102-103)

1. **fratricide.** The killing of a brother; may also refer to the killing of a sister.

2. **corpulent.** Fat; fleshy; obese.

3. **mortify.** To cause to feel shame; to punish (one's body) or control (one's physical desires or passions) by self-denial, fasting, and the like, as a means of religious or ascetic (severe) discipline.

4. **amortize.** The gradual extinction of a debt such as a mortgage or a bond issue by payment of a part of the principal at the time of each periodic interest payment.

5. **caption.** The heading of a chapter, section, or page in a book; a title or subtitle of a picture.

6. **capitulate.** To give up; surrender.

7. **symbol.** Something that stands for or represents another thing; an object used to represent something abstract.

8. **syllable.** A letter or a group of letters with one vowel sound.

9. **monosyllable.** A word consisting of a single syllable.

10. **symphony.** Harmony of sound; harmony of any kind.

11. **symptom.** In medicine, a condition that results from a disease and serves as an aid in diagnosis; a sign or token that indicates the existence of something else.

12. **synthesis.** A putting together of two or more things to form a whole.

13. **symmetry.** Balanced form or arrangement; balance on both sides.

Practice for Additional Words Derived from Combining Forms (p. 103)

(1) i, (2) m, (3) b, (4) a, (5) d, (6) j, (7) c, (8) l, (9) f, (10) h, (11) g, (12) e, (13) k.

Exercise 9 (p. 104-113)

Practice A

(1) pseudonym, (2) misnomer, (3) antonym, (4) synonym, (5) anonymous, (6) manual, (7) manuscript, (8) manicure, (9) factory, (10) benefactor, (11) beneficiary, (12) benefit, (13) manufacture, (14) affect, (15) effect, (16) effective, (17) auditorium, (18) audience, (19) audible, (20) audiovisual, (21) audition, (22) audit, (23) allocate, (24) location, (25) local, (26) homonym.

Practice B

(1) beneficiary, (2) factory, (3) pseudonym, (4) anonymous, (5) manuscript, (6) auditorium, (7) effect, (8) affect, (9) synonym, (10) antonym, (11) homonym, (12) effective, (13) allocated, (14) audible, (15) local, (16) audit, (17) audition.

Practice C

(1) manual, (2) benefit, (3) factory, (4) manufacture, (5) benefactor, (6) beneficiary, (7) factory, (8) location, (9) audience, (10) effective, (11) effect, (12) audible, (13) local, (14) audition, (15) manicure, (16) audition, (17) location, (18) audible, (19) manicure, (20) pseudonym.

Additional Words Derived from Combining Forms (pp. 111-112)

1. **audiometer.** An instrument used to measure hearing.

2. **audiology.** The study of hearing.

3. **benediction.** A blessing; the expression of good wishes.

4. **antipathy.** A dislike for someone.

5. **pseudopodium.** False foot.

6. **curator.** Head of a department of a museum; one in charge.

7. **pedicure.** Care of the feet, toes, and nails.

8. **pseudoscience.** A false science.

9. **manipulation.** The act of handling or operating; the act of managing or controlling skillfully or by shrewd use of influence; the act of changing or falsification for one's own purposes or profit.

10. **emancipate.** To set free from servitude or slavery; to set free.

11. **personification.** A figure of speech in which a nonliving thing or idea is made to appear as having the qualities of a person.

12. **facsimile.** An exact copy; to make an exact copy of.

13. **faction.** A number of persons in an organization, group, government, party, and so on, having a common goal, often self-seeking and reckless of the common good.

Practice for Additional Words Derived from Combining Forms (p. 113)

(1) h, (2) i, (3) a, (4) e, (5) l, (6) g, (7) m, (8) j, (9) k, (10) c, (11) d, (12) b, (13) f.

Crossword Puzzle 3 (pp. 114-115)

135

Word Scramble 3 (pp. 115–116)

(1) vision, (2) television, (3) invisible, (4) provisions, (5) evidence, (6) science, (7) astrology, (8) astronomy, (9) astronaut, (10) aquatic, (11) convene, (12) convenient, (13) potent, (14) potential, (15) omnipresent, (16) homicide, (17) apathy, (18) genocide, (19) empathy, (20) capitalism, (21) incorporate, (22) corpse, (23) immortal, (24) mortgage, (25) manual, (26) benefactor, (27) factory, (28) effect, (29) affect, (30) audible, (31) audit, (32) allocate, (33) pseudonym, (34) synonym, (35) anonymous.

Analogies 3 (p. 117)

(1) underwater, (2) omnipresent, (3) impotent, (4) convene, (5) pseudoscience, (6) pseudopodal, (7) mortify, (8) caption, (9) visage, (10) facsimile, (11) audiology, (12) homicide, (13) corpulent, (14) antipathy, (15) convenient, (16) apathy, (17) creed, (18) effect, (19) anonymous, (20) capitulate.

Multiple-Choice Vocabulary Test 3 (pp. 118–123)

Exercise 7

(1) c, (2) c, (3) b, (4) a, (5) a, (6) a, (7) a, (8) d, (9) b, (10) a, (11) d, (12) b, (13) c, (14) c, (15) c, (16) b, (17) a, (18) c, (19) b, (20) a, (21) d.

Exercise 8

(22) c, (23) a, (24) b, (25) d, (26) b, (27) c, (28) a, (29) c, (30) d, (31) a, (32) b, (33) c, (34) a, (35) b, (36) d, (37) d, (38) b, (39) d, (40) d, (41) d.

Exercise 9

(42) a, (43) d, (44) c, (45) c, (46) d, (47) b, (48) c, (49) a,[2] (50) d, (51) b, (52) d, (53) c, (54) d, (55) a, (56) b, (57) d, (58) d, (59) a, (60) b, (61) c, (62) b, (63) d, (64) c, (65) d, (66) d, (67) c.

True/False Test 3 (pp. 124–125)

(1) T,[3] (2) F,[4] (3) T, (4) F, (5) F,[5] (6) F, (7) F, (8) F, (9) F, (10) F, (11) T,

---

[2] *Performance* or *charity* is not specific enough by itself. A benefit performance is a performance for some charity or cause. Not *all* performances are for benefits.

[3] Although a fratricide is the killing of a brother or a sister, it is also a homicide.

[4] A suicide is *not* a homicide because it does not involve another person.

[5] As proportionally more minority group children die than children as a whole, the mortality or death rate for minority group children would be *higher*.

(12) T[6], (13) F, (14) F, (15) T, (16) T, (17) T, (18) F, (19) F,[7] (20) T, (21) T, (22) F, (23) F, (24) T, (25) F.

STOP. Turn to p. 125 for the scoring of the tests.

Additional Practice Sets (pp. 125-131)

Additional Practice 1

A. (1) c, (2) h, (3) g, (4) b, (5) f, (6) a, (7) e, (8) d.
B. (1) vision, (2) invisible, (3) television, (4) visible,[8] (5) provisions, (6) science, (7) evidence, (8) evident,[8] (9) astrology, (10) astronauts, (11) aquanauts, (12) astronomy, (13) aquatic, (14) aquarium, (15) convene, (16) conventions, (17) convenient, (18) potent, (19) impotent, (20) potential, (21) omnipresent.

Additional Practice 2

A. (1) b, (2) f, (3) d, (4) e, (5) c, (6) g, (7) h, (8) a.
B. (1) homicide, (2) genocide, (3) empathy, (4) apathy, (5) sympathy, (6) suicide, (7) fraternity, (8) corporation, (9) capitalism, (10) incorporate, (11) mortals, (12) immortal, (13) corpse, (14) capital punishment, (15) corporal punishment, (16) mortality, (17) morgue, (18) mortgage, (19) mortician, (20) capital.

Additional Practice 3

A. (1) h, (2) a, (3) b, (4) f, (5) g, (6) c, (7) d, (8) e.
B. (1) manicure, (2) manuscript, (3) factory, (4) benefactor, (5) manual, (6) audible, (7) audit, (8) audition, (9) audiovisual, (10) effective, (11) auditorium, (12) manufacture, (13) effect, (14) beneficiary, (15) benefit, (16) audience, (17) affect, (18) homonyms, (19) synonyms, (20) antonyms, (21) pseudonyms, (22) misnomer, (23) anonymous, (24) local, (25) allocate, (26) location.

---

[6] Only for empathy must you experience how the other person feels.

[7] A morgue is a place where only accident victims and other unidentified bodies are kept.

[8] Although *visible* and *evident* are synonyms, *visible* is the more specific and therefore *better* answer for 4; *evident* is the *better* answer for 8.

CHAPTER FIVE

EXERCISE 10

Step I. Combining Forms

A. Directions: A list of combining forms with their meanings follows. Look at the combining forms and their meanings. Concentrate on learning each combining form and its meaning. Cover the meanings, read the combining forms, and state the meanings to yourself. Check to see if you are correct. Now cover the combining forms, read the meanings, and state the combining forms to yourself. Check to see if you are correct.

Combining Forms	*Meanings*
1. dia	through
2. cata	down
3. log, logo	speech; word
4. fin	end
5. biblio	book
6. fer	bring; bear; yield (give up)
7. epi	upon; beside; among
8. pro	before; forward

B. Directions: Cover the preceeding meanings. Write the meanings of the following combining forms.

Combining Forms   *Meanings*

  1. dia   _____

  2. cata   _____

  3. log, logo   _____

  4. fin   _____

  5. biblio   _____

  6. fer   _____

  7. epi   _____

  8. pro   _____

Step II. Words Derived from Combining Forms

1. **logical** (log · i · cal) (loj′ i · kal) *adj.* Relating to the science concerned with correct reasoning. *The arguments that you are giving are not very **logical** because the reasoning is faulty.*

2. **prologue** (prō′ logŭe) *n.* An introduction, often in verse (poetry), spoken or sung before a play or opera; any introductory or preceding event; a preface. *The **prologue** of the play comes at the beginning and sometimes introduces the characters or sets the mood for the play.*

3. **epilogue** (ep′ i · logŭe) *n.* A short section added at the end to a book, poem, and so on; a short speech added to a play and given at the end. *We were very moved by the actor's **epilogue** at the end of the play.*

4. **catalog** (kat′ a · log) *n.* A listing of names, titles, and so on, in some order; a book containing such a list. *v.* To make a catalog. *The card **catalog** in the library lists books in alphabetical order according to topics, authors, and titles.*

5. **dialogue** (dī′ a · logŭe) *n.* A conversation in which two or more take part; the conversation in a play. *John and Mary had such a good **dialogue** going that when the bell rang, they still continued their conversation.*

6. **diagram** (dī′ a · gram) *n.* An outline figure that shows the relationship among parts or places; a graph or chart. *The **diagram** showing the circulatory system of the body helped me to see the relationship between the veins and arteries.*

7. **diameter** (dī · am′ e · ter) *n.* A straight line passing through the center of a circle. *The **diameter** of a circle divides the circle in half because it passes through the center of it from one end to the other.*

8. **bibliography** (bib · li · og · ra · phy) (bib · lē · og′ ra · fē) *n.* (*pl.* **phies**) A listing of books on a subject or by an author (the description includes author's name, title, publisher, date of publication, and so on). *The **bibliography** for my paper was large because our teacher wanted us to list at least twenty books on the topic we were writing about.*

9. **final** (fī′ nal) *adj.* Conclusive; last; coming at or relating to the end. *Most instructors give a **final** examination at the end of the semester.*

10. **finite** (fī′ nīt∉) *adj.* Having a limit or end; able to be measured. *Because there are a **finite** number of places where the missing item can be, we'll find it.*

11. **infinite** (in′ fi · nit∉) *adj.* Having no limit or end; not able to be measured. *If the universe is **infinite**, it has no beginning or end.*

12. **fertile** (fer′ til∉) *adj.* Able to produce a large crop; able to produce; capable of bearing offspring, seeds, fruit, and so on; productive in mental achievements; inventive; having abundant resources. *The land was so **fertile** that each year it produced a very large crop*

13. **fertilization** (fer · til · i · za · tion) (fer · til · i · zā′ shun) *n.* The act of making something able to produce; in biology, the union of a male and female germ cell; impregnation. *Human **fertilization** takes place when a sperm cell and egg cell unite.*

14. **reference** (ref′ er · ens∉) *n.* A referring or being referred; the giving of a problem to a person, a committee, or an authority for settlement; a note in a book that sends the reader for information to another book; the name of another person who can offer information or recommendation; the mark or sign, as a number or letter, directing the reader to a footnote, and so on; a written statement of character, qualification, or ability; testimonial. *My biology and geology instructors said that they would give me good **references** for a job after college.*

15. **preference** (pref′ er · ens∉) *n.* The choosing of one person or thing over another; the valuing of one over another; a liking better. *Her **preference** for science courses is obvious, for she chooses those over all others.*

16. **transfer** (trans′ fer) *v.* To carry or send from one person or place to another; to cause to pass from one person or place to another. *n.* An act of transferring or being transferred. *When my boss said he would **transfer** me to another department, I was very pleased because I wanted to go to the other place.*

17. **conference** (con · fer · ence) (kon′ fer · ens∉) *n.* A discussion or meeting on some important matter. *Because the dean wanted a **conference** with*

the students involved in the fight, he asked his secretary to call in the students for a meeting with him.

18. **suffer** (suf' · fer) *v.* To feel pain or distress. *The woman who lost five sons in World War II must have **suffered** a great deal of pain and distress.*

19. **circumference** (cir · cum · fer · ence) (sir · kum' fer · ens¢) *n.* The distance around a circle; a boundary line of any rounded area. *When we speak of the **circumference** of the globe, we refer to the distance around the globe.*

Special Notes

1. *Prologue* and *preface* are both introductory statements. However, a *prologue* is usually found at the beginning of a play or poem but usually not in a book such as a novel or textbook. In a book, article, or speech, the introduction found at the beginning is usually called a *preface*. The preface sets forth the plan, purpose, and so on, of the book, article, or speech.

2. **logical.** Relating to correct reasoning. A person who is *logical* is able to present arguments in a carefully thought out manner so that each statement correctly follows the other.

Step III. Practice

A. Directions: Following are a number of sentences with missing words. Fill in the word that *best* fits the sentence. Two choices are given for each sentence.

1. _____in plants also involves the union of egglike and spermlike cells. (circumference; fertilization)

2. A _____ is an outline figure that shows the relationship between parts or places. (diameter; diagram)

3. A(n) _____ is found at the end of a book. (prologue; epilogue)

4. In order to engage in a_____, you need two or more people interested in the topic of discussion. (dialogue; prologue)

5. When a limited number of something exists, it means that the number is _____. (final; finite)

6. The biologists held a number of_____s to discuss important topics. (conference; circumference)

7. The _____ is a listing of books that usually comes at the end of a research paper, a report, or an essay. (bibliography; catalog)

8. When someone has a_____._____ for something, he or she usually chooses that thing over another. (reference; preference)

9. An introduction to a play or poem is called a_____. (dialogue; prologue)

10. The _____ exam will come on the last day of class. (finite; final)

11. Time is considered_____ because it goes on without end. (infinite; final)

12. A(n) _____ lists items in some kind of order. (epilogue; catalog)

13. Both lawyers presented arguments that sounded reasonable and appeared _____. (logical; fertile)

14. The author of the book I am reading made a _____to another author who has written on the same topic. (reference; preference)

15. When a tomato plant is_____, it can produce a lot. (fertile; finite)

STOP. Check answers at the end of the chapter.

B. Directions: Following are a number of sentences with missing words. Choose the word that *best* fits the sentence. Put the word in the blank. *All words fit in.*

Word List

diagram, infinite, circumference, fertile, transfer, fertilization, suffer, catalog, diameter, finite, epilogue, dialogue, final, logical, preference, prologue, bibliography, reference, conference.

1. At the beginning of some plays there may be a(n)_____.

2. The _____ between the main characters in the play was interesting to listen to.

3. Some authors add a(n) _____ at the end of their books.

4. _____s have always helped me in learning something because I can understand better when I see an outline picture.

5. Our instructor asked us to list at least twenty-five books for our topic and to make sure that we gave the author, name of book, publisher, and date in the proper form for our_____.

6. As a senior, do you have to take _____ s at the end of the semester?

7. Only a(n)_____ number of people can attend the jazz concert because there is limited seating.

8. The number system is_____ because you can go on counting numbers without end.

9. At the science convention, a group of scientists had_____ s to discuss some important matters.

10. The _____ cuts a circle in half.

11. The boundary of a circle is called its_____.

12. I am going to _____ my funds from the State National Bank to the Security Bank because the Security Bank pays more interest.

13. Because your argument is full of holes, it is not very_____.

14. A file clerk has to _____ things in some order.

15. The soil in our garden is so _____ that we can grow practically anything.

16. I asked Professor Jones, from whom I received an *A*, if I could use his name as a(n)_____ for a job.

17. Because she has a(n) _____ for certain kinds of clothing, I know exactly what she will choose.

18. He was willing to_____ and bear the pain of another operation if it meant that he would walk again.

19. In the process of sexual reproduction, the union of sperm and egg is called _____ .

STOP. Check answers at the end of the chapter.

C. Directions: The Combining Form and Word Square that follows contains the combining forms from this exercise as well as the words derived from these combining forms. Definitions of the combining forms and words follow. There are *more definitions* than words in the square. Some of the definitions are for words from previous exercises.

1. Fill in the combining form that matches the meaning. Find the combining form in the square.

2. Fill in the blanks of those vocabulary definitions that have words in the square.

3. List the letters of the vocabulary definitions that do not have words in the square.

4. List the words that *best* fit the definitions that do not have words in the square.

COMBINING FORM AND WORD SQUARE

I	P	C	C	O	T	E	F	I	N	A	L	C
A	R	I	A	B	R	P	B	I	B	L	I	O
F	E	R	T	I	L	I	Z	A	T	I	O	N
D	F	C	A	B	A	L	B	I	O	E	C	F
I	E	U	L	L	L	O	G	I	C	A	L	E
A	R	M	O	I	S	G	D	N	F	P	O	R
M	E	F	G	O	U	U	I	F	E	R	R	E
E	N	E	E	G	F	E	A	I	R	O	A	N
T	C	R	E	R	F	O	G	N	T	S	R	C
E	E	E	R	A	E	A	R	I	I	C	C	E
R	M	N	E	P	R	I	A	T	L	I	H	O
O	A	C	I	H	L	A	M	E	E	I	S	T
R	B	E	C	Y	D	I	A	L	O	G	U	E

1. Combining Forms
    a. through_____
    b. down _____
    c. speech; word _____
    d. end _____
    e. book _____
    f. bring; bear, yield _____
    g. upon; beside; among_____
    h. before; forward _____

2. Vocabulary Definitions

   a. Endless _____

   b. A listing of books _____

   c. Last _____

   d. Killing of oneself _____

   e. An introduction _____

   f. Not believable _____

   g. Not legal _____

   h. Able to produce _____

   i. Able to be measured; having an end _____

   j. Relating to correct reasoning _____

   k. A listing of names, titles, and so on, in some order _____

   l. A conversation _____

   m. The act of making something able to produce _____

   n. The distance around a circle _____

   o. A straight line passing through the center of a circle _____

   p. A short section added to the end of a book _____

   q. An outline figure that shows the relationship among parts _____

   r. To feel pain or distress _____

   s. A note in a book that sends the reader to another book _____

   t. The choosing of one person or thing over another _____

   u. A discussion or meeting of some important matter _____

   v. To carry from one place to another _____

3. List the letters of the vocabulary definitions that do not have words in the square. _____

4. List the words that *best* fit the definitions that do not have words in the square. _____

_____

STOP. Check answers at the end of the chapter.

im, in. Into. **in, im, il, ir.** Not. Note than when *in* is placed at the beginning of a word, it can mean either "into" or "not." Note also that the *n* changes to an *m* when *in* is added to a word beginning with an *m*, *b*, or *p*. Example of *in* meaning "into": *inspection*—the act of looking into something. *The inspector gave the restaurant a careful **inspection** to see if everything was in order.* Examples of *in* meaning "not": *infinite*—not ending; *ineffectual*—not being able to bring about results. *The lifeguard was **ineffectual** in his efforts to save the drowning child.* Examples of *in* meaning "into" changing to *im*: *import*—to carry in; *important*—deserving of notice; of great value. *The materials being **imported** were so **important** that fifteen extra guards were hired to watch them as they came off the ship.* Examples of *in* meaning "not" changing to *im*: *imperfect*—not perfect; having a fault. Note that *in* meaning "not" also changes to *il* and *ir* when *in* is added to words beginning with *l* or *r*. For example: *illegal*—not legal; *irregular*—not uniform; not the same.

trans. Across; beyond; through; on the other side of; over. When *trans* is placed at the beginning of a word such as the following, it means "across," "beyond," "through," "on the other side of." For example: *transatlantic*—across the Atlantic; on the other side of the Atlantic; *transhuman*—beyond human limits; *transport*—to carry from one place to another; *transparent*—able to be seen through; *transfer*—to move from one place to another.

Additional Words Derived from Combining Forms

From your knowledge of combining forms, can you define the following words?

1. **inference** (in′ fer · ens̸) *n.* *Although he did not say it exactly, the **inference** I got was that he was quitting his job.*

2. **proficient** (pro · fi · cient) (pro · fish′ ent) *adj.* *It was obvious that he was a proficient skier because he was able to ski from the highest and steepest mountain paths with ease.*

3. **dialect** (dī′ a · lekt) *n.* *It's evident that Jane comes from the South because she speaks a Southern dialect.*

4. **monologue** (mon′ o · logue) *n.* *Jim's monologue was so long that after a while nobody was listening to what he was saying.*

5. **definitive** (de · fin′ i · tive) *adj.* *The results from the studies are not definitive because there are too many different conclusions.*

6. **finale** (fi · na′ lē) *n.* *The play's finale was completely unexpected on the basis of everything that went before.*

7. **affinity** (af · fin′ i · tē) *n.* *We knew that our relationship would grow into more than just being acquaintances, because of the affinity we had for one another when we first met.*

8. **infinitesimal** (in · fin · i · tes′ i · mal) *adj.* *The size of the microorganism was almost infinitesimal because it could be seen only with the most high-powered microscope.*

9. **deference** (def′ er · ense) *n.* *In deference to his age and position, the group decided to give him a chance to speak.*

10. **defer** (de · fer′) *v.* *I will defer to my partner because he has studied the matter very closely.*

STOP. Check answers at the end of the chapter.

Practice for Additional Words Derived from Combining Forms

Directions: Match each word with the *best* definition.

_____ 1. inference		a. respect
_____ 2. proficient		b. too small to be measured
_____ 3. dialect		c. able to do something very well
_____ 4. monologue		d. a conclusion drawn from statements
_____ 5. infinitesimal		e. to leave to another's opinion
_____ 6. affinity		f. conclusive
_____ 7. definitive		g. long speech by one person
_____ 8. finale		h. close relationship
_____ 9. deference		i. the last part
_____ 10. defer		j. a variety of speech

STOP. Check answers at the end of the chapter.

©1960 United Feature Syndicate, Inc.

EXERCISE 11

Step I. Combining Forms

A. Directions: A list of combining forms with their meanings follows. Look at the combining forms and their meanings. Concentrate on learning each combining form and its meaning. Cover the meanings, read the combining forms, and state the meanings to yourself. Check to see if you are correct. Now cover the combining forms, read the meanings, and state the combining forms to yourself. Check to see if you are correct.

Combining Forms	Meanings
1. cap, cep	take, receive
2. gnosi, gnosis	knowledge
3. ped, pedo	child

4. tox, toxo	poison
5. gyn, gyno	woman
6. temp, tempo, tempor	time
7. hypo	under
8. derm, dermo	skin
9. ri, ridi, risi	laughter

B. Directions: Cover the preceding meanings. Write the meanings of the following combining forms.

Combining Forms	*Meanings*
1. cap, cep	————
2. gnosi, gnosis	————
3. ped, pedo	————
4. tox, toxo	————
5. gyn, gyno	————
6. temp, tempo, tempor	————
7. hypo	————
8. derm, dermo	————
9. ri, ridi, risi	————

Step II. Words Derived from Combining Forms

1. **capable** (ca · pa · ble) (kā′ pa · bul) *adj.* Able to be affected; able to understand; having ability; having qualities that are able to be developed. *Although he is* ***capable*** *of many things, time will tell whether he will use all his abilities.*

2. **captive** (kap′ tiv̸) *n.* One who is taken prisoner; one who is dominated. *When the daughter of a wealthy man was held a* ***captive*** *by dangerous criminals, one million dollars was paid to the criminals to release the girl.*

3. **conceive** (kon · sēiv̸′) *v.* To become pregnant with; to form in the mind; to understand; to think; to believe; to imagine; to develop mentally. *I cannot* ***conceive*** *of him as a scientist because the image I have of him is as a playboy.*

4. **deceive** (de · sēiv̸′) *v.* To mislead by lying; to lead into error. *I couldn't believe that my best friend told all those lies to* ***deceive*** *me.*

5. **reception** (re · cep · tion) (re · sep′ shun) *n.* The act of receiving or being received; a formal social entertainment; the manner of receiving someone;

150

the receiving of a radio or television broadcast. *I received a warm reception when I attended Laura's wedding reception, which was the social event of the year.*

6. **exception** (ex · cep · tion) (ek · sep′ shun) *n.* The act of taking out; something or one that is taken out or left out; an objection. *In English spelling rules there always seems to be an exception to which the rule does not apply.*

7. **perception** (per · cep · tion) (per · sep′ shun) *n.* The act of becoming aware of something through the senses of seeing, hearing, feeling, tasting and/or smelling. *If you have something wrong with your senses, your perception will be faulty.*

8. **capsule** (kap′ sul̸e) *n.* A small container made of gelatin (or other material that melts) that holds a dose of medicine; a special removable part of an airplane or rocket. *Each capsule contained the exact amount of medicine the doctor wanted me to take.*

9. **ridiculous** (ri · dic · u · lous) (ri · dik′ yu · l̸ous) *adj.* Unworthy of consideration; absurd (senseless); preposterous. *His suggestion was so ridiculous that no one would even consider it.*

10. **ridicule** (rid′ i · kūl̸e) *n.* The language or actions that make a person the object of mockery or cause one to be laughed at or scorned. *v.* To mock or view someone in a scornful way; to hold someone up as a laughingstock; to make fun of. *I think it is cruel when someone ridicules another person and holds him or her up as a laughingstock.*

11. **diagnose** (dī · ag · nōs̸e′) *v.* To determine what is wrong with someone after an examination. *It is very important for a doctor to be able to diagnose a person's illness correctly so that the doctor will know how to treat it.*

12. **prognosis** (prog · nō′ sis) *n.* (*pl.* **ses**) (sēz) A prediction or conclusion regarding the course of a disease and the chances of recovery; a prediction. *Because the doctor's prognosis regarding John's illness was favorable, we knew that he would recover.*

13. **pediatrician** (pe · di · a · tri · cian) (pē · dē · a · trish′ un) *n.* A doctor who specializes in children's diseases. *I like to take my children to a pediatrician for a checkup rather than to a general doctor because a pediatrician deals only with children's diseases.*

14. **gynecologist** (gyn · e · col · o · gist) (gi · ne · kol′ o · jist) *n.* A doctor dealing with women's diseases, especially in reference to the reproductive organs. *Many women go to a gynecologist for an annual checkup even if they have no symptoms of anything wrong.*

15. **toxic** (tox · ic) (tok′ sik) *adj.* Relating to poison. *Children should not be allowed to lick the walls because some of the paints have toxic materials in them.*

16. **dermatologist** (der · ma · tol' o · jist) *n.* A doctor who deals with skin disorders. *When I broke out in a rash, I went to a **dermatologist** to find out what was wrong with me.*

17. **hypodermic** (hy · po · der · mic) (hī · po · der' mik) *adj.* Referring to the area under the skin; used for injecting under the skin. *n.* A hypodermic injection; a hypodermic syringe or needle. *The doctor injected the **hypodermic** needle so far under my skin that my arm hurt all day.*

18. **hypothesis** (hī · poth' e · sis) *n.* (*pl.* **ses**) (sēz). An unproved scientific conclusion drawn from known facts; something assumed as a basis for argument; a possible answer to a problem that requires further investigation. *The **hypothesis** that was put forth as the solution to the problem seemed logical, but it required further investigation to prove whether it was correct.*

19. **temporary** (tem' po · rar · ē) *adj.* Lasting for a short period of time. *I was not upset when I was dismissed from my job because I had been told, when hired, that it was only a **temporary** position.*

20. **contemporary** (con · tem · po · rar · y) (kon · tem' po · rar · ē) *adj.* Belonging to the same age; living or occurring at the same time; current. *n.* (*pl.* **ies**) One living in the same period as another or others; a person or thing of about the same age or date of origin. *Even though they act like **contemporaries**, they are a generation apart.*

Special Notes

1. The term *exception,* meaning "something or one that is left out," has a special meaning when it is used in the phrase *to take exception. To take exception* means "to disagree," "to object." For example: *I take exception to what you are saying.*

2. *Hypothesis* is a term that is much used in the area of logic and science. A hypothesis may be defined as an unproved scientific conclusion drawn from known facts and used as a basis for further investigation. In science, a *hypothesis* is thus a possible explanation of observed facts and must be found true or false by more experiments.

3. You met the combining forms *ped, pod* in Exercise 1 of Chapter One. *Ped, pod* means "foot" in such words as *biped, pedestrian, apodal, pseudopodia,* and *podiatrist. Ped, pedo* means "child" in such words as *pediatrician* and *pedagogue.*

Step III. Practice

A. Directions: Following are the words presented in Exercise 11. Match the word with its meaning.

_____ 1. diagnose

_____ 2. prognosis

_____ 3. pediatrician

_____ 4. gynecologist

_____ 5. toxic

_____ 6. dermatologist

_____ 7. capable

_____ 8. captive

_____ 9. deceive

_____ 10. reception

_____ 11. conceive

_____ 12. perception

_____ 13. exception

_____ 14. ridicule

_____ 15. capsule

_____ 16. ridiculous

_____ 17. hypodermic

_____ 18. hypothesis

_____ 19. temporary

_____ 20. contemporary

a. having ability

b. a small container that holds a dose of medicine

c. the act of taking out

d. to become pregnant with; to think

e. a prisoner

f. a formal social entertainment; act of receiving

g. the act of becoming aware of something through the senses

h. to mislead by lying

i. referring to the area under skin

j. an unproved scientific conclusion

k. to mock or view someone in a scornful way

l. absurd; beyond belief

m. a doctor who specializes in skin diseases

n. referring to poison

o. a doctor who specializes in children's diseases

p. a prediction

q. to determine what is wrong with someone after an examination

r. a doctor who specializes in women's diseases

s. of the same age; current

t. for a short period of time

STOP. Check answers at the end of the chapter.

B. Directions: Each sentence has a missing word. Choose the word that *best* completes the sentence. Write the word in the blank. *Each word is used only once.*

Word List

diagnose, hypothesis, perception, hypodermic, prognosis, contemporary, conceive, ridiculous, ridicule, dermatologist, capsule, captive, temporary, toxic, capable, exception, reception, pediatrician, deceive, gynecologist.

1. The scientists came up with a(n) _____, which they felt needed further testing to determine if it was the solution to their problem.

2. It is _____ to believe that an eighty-five-year-old man can ride a bicycle across the whole United States, so I will not even consider the idea.

3. As I don't know what these spots on my face and hands are, I'm going to visit a(n) _____ .

4. The space _____ left the rocket at the proper time.

5. Because the patient could not take any medicine by mouth, the doctor told the nurse to give the patient the medicine using a(n)_____ needle.

6. When I am ill, I want a doctor who is able to_____ what is wrong with me.

7. After being _____ s for three years or more, some prisoners of war had a difficult time adjusting to normal life.

8. The help I need is _____ because we are leaving in a short period of time.

9. The doctor's _____ for the patient's recovery was favorable.

10. _____materials are dangerous and should be clearly marked as poisonous.

11. It's a shame that someone who is as _____ as you are is not doing anything with his ability.

12. I dislike people who _____ others by making fun of them.

13. It is incredible that in_____times there are still people in the United States who do not have indoor bathrooms and other modern conveniences.

14. A(n) _____ to a rule is something that does not fit in.

15. The wedding_____ of the two wealthiest persons in the world was held in the largest ballroom the reporters ever saw, and it was a spectacular affair.

16. Many parents like to take their young children to_____s because they prefer doctors who specialize in children's diseases.

17. Nobody was able to_____of a plan that was agreeable to all because everyone thought of a different one.

18. Some husbands or wives _____ their spouses by telling them lies.

19. Because I prefer a doctor who specializes in women's diseases, I go to a(n)_____.

20. A person who is deaf has no _____ of what it is to hear.

STOP. Check answers at the end of the chapter.

C. Directions: Following are twenty sentences containing the meanings of vocabulary presented in Exercise 11. Choose the word that *best* fits the meaning of the word or phrase underlined in the sentence.

Word List

ridiculous, reception, ridicule, hypothesis, capable, contemporaries, toxic, captive, hypodermic, temporary, gynecologist, dermatologist, diagnose, prognosis, capsules, deceive, conceive, exception, pediatrician, perception.

1. As a person having ability, you should do well in college. _____

2. I knew they were happy to see us because of the manner in which they received us when we visited them. _____

3. I become very upset when I learn how some leaders of our country mislead us by lying to us. _____

4. I can't think of you as someone interested in astrology. _____

5. What you have said is so unworthy of consideration that I will not even repeat it to anyone. _____

6. How cruel of those children to make fun of the poor man. _____

7. Would you believe that I have to take ten tiny containers of medicine like this every day? _____

8. Blind persons seem to have a more developed sense of hearing because they seem to be able to hear things that others can't. _____

9. Almost every general rule has an example that does not belong. _____

10. When I received an injection by needle under my skin, I broke out in a cold sweat. _____

11. The geologist has come up with a possible solution to a problem he has been working on, and now he would like to test it to determine if it is correct. _____

12. At the political rally, I met a lot of <u>people of my same age group.</u>
_____

13. We waited anxiously to hear what the doctor's <u>prediction</u> would be concerning our mother's heart condition. _____

14. <u>After an examination</u>, the doctor was able to tell <u>what was wrong</u> with our mother. _____

15. I feel that it's best to take a child to <u>a doctor who specializes in children's diseases.</u> _____

16. I feel that <u>a doctor who specializes in women's diseases</u> would know more about some female problems than other doctors. _____

17. When I have a skin problem, I go to <u>a doctor who specializes in skin disorders.</u> _____

18. Parents should keep <u>poisonous</u> materials out of the reach of children.
_____

19. Although this job will be <u>lasting for a short period of time</u> only, I will still try to do my best at it. _____

20. The warden of the jail was held <u>a prisoner</u> by three men who were trying to escape. _____

STOP. Check answers at the end of the chapter.

EXTRA WORD
POWER

ex, e. Out of; from; lacking. When *ex* or *e* is placed at the beginning of a word, it means "out of" or "from." When *ex* is placed at the beginning of a word and a hyphen (-) is attached to the word, *ex* means "former" or "sometime." For example: *ex-president*—former president; *ex-wife*—former wife. Examples of *ex* meaning "out of" or "from": *exclude*—to keep from; *exit*—to go out of; *expect*—to look out for; *excuse*—to forgive; to apologize for; *exhale*—to breathe out.

de. Away; from; off; completely. *De* is found at the beginning of many words. For example: *deport*—to send someone away. *An alien who was involved in many holdups was **deported** to his own country.* Other words with *de*: *deflea*—to take off fleas; *delouse*—to free from lice; *decolor*—to take color away; *decode*—to change from code to plain language; *dextoxify*—to take away poison; to destroy

156

the poison; *decapitate*—to take off the head; to kill; *deprive*—to take something away from; *denude*—to strip the covering from completely. Can you supply more words with *ex, e,* or *de*?

Additional Words Derived from Combining Forms

From your knowledge of combining forms, can you define the following words?

1. **misogynist** (mi · sog · y · nist) (mi · soj′ i · nist) *n.* *Although Tom is a misogamist, he isn't a* **misogynist** *because he likes women.*

   _____

2. **agnostic** (ag · nos′ tik) *adj. n.* *Pat must be an* **agnostic** *because she believes that there is no way for anyone to know for sure about the existence of God.*

   _____

3. **epidermis** (ep · i · der′ mis) *n.* *The* **epidermis** *is the layer of skin that is the most exposed.*

   _____

4. **pedagogue** (ped′ a · gog/g̸) *n.* *A* **pedagogue** *is a person who teaches students.*

   _____

5. **antitoxin** (an · ti · tox · in) (an · ti · tok′ sin) *n.* *The doctor injected my brother with an* **antitoxin** *in order to prevent his getting a certain disease.*

   _____

6. **toxicologist** (tox · i · col · o · gist) (tok · si · kol′ o · jist) *n.* *A* **toxicologist** *was called in to help in the homicide investigation because all symptoms pointed to a possible death by poisoning.*

   _____

7. **derisive** (de · rī′ siv̸) *adj.* *The* **derisive** *laughter of the class toward all student comments kept me from saying anything because I did not want to be ridiculed.*

   _____

8. **intercept** (in · ter · sept′) *v.* *When the ball was* **intercepted** *before a goal could be made, the home team audience screamed with delight.*

   _____

9. **susceptible** (sus · cep · ti · ble) (sus̸ · sep′ ti · bul) *adj.* *When he heard that he was* **susceptible** *to tuberculosis, he asked the doctor to help him to prevent the onset of the disease.*

   _____

10. **perceptive** (per · sep′ tiv) *adj.* *Being a* **perceptive** *individual, she knew that this was not the right time to ask her father for use of the car.*

---

11. **tempo** (tem′pō) *n.* (*pl.* **tempi**) *The* **tempo** *of modern living is very fast.*

---

12. **extemporaneous** (ex · tem · po · ra · ne · ous) (ek · stem · po · rā′ nē · us) *adj.* *When she was called upon to express her views, her* **extemporaneous** *talk was so logical and well expressed that she couldn't have done better if she had spent hours preparing it.*

STOP. Check answers at the end of the chapter.

Practice for Additional Words Derived from Combining Forms

Directions: Match each word with the *best* definition.

_____ 1. misogynist	a. outermost layer of skin
_____ 2. agnostic	b. rate of speed
_____ 3. pedagogue	c. being aware
_____ 4. antitoxin	d. hater of women
_____ 5. epidermis	e. mocking; jeering
_____ 6. toxicologist	f. something used against poison
_____ 7. derisive	g. done or spoken without preparation
_____ 8. intercept	
_____ 9. susceptible	h. professing uncertainty about ultimates
_____ 10. perceptive	i. specialist in poisons
_____ 11. extemporaneous	j. a teacher
_____ 12. tempo	k. especially liable to
	l. to stop or interrupt the course of

STOP. Check answers at the end of the chapter.

158

EXERCISE 12

Step I. Combining Forms

A. Directions: A list of combining forms with their meanings follows. Look at the combining forms and their meanings. Concentrate on learning each combining form and its meaning. Cover the meanings, read the combining forms, and state the meanings to yourself. Check to see if you are correct. Now cover the combining forms, read the meanings, and state the combining forms to yourself. Check to see if you are correct.

Combining Forms	*Meanings*
1. ten, tent, tain	hold
2. cede, ceed	go; give in; yield (give in)
3. sequi	follow
4. cycl, cyclo	circle; wheel
5. chron, chrono	time
6. archae, archaeo	ancient
7. crypto, crypt	secret; hidden
8. duc	lead
9. brevi	short; brief

B. Directions: Cover the preceding meanings. Write the meanings of the following combining forms.

Combining Forms	*Meanings*
1. ten, tent, tain	_____
2. cede, ceed	_____
3. sequi	_____
4. cycl, cyclo	_____
5. chron, chrono	_____
6. archae, archaeo	_____
7. crypto, crypt	_____
8. duc	_____
9. brevi	_____

159

1. **tenant** (ten' ant) *n.* A person who holds property; one who lives in property belonging to another; one who rents or leases from a landlord; one who lives in a place. *The tenants told the landlord, who owned the building, that they would not pay the rent unless the landlord made the needed repairs to their apartments.*

2. **content** (kon' tent) *n.* What something holds (usually plural in this sense); subject matter; the material that something is made up of; the main substance or meaning. *The course content was supposed to deal with the earth's crust or makeup, but the instructor had not yet covered any subject matter related to geology.*

3. **content** (kon · tent') *adj.* Satisfied; not complaining; not desiring something else. *It is obvious that Sally is content with her life because she never complains and always seems free from worry.*

4. **maintain** (main · tain') *v.* To carry on or continue; to keep up; to keep in good condition. *When Mr. Jones lost his job, he found that he could not maintain his house because the needed repairs were too costly.*

5. **sequence** (se · quence) (sē' kwens) *n.* The following of one thing after another; order; a continuous or related series, with one thing following another. *The detectives investigating the suicide were trying to get the sequence of events, step-by-step and in order, to try to figure out why the man took his life.*

6. **consequence** (con · se · quence) (kon' se · kwens) *n.* That which follows from any act; a result; an effect. *I had no idea what the consequence of my leaving home would be until I found out that my mother became ill as a result of it.*

7. **subsequent** (sub · se · quent) (sub' se · kwent) *adj.* Following soon after; following in time, place, or order; resulting. *The subsequent chapter, which follows this one, is the last chapter in Part I of this book.*

8. **cycle** (cy · cle) (sī' kul) *n.* A period that keeps coming back, in which certain events take place and complete themselves in some definite order; a round of years or ages; a pattern of regularly occurring events; a series that repeats itself. *We seem to be going through an economic cycle that is similar to one we had a decade ago.*

9. **cyclone** (cy · clone) (sī' klōn) *n.* A system of violent and destructive whirlwinds. *When the cyclone hit the small town, its winds were so strong that it destroyed everything in its path.*

10. **archaeology** (ar · chae · ol · o · gy) (ar · kē · ol' o · jē) *n.* The study of the life and culture of ancient people, as by the digging up of old settlements, ruins from the past, and old man-made or other objects. *I knew*

that I'd enjoy studying **archaeology** *because I have always loved to dig in old places and hunt for things from the past so that I could learn more about ancient times.*

11. **archaic** (ar · cha · ic) (ar · kā′ ik) *adj.* Belonging to an earlier period; ancient; old-fashioned; no longer used. *It is surprising to find someone in our times who believes in such an* **archaic** *practice as bloodletting for curing disease.*

12. **chronological** (chron · o · log · i · cal) (kron · o · loj′ i · kal) *adj.* Arranged in time order (earlier things or events precede later ones). *In order to arrange our outline on wars in the United States in* **chronological** *order, we needed to know the dates of the wars.*

13. **chronic** (chron′ ic) (kron′ ik) *adj.* Continuing for a long time; prolonged; recurring. *Because he had a* **chronic** *cough, it lasted for a long period of time and always came back.*

14. **concede** (con · cede) (kon · sēde′) *v.* To give in; surrender; yield; grant; admit. *After a long discussion and debate on an issue, the union said it would* **concede** *on this particular issue because the employers had given in on other issues.*

15. **precede** (prē · sēde′) *v.* To go or come before. *In the circus parade the clowns were to* **precede** *the others because, by entering first, they would put the spectators in a good mood for the rest of the show.*

16. **proceed** (prō · sēed′) *v.* To go on; to go forward; to carry on an action. *We will* **proceed** *the way we have been going unless someone knows some reason why we should not continue.*

17. **succeed** (suc · ceed) (suk · sēed′) *v.* To accomplish what is attempted; to come next in order; to come next after or replace another in an office or position. *The people who* **succeed** *seem to be those who do not stop until they have accomplished what they set out to do.*

18. **abbreviation** (ab · bre · vi · a · tion) (ab · brē · vē · ā′ shun) *n.* A shortened form of a word or phrase. *It is usual to give an* **abbreviation** *of the spelling of the states rather than write them out completely because it's much faster and easier.*

19. **conductor** (con · duc · tor) (kon · duk′ tor) *n.* One who guides or leads; a guide or director; one who has charge of a railroad train; the director of an orchestra or chorus; any substance that conducts electricity, heat, and so on. *You could tell from the applause that the* **conductor** *of the orchestra was greatly admired by the large audience that had come to see him lead the orchestra.*

20. **deduction** (de · duc · tion) (de · duk′ shun) *n.* The act of drawing a conclusion by reasoning or reasoning that goes from the general to the particular; the subtraction of something; an inference or conclusion. *How much money are you able to get back by having so many* **deductions** *on your income tax?*

161

21. **cryptic** (cryp · tic) krip' tik) *adj.* Having a hidden or secret meaning; mysterious. *The **cryptic** message was very difficult to decode because no one was familiar with the meanings of the letters used in the code.*

22. **crypt** (kript) *n.* An underground vault. *The **crypt** was buried fifty feet underground in a special cave.*

Special Notes

1. Note that the terms *content* (con' tent) *n.* and *content* (con · tent') *adj.* are spelled identically but are *pronounced differently* and have *different meanings.* Many of the words you have met have had more than one meaning. However, they were *pronounced identically.* Because *content* (con' tent) *n.* and *content* (con tent') *adj.* are pronounced differently and each word has meanings different from those of the other, they are presented separately.
   a. **content** (con' tent) *n.* What something holds (usually plural in this sense). *The **contents** of the box contained all her childhood toys.*
   b. **content** (con' tent) *n.* Subject matter. *The course **content** was so boring that I decided not to take any other courses in that subject.*
   c. **content** (con' tent) *n.* The material that something is made up of. *When I checked the **content** of the ice cream I was eating, I found that it was made up almost completely of artificial products.*
   d. **content** (con · tent') *adj.* Satisfied; not complaining; not desiring something else. *I am **content** with my job, so there is no need for me to look for another.*

2. You met the term *bicycle,* meaning "two-wheeler," in Exercise 1. You can now see that *cycle* in *bicycle* comes from the combining form *cyclo* meaning *wheel.*

3. The term **deduction** has a few meanings.
   a. **deduction.** A subtraction; something taken away. A *deduction* refers to your being able to subtract or take away a certain amount from something else. This meaning of *deduction* is much used in relation to the income tax. You can subtract or take away a certain amount of money from your income taxes on the basis of the number of *deductions* you have.
   b. **deduction.** Reasoning from the general to the particular or reasoning from given statements to conclusions. This meaning of *deduction* is used in *logic,* which is the *science of correct reasoning.* You met the term *logical,* which deals with correct reasoning, in Exercise 10. An example of deduction—going from the general to the specific—follows:

      All men are good.
      Arthur is a man.
      Therefore, Arthur is good.

   In the preceding example, we can decide, on the basis of a general statement that all men are good, that a particular man, Arthur, must be good.

162

c. **deduction.** An inference; a conclusion. It is important for readers to be able to make *deductions* in reading because many times writers do not directly state what they mean but present ideas in a more "roundabout" way, or *indirectly*.

In Exercise 10 you met the word *inference* in the section entitled Additional Words Derived from Combining Forms. *Deduction* and *inference* have the same meaning. Remember that an *inference* is drawn from information that is not directly stated. The same is true of *deduction*. When all the information is given in statements but the information is given indirectly, you must make *deductions* or *inferences*. In order to get the information, you must "read between the lines." Mystery writers often use *inference* to make their stories more interesting and enjoyable. Following is an example of inference. Can you draw the proper inferences or make the correct deductions from the information given?

Read the following short selection, and answer the two questions.

The six remaining boys were worn out from walking all day with such heavy knapsacks. They headed toward the mountain range, hoping to reach it before the sun finally set behind it. One third of their original number had turned back earlier.

(1) In what direction were the six boys headed?

(2) How many boys had there been at the beginning of the trip?

In order to answer the first question, you must collect the following clues:

(1) Boys walking toward mountain range.

(2) Sun sets behind the mountain range.

From this information you should conclude that the answer to the first question is "west" because the sun sets in the west and the boys were heading toward the setting sun.

To answer the second question, you must collect the following clues:

(1) Six boys remaining.

(2) One third had turned back.

From this information you should conclude that the answer to the second question is "nine" because two thirds of the boys equals six, one third must be three, and six plus three equals nine.

PEANUTS ®   **By Schulz**

A. Directions: Each sentence has a missing word. Choose the word that *best* completes the sentence. Write the word in the blank. Note that one word is used in two sentences, once as a noun and once as an adjective.

Word List

concede, maintain, cycle, abbreviation, subsequent, precede, proceed, chronic, cyclone, conductor, archaic, cryptic, content, sequence, crypt, succeed, chronological, deduction, archaeology, tenant, consequence.

1. As that is a(n)_____word, it is not used anymore.

2. Whenever I have an argument with anyone, it always seems that I'm the one to _____ , because the other person just won't give in.

3. The _____ writing that they found on the box has still not been decoded because no one can figure out the code.

4. I've heard that some banks store their gold in a_____ that is buried so far in the ground that it is almost impossible for robbers to get to it.

5. A(n) _____ is a person who usually pays rent to occupy property.

6. I am perfectly _____ with the place where I live, so there is no reason for me to complain about it.

7. Because our landlord will not_____the property and keep it in good condition, we are withholding our rent.

8. The_____of events was easy to follow because there was a definite order to the events.

9. After the fire it was difficult to tell what the_____s of the house had been because everything in the house was so badly burned.

10. The doctor told my friend that unless he followed the doctor's orders, the _____s would be bad, and he might have to go to the hospital.

11. How many_____s will you be able to subtract from your income tax this year?

12. Because _____ deals with ancient cultures, we are going to visit an ancient cave and dig for things from the past for our _____ class.

13. The dates were listed in _____ order, starting with ancient times and continuing to contemporary times.

14. I can tell that I'm starting my losing _____ all over again because the events that happened before seem to be repeating themselves.

15. The problem with a(n) _____ illness is that even though it may go away, it always comes back.

16. When the _____ hit our area, we were lucky that our house was not in the path of the violent winds because it would have been completely destroyed.

17. I attempt to do only things that I feel I can accomplish because I like to _____ in what I do.

18. You usually use a(n) _____ for name titles rather than write out the whole word.

19. _____ with your work because you seem to be doing it correctly.

20. I was surprised that you did not _____ him in the lineup of players because you always go up to bat before he does.

21. The audience was quiet when the _____ came on stage to begin directing the orchestra.

22. The _____ chapters should be easier for you because they come after the more difficult material.

STOP. Check answers at the end of the chapter.

B. Directions: A short story with missing words follows. Fill in the blanks with the words that *best* fit. Words are used only once. Note that *content* is given twice because it us used in two different ways.

Word List

cyclone, homicide, corpse, morgue, television, consequence, description, sequence, local, cryptic, conductor, deduction, hypothesis, illegal, tenant, maintain, chronic, succeed, concede, content, content, abbreviation, subsequent, cycle, proceed.

I am a(n) 1 _____ in a large apartment building. I have been 2 _____ living there and really had nothing much to complain about until last month. A(n) 3 _____ of events took place that has made it very difficult for me to 4 _____ my former way of living. What I am saying is that as a(n) 5 _____ of one particular night my whole life has changed.

I remember the night very well for three reasons. First, we had such a violent 6 _____ during the day that some of my windows had been broken. Second, the night was very dark because the moon was completing its monthly 7 _____ just before the new moon. Third, a(n) 8 _____ took place right outside my broken window.

I should tell you that I live on the ground floor in a rather quiet neighborhood. My building is across the street from a large park, and during the summers we have many famous 9 _____ s leading orchestras in outdoor concerts. I live on the ground floor because I have a(n) 10 _____ back problem, and I never know when it will give me trouble.

Let me 11 _____ with my story of the murder. At about 10 P.M. I thought I heard some sounds from outside, but I had the 12 _____ on, so I wasn't sure. The third time I thought I heard something, I went to my broken window to look outside. It was so dark that I saw nothing. However, on my floor I found a paper attached to a broken piece of glass. Although I tried to read it, I did not 13 _____ in figuring out the 14 _____ s of the paper. The paper contained a(n) 15 _____ message, which I could not decode. The only thing I could make out was *Dr.*, a(n) 16 _____ of the word *doctor*.

I immediately phoned the police. While waiting for the police, I again tried to decode the message. I finally had to 17 _____ to myself that I could not figure it out. The police arrived. I told them my story. They went out to investigate. It was then that they found the 18 _____ . I was asked to look at the body. Frightened and trembling, I did. However, I had never seen the person before. The dead body was then taken to the 19 _____ because there was no identification on it. 20 _____ to that, the police came to question me. They wanted to know if I had any 21 _____ that might be a possible explanation for the murder. I stated that I had none and that I knew nothing.

I told them that the only 22 _____ I could make or conclude was that the person couldn't have died right away because he had time to pick up a piece of broken glass, attach some paper to it and throw it through my already broken window.

The police were able to decode the message. The message gave such a good 23 _____ of the murderer that the police were able to have a picture drawn of him. It turned out to be a(n) 24 _____ doctor from the neighborhood who was involved with the 25 _____ sale of drugs.

STOP. Check answers at the end of the chapter.

C. Directions: In the Word Square there are fifteen words from Exercise 12. Find the words in the square, and match them with their correct meanings. Note that there are *more* meanings than words.

Word Square

D	E	D	U	C	T	I	O	N	E	S	A
C	O	N	S	E	Q	U	E	N	C	E	B
R	A	C	U	M	A	I	N	T	H	E	B
Y	R	Y	B	C	Y	C	L	E	R	M	R
P	C	C	S	O	P	C	E	N	O	A	E
T	H	L	E	N	U	O	C	A	N	I	V
I	O	O	Q	T	C	N	O	N	I	N	I
C	O	N	U	E	O	T	N	T	C	T	A
H	L	E	E	N'	N	E	T	E	A	A	T
R	O	I	N	T	A	N	E	O	N	I	I
O	G	N	T	C	O	T	C	E	D	N	O
N	Y	A	R	C	H	A	I	C	A	O	N

Meanings

1. Satisfied; not complaining

2. To continue; to keep up; to keep in good condition

3. A continuous series

4. A result; an effect

5. A person who rents or leases from a landlord

6. Following soon after

7. The study of the life and culture of ancient people

8. Referring to what is ancient

9. A round of years or ages

10. A violent, destructive whirlwind

11. Arranged in time order

12. To go forward

Words

1. _____

2. _____

3. _____

4. _____

5. _____

6. _____

7. _____

8. _____

9. _____

10. _____

11. _____

12. _____

13. To give in   _____

14. To go or come before   _____

15. Continuing for a long time and
    coming back   _____

16. To accomplish what is attempted;
    to come after   _____

17. A shortened form of a word or
    phrase   _____

18. One who guides or leads   _____

19. The act of drawing a conclusion
    by reasoning; an inference   _____

20. Having a hidden meaning   _____

21. An underground vault   _____

22. Subject matter   _____

STOP. Check answers at the end of the chapter.

EXTRA WORD
POWER

> **dis.** Away from; apart; not. When *dis* is placed in
> front of a word, it may give it the opposite meaning.
> It may result in undoing something that was done.
> It may take away some quality, power, rank, and so
> on. For example: *disrobe*—take off clothes; *disband*—
> break up the group; *disable*—make an object or some-
> one not able to do something; *disloyal*—not loyal;
> *disapprove*—to not approve of; to regard as not worthy;
> *dishonest*—not honest; not to be trusted. How many
> more words with *dis* can you supply?
>
> **sub.** Under; beneath; below; lower in rank. *Sub* is
> added to the beginning of many words. For example:
> *submarine*—undersea ship; *subfloor*—floor beneath;
> *subtraction*—the act of taking something away; *sub-
> set*—something that is under the larger set; *subcom-
> mittee*—a committee under the original committee.
> Check your dictionary to find many more words be-
> ginning with *sub*.

Additional Words Derived from Combining Forms

From your knowledge of combining forms, can you define the following words?

1. **chronometer** (kro · nom′ e · ter) *n.* *As the car's **chronometer** was always correct, I usually went by that time.*

_____

2. **anachronism** (a · nach · ro · nism) (a · nak′ ro · niz · um) *n.* *An example of an **anachronism** in a film would be to have an automobile present in a set representing the Middle Ages.*

_____

3. **synchronize** (syn · chro · nize) (sin′ kro · nīze) *v.* *We **synchronized** our watches to make sure that we all had the same time.*

_____

4. **concession** (con · ces · sion) (kon · sesh′ un) *n.* *In order to settle the strike, both sides had to make a number of **concessions**.*

_____

5. **procession** (pro · ces · sion) (pro · sesh′ un) *n.* *The **procession** continued to move forward in an orderly manner even though it was raining very hard.*

_____

6. **recession** (re · ces · sion) (re · sesh′ un) *n.* *During a **recession**, when unemployment is high, economists try to figure out ways to stimulate the economy.*

_____

7. **secede** (se · sēde′) *v.* *During the Civil War, the South **seceded** from the Union.*

_____

8. **subscription** (sub · scrip · tion) (sub · skrip′ shun) *n.* *Each year when I take out a **subscription** for my favorite magazine, I sign a form promising to pay a certain amount of money for the delivery of the magazine.*

_____

9. **untenable** (un · ten′ a · bul) *adj.* *Her position on the issue was such an **untenable** one that we all agreed not to support her.*

_____

10. **detain** (de · tāin′) *v.* *The man at the airport was **detained** by the police because they thought that he was a criminal attempting to flee the country.*

_____

11. **retentive** (re · ten′ tive) *adj.* *Arthur has such a **retentive** memory that he can recall details from things he studied or read over twenty years ago.*

_____

12. **tenacious** (te · na · cious) (te · nā′ shus) *adj. He had such **tenacious** feelings on that issue that no one could change his mind.*

STOP. Check answers at the end of the chapter.

©1966 United Feature Syndicate, Inc.

Practice for Additional Words Derived from Combining Forms

Directions: Match each word with the *best* definition.

_____ 1. chronometer

_____ 2. concession

_____ 3. anachronism

_____ 4. recession

_____ 5. synchronize

_____ 6. untenable

_____ 7. tenacious

_____ 8. retentive

_____ 9. secede

a. having the ability to keep things in

b. to withdraw from

c. an instrument used to measure time

d. the act of going back

e. a parade

f. an act of giving in

g. something out of time order

h. to cause to agree in rate or speed

_____ 10. subscription

_____ 11. procession

_____ 12. detain

i. an agreement to pay some money for something

j. to stop; to delay

k. stubborn

l. not able to be held or defended

STOP. Check answers at the end of the chapter.

CROSSWORD PUZZLE 4

Directions: The meanings of many of the combining forms from Exercises 10–12 follow. Your knowledge of these combining forms will help you to solve this crossword puzzle. Note that *combining form* is abbreviated as *comb. f.*

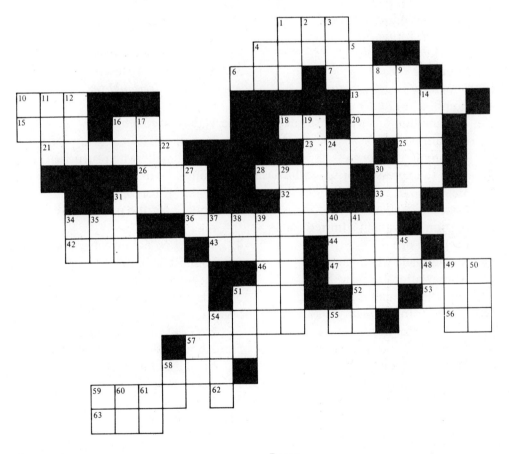

Across

1. Meaning of comb. f. *deca*

Down

1. You pay this on money you earn

4. Salesmen like to make lots of
6. Comb. f. for *poison*
7. Comb. f. for *skin*
10. Comb. f. for *other*
13. Sound a duck makes
15. Homonym of *two*
16. Comb. f. for *one who*
18. Rhymes with *ham*
20. Until, to
21. Comb. f. for *knowledge*
23. Comb. f. for *upon*
25. Homonym of *two*
26. Comb. f. for *lead*
28. Comb. f. for *down*
30. Comb. f. for *take*
31. Belonging to me
32. Comb. f. for *back*
33. Abbreviation for *railroad*
34. Comb. f. for *before*
36. Rule by the people
42. Intention
43. Geometry is a ____ course
44. Comb. f. for *under*
46. Exclamation of surprise, suspicion or triumph
47. Antonym of *actor*
51. Used to express surprise, enthusiasm
52. Means *look*; ____ and behold
53. Comb. f. for *through*
54. A courageous man admired for his brave deeds
55. Sound made when laughing
56. Abbreviation for *New York*
57. Something small is a little ____
58. Comb. f. for *woman*
59. Comb. f. for *time*
62. Fourth letter of the alphabet
63. Meaning of *uni*

2. Abbreviation for *elevated train*
3. Boy's name
4. Homonym of *sew*
5. Comb. f. for *follow*
8. You ____ faster than you walk
9. What a thing is made of
10. A preposition meaning "on" or "near"
11. Comb. f. for *speech; word*
12. Comb. f. for state of, act of, or result of
14. Home for chickens
16. Rhymes with *has*
17. Comb. f. for *laughter*
18. Comb. f. for *without*
19. Comb. f. for *measure*
22. On a nice day it shines
24. Way of saying *father*
27. Comb. f. for *go*
29. Comb. f. for *ancient*
30. Comb. f. for *secret*
31. Way of saying *mother*
34. Same as # 24 Down
35. Comb. f. for *laughter*
37. Comb. f. for *in*
38. Way of saying *mother*
39. Meaning of *ali*
40. Sound made when surprised
41. Comb. f. for *circle*; *wheel*
45. Comb. f. for *one who*
48. Ending for the past tense of regular verbs
49. When you do a wrong, you commit a ____
50. Meaning of *dict*
51. Rhymes with *let*
54. Refers to the rear
57. You say this when you leave
58. Abbreviation for a doctor who has a general practice
59. Same as # 25 Across
60. Comb. f. for *in*
61. A pronoun

STOP. Check answers at the end of the chapter.

WORD SCRAMBLE 4

Directions: Word Scramble 4 is based on words from Exercises 10–12. The meanings are your clues to arranging the letters in correct order. Write the correct word in the blank.

Meanings

1. aenttn   _____ a person who occupies property

2. nctonte   _____ subject matter

3. cuneqsee   _____ the following of one thing after another

4. busqseetnu   _____ following soon after

5. rhicaac   _____ belonging to an earlier period

6. iloglohcnroac   _____ arranged in time order

7. eenocdc   _____ to give in

8. cereped   _____ to go before

9. yccrtip   _____ mysterious

10. onedidtuc   _____ the act of drawing a conclusion

11. noceylc   _____ system of violent and destructive whirlwinds

12. notcroucd   _____ one who leads or guides

13. geuorplo   _____ an introduction to a play

14. gloclia   _____ relating to correct reasoning

15. eeiuoglp   _____ something added to the end of a book

16. metadire   _____ a straight line passing through the center of a circle

17. ffuesr   _____ to feel pain

18. enofrencec   _____ a discussion or meeting on some important matter

19. libbyoipragh   _____ a listing of books

20. eiifnt   _____ having a limit or end

21. literef   _____ able to produce a large crop

22. laeapcb   _____ having ability

23. pitacve   _____   a prisoner

24. onticpere   _____   the manner of receiving someone

25. cceeiovn   _____   to think; to believe

26. ceideve   _____   to mislead by lying

27. urdiclei   _____   to make fun of

28. cionxpete   _____   something or one that is left out

29. rontippece   _____   the act of being aware of something through the senses

30. nosegdai   _____   to determine what is wrong with

31. orgpsonsi   _____   a prediction or conclusion regarding the course of a disease

32. armedlottsigo   _____   a skin doctor

33. dipetraiinac   _____   a children's doctor

34. oxict   _____   referring to poison

35. ropetmrya   _____   lasting for a short period of time

36. redopyhcim   _____   under the skin

STOP. Check answers at the end of the chapter.

ANALOGIES 4

Directions: Find the word from the following list that *best* completes each analogy. There are more words listed than you need.

Word List

infinitesimal, infinite, dialogue, dialect, finite, diagram, diameter, chronometer, reference, captor, bibliography, biography, pediatrician, epilogue, inference, deride, prognosis, diagnosis, catalog, tenacious, deceive, transparent, toxicologist, preface, procession, agnostic, adult, decimate, pedagogue, content, fertile, mouth, visage, cyclone, contemporary, ancient, archaic, consequence.

1. Clock : chronometer :: stubborn :_____.

2. Beginning : end :: prologue :_____.

3. Enthusiasm : apathy :: immeasurable : _____ .

4. Deference : respect :: ridicule : _____.

5. Skin : dermatologist :: poison :_____.

6. Limp : wilted :: parade :_____.

7. Extemporaneous : prepared :: dissatisfied :_____ .

8. Woman : gynecologist :: child :_____.

9. Lawyer : counselor :: teacher :_____.

10. Potentate : monarch :: current :_____.

11. Deportment : behavior :: effect :_____.

12. Snow : blizzard :: wind : _____.

13. Wrist : arm :: nose : _____ .

14. Archaic : ancient :: bluff :_____ .

15. Salary : employee :: ransom :_____ .

16. Alarm : warn :: dynamite : _____.

17. Sheer : opaque :: sterile : _____.

18. God : atheist :: knowing :_____.

19. Shawl : scarf :: deduction : _____.

20. Gait : trot :: speech :_____.

STOP. Check answers at the end of the chapter.

MULTIPLE-CHOICE VOCABULARY TEST 4

Directions: This is a test on words in Exercises 10–12. Words are presented according to exercises. *Do all exercises before checking answers.* Underline the meaning that *best* fits the word.

Exercise 10

1. prologue
   a. added to the end of a book
   b. introduction to a play
   c. correct reasoning
   d. conversation

2. logical
   a. relating to correct reasoning
   b. relating to an introduction
   c. a listing of names
   d. added to the end of a book

3. catalog
   a. added to the end of a book
   b. an introduction
   c. conversation
   d. a listing of names, titles, and so on, in some order

4. epilogue
   a. conversation
   b. a listing of books
   c. addition to the end of a book
   d. an introduction

5. dialogue
   a. introduction
   b. conversation
   c. at the end of a book
   d. refers to reasoning

6. diagram
   a. divides circle in half
   b. conversation
   c. outline figure showing relationships
   d. introduction

7. diameter
   a. line dividing a circle in half
   b. an outline showing relationships in a circle
   c. an outline
   d. a map

8. bibliography
   a. a listing of books on a subject
   b. a note in a book
   c. refers to books
   d. the study of spelling

9. final
   a. able to produce
   b. limited number
   c. last
   d. refers only to tests

10. finite
    a. the end of a play
    b. at the end of a book
    c. added to a book
    d. having a limit or an end

11. infinite
    a. ends in time
    b. endless
    c. ends
    d. certain number

12. fertile
    a. a producer
    b. able to produce a large crop
    c. refers to soil
    d. refers to children

13. fertilization
    a. a producer
    b. what one puts on soil
    c. union of sperm and egg
    d. refers to children

14. reference
    a. a person who sends things
    b. a chapter in a book
    c. a recommendation from a person
    d. a letter

15. preference
    a. a note in a book
    b. a note in a book sending you for information
    c. a recommendation
    d. someone or something you choose over another

16. transfer
   a. to carry or send from one place to another
   b. a sender
   c. a carrier
   d. to cross

17. conference
   a. a convention
   b. a friendly get-together
   c. a discussion or meeting on some important matters
   d. refers to science meetings

18. suffer
   a. to be able to take pain
   b. to put up with pain
   c. to feel pain
   d. refers to pain

19. circumference
   a. the distance across a circle
   b refers to measurement
   c. the distance around a circle
   d. refers to a globe

Exercise 11

20. capable
   a. something for the head
   b. able to wear hats
   c. refers to power
   d. having ability

21. captive
   a. a prisoner
   b. a hunter
   c. a kidnapper
   d. a searcher

22. conceive
   a. to learn
   b. to conceal
   c. to teach
   d. to think

23. deceive
   a. to believe
   b. to lead
   c. to mislead by lying
   d. to tell

24. reception
   a. to receive something
   b. the manner of receiving someone
   c. the manner of thinking
   d. the act of taking

25. exception
   a. something or one that is left out
   b. being included
   c. being invited
   d. refers to leaving

26. perception
   a. a sense
   b. senses of seeing and hearing
   c. act of knowing something
   d. act of becoming aware of something through the senses

27. capsule
   a. a spaceship
   b. a rocket
   c. an instrument
   d. a removable part of a rocket or an airplane

177

28. ridiculous   a. funny   c. something not nice
                    b. unworthy of consideration   d. something not helpful

29. ridicule   a. to laugh   c. to make someone the object of mockery
                    b. to joke   d. to be cruel

30. diagnose   a. to make a predicdiction   c. to give an examination
                    b. to make a prediction concerning someone's illness   d. to determine what is wrong with someone after an examination

31. prognosis   a. refers to recovery   c. refers to knowing what is wrong
                    b. refers to illness   d. a prediction concerning an illness

32. pediatrician   a. a woman who is a doctor   c. a doctor who specializes in foot diseases
                    b. a doctor   d. a children's doctor

33. gynecologist   a. a woman who is a doctor   c. a doctor who is a specialist
                    b. a doctor   d. a doctor who specializes in women's diseases

34. toxic   a. deadly   c. unsafe
                    b. poisonous   d. unclear

35. dermatologist   a. a skin disease   c. a skin doctor
                    b. a doctor   d. refers to skin

36. hypodermic   a. a needle   c. area above the skin
                    b. referring to the area under the skin   d. skin

37. hypothesis   a. any guess   c. an unproved conclusion
                    b. any idea   d. an unproved conclusion drawn from known facts

38. temporary   a. referring to time   c. referring to a short time period
                    b. referring to a waiting period   d. referring to a time period

39. contemporary   a. referring to what is ancient   c. referring to a short period of time
                    b. referring to a time period   d. referring to what is modern

40. tenant
   - a. one who takes care of apartments for a salary
   - b. one who lives on property belonging to another
   - c. one who takes care of buildings for a salary
   - d. one who holds things

41. content
   - a. subject matter
   - b. refers to courses
   - c. refers to teaching
   - d. refers to learning

42. maintain
   - a. to keep up in good repair
   - b. to help someone
   - c. to carry
   - d. to hold

43. content
   - a. worried
   - b. unsure
   - c. unhappy
   - d. satisfied

44. sequence
   - a. coming before
   - b. coming after
   - c. following
   - d. following one after the other

45. consequence
   - a. an arrangement
   - b. in order
   - c. an effect
   - d. following

46. subsequent
   - a. in order
   - b. following
   - c. a result
   - d. an arrangement

47. cycle
   - a. refers to time
   - b. refers to the wind
   - c. refers to the mind
   - d. a round of years or ages

48. cyclone
   - a. a wind
   - b. a rainstorm
   - c. system of violent and destructive whirlwinds
   - d. a round of years or ages

49. archaeology
   - a. study of rocks
   - b. study of rulers
   - c. ancient life
   - d. study of the life and culture of ancient people

50. archaic
   - a. refers to rulers
   - b. the study of ancient cultures
   - c. ancient
   - d. a time period

51. chronological   a. referring to disease   c. referring to an outline
                               b. arranged in time order   d. referring to an ancient time

52. chronic   a. time   c. continuing for a long time
                      b. time period   d. not returning

53. concede   a. going before   c. to accomplish what one started out to do
                      b. coming after   d. to give in

54. precede   a. to go forward   c. to give in
                      b. to come before   d. to accomplish things

55. proceed   a. to come before   c. to go back
                      b. to go forward   d. to give in

56. succeed   a. to accomplish what one started out to do   c. to go forward
                      b. to give in   d. to go back

57. abbreviation   a. a short person   c. refers to short
                          b. a shortened form of a word or phrase   d. a cutoff of something

58. conductor   a. head of a company   c. one who takes
                       b. an orchestra leader   d. one who takes away

59. deduction   a. act of leading away   c. a conclusion
                       b. act of leading   d. act of leading to

60. cryptic   a. a hidden vault   c. an underground vault
                      b. a mysterious vault   d. having a hidden or secret meaning

61. crypt   a. having a hidden meaning   c. a vault
                     b. having a secret meaning   d. an underground vault

TRUE/FALSE TEST 4

Directions: This is a true/false test on Exercises 10–12. Read each sentence carefully. Decide whether it is true or false. Put a *T* for *true* or an *F* for *false* in the blank. The number after the sentence tells you if the word is from Exercise 10, 11, or 12.

_____ 1. A bibliography is a listing of reference words. 10

180

_____ 2. _Prologue_ and _dialogue_ are antonyms. 10

_____ 3. A <u>diagram</u> helps to give a description of something by using an outline figure to show relationships among things.

_____ 4. _Podiatrist_ and _pediatrician_ are synonyms. 11

_____ 5. Something <u>contemporary</u> must be <u>archaic</u>. 11, 12

_____ 6. _Content_ meaning "subject matter" and _content_ meaning "satisfied" are homographs. 12

_____ 7. When I was <u>preceded</u> by Alan in the parade, Alan came after me. 12

_____ 8. The number of <u>deductions</u> on my paycheck refers to money I get from savings bonds. 12

_____ 9. <u>Antitoxin</u> is used by scientists to <u>diagnose</u> a patient's condition. 11

_____ 10. A <u>prognosis</u> is usually based on a doctor's <u>diagnosis</u> and makes a prediction about a patient's recovery. 11

_____ 11. An <u>agnostic</u> is one who is sure of his or her beliefs. 11

_____ 12. _Demagogue_ and _pedagogue_ are synonyms. 11

_____ 13. A <u>pediatrician</u> is a foot doctor. 11

_____ 14. A misanthrope is also a <u>misogynist</u>. 11

_____ 15. A bachelor must be a <u>misogynist</u>. 11

_____ 16. An <u>archaeologist</u> is one who is ancient. 12

_____ 17. The word _conceive_ can mean "to become pregnant" and "to think of." 11

_____ 18. Something that is <u>finite</u> must end. 10

_____ 19. When something is an <u>exception</u> to a rule, it means that it belongs to the rule. 11

_____ 20. _Crypt_ refers to a hidden message. 12

_____ 21. In order to be <u>logical</u>, you must use correct reasoning. 10

_____ 22. An <u>epilogue</u> is what is sometimes given at the beginning of a play to the audience. 10

_____ 23. A <u>capable</u> person is one with ability. 11

_____ 24. _Consequence_ and _affect_ are synonyms. 12

_____ 25. When something is <u>subsequent</u> to something else, it comes before it. 12

_____ 26. <u>Chronological</u> order does not have to refer to time order. 12

_____ 27. When someone <u>maintains</u> something, he or she keeps it up. 12

_____ 28. It is <u>logical</u> to assume that if *A* is taller than *B* and *B* is taller than *C,* then *A* is taller than *C.* 10

_____ 29. The <u>consequences</u> of actions would be the results of them. 12

_____ 30. The terms *deduction* and *inference* can be synonyms. 12, 10

_____ 31. When someone is able to make a conclusion from the general to the particular, that is a <u>deduction</u>. 12

_____ 32. When someone is able to gain information from statements that are indirectly stated, that is a <u>deduction.</u> 12

_____ 33. When you are a <u>captive</u>, you are always a prisoner in jail. 11

_____ 34. Something <u>temporary</u> can last for an infinite time period. 11

_____ 35. When <u>fertilization</u> takes place, it means a woman has <u>conceived</u> 10, 11

STOP. Check answers for both tests at the end of the chapter.

SCORING OF TESTS

Multiple-Choice Vocabulary Test			True/False Test	
Number Wrong	*Score*		*Number Wrong*	*Score*
0–4	Excellent		0–4	Excellent
5–9	Good		5–7	Good
10–13	Weak		8–10	Weak
Above 13	Poor		Above 10	Poor
Score_____			Score_____	

1. If you scored in the excellent or good range on *both tests,* you are doing well. Go on to Chapter Six.

2. If you scored in the weak or poor range on either test, turn to the next page and follow directions for Additional Practice. Note that the words on the test are arranged so that you can tell in which exercise to find them. This will help you if you need additional practice.

ADDITIONAL PRACTICE SETS

A. Directions: Write the words you missed on the tests from the three exercises in the space provided. Note that the tests are presented so that you can tell to which exercises the words belong.

Exercise 10 Words Missed

1. _____   6. _____

2. _____   7. _____

3. _____   8. _____

4. _____   9. _____

5. _____   10. _____

Exercise 11 Words Missed

1. _____   6. _____

2. _____   7. _____

3. _____   8. _____

4. _____   9. _____

5. _____   10. _____

Exercise 12 Words Missed

1. _____   6. _____

2. _____   7. _____

3. _____   8. _____

4. _____   9. _____

5. _____   10. _____

B. Directions: Restudy the words that you have written down on this page. Study the combining forms from which those words are derived. Do Step I and Step II for those you missed. Note that Step I and Step II of the combining forms and vocabulary derived from these combining forms are on the following pages:

Exercise 10—pp. 139–142.

Exercise 11—pp. 149–152.

Exercise 12—pp. 159–163.

C. Directions: Do Additional Practice 1 on pp. 184–185 if you missed words from Exercise 10. Do Additional Practice 2 on pp. 185–186 if you missed words from Exercise 11. Do Additional Practice 3 on pp. 186–188 if you missed words from Exercise 12. Now go on to Chapter Six.

A. Directions: Following are the combining forms presented in Exercise 10. Match the combining form with its meaning.

_____ 1. dia   a. end

_____ 2. cata   b. down

_____ 3. log, logo   c. through

_____ 4. fin   d. book

_____ 5. biblio   e. speech; word

_____ 6. fer   f. before; forward

_____ 7. epi   g. bring; bear; yield (give up)

_____ 8. pro   h. upon; beside; among

STOP. Check answers at the end of the chapter.

B. Directions: Following are the words presented in Exercise 10. Match the word with its meaning.

_____ 1. prologue   a. to feel pain

_____ 2. logical   b. outline figure showing relationships

_____ 3. catalog

_____ 4. epilogue   c. last

_____ 5. dialogue   d. someone or something chosen over another

_____ 6. diagram

_____ 7. diameter   e. a listing of books on a subject

_____ 8. bibliography   f. endless

_____ 9. final   g. a discussion or meeting on an important matter

_____10. finite

_____11. infinite   h. section added to the end of a book

_____12. fertile

_____13. reference   i. a listing of names, titles, and so on, in some order

_____14. fertilization

_____15. preference   j. distance around a circle

                                     k. having an end

                                     l. the union of sperm and egg

_____16. transfer

_____17. conference

_____18. suffer

_____19. circumference

m. able to produce

n. referring to correct reasoning

o. a recommendation

p. introduction to a play

q. to carry or send from one place to another

r. a line that divides a circle in half

s. conversation

STOP. Check answers at the end of the chapter.

Additional Practice 2 for Exercise 11

A. Directions: Following are the combining forms presented in Exercise 11. Match the combining form with its meaning.

_____ 1. cap, cep

_____ 2. gnosi, gnosis

_____ 3. ped, pedo

_____ 4. tox, toxo

_____ 5. gyn, gyno

_____ 6. temp, tempo, tempor

_____ 7. hypo

_____ 8. derm, dermo

_____ 9. ri, ridi, risi

a. skin

b. laughter

c. under

d. take; receive

e. child

f. woman

g. knowledge

h. time

i. poison

STOP. Check answers at the end of the chapter.

B. Directions: Following are the words presented in Exercise 11. Match the word with its meaning.

_____ 1. capable

_____ 2. captive

_____ 3. conceive

_____ 4. deceive

_____ 5. reception

a. to mock or view in a scornful way

b. modern

c. a children's doctor

d. prediction concerning an illness

e. poisonous

_____ 6. exception

_____ 7. perception

_____ 8. capsule

_____ 9. ridiculous

_____10. ridicule

_____11. diagnose

_____12. prognosis

_____13. pediatrician

_____14. gynecologist

_____15. toxic

_____16. dermatologist

_____17. hypodermic

_____18. hypothesis

_____19. temporary

_____20. contemporary

f. having ability

g. doctor who specializes in women's diseases

h. an unproved conclusion drawn from known facts

i. to think

j. something or one that is left out

k: to mislead by lying

l. referring to the area under the skin

m. unworthy of consideration

n. a becoming aware of something through the senses

o. a prisoner

p. manner of receiving someone

q. lasting for a short period of time

r. to determine what is wrong with someone after an examination

s. a removable part of a rocket or airplane

t. a skin doctor

STOP. Check answers at the end of the chapter.

Additional Practice 3 for Exercise 12

A. Directions: Following are the combining forms presented in Exercise 12. Match the combining form with its meaning.

_____ 1. ten, tent, tain

_____ 2. cede, ceed

_____ 3. sequi

_____ 4. cycl, cyclo

a. short; brief

b. ancient

c. hold

d. lead

_____ 5. chron, chrono   e. circle; wheel

_____ 6. archae, archaeo   f. secret; hidden

_____ 7. crypto, crypt   g. follow

_____ 8. duc   h. go; give in; yield (give in)

_____ 9. brevi   i. time

STOP. Check answers at the end of the chapter.

B. Directions: Following are the words presented in Exercise 12. Match the word with its meaning.

_____ 1. tenant

_____ 2. content

_____ 3. content

_____ 4. maintain

_____ 5. sequence

_____ 6. consequence

_____ 7. subsequent

_____ 8. cycle

_____ 9. cyclone

_____ 10. archaeology

_____ 11. archaic

_____ 12. chronological

_____ 13. chronic

_____ 14. concede

_____ 15. precede

_____ 16. proceed

_____ 17. succeed

_____ 18. abbreviation

_____ 19. conductor

_____ 20. deduction

_____ 21. cryptic

_____ 22. crypt

a. the study of the life and culture of ancient people

b. to go forward

c. to come before

d. to give in

e. one who lives on property belonging to another

f. a result

g. satisfied

h. a round of years or ages

i. the following of one thing after another

j. a system of violent and destructive whirlwinds

k. subject matter

l. to keep up

m. following

n. a shortened form of a word or phrase

o. ancient

p. having a hidden meaning

q. a conclusion

r. underground vault

s. continuing for a long time
and returning

t. orchestra leader; one in charge
of a train

u. arranged in time order

v. to accomplish what one started
out to do

STOP. Check answers at the end of the chapter.

ANSWERS

Exercise 10 (pp. 139-149)

Practice A

(1) fertilization, (2) diagram, (3) epilogue, (4) dialogue, (5) finite, (6) conference, (7) bibliography, (8) preference, (9) prologue, (10) final, (11) infinite, (12) catalog, (13) logical, (14) reference, (15) fertile.

Practice B

(1) prologue, (2) dialogue, (3) epilogue, (4) diagram, (5) bibliography, (6) final, (7) finite, (8) infinite, (9) conference, (10) diameter, (11) circumference, (12) transfer, (13) logical, (14) catalog, (15) fertile, (16) reference, (17) preference, (18) suffer, (19) fertilization.

Practice C

1. (a) dia, (b) cata, (c) log, (d) fin, (e) biblio, (f) fer, (g) epi, (h) pro.
2. (a) infinite, (b) bibliography, (c) final, (h) fertile, (i) finite, (j) logical, (k) catalog, (l) dialogue, (m) fertilization, (n) circumference, (o) diameter, (p) epilogue (q) diagram, (r) suffer, (s) reference, (t) preference, (u) conference.
3. d, e, f, g, v.
4. (d) suicide, (e) prologue, (f) incredible, (g) illegal, (v) transfer.

Combining Form and Word Square

```
I  P  C  C  O  T  E  F  I  N  A  L  C
A  R  I  A  B  R  P  B  I  B  L  I  O
F  E  R  T  I  L  I  Z  A  T  I  O  N
D  F  C  A  B  A  L  B  I  O  E  C  F
I  E  U  L  L  L  O  G  I  C  A  L  E
A  R  M  O  I  S  G  D  N  F  P  O  R
M  E  F  G  O  U  U  I  F  E  R  R  E
E  N  E  E  G  F  E  A  I  R  O  A  N
T  C  R  E  R  F  O  G  N  T  S  R  C
E  E  E  R  A  E  A  R  I  I  C  C  E
R  M  N  E  P  R  I  A  T  L  I  H  O
O  A  C  I  H  L  A  M  E  E  I  S  T
R  B  E  C  Y  D  I  A  L  O  G  U  E
```

Additional Words Derived from Combining Forms (pp. 147–148)

1. **inference.** Something derived by reasoning; something that is not directly stated but suggested in the statement; a logical conclusion that is drawn from statements; a deduction.

2. **proficient.** Knowing something very well; able to do something very well.

3. **dialect.** A variety of speech; a regional form of a standard language.

4. **monologue.** A long speech by one person; a dramatic sketch performed by one actor.

5. **definitive.** Conclusive; final; most nearly complete or accurate.

6. **finale.** The last part; end; the concluding movement of a musical composition; the last scene of an entertainment.

7. **affinity.** Close relationship; attraction to another.

8. **infinitesimal.** Too small to be measured; very minute.

9. **deference.** Respect; a giving in to another's opinion or judgment.

10. **defer.** To leave to another's opinion or judgment; to delay; to postpone; to put off for a future time.

Practice for Additional Words Derived from Combining Forms (p. 149)

(1) d, (2) c, (3) j, (4) g, (5) b, (6) h, (7) f, (8) i, (9) a, (10) e.

Exercise 11 (pp. 149–158)

Practice A

(1) q, (2) p, (3) o, (4) r, (5) n, (6) m, (7) a, (8) e, (9) h, (10) f, (11) d, (12) g, (13) c, (14) k, (15) b, (16) l, (17) i, (18) j, (19) t, (20) s.

Practice B

(1) hypothesis, (2) ridiculous, (3) dermatologist, (4) capsule, (5) hypodermic, (6) diagnose, (7) captive, (8) temporary, (9) prognosis, (10) toxic, (11) capable, (12) ridicule, (13) contemporary, (14) exception, (15) reception, (16) pediatrician, (17) conceive, (18) deceive, (19) gynecologist, (20) perception.

Practice C

(1) capable, (2) reception, (3) deceive, (4) conceive, (5) ridiculous, (6) ridicule, (7) capsules, (8) perception, (9) exception, (10) hypodermic, (11) hypothesis, (12) contemporaries, (13) prognosis, (14) diagnose, (15) pediatrician, (16) gynecologist, (17) dermatologist, (18) toxic, (19) temporary, (20) captive.

Additional Words Derived from Combining Forms (pp. 157–158)

1. **misogynist.** Hater of women.

2. **agnostic.** Professing uncertainty; one who is not for or against; one who doubts that the ultimate cause (God) and the essential nature of things are knowable.

3. **epidermis.** Outermost layer of skin.

4. **pedagogue.** A teacher.

5. **antitoxin.** Something used against bacterial poison; a substance formed in the body that counteracts a specific toxin; the antibody formed in immunization with a given toxin, used in treating certain infectious diseases or in immunizing against them.

6. **toxicologist.** One who specializes in the study of poisons.

7. **derisive.** Mocking; jeering.

8. **intercept.** To stop or interrupt the course of.

9. **susceptible.** Easily influenced by or affected with; especially liable to.

10. **perceptive.** Being aware; having insight, understanding, or intuition, as a *perceptive* analysis of the problems involved.

11. **tempo.** The rate of speed at which a musical composition is supposed to be played; rate of activity.

12. **extemporaneous.** Done or spoken without special preparation; makeshift.

Practice for Additional Words Derived from Combining Forms (p. 158)

(1) d, (2) h, (3) j, (4) f, (5) a, (6) i, (7) e, (8) l, (9) k, (10) c, (11) g, (12) b.

Exercise 12 (pp. 159–171)

Practice A

(1) archaic; (2) concede; (3) cryptic, (4) crypt, (5) tenant; (6) content;
(7) maintain; (8) sequence; (9) content; (10) consequence; (11) deduction
(12) archaeology; (13) chronological; (14) cycle; (15) chronic; (16) cyclone;
(17) succeed; (18) abbreviation; (19) proceed; (20) precede; (21) conductor
(22) subsequent.

Practice B

(1) tenant, (2) content, (3) sequence, (4) maintain, (5) consequence, (6) cyclone, (7) cycle, (8) homicide, (9) conductor, (10) chronic, (11) proceed, (12) television, (13) succeed, (14) content, (15) cryptic, (16) abbreviation, (17) concede, (18) corpse, (10) morgue, (20) subsequent, (21) hypothesis, (22) deduction, (23) description, (24) local, (25) illegal.

Practice C

(1) content, (2) maintain, (3) sequence, (4) consequence, (5) tenant, (6) subsequent, (7) none—archaeology, (8) archaic, (9) cycle, (10) cyclone, (11) none—chronological, (12) none—proceed, (13) none—concede, (14) none—precede, (15) chronic, (16) none—succeed, (17) abbreviation, (18) none—conductor, (19) deduction, (20) cryptic, (21) crypt, (22) content.

WORD SQUARE

D	E	D	U	C	T	I	O	N	E	S	A
C	O	N	S	E	Q	U	E	N	C	E	B
R	A	C	U	M	A	I	N	T	H	E	B
Y	R	Y	B	C	Y	C	L	E	R	M	R
P	C	C	S	O	P	C	E	N	O	A	E
T	H	L	E	N	U	O	C	A	N	I	V
I	C	O	Q	T	C	N	O	N	I	N	I
C	O	N	U	E	O	T	N	T	C	T	A
H	L	E	E	N	N	E	T	E	A	A	T
R	O	I	N	T	A	N	E	O	N	I	I
O	G	N	T	C	O	T	C	E	D	N	O
N	Y	A	R	C	H	A	I	C	A	O	N

Additional Words Derived from Combining Forms (pp. 169–170)

1. **chronometer.** A very accurate clock or watch; an instrument used to measure time.

2. **anachronism.** Something out of time order; an error in chronology (the science of measuring time in fixed periods, and arranging dates in their proper order) in which a person, an object, or an event is assigned an incorrect date or period.

3. **synchronize.** To cause to agree in rate or speed; to happen or take place at the same time.

4. **concession.** An act of giving in; a right granted by the government or other authority for a specific purpose.

5. **procession.** A parade, as a funeral *procession*; any continuous course.

6. **recession.** The act of going back; in economics, the decline of business activity.

7. **secede.** To withdraw from.

8. **subscription.** An agreement; a promise in writing to pay some money; an agreement to receive something and pay for it.

9. **untenable.** Not able to be held or defended.

10. **detain.** To stop; to hold; to keep from proceeding; to delay.

11. **retentive.** Having the ability to retain or keep in things; tenacious, as a *retentive* memory; having a good memory.

12. **tenacious.** Stubborn; tough; holding or tending to hold strongly to one's views, opinions, rights, and so on; retentive, as a *tenacious* memory.

Practice for Additional Words Derived from Combining Forms (pp. 170–171)

(1) c, (2) f, (3) g, (4) d, (5) h, (6) l, (7) k, (8) a, (9) b, (10) i, (11) e, (12) j.

Crossword Puzzle 4 (pp. 171–172)

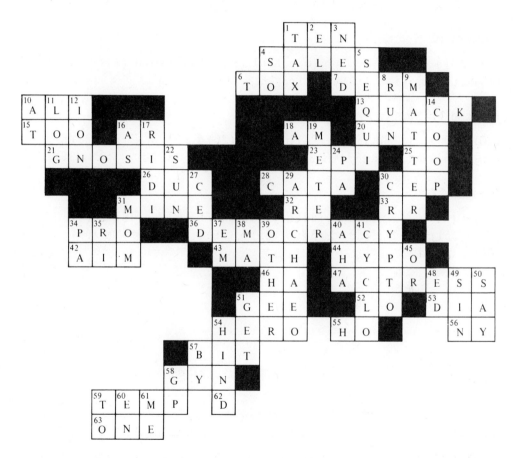

Word Scramble 4 (pp. 173–174)

(1) tenant, (2) content, (3) sequence, (4) subsequent, (5) archaic, (6) chronological, (7) concede, (8) precede, (9) cryptic, (10) deduction, (11) cyclone, (12) conductor, (13) prologue, (14) logical, (15) epilogue, (16) diameter, (17) suffer, (18) conference, (19) bibliography, (20) finite, (21) fertile, (22) capable, (23) captive, (24) reception, (25) conceive, (26) deceive, (27) ridicule, (28) ex-

ception, (29) perception, (30) diagnose, (31) prognosis, (32) dermatologist, (33) pediatrician, (34) toxic, (35) temporary, (36) hypodermic.

Analogies 4 (pp. 174-175)

(1) tenacious, (2) epilogue, (3) finite, (4) deride, (5) toxicologist, (6) procession, (7) content, (8) pediatrician, (9) pedagogue, (10) contemporary, (11) consequence, (12) cyclone, (13) visage, (14) deceive, (15) captor, (16) decimate, (17) fertile, (18) agnostic, (19) inference, (20) dialect.

Multiple-Choice Vocabulary Test 4 (pp. 175-180)

Exercise 10

(1) b, (2) a, (3) d, (4) c, (5) b, (6) c, (7) a, (8) a, (9) c, (10) d, (11) b, (12) b, (13) c, (14) c, (15) d, (16) a, (17) c, (18) c, (19) c.

Exercise 11

(20) d, (21) a, (22) d, (23) c, (24) b, (25) a, (26) d, (27) d, (28) b, (29) c, (30) d, (31) d, (32) d, (33) d, (34) b, (35) c, (36) b,[1] (37) d,[2] (38) c, (39) d.

Exercise 12

(40) b, (41) a, (42) a, (43) d, (44) d, (45) c, (46) b, (47) d, (48) c,[3] (49) d, (50) c, (51) b, (52) c, (53) d, (54) b, (55) b, (56) a, (57) b, (58) b, (59) c, (60) d, (61) d.

---

[1]*Referring to the area under the skin* is a better answer than a *needle* because *hypodermic* refers to an area under the skin. The term *hypodermic* also means "a needle that is injected under the skin" or "a hypodermic needle." However, the best answer is *b* because a needle could refer to any needle, including a sewing needle.

[2]*An unproved conclusion drawn from known facts* is a better answer than *an unproved conclusion* because it is a more complete answer.

[3]*System of violent and destructive whirlwinds* is a better answer than *a wind* because it is more complete and less general. This is also true for numbers 32, 33, and 35 in Exercise 11. It is not enough to state *doctor* as the answer. That is too general. You must state the kind of doctor the person is.

True/False Test 4 (pp. 180–182)

(1) F, (2) F, (3) T, (4) F, (5) F, (6) T, (7) F, (8) F, (9) F, (10) T, (11) F, (12) F, (13) F, (14) T[4], (15) F[5], (16) F, (17) T, (18) T, (19) F, (20) F, (21) T, (22) F, (23) T, (24) F[6], (25) F, (26) F, (27) T, (28) T, (29) T, (30) T, (31) T, (32) T, (33) F, (34) F, (35) T.

STOP. Turn to p. 182 for the scoring of the tests.

Additional Practice Sets (pp. 183–188)

Additional Practice 1

A. (1) c, (2) b, (3) e, (4) a, (5) d, (6) g, (7) h, (8) f.
B. (1) p, (2) n, (3) i, (4) h, (5) s, (6) b, (7) r, (8) e, (9) c, (10) k, (11) f, (12) m, (13) o, (14) l, (15) d, (16) q, (17) g, (18) a, (19) j.

Additional Practice 2

A. (1) d, (2) g, (3) e, (4) i, (5) f, (6) h, (7) c, (8) a, (9) b.
B. (1) f, (2) o, (3) i, (4) k, (5) p, (6) j, (7) n, (8) s, (9) m, (10) a, (11) r, (12) d, (13) c, (14) g, (15) e, (16) t, (17) l, (18) h, (19) q, (20) b.

Additional Practice 3

A. (1) c, (2) h, (3) g, (4) e, (5) i, (6) b, (7) f, (8) d, (9) a.
B. (1) e, (2) g,[7] (3) k,[8] (4) l, (5) i, (6) f, (7) m, (8) h, (9) j, (10) a, (11) o, (12) u, (13) s, (14) d, (15) c, (16) b, (17) v, (18) n, (19) t, (20) q, (21) p, (22) r.

---

[4] Because a misanthrope is a hater of mankind, in the generic sense, he or she would also have to be a hater of women.

[5] It does not necessarily follow that a man who is not married is a hater of women. He may be unmarried for many reasons—one might be that he likes many women a lot.

[6] *Consequence* and *effect* have the same meanings. *Affect* means "to influence."

[7] The answer for 2 can be either *g* or *k*.

[8] The answer for 3 can be either *k* or *g*.

CHAPTER SIX

EXERCISE 13

Step I. Combining Forms

A. Directions: A list of combining forms with their meanings follows. Look at the combining forms and their meanings. Concentrate on learning each combining form and its meaning. Cover the meanings, read the combining forms, and state the meanings to yourself. Check to see if you are correct. Now cover the combining forms, read the meanings, and state the combining forms to yourself.

Combining Forms	*Meanings*
1. tend, tens, tent	stretch; strain
2. bello, belli	war
3. civ, civis	citizen
4. polis	city
5. pac, pax	peace
6. voc, vox	voice; call
7. post	after
8. ambi	both

197

B. Directions: Cover the preceding meanings. Write the meanings of the following combining forms.

Combining Forms	Meanings
1. tend, tens, tent	_____
2. bello, belli	_____
3. civ, civis	_____
4. polis	_____
5. pac, pax	_____
6. voc, vox	_____
7. post	_____
8. ambi	_____

Step II. Words Derived from Combining Forms

1. **attention** (at · ten · tion) (at · ten′ shun) *n.* Mental concentration; care; a position of readiness; act of courtesy. *When children are tired, they cannot pay attention because they have lost their ability to concentrate.*

2. **intention** (in · ten · tion) (in · ten′ shun) *n.* Aim; goal; purpose. *Although, as a child, her intention was to become a famous archaeologist, she never thought that she would achieve her goal.*

3. **tension** (ten · sion) (ten′ shun) *n.* The act of stretching or the condition of being stretched tight; mental strain. *The parents' tension was so great when their child was kidnapped that they did not know how long they could stand the mental strain.*

4. **intense** (in · tense′) *adj.* Having great or extreme force; very strong; existing or occurring to a high or extreme degree. *The heat was so intense from the fire that the firemen could not enter the building.*

5. **belligerent** (bel · lij′ er · ent) *adj.* Warlike. *n.* Any nation, person, or group engaged in fighting or war. *Because he has such a belligerent manner, he gets into a lot of fights.*

6. **civilian** (ci · vil · ian) (si · vil′ yun) *n.* One who is not in the military; *adj.* Of civilians; nonmilitary. *It is good to be a civilian again after spending three years in the army.*

7. **civics** (civ · ics) (siv′ iks) *n.* (Used in the singular.) The part of political science dealing with the study of civic affairs and the rights and responsibilities of citizenship. *In school I took a course in civics because I wanted to learn more about the individual citizen's rights and responsibilities.*

198

8. **civilization** (civ · i · li · za · tion) (siv′ i · li · zā · shun) *n.* A state of human society that has a high level of intellectual, social, and cultural development; the cultural development of a specific people, country, or region. *In a **civilization**, a high level of intellectual, social, and cultural development is supposed to exist.*

9. **civil** (siv′ il) *adj.* Of a citizen or citizens; relating to citizens and their government; relating to ordinary community life as distinghished from military or church affairs; courteous or polite. ***Civil** liberties are the rights that individual citizens have.*

10. **politics** (pol′ i · tiks) *n.* (Although plural, it is usually looked upon as singular.) The science or art of government or of the direction and management of public or state affairs. *Person who are in **politics** are interested in the management of public or state affairs.*

11. **politician** (pol · i · ti · cian) (pol′ i · tish · un) *n.* A person engaged in politics; a person involved in the science or art of government; a person who seeks advancement or power within an organization by dubious (doubtful) means. *The **politicians** met to determine whom they would support for office.*

12. **metropolitan** (met · ro · pol′ i · tun) *adj.* Referring to a major city center and its surrounding area. *n.* A person who inhabits a metropolis or one who has the manners and tastes associated with a metropolis. *I like to live in a **metropolitan** area so that I can be close to the kinds of stores, theaters, and restaurants that are found in large cities.*

13. **vocal** (vo · cal) (vō′ kul) *adj.* Referring to the voice; having voice; oral; freely expressing oneself in speech, usually with force; speaking out. *When we strained our **vocal** cords from yelling at the basketball game, we could hardly use our voices the next day.*

14. **vocabulary** (vo · cab · u · lar · y) (vō · kab′ yu · lar · ē) *n.* (*pl.* **ies**) A list of words and phrases, usually arranged alphabetically, that are defined or translated from another language; a stock of words possessed by an individual or a group. *You are gaining a larger **vocabulary** from doing the exercises involving lists of words and their definitions.*

15. **vocation** (vo · ca · tion) (vō · kā′ shun) *n.* A calling; a person's work or profession. *Sharon chose a **vocation** similar to her father's because she wanted to follow in his footsteps.*

16. **ambiguous** (am · big′ ū · øus) *adj.* Having two or more meanings. *What he said was so **ambiguous** that I couldn't figure out if he wanted me to stay or go.*

SMIDGENS   by Bob Cordray

© 1973 National News Syndicate. Reprinted by permission of Bob Cordray.

17. **postscript** (pōst′ skript) *n.* Something added to a letter after the writer's signature; something added to written or printed legal papers. *The abbreviation of* **postscript**, *something added to a letter after the writer has signed his name, is P.S.*

18. **pacify** (pac · i · fy) (pas′ i · fī) *v.* To bring peace to; to calm; to quiet. *The speaker tried to* **pacify** *the mob, but he could not calm them down.*

Special Note

The term *civilian,* which refers to someone who is not in the military, is used also by policemen and by others who wear special uniforms to refer to someone out of uniform.

Step III. Practice

A. Directions: Each sentence has a missing word. Choose the word that *best* completes the sentence. Write the word in the blank. *All words fit in.*

Word List

postscript, metropolitan, attention, vocabulary, vocal, pacify, intention, belligerent, ambiguous, tension, civics, politics, vocation, civil, intense, civilian, civilization, politician.

1. Some people pay a lot of _____ to their appearance because they want to look their best.

2. His _____ is to be on time, but he is always late.

3. Too much _____ gives me a headache because I can't take mental strain.

4. Try to be less _____ about everything you do because your forcefulness is beginning to annoy us.

200

5. The homeowners were so angry at their increase in taxes that it was difficult to _____ them.

6. The crowd had become so_____ that the police had to call for reinforcements to help control the crowd.

7. My course in _____ helped me gain a better understanding of the individual citizen's rights and responsibilities.

8. After being in military service for a decade, I decided to leave and become a(n)_____ again.

9. Being in _____ has opened my eyes to a lot of problems that exist in the management and direction of state affairs.

10. As a(n) _____who was elected to office, I hope to be able to make some contribution to society.

11. Some people are _____ on purpose because they do not want to say exactly how they stand on an issue.

12. This is not the_____ I planned for in school, but it's the only work I could get.

13. Although we have reached a high level of_____ , wars still exist among nations.

14. Persons involved in the_____ rights movement try to protect citizens' rights as established in the Constitution.

15. The singer had to cancel her performance because she had something wrong with her_____cords.

16. Because I need a good_____to read successfully, I am studying words and their meanings.

17. After I signed my name to the letter I was writing, I had to add a(n) _____because I thought of something else I wanted to say.

18. When we moved to a(n)_____ area, I sold my car and decided to become a pedestrian because it was too difficult to keep a car in the city.

STOP. Check answers at the end of the chapter.

B. Directions: Underline the word that *best* fits the definition(s).

1. Mental concentration; act
   of courtesy
   a. tension   c. attention
   b. intense   d. intention

2. Aim; goal
   a. attention   c. tension
   b. intense   d. intention

3. Mental strain   a. intense   c. attention

                                 b. tension   d. intention

4. Very strong   a. tension   c. intention

                                 b. attention   d. intense

5. Warlike   a. intense   c. belligerent

                                 b. tension   d. civil

6. One not in the military   a. civil   c. civilian

                                 b. civilization   d. civics

7. Cultural development of   a. civics   c. civilian

    a people   b. civilization   d. civil

8. Polite; of a citizen or   a. civics   c. civilian

    citizens   b. politician   d. civil

9. Science of government dealing   a. civilization   c. politics

    with the management of public   b. civics   d. civilian

    affairs

10. The part of political science   a. civics   c. civilization

    dealing with citizens' rights   b. politics   d. civilian

    and responsibilities

11. A person involved in the   a. civilian   c. politics

    science or art of government   b. vocation   d. politician

12. Referring to a major city   a. civilization   c. politics

    center and its surrounding   b. metropolitan   d. civilian

    area

13. Something added to a letter   a. vocabulary   c. metropolitan

    after the signature   b. ambiguous   d. postscript

14. List of words that are defined   a. vocation   c. vocal

                                     b. vocabulary   d. postscript

15. Referring to the voice   a. vocal   c. vocabulary

                                     b. vocation   d. ambiguous

16. A person's work   a. vocation   c. politics

                                   b. civilization   d. vocal

17. To calm   a. civil   c. pacify

                                   b. vocal   d. postscript

18. Having two or more meanings   a. vocabulary   c. vocal

                                   b. attention   d. ambiguous

STOP. Check answers at the end of the chapter.

C. Directions: In the following sentences give the meaning that *best* fits the underlined word.

1. During the president's speech we paid very close <u>attention</u> to what he was saying because we did not want to miss one word. _____

2. From his conflicting actions, I can't figure out what his <u>intentions</u> are. _____

3. There was considerable <u>tension</u> in the room after the instructor told the students that they needed to do more work. _____

4. The light was so <u>intense</u> that it hurt my eyes. _____

5. I avoid <u>belligerent</u> people because I am peaceful. _____

6. How do you feel now that you're out of uniform and a <u>civilian</u> again? _____

7. I think that courses in <u>civics</u> will help me because I want to become a politician. _____

8. Western <u>civilization</u> is different from Eastern <u>civilization</u> because the cultural development of the West and that of the East have been different. _____

9. There have been so many scandals in <u>politics</u> in the past decade that many people feel that elected officials are more concerned with selfish interests than with the proper management of public affairs. _____

10. It is sometimes difficult to be <u>civil</u> to persons who are rude and impolite. _____

11. As a <u>politician</u>, I intend to serve wisely the people who elected me to office. _____

12. What a change it was when we moved from a rural area, which is all farmland, to a <u>metropolitan</u> area. _____

13. The students were very <u>vocal</u> in their demands. _____

14. After studying so many words and their meanings, I have a larger <u>vocabulary</u>. _____

15. My <u>vocation</u> is one that requires a lot of time, effort, and study. _____

16. The directions for the exam were so <u>ambiguous</u> that half the class did one thing, and the other half did something else. _____

17. I needed to add a <u>postscript</u> to my letter because I thought of more things to say after I had already signed my letter. _____

18. The mother tried to <u>pacify</u> her screaming child by giving him a toy. _____

STOP. Check answers at the end of the chapter.

ance, ence. Act of; state of; quality of. When *ance* is found at the end of a word, it means "act of," "state of," or "quality of." In an earlier exercise you met *tion,* which also means "state of" or "act of." If *ance* or *ence* is added to a word, the word changes to a noun. For example: **maintain.** To carry on or continue; to keep up. *I will maintain your car while you are away so that it will be in good working condition when you get home.* **maintenance.** The act of keeping up. *The maintenance of your car is important if it is to stay in good running condition.* Examples of words with *ance, ence: dependence*—act of trusting; act of relying on someone for support; *assistance*—act of helping; *sequence*—the state of following; *conferance*—the act of meeting in a group. How many more words can you supply?

al. Relating to. When *al,* meaning "relating to," is added to the end of a word, the word is usually an adjective. For example: *vocal*—relating to the voice; *local*—relating to a place; *manual*—relating to the hand; *annual*—relating to the year; *universal*—relating to all; *legal*—relating to law; *apodal*—relating to being without feet; *nautical*—relating to sailing. How many more words can you supply?

Additional Words Derived from Combining Forms

From your knowledge of combining forms, can you define the following words?

1. **postmortem** (pōst · mor′ tem) *adj. n. The doctor performed a **postmortem** examination on the victim in order to determine the cause of his death.*

   _____

2. **posterior** (pos · te · ri · or) (pos · tir′ ē · or) *adj. n. This blueprint shows the **posterior** section of the new airplane our company is building.*

   _____

3. **posterity** (pos · ter′ i · tē) *n. Artists hope that their works will be admired by **posterity**.*

   _____

4. **posthumously** (post · hu · mous · ly) (pos′ chū · møus · lē) *adv. Many artists gain recognition **posthumously** rather than during their lifetime.*

---

5. **provoke** (pro · vōkǿ′) *v. The speaker's words so **provoked** some of the people in the audience that they stood up and booed.*

---

6. **pacifist** (pas′ i · fist) *n. As George was a **pacifist**, he would not join the armed forces or any other military organization.*

---

7. **megalopolis** (meg · a · lop′ o · lis) *n. The area between Boston and Washington, D.C., is considered one **megalopolis** because of the high density of population between these two cities.*

---

8. **ambidextrous** (am · bi · dex · trous) (am · bē · dek′ strøus) *adj. Some **ambidextrous** people use their left hands for writing and their right hands for everything else.*

---

9. **vociferous** (vō · sif′ er · øus) *adj. The couple in the apartment above us were so **vociferous** that the neighbors called the police to complain about the noise.*

---

10. **convocation** (con · vo · ca · tion) (kon · vo · kā′ shun) *n. At the beginning of the college year, a **convocation** is held, at which time the president of the college gives his welcoming address.*

---

11. **avocation** (av · o · ca · tion) (av · o · kā′ shun) *n. Stamp collecting is my father's **avocation**.*

---

12. **detention** (de · ten · tion) (de · ten′ shun) *n. The accused person was held in **detention** until bail was raised for him.*

---

13. **detente** (de · tente) (dā · tantǿ′) *n. The president said that **detente** between the two nations would continue if each country lived up to its agreements.*

STOP. Check answers at the end of the chapter.

Practice for Additional Words Derived from Combining Forms

Directions: Match each word with the *best* definition.

_____ 1. postmortem		a. a group of people called together
_____ 2. posterity		b. easing of strained relations
_____ 3. posterior		c. one very large city
_____ 4. provoke		d. an autopsy
_____ 5. pacifist		e. one who is against war
_____ 6. ambidextrous		f. confinement; a keeping back
_____ 7. convocation		g. in the rear
_____ 8. detente		h. after death
_____ 9. vociferous		i. future generations
_____ 10. posthumously		j. to stir up; irritate
_____ 11. detention		k. able to use both hands equally well
_____ 12. megalopolis		l. hobby
_____ 13. avocation		m. clamorous

STOP. Check answers at the end of the chapter.

EXERCISE 14

Step I. Combining Forms

A. Directions: A list of combining forms with their meanings follows. Look at
   the combining forms and their meanings. Concentrate on learning each combining form and its meaning. Cover the meanings,
   read the combining forms, and state the meanings to yourself.
   Check to see if you are correct. Now cover the combining forms,
   read the meanings, and state the combining forms to yourself.
   Check to see if you are correct.

Combining Forms	*Meanings*
1. luc, lum	light; clear
2. err	wander
3. soph	wise

4. sist, sta	stand
5. nov	new
6. dorm	sleep
7. peri	around
8. hyper	over; above; excessive (very much)
9. ego	I; me; the self

B. Directions: Cover the preceding meanings. Write the meanings of the following combining forms.

Combining Forms	Meanings
1. luc, lum	_____
2. err	_____
3. soph	_____
4. sist, sta	_____
5. nov	_____
6. dorm	_____
7. peri	_____
8. hyper	_____
9. ego	_____

Step II. Words Derived from Combining Forms

1. **lucid** (lū′ sid) *adj.* Clear; easily understood; bright; shining. *When I ask a question about something I don't understand, I like to receive a **lucid** explanation.*

2. **translucent** (trans · lū′ sent) *adj.* Permitting light to go through but not permitting a clear view of any object. *We had a **translucent** screen on our window that allowed light to go through, but persons looking through the screen could not get a clear view of what was in the room.*

3. **error** (er′ ŗor) *n.* A mistake; something done, said, or believed incorrectly; a wandering from what is correct. *The **error** in judgment seemed like a very small mistake, but it caused a great deal of suffering for others.*

4. **sophisticated** (so · phis · ti · cat · ed) (so · fis′ ti · kāt · id) *adj.* Not in a simple, natural, or pure state; worldly-wise; not naive; cultured; highly complicated; complex; experienced. *Because she has traveled quite a lot and is very cultured, she always acts in a **sophisticated** manner.*

5. **sophomore** (sof′ o · mor∉) *n.* A second-year student in American high schools or colleges; an immature person; one who thinks he or she knows more than is the case. *As a college* **sophomore**, *I have two more years to go before I graduate.*

6. **philosophy** (phi · los · o · phy.) (fi · los′ o · fē) *n.* (*pl.* **phies**) The study of human knowledge; the love of wisdom and the search for it; a search for the general laws that give a reasonable explanation of something. *Students of* **philosophy** *seek to understand various ideas better.*

7. **circumstance** (cir · cum · stance) (sir′ kum · stans∉) *n.* Something connected with an act, an event, or a condition; (*often pl.*): the conditions, influences, and so on surrounding and influencing persons or actions; formal display, as in *pomp and circumstance. The* **circumstances** *of the suicide were so suspicious that a full-scale investigation was started.*

8. **substitute** (sub′ sti · tūt∉) *v.* To put in place of another person or thing. *n.* One who takes the place of another person; something that is put in place of something else or is available for use instead of something else. *When our teacher was absent, a* **substitute** *took her place.*

9. **consist** (kon · sist′) *v.* To be made up of. *I know what the plan* **consists** *of because I made it up myself.*

10. **assist** (a∂ · sist′) *v.* To give help to. *n.* An act of helping. *John* **assisted** *his friend because his friend had always helped him.*

11. **distant** (dịs′ tant) *adj.* Separated or apart by space and/or time; away from; far apart; not closely related. *A* **distant** *relative came to visit us, but I had never met her before because I am not closely related to her.*

12. **obstacle** (ob · sta · cle) (ob′ sta · kul) *n.* Something that stands in the way or opposes; something that stops progress; an obstruction. *There were many* **obstacles** *that stood in the way of my going to college, but I was able to overcome each of them.*

13. **persist** (per · sist′) *v.* To continue in some course or action even though it is difficult. *Even though she knew that it would be difficult to become an actress, she* **persisted** *in trying.*

14. **innovation** (in · no · va · tion) (in · ∤o · vā′ shun) *n.* Something newly introduced; a new method; something new. *The man's* **innovation** *saved his company millions of dollars because his new method made it possible to manufacture the product cheaper.*

15. **novel** (nov′ el) *n.* A work of fiction of some length. *adj.* New; strange; unusual. *It takes some people a while to get used to* **novel** *ideas because they do not like anything new or different.*

16. **dormitory** (dor · mi · to · ry) (dor′ mi · tor · ē) *n.* (*pl.* **ries**) A large room in which many persons sleep; a building providing sleeping and living quarters, especially at a school, college, or resort (summer or winter hotel). *Our college **dormitory** houses one hundred students.*

17. **dormant** (dor′ mant) *adj.* Asleep or as if asleep; not active. *Bears are **dormant** during the winter.*

18. **period** (pe · ri · od) (pir′ ē · od) *n.* A portion of time; a portion of time into which something is divided; a punctuation mark that signals a full stop at the end of a sentence, also used after abbreviations. *In high school, the school day was divided into seven class **periods**.*

19. **periodical** (pe · ri · od · i · cal) (pir · ē · od′ i · kul) *adj.* Referring to publications, such as magazines, that appear at fixed time intervals. *n.* A periodical publication. *I have a subscription to a **periodical** that is published every month.*

20. **hypertension** (hy · per · ten · sion) (hī · per · ten′ shun) *n.* High blood pressure. *When someone is diagnosed as having **hypertension**, he or she should have his or her blood pressure checked frequently to make sure that it doesn't get too high.*

21. **egocentric** (e · go · cen · tric) (ē · gō · sen′ trik) *adj.* Self-centered; relating everything to oneself. *He is so **egocentric** that everything he says seems to start with* I, me, *or* my.

Special Note

Hyper, meaning "over," "above," "excessive" (very much), is placed at the beginning of a great number of words. For example:

1. *Hypersensitive*—oversensitive.

2. *Hyperactive*—overactive.

3. *Hyperproductive*—overproductive.

Check your dictionary for more words with *hyper.*

Step III. Practice

A. Directions: Following are a number of sentences with missing words. Choose the word that *best* fits the sentence from the following words, and write it in the blank. *All words fit in.*

Word List

translucent, assist, lucid, circumstance, persist, error, philosophy, distant, substitute, dormitory, sophomore, obstacle, novel, sophisticated, consist, innovation, dormant, hypertension, period, egocentric, periodical.

1. I make the most _____s when I am very excited about something because I don't stop to think.

2. He was not very _____ when he spoke; so we still do not know
   what took place.

3. I like the _____ glass we have in our living room because
   it allows light to come in, but people can't see clearly inside the room.

4. Some scientists may take courses in _____ because they
   are interested in general laws that give reasonable explanations that apply
   to the whole field of science.

5. Under what _____s would you consider taking this job?

6. Now that I'm a(n) _____, I have only two more years after
   this one to graduation.

7. Doctors have more _____equipment today, which helps
   them to diagnose illnesses better.

8. We had a(n) _____ in our geometry class because our regular teacher was out ill.

9. The man needed a(n) _____ to get his car started, but no
   one seemed to want to stop to help.

10. In the not too _____ future, I intend to become a geol-
    ogist.

11. Although I will probably meet many_____s in my life, I
    intend to overcome them.

12. I want to know what the medicine_____ s of because I
    am allergic to some drugs.

13. In the past four decades, many_____ s have been developed
    by man that were never dreamed possible a century ago.

14. Ms. Smith uses_____approaches in teaching her course
    because she finds that students enjoy new ways of learning.

15. The doctor said that the disease was _____ at the moment,
    but it could become active at any time.

16. We have both males and females living in our college_____.

17. I am the kind of person who will_____until I achieve what
    I started out to achieve.

18. Some people are so _____ that they talk only about them-
    selves.

19. The doctor's prognosis for Nancy's mother was not too good because her mother suffers from _____ and has already had one stroke.

20. If this _____ of drought does not end, the farmers will not be able to produce the crops that are needed.

21. I receive a few _____ s every month, but I don't always have time to read all the articles in them.

STOP. Check answers at the end of the chapter.

B. Directions: In the Word Square there are seventeen words from Exercise 14. Find the words in the square and match them with their correct meanings. Note that there are more meanings than words. If there is no word in the square for a meaning, write *none*, and give the word.

WORD SQUARE

I	N	N	O	V	A	T	I	O	N	P	T	S
I	S	P	E	R	S	I	S	T	O	H	R	Q
D	O	D	I	S	T	A	N	T	V	I	A	W
O	P	O	B	S	T	A	C	L	E	L	N	K
R	H	R	L	U	S	S	O	E	L	O	S	T
M	O	M	O	B	Y	S	N	R	I	S	L	D
A	M	I	O	S	N	I	S	R	N	O	U	L
N	O	T	M	T	O	S	I	O	G	P	C	Y
T	R	O	E	I	N	T	S	R	S	H	E	H
R	E	R	R	T	Y	O	T	E	E	Y	N	W
O	L	Y	R	U	L	U	C	I	D	E	T	N
P	M	Y	O	T	O	D	U	E	E	O	R	A
H	O	M	P	E	R	I	O	D	I	C	A	L

Meanings

Words

1. Clear; easily understood   _____

2. Permitting light to go through   _____

3. A mistake _____

4. Worldly-wise _____

5. Second-year student _____

6. The study of human knowledge _____

7. Conditions or influences connected
with an act or event _____

8. To put in place of _____

9. To be made up of _____

10. Give help to _____

11. Separated or apart by space and/or time _____

12. Something in the way of _____

13. Continue in some course even
though it's difficult _____

14. A new idea _____

15. Strange; unusual; long work of fiction _____

16. Large room in which many people sleep _____

17. Asleep; not active _____

18. Portion of time _____

19. Referring to a publication that
is put out at regular intervals _____

20. High blood pressure _____

21. Self-centered _____

STOP. Check answers at the end of the chapter.

C. Directions: In the following sentences, give the meaning that *best* fits the
underlined word.

1. We were able to view a distant star through the telescope. _____

2. The dormant volcano had been inactive for so long that no one expected it
to erupt when it did. _____.

3. Under what circumstances do you feel we should allow such things to take
place?_____

4. The light that shone through the translucent glass made different designs in
our room, depending on the time of day._____

5. Your <u>error</u> in auditing the books is so serious that the mistake could cost you your job. _____

6. Jean was not very <u>lucid</u> when she awakened after having been attacked; so we had to wait until she could be clearer about what had happened. _____

7. Because I don't know what that travel package <u>consists</u> of, I'd like you to tell me exactly what is included._____

8. I took a course in <u>philosophy</u> because I love to examine ideas and deal with such questions as "What is good?" and "What is truth?" _____

9. At college some persons live off campus rather than in a <u>dormitory</u>. _____

10. What picture will you <u>substitute</u> to take the place of the one you took out? _____

11. It gives me a good feeling to be able to <u>assist</u> people when they need help. _____

12. Whenever an <u>obstacle</u> is put in my way that makes things difficult for me, I try to think of ways to remove it. _____

13. The doctors were hoping that the <u>innovations</u> in heart surgery that had just been introduced at the hospital would help to save patients' lives. _____

14. I will <u>persist</u> in doing my work this way, even though it is more difficult, because I know that it is the correct way. _____

15. I always forget to put a <u>period</u> after abbreviations._____

16. When my <u>periodical</u> did not arrive for three months in a row, I wrote to the magazine publisher's office to complain. _____

17. <u>Hypertension</u> is called the "silent killer" because many people are not aware that they have high blood pressure. _____

18. It is difficult to carry on a dialogue with an <u>egocentric</u> person because he or she always seems to be interested only in himself or herself. _____

19. Whenever someone says that I'm behaving like a <u>sophomore</u>, I know that he or she is not giving me a compliment. _____

20. I like to go out with <u>sophisticated</u> people because they are cultured and know how to behave properly. _____

21. I enjoy reading books with <u>novel</u> plots because I like strange or unusual stories._____

STOP. Check answers at the end of the chapter.

inter. Between; among. When *inter* comes at the beginning of a word, it means "between" or "among." *Do not* confuse *inter* with *intra.* For example: *inter-departmental*—between departments; *interdependent*—dependent upon one another; *interstate*—between states; *intercollegiate*—between colleges.

intra. Within; inside of. *Intra* comes at the beginning of a word. It means "within." Do not confuse *intra* with *inter.* For example: *intradepart-mental*—within the department; *intracollegiate*—within the college; *intramural*—within a school or an institution. Can you supply more words beginning with *inter* and *intra?* Check your dictionary for a large list of such words.

Additional Words Derived from Combining Forms

From your knowledge of combining forms, can you define the following words?

1. **perimeter** (pe · rim′ e · ter) *n. The **perimeter** of a circle would be its circumference.*

   _____

2. **periphery** (pe · riph · er · y) (pe · rif′ er · ē) *n. (pl. **eries**) **Periphery** and* perimeter *are synonyms.*

   _____

3. **periscope** (per′ i · skōpe) *n. The sailor in the submarine used the **periscope** to view the approaching destroyer.*

   _____

4. **hyperbole** (hī · per′ bo · lē) *n. When Sharon said that she had walked a million miles today, she was using **hyperbole.***

   _____

5. **illuminate** (il · lū′ · mi · nate) *v. The lights so **illuminated** the room that everything could be seen clearly.*

   _____

6. **egotistic** (ē · gō · tis′ tik) *adj.* *I do not enjoy being in the company of* **egotistic** *people because they are too concerned with themselves.*

_____

7. **novice** (nov′ is) *n.* *Everyone thought that he was an expert rather than a* **novice** *because of the way he handled himself on the tennis court.*

_____

8. **stamina** (stam′ i · na) *n.* *Professional athletes need a lot of* **stamina** *in order to keep playing.*

_____

9. **obstinate** (ob · sti · nate) (ob′ sti · nit) *adj.* *My friend is so* **obstinate** *that once he makes up his mind, he will never change it.*

_____

10. **sophistry** (soph · ist · ry) (sof′ ist · rē) *n.* (*pl.* **ies**) *Some persons are so clever in presenting their illogical arguments that it is difficult to recognize that the arguments are filled with* **sophistry.**

_____

11. **erratic** (er · rat′ ik) *adj.* *Her behavior was so* **erratic** *that we wondered if she was mentally ill.*

_____

12. **periodic** (pe · ri · od · ic) (pir · ē · od′ ik) *adj.* *The phases of the moon are periodic.*

_____

STOP. Check answers at the end of the chapter.

Practice for Additional Words Derived from Combining Forms

Directions: Match each word with the *best* definition.

_____ 1. perimeter	a. to give light to
_____ 2. periphery	b. a beginner
_____ 3. periscope	c. staying power
_____ 4. hyperbole	d. faulty reasoning
_____ 5. egotistic	e. the outer part or boundary of something
_____ 6. illuminate	f. conceited
_____ 7. novice	g. great exaggeration
_____ 8. erratic	

_____ 9. obstinate

_____10. stamina

_____11. sophistry

_____12. periodic

h. an instrument used by a submarine to see all around

i. a measure of the outer part of
   a closed plane figure

j. not regular; not stable

k. stubborn

l. taking place at regular intervals

STOP. Check answers at the end of the chapter.

EXERCISE 15

Step I. Combining Forms

A. Directions: A list of combining forms with their meanings follows. Look
   at the combining forms and their meanings. Concentrate on
   learning each combining form and its meaning. Cover the
   meanings, read the combining forms, and state the meanings to
   yourself. Check to see if you are correct. Now cover the combining forms, read the meanings, and state the combining forms
   to yourself. Check to see if you are correct.

Combining Forms	*Meanings*
1. mitt, miss	send
2. pos, pon	place; set
3. animus, anima	spirit; mind; soul
4. magna	great; large
5. hypn, hypno	sleep
6. feder, fid, fide	trust; faith
7. nasc, nat	born
8. equi	equal
9. pop	people

B. Directions: Cover the preceding meanings. Write the meanings of the following combining forms.

Combining Forms	*Meanings*
1. mitt, miss	_____

2. pos, pon   _____

3. animus, anima   _____

4. magna   _____

5. hypn, hypno   _____

6. feder, fid, fide   _____

7. nasc, nat   _____

8. equi   _____

9. pop   _____

Step II. Words Derived from Combining Forms

1. **mission** (mis · sion) (mish′ un) *n.* Group or team of persons sent some place to perform some work; the task, business, or responsibility that a person is assigned; the place where missionaries carry out their work; a place where poor people may go for assistance. *The astronauts were sent on a special mission to try to locate a missing spaceship.*

2. **permission** (per · mis · sion) (per · mish′ un) *n.* Act of allowing the doing of something; a consent. *I received permission from the instructor to audit her class.*

3. **dismiss** (dis · miss′) *v.* To tell or allow to go; to discharge, as from a job; to get rid of; to have done with quickly; to reject. *The class was dismissed when the period was over.*

4. **admission** (ad · mis · sion) (ad · mish′ un) *n.* Act of allowing to enter; entrance fee; a price charged or paid to be admitted; acknowledgment; a confession, as to a crime. *We did not know we had to pay admission to enter the fair.*

5. **submit** (sub · mit′) *v.* To give in to another; to surrender; to concede; to present for consideration or approval; to present as one's opinion. *I will submit my manuscript to a publisher for possible publication.*

6. **transmit** (trans · mit′) *v.* To send from one place to another; to pass on by heredity; to transfer; to pass or communicate news, information, and so on. *Certain diseases are transmitted from the parent to the child through heredity.*

7. **intermission** (in · ter · mis · sion) (in · ter · mish′ un) *n.* Time between events; recess. *The intermissions between acts in the play were each fifteen minutes long.*

8. **position** (po · si · tion) (po · zish′ un) *n.* An act of placing or arranging; the manner in which a thing is placed; the way the body is placed, as in *sitting position*; the place occupied by a person or thing; the proper or appropriate place, as *in position*; job; a feeling or stand; social standing.

*He had been sitting in that **position** for so long that if he hadn't moved a
little, his legs would have fallen asleep.*

9. **postpone** (pōst · pōng̸') *v.* To put off to a future time; to delay *They had
to **postpone** their annual reading convention for another month because
many members could not come at the scheduled time.*

10. **positive** (poz' i · tiv̸) *adj.* Being directly found to be so or true; real; actual;
sure of something; definitely set; confident. *She was **positive** that she could
describe the men who kidnapped her because they hadn't bothered to blind-
fold her.*

11. **posture** (pos · ture) (pos' chur) *n.* The placing or carriage of the body or
parts of the body; a mental position or frame of mind. *His sitting **posture**
is so poor that after a while it may cause him to have back problems.*

12. **post** (pōst) *n.* A position or employment, usually in government service;
an assigned beat; a piece of wood or other material to be used as a support;
a place occupied by troops. *v.* To inform; to put up (as on a wall); to mail
(as a letter). *Do you like the **post** you have with the government?*

13. **proposal** (pro · po · sal) (pro · pō' zul) *n.* An offer put forth to be accepted or adopted; an offer of marriage; a plan. *As the governor's **proposal**
for a tax plan was not acceptable to the people, the legislators voted against
it.*

14. **animosity** (an · i · mos' i · tē) *n.* (*pl.* **ties**) Hatred; resentment. *She felt great
animosity toward the persons who attacked her father and beat him so badly
that he had to go to the hospital.*

15. **magnanimous** (mag · nan' i · møus) *adj.* Forgiving of insults or injuries; high-
minded; great of soul. *The speaker was very **magnanimous** to overlook the
insults that were yelled at him.*

16. **magnify** (mag' ni · fī) *v.* To increase the size of; to make larger. *The microscope **magnifies** very small objects so that they can be viewed easily.*

17. **magnificent** (mag · nif' i · sent) *adj.* Splendid; beautiful; superb. *The
palace was so **magnificient** that it was difficult to find words to describe
its splendor.*

18. **hypnosis** (hip · nō' sis) *n.* (*pl.* **ses; sēz**) A sleeplike trance that is artificially brought about. *I can't believe that I was put in a state of **hypnosis**
and did all those silly things, because I do not remember anything that
took place.*

19. **federal** (fed' er · al) *adj.* Of or formed by a compact relating to or formed
by an agreement between two or more states, groups, and so on; relating to
a union of states, groups, and so on in which central authority in common
affairs is established by consent of its members. *All the states in the*

*United States joined to form a **federal** government in which common affairs, such as foreign policy, defense, and interstate commerce, are controlled by the government.*

20. **confide** (con · fīdé) *v.* To tell in trust; to tell secrets trustingly. *If you do not want others to know your secrets, **confide** only in people you can trust.*

21. **innate** (iń · nāté) *adj.* Inborn; born with; not acquired from the environment; belonging to the fundamental nature of something; beginning in; coming from. ***Innate** characteristics are those that cannot be acquired after birth.*

22. **postnatal** (pōst · nāt′ ul) *adj.* Occurring after birth. *It is important that all infants receive good **postnatal** care.*

23. **prenatal** (prē · nāt′ ul) *adj.* Being or taking place before birth. *A pregnant woman should take good care of herself so that her unborn child will be receiving good **prenatal** care.*

24. **nature** (na · ture) (nā′ chur) *n.* The necessary quality or qualities of something; sort; kind; wild state of existence; uncivilized way of life; overall pattern or system; basic characteristic of a person; inborn quality; the sum total of all creation; the whole physical universe. *It seems to be his **nature** to behave in such a friendly manner all the time.*

25. **popular** (pop · u · lar) (pop′ yu · lar) *adj.* Referring to the common people or the general public; approved of; admired; liked by most people. *Jack and Herb were voted the most **popular** boys in their class because they were liked by the most people.*

26. **population** (pop · u · la · tion)(pop · u · lā′ shun) *n.* Total number of people living in a country, city, or any area. *According to the census figures, the **population** in the United States is about 220,000,000 people.*

27. **equivalent** (e · quiv · a · lent) (e · kwiv′ a · lent) *adj.* Equal in value, meaning, force, and so on. *The amounts were **equivalent**, so that each person had exactly the same number.*

Special Notes

1. Do not confuse the word *post*, meaning "a position or employment," "a support for a sign," "to inform," and so on, with the combining form *post* meaning "after." The word *post* comes from the combining form *pos, pon,* meaning "place" or "set."

2. The word *innate* meaning "born with" refers to characteristics or qualities with which you are born. You cannot acquire these after birth. The term *innate* can also be applied to things about which you say that something is such an important part of the thing in question that it is necessarily a part of

it. For example: the *innate* weakness of certain kinds of government. Note that "innate weakness" does not mean "inborn weakness." *Inborn* can apply only to living beings.

3. When the term *Federal* is spelled with a capital letter, it means "relating to or supporting the central government of the United States" or "relating to or loyal to the Union cause in the American Civil War of 1861–1865."
   a. The *Federal* Bureau of Investigation is an agency of the United States that investigates violations of *Federal* criminal laws.
   b. The *Federal* soldiers were those who fought for the Union cause in the Civil War.

Step III. Practice

A. Directions: Following are a number of sentences with missing words. Choose the word that *best* fits the sentence. Put the word in the blank. Each word is used only once. *All words fit in.*

Word List

dismiss, mission, population, popular, submit, animosity, equivalent, intermission, admission, transmit, positive, post, magnify, position, prenatal, postnatal, proposal, postpone, posture, magnanimous, confide, federal, magnificent, hypnosis, nature, innate, permission.

1. Tom has to _____ his report to his advisor for approval.

2. The _____ in some cities is so large that there are not enough jobs for all the people.

3. A misanthrope would have _____ toward all people because he or she is a hater of mankind.

4. The men are going on such a secret _____ that even they do not yet know what they are supposed to accomplish.

5. It appears that our jobs are _____ because we have the same duties to perform and we're getting paid the same.

6. I wonder how it feels to be the most _____ person in school and be admired by practically everyone?

7. Have you gained _____ to the school you want to go to in the fall?

8. Did you know that the company will have to _____ a number of persons because it is not as productive as it was?

9. Tonight the network is going to _____ the television program from England to the United States.

10. Will the _____ between events be long or short?

11. Try to _____ the conference for as long as you can so that we can gather more information.

12. The politician running for office was presenting his _____ on the issue of school busing.

13. If you always sit slouched over and never stand up straight, you will have bad _____ .

14. I am _____ that the capital of the United States is Washington, D.C.

15. She has been employed in a very important _____ in government service for the past decade.

16. When Ms. Smith was pregnant, she visited her obstetrician every month to make sure that she was receiving proper _____ care.

17. When Jim's third _____ of marriage was turned down, he began to wonder whether there was something wrong with him.

18. Babies who are born prematurely need special _____ care.

19. _____ people are so great of spirit that they can overlook many things that others of us may not be able to overlook.

20. Some people _____ their errors so that they seem larger than they are.

21. One of the wealthiest men in the world built himself the most _____ mansion that has ever been seen.

22. While under the spell of _____ , I did some very embarrassing things that I would not have done if I had been awake.

23. As she was born with that defect, it is _____ .

24. When we went on our camping trip, we went to a place that was away from all civilization, and we lived in a state of _____ .

25. I _____ only in people I know I can trust.

26. Although in a(n) _____ government all states must obey laws that are common to all, each state does have control of its own internal affairs.

27. In many states you need your parents' _____ in order to be allowed to marry under the age of eighteen.

STOP. Check answers at the end of the chapter.

B. Directions: A list of definitions follows. Give the word that *best* fits the definition. Try to relate the definition to the meanings of the combining forms

Word List

dismiss, admission, submit, transmit, intermission, position, postpone, positive, posture, post, proposal, magnanimous, permission, magnify, magnificent, hypnosis, federal, confide, innate, postnatal, prenatal, nature, popular, population, equivalent, animosity, mission.

1. To send from one place to another _____

2. Sure of something _____

3. A piece of wood or other material to be used as a support_____

4. The manner in which a thing is placed_____

5. Forgiving of insults or injuries _____

6. The placing or carriage of the body _____

7. Time between events_____

8. A sleeplike trance that is artificially brought about _____

9. Splendid _____

10. An offer put forth to be accepted or adopted _____

11. Being before birth_____

12. Born with _____

13. Occurring after birth_____

14. The necessary qualities of something _____

15. Relating to or formed by an agreement among two or more states _____

16. To reveal in trust _____

17. To enlarge _____

18. Hatred_____

19. Total number of people living in a country_____

20. Entrance fee_____

21. Task or responsibility _____

22. Equal in value, meaning, and so on _____

23. Liked by most people _____

24. To delay_____

25. To tell or allow to go _____

26. To give in to another _____

27. A consent _____

STOP. Check answers at the end of the chapter.

C. Directions: Following are sentences containing the meaning of vocabulary presented in Exercise 15. Choose the word that *best* fits the meaning of the word or phrase underlined in the sentence. Put the word in the blank.

Word List

admission, dismissed, popular, position, mission, submit, intermission, equivalent, magnanimous, posts, positive, posture, innate, nature, prenatal, postnatal, magnify, magnificent, postpone, transmit, hypnosis, federal, population, confide, animosity, proposal, permission.

1. Because I did not have the entrance fee, I could not enter the park.
   _____

2. I refuse to give in to that group of people's way of doing things.
   _____

3. After working there for a decade, I was told that I was going to be let go.
   _____

4. I am certain that this is the correct way to put that together. _____

5. The city we visited was exceptionally impressive. _____

6. Could you please put off going on that trip for another two weeks?
   _____

7. Your carriage is so poor when you walk. Can't you straighten up?
   _____

8. We used strong timber to hold up our birdhouse. _____

9. Will there be a break between the acts in the show? _____

10. All week the newsreporters had to pass on information about the floods so that people would know when they could return to their homes.
    _____

11. It's rare to meet someone who can turn the other check and be so forgiving of insults. _____

12. I need something that will increase the size of this print so that I can see it better. _____

223

13. The doctor gave me <u>suggestions to induce a sleeplike trance</u> so that he could try to cure me of my phobia of heights. _____

14. Have you read my <u>plan</u> in full? _____

15. Children need good <u>after birth</u> care._____

16. It's difficult to determine <u>the basic characteristic</u> of a person. _____

17. The color of your eyes is determined by your genes and is an <u>inborn</u> characteristic. _____

18. I always try to give the twins <u>equal</u> attention. _____

19. I am shocked at what my best friend will <u>reveal</u> to me <u>in trust.</u> _____

20. In order to have a good start in life, a child needs good <u>before birth</u> care. _____

21. What type of government are we talking about when we say "relating to a <u>union of states in which central authority in common affairs is established by consent of its members</u>"? _____

22. Some leaders tend to be more <u>admired</u> than others. _____

23. Do you know <u>the total number of people</u> in your community? _____

24. The government would not give its <u>consent</u> to some aliens to remain in this country when it was found out that the aliens had criminal records in their own countries. _____

25. Do you have a <u>special task</u> that you must accomplish? _____

26. Is this <u>the proper place</u> for the chair? _____

27. <u>The hatred</u> that the people felt for the demagogue who attempted to deceive them was evident in their faces. _____

STOP. Check answers at the end of the chapter.

EXTRA WORD
POWER

> **mal.** Bad; ill; evil; wrong; not perfect. *Mal* is found at the beginning of a great number of words. Examples: *malfunction*—to function badly; *malnourished*—badly nourished; *malformed*—abnormally formed; *maltreated*—treated badly. How many more words with *mal* can you supply? Check your dictionary for a list of words beginning with *mal*.
>
> **semi.** Half; not fully; partly; occurring twice in a

period. *Semi* is found at the beginning of a great number of words. For example: *semiblind*—partly blind; *semicircle*—half circle; *semiannual*—twice in a year, every half year; *semistarved*—partly starved; *semiwild*—partly wild. How many more words with *semi* can you supply? Check your dictionary for a long list of words beginning with *semi*.

Additional Words Derived from Combining Forms

From your knowledge of combining forms, can you define the following words?

1. **equivocate** (e · quiv · o · cate) (e · kwiv′ o · cāt₡) *v. He always seems to **equivocate** when he does not want to commit himself to giving an exact answer.*

2. **missile** (mis′ ₡il₡) *n. That big stone, which he used as a **missile**, hit its target.*

3. **remission** (re · mis · sion) (re · mish′ un) *n. The doctors were delighted that the disease had reached a state of **remission** and was now dormant.*

4. **emissary** (em′ i₡ · sa · rē) *n. Usually, an **emissary** is sent to another country to try to learn about the other country's plans and to try to influence the plans.*

5. **intermittent** (in · ter · mit′ ent) *adj. Because the pain was **intermittent**, he had some pain-free moments.*

6. **intercede** (in · ter · sēd₡′) *v. The company's troubleshooter was called upon to **intercede** in the dispute that had hurt relations between the company and the town.*

7. **intervene** (in · ter · vēn¢') v. *Because the strike had been going on for so long, the courts decided to* **intervene** *by asking for a "cooling off" period for both sides.*

_____

8. **proposition** (prop · o · si · tion) (prop · o · zish' un) n. *His* **proposition** *sounded like a very sophisticated plan; so we decided to consider it at our next conference.*

_____

9. **disposition** (dis · po · si · tion) (dis · po · zish' un) n. *Because he has such a good* **disposition**, *I'm sure that he will be very nice to you.*

_____

10. **depose** (de · pōz¢') v. *After some monarchs have been* **deposed**, *they have been executed.*

_____

11. **expound** (ex · pound) (ik · spound') v. *As the class had difficulty understanding the concept of intelligence, the professor* **expounded** *further on it.*

_____

12. **infidelity** (in · fi · del' i · tē) n. *Both spouses were suing for divorce on the grounds of* **infidelity** *because each had found that the other had been unfaithful.*

_____

13. **perfidious** (per · fid' ē · ¢us) adj. *I did not know that I had a* **perfidious** *friend until I heard from others that my secrets had all been told.*

_____

14. **magnate** (mag' nāt¢) n. *Howard Hughes, a* **magnate** *of considerable wealth, lived in seclusion the last years of his life.*

_____

15. **malediction** (mal · e · dic · tión) (mal · e · dik' shun) n. *The words* **malediction** *and* benediction *are antonyms.*

_____

16. **malefactor** (mal' e · fak · tor) n. *When a* **malefactor** *is caught by the police, he usually is sent to jail for his crimes.*

_____

17. **animate** (an' i · māt¢) v. *When Arthur tells a story, he becomes so* **animated** *that every part of him is alive and active.*

_____

STOP. Check answers at the end of the chapter.

Practice for Additional Words Derived from Combining Forms

Directions: Match each word with the *best* definition.

_____ 1. equivocate	a. a criminal; one who does something bad
_____ 2. missile	
_____ 3. remission	b. breach of trust; adultery
_____ 4. proposition	c. a speaking badly of someone
_____ 5. disposition	d. to come between
_____ 6. animate	e. starting or stopping again
_____ 7. malediction	f. a person sent on a special mission
_____ 8. infidelity	
_____ 9. malefactor	g. a temporary stopping of a disease
_____ 10. intervene	h. to remove from a throne or other high position
_____ 11. intercede	
_____ 12. intermittent	i. to come between
_____ 13. emissary	j. to use ambiguous language on purpose
_____ 14. perfidious	
_____ 15. depose	k. a very important or influential person
_____ 16. expound	
_____ 17. magnate	l. a plan put forth for consideration

m. one's usual frame of mind

n. to state in detail

o. to make alive

p. a weapon intended to be thrown

q. treacherous

STOP. Check answers at the end of the chapter.

CROSSWORD PUZZLE 5

Directions: The meanings of many of the combining forms from Exercises 13–15 follow. Your knowledge of these combining forms will help you to solve this crossword puzzle. Note that *combining form* is abbreviated as *comb. f.*

Across

1. Slang for a large crowd
3. A musical syllable
5. Same as # 4 Down
6. Comb. f. for *equal*
7. Comb. f. for *out of; from; lacking*
8. Abbreviation of *mail*
9. Comb. f. for *sleep*
11. A friend
12. Ready to eat

Down

1. Way of saying *mother*
2. Comb. f. for *war*
3. Comb. f. for *faith*
4. Comb. f. for *without*
7. Comb. f. for *wander*
8. Meaning of *homo*
10. Comb. f. for *wrong*
11. Comb. f. for *peace*
13. Comb. f. for *after*

15. Comb. f. for *spirit; mind*
19. You feel this way when you ache
21. Abbreviation of *masculine*
24. An insect
25. Antonym of *happy*
26. Comb. f. for *I; me*
27. An insect
29. Rhymes with *hat*
30. Antonym of *bottom*
31. Meaning of *mono* and *uni*
32. Comb. f. for *one who*
34. Same as # 32 Across
35. Eighth letter of the alphabet
36. Antonym of *actress*
37. Comb. f. for *new*
39. Sixteenth letter of the alphabet
40. Same as # 7 Across
41. Meaning of *hyper*
44. Meaning of *dorm*
48. Meaning of *cura*
49. On a nice day it shines
50. Antonym of *off*
52. Third letter of the alphabet
53. A number rhyming with *fine*
55. The highest card is an _____
56. Another word for *clear*
58. Comb. f. for *one who*
59. Eighteenth letter of the alphabet
60. Thirteenth letter of the alphabet
61. Meaning of *en; em*
62. Same as # 38 Down
64. Pronoun referring to *us*
65. Twenty-fifth letter of the alphabet
66. Antonym of *no*
67. Same as # 61 Across
68. Same as # 18 Down

14. Time period
16. Comb. f. for *large*
17. Not required
18. Comb. f. for *stand*
20. Ending added to form past tense of regular verbs
21. A subway in Paris
22. Something that happened long_____
23. Comb. f. for *wise*
28. Homonym of *two*
29. Same as # 4 Down
33. Abbreviation of *railroad*
34. Antonym of *off*
38. Comb. f. for *voice*
39. Comb. f. for *around*
42. A truck for moving
43. When you take the same books out of the library, you__them
45. Comb. f. for *clear; light*
46. Antonym of *friend*
47. Comb. f. for *city*
51. A woman who lives in a convent
52. Comb. f. for *citizen*
54. Poetic way of saying *before*
57. Contraction for *do not*
63. Same as #52 Across

STOP. Check answers at the end of the chapter.

WORD SCRAMBLE 5

Directions: Word Scramble 5 is based on words from Exercises 13–15. The meanings are your clues to arranging the letters in correct order. Write the correct word in the blank.

1. netttaino   _____ mental concentration

2. stneoin   _____ mental strain

3. gllieeebtnr   _____ warlike

4. aciliinv   _____ one not in the military

5. vlcii   _____ polite

6. tiocispl   _____ the science or art of government

7. locav   _____ referring to voice

8. tocovain   _____ a person's work

9. goubumais   _____ having two or more meanings

10. cayfip   _____ to quiet

11. cludi   _____ clear

12. rerro   _____ mistake

13. phosreomo   _____ second-year student

14. crmuctinecas   _____ something connected with an act

15. bistttuues   _____ to put in place of

16. tasiss   _____ aid

17. blaceost   _____ something in the way

18. stpresi   _____ to continue in some course

19. loven   _____ new

20. mordtan   _____ inactive

21. rediop   _____ a portion of time

22. tegrccineo   _____ self-centered

23. ismnosi   _____ the task or responsibility a person is assigned

24. smissid   _____ to tell to go

25. dimsonias   _____ entrance

26. tusbim   _____ to give in to another

27. trinessimnoi   _____ time between events

28. tenoospp   _____ to put off

29. sitviope   _____ definitely set; sure

30. stop	_____	to inform; piece of timber
31. sloprpao	_____	an offer
32. gaimyfn	_____	to enlarge
33. nosyhpsi	_____	sleeplike trance artificially brought on
34. nodifec	_____	to reveal in trust
35. tanine	_____	born with
36. ratneu	_____	necessary qualities of something
37. luoppra	_____	liked by most people
38. quelineavt	_____	equal to
39. timanysio	_____	hatred

STOP. Check answers at the end of the chapter.

ANALOGIES 5

Directions: Find the word from the following list that *best* completes each analogy. *There are more words in the list than you need.*

Word List

avocation, vocation, vacation, civilian, persist, polite, malediction, convocation, infidelity, tense, intention, novel, malefactor, active, peace, lucid, impolite, intense, expert, novice, inactive, innate, nature, aid, magnificent, dismiss, confide, animosity, oral, vocabulary, civilization, knowledge, proposal, politics, politician, attorney, stubborn, visage, consequence, sequence, affect, cyclone, decimate, fertilization, fertile, agnostic, concession, procession, antitoxin, contemporary, toxicologist, content.

1. Credible : incredible :: benediction :_____ .

2. Uniform : same :: criminal : _____ .

3. Hyper : hypo :: ambiguous :_____ .

4. Admit : deny :: civil :_____ .

5. Independent : dependent :: veteran :_____ .

6. Intention : aim :: assembly : _____ .

7. Quiet : vociferous :: relaxed : _____ .

8. Entrance : exit :: dormant : _____

9. Shy : bashful :: tenacious : _____.

10. Magnify : enlarge :: unfaithfulness : _____

11. Belligerent : war :: pacifist : _____

12. Content : dissatisfied :: love : _____

13. Pine : tree :: banking : _____

14. Infinite : finite :: military : _____

15. Unpopular : popular :: weak : _____

16. Error : mistake :: assist : _____

17. Monotonous : changeless :: continue : _____

18. Provoke : irritate :: unusual : _____

19. Astronomer : stars :: philosopher : _____

20. Position : post :: vocal : _____

STOP. Check answers at the end of the chapter.

MULTIPLE-CHOICE VOCABULARY TEST 5

Directions: This is a test on words in Exercises 13–15. Words are presented according to exercises. *Do all exercises before checking answers.* Underline the meaning that *best* fits the word.

Exercise 13

1. attention
   a. aim
   b. mental strain
   c. mental concentration
   d. very strong

2. intention
   a. mental concentration
   b. extreme force
   c. mental strain
   d. aim

3. tension
   a. mental strain
   b. aim
   c. mental concentration
   d. very strong

4. intense
   a. mental strain
   b. very strong
   c. mental concentration
   d. aim

5. belligerent
   a. aim
   b. very strong
   c. hatred
   d. warlike

6. civilian
   a. polite
   b. a state of human society
   c. refers to citizenship
   d. person not in the military

7. civics
   a. cultural development
   b. not in uniform
   c. polite
   d. the study of the rights and responsibilities of citizenship

8. civilization
   a. dealing with citizens
   b. polite
   c. cultural development, as of a people
   d. not in the military

9. civil
   a. not in uniform
   b. polite
   c. cultural development
   d. the study of the rights and responsibilities of citizens

10. politics
   a. science or art of government
   b. cultural development
   c. rule by people
   d. refers to a city

11. politician
   a. science or art of government
   b. refers to citizens
   c. refers to a city
   d. person engaged in the science or art of government

12. metropolitan
   a. surrounding area of a city
   b. a person involved in city government
   c. city government
   d. referring to a major city center and its surrounding area

13. vocal
   a. manner of speaking
   b. referring to the voice
   c. referring to a person's work
   d. referring to peace

14. vocabulary
   a. refers to work
   b. refers to the voice
   c. refers to new words
   d. list of words that are defined

15. vocation
   a. one's work
   b. voice
   c. outspoken
   d. list of words

16. ambiguous
   a. referring to two
   b. having two or more meanings
   c. referring to many words
   d. referring to words with the same meanings

17. postscript
   a. a letter
   b. something written
   c. a signature
   d. something added to a letter after the writer's signature

18. pacify
   a. an agreement
   b. to calm
   c. to help
   d. to work with

19. lucid
   a. a light
   b. clear
   c. permitting light to go through
   d. to view

20. translucent
   a. a clear view
   b. light
   c. permitting light to go through but not allowing a clear view
   d. light can go through and permits a clear view

21. error
   a. to walk around
   b. to wander off walking
   c. a mistake
   d. to lie

22. sophisticated
   a. worldly-wise
   b. very knowledgeable
   c. not clever
   d. to know how to dress

23. sophomore
   a. third-year student
   b. immature person
   c. someone who is knowledgeable
   d. someone not too smart

24. philosophy
   a. refers to knowledge
   b. wise man
   c. the study of human knowledge
   d. charity

25. circumstances
   a. the conditions surrounding an act
   b. the acts
   c. the events
   d. aims

26. substitute
   a. to put in place of
   b. to place
   c. to set
   d. to take

27. consist
   a. to place
   b. to stand
   c. to put together
   d. to be made up of

28. assist
   a. to stand by
   b. to stand off
   c. to help
   d. to place

29. distant
   a. separated by time and/or space
   b. a relation
   c. refers to space
   d. to stand by

30. obstacle
   a. something helpful
   b. something harmful
   c. something that stands in the way
   d. a large rock

31. persist
   a. to stand around
   b. to move on
   c. to stand for
   d. to continue in some course even when it is difficult

32. innovation
   a. a book
   b. a strange idea
   c. something newly introduced
   d. an immunization

33. novel
   a. refers to a nonfiction book
   b. new
   c. something done over
   d. refers to a biography

34. dormitory
   a. a house
   b. a room
   c. a resort
   d. a building providing sleeping and living quarters at a school

35. dormant
   a. active
   b. inactive
   c. awake
   d. referring to door

36. period
   a. a circle
   b. time
   c. portion of time
   d. portion of something

37. hypertension
   a. mental strain
   b. very strong force
   c. very tired
   d. high blood pressure

38. egocentric
   a. not concerned with self
   b. self-centered
   c. self-sufficient
   d. able to help self

Exercise 15

39. mission
   a. the task or responsibility a person is assigned
   b. a vacation trip
   c. a house
   d. atomic particles

40. permission
   a. weekly allowance
   b. a consent
   c. to give in to
   d. to give

41. dismiss
   a. to leave
   b. to let alone
   c. to tell to go
   d. to go

42. admission
   a. act of allowing to enter
   b. allow to do
   c. refers to money
   d. an allowance

43. submit
   a. to allow to do
   b. to let go
   c. to give in to
   d. to help

44. transmit
   a. to send away
   b. to give in
   c. to let go
   d. to send from one place to another

45. intermission
a. a space
b. time period
c. a responsibility
d. time between events

46. position
a. place occupied by a thing
b. to put off
c. something proper
d. to put away

47. postpone
a. to mail
b. to delay
c. to put away
d. to stay

48. positive
a. the manner of sitting
b. to put off
c. sure of
d. not confident

49. posture
a. a place
b. a setting
c. the manner of carrying the body
d. mental strain

50. post
a. a government job
b. government
c. to put off
d. to serve

51. proposal
a. to put off
b. to send away
c. an acceptance
d. an offer

52. magnanimous
a. large
b. highly spirited
c. forgiving of insults
d. splendid

53. magnify
a. to see from
b. something large
c. to help
d. to enlarge

54. magnificent
a. forgiving of insults
b. large of spirit
c. splendid
d. large

55. animosity
a. full of spirit
b. refers to the mind
c. hatred
d. large of soul

56. hypnosis
a. sleep
b. put to sleep
c. a sleeplike trance artificially brought on
d. a drug

57. federal
a. government
b. relating to states
c. faith in government
d. relating to an agreement between two or more states to join into a union

58. confide
a. faith in
b. to tell in trust
c. to tell everything
d. to give information

59. innate
a. not born
b. acquired after birth
c. birth
d. born with

60. postnatal   a. refers to nose condition   c. born with
     b. occurring before birth   d. occurring after birth

61. prenatal   a. refers to birth   c. occurring before birth
     b. born with   d. occurring after birth

62. nature   a. outside   c. the necessary qualities of something
     b. flowers   d. a person

63. popular   a. people   c. the number of people
     b. approved of   d. lots of people

64. population   a. people   c. liked by people
     b. total number of people living in an area   d. an area in which people live

65. equivalent   a. equal to   c. a comparison
     b. unlike   d. a mathematical sign

TRUE/FALSE TEST 5

Directions: This is a true/false test on Exercises 13–15. Read each sentence carefully. Decide whether it is true or false. Put a *T* for *true* or an *F* for *false* in the blank. The number after the sentence tells you if the word is from Exercise 13, 14, or 15.

_____ 1. When you pay attention to something, you do not need to concentrate. 13

_____ 2. A pacifist is belligerent. 13

_____ 3. A civilian is a member of the armed forces. 13

_____ 4. *Intense* and *tension* are synonyms. 13

_____ 5. If you live in a metropolitan area, you are in or near a major city. 13

_____ 6. If you postpone something, you are putting it off. 15

_____ 7. A proposal is something you must accept. 15

_____ 8. All intermissions are at least ten minutes. 15

_____ 9. A sophisticated plan is a complex plan. 14

_____10. You can clearly see through something translucent. 14

_____11. Politics is the science of people. 13

_____12. Civilization can exist in the wilderness without people. 13

_____13. Your vocation is what you are called. 13

_____14. A postscript is the last paragraph of your essay. 13

_____15. When you are ambiguous, what you say can be taken two ways. 13

_____16. The way you dress would be due to innate factors. 15

_____17. *Equivalent* and *similar* are synonyms. 15

_____18. An egocentric person is concerned with himself or herself. 14

_____19. To persist in a course means you need an assist. 14

_____20. *Civil* and *rude* are antonyms. 13

_____21. An innovation is an archaic plan. 14

_____22. A dormant disease is in remission. 14, 15

_____23. To transmit information means that you send it from one place to another. 15

_____24. *Hypnosis* and *dormant* are synonyms. 15, 14

_____25. *Animosity* and *love* are antonyms. 15

_____26. *Submit* and *concede* are synonyms. 15

_____27. A person who behaves like a sophomore is someone who is worldly-wise. 14

_____28. Federal refers to all unions. 15

_____29. Only astronauts can go on missions. 15

_____30. A novel can be an autobiography. 14

STOP. Check answers for both tests at the end of the chapter.

SCORING OF TESTS

Multiple-Choice Vocabulary Test

Number Wrong	Score
0–4	Excellent
5–10	Good
11–14	Weak
Above 14	Poor
Score _____	

True/False Test

Number Wrong	Score
0–3	Excellent
4–6	Good
7–9	Weak
Above 9	Poor
Score _____	

1. If you scored in the excellent or good range on *both tests,* you are doing well. Go on to Part II.

2. If you scored in the weak or poor range on either test, look below and follow directions for Additional Practice. Note that the words on the tests are arranged so that you can tell in which exercise to find them. This will help you if you need additional practice.

ADDITIONAL PRACTICE SETS

A. Directions: Write the words you missed on the tests from the three exercises in the space provided. Note that the tests are presented so that you can tell to which exercises the words belong.

Exercise 13 Words Missed

1. _____   6. _____
2. _____   7. _____
3. _____   8. _____
4. _____   9. _____
5. _____   10. _____

Exercise 14 Words Missed

1. _____   6. _____
2. _____   7. _____
3. _____   8. _____
4. _____   9. _____
5. _____   10. _____

Exercise 15 Words Missed

1. _____   6. _____
2. _____   7. _____
3. _____   8. _____
4. _____   9. _____
5. _____   10. _____

B. Directions: Restudy the words that you have written down on this page. Study the combining forms from which those words are derived.

Do Step I and Step II for those you missed. Note that Step I and Step II of the combining forms and vocabulary derived from these combining forms are on the following pages:

Exercise 13—pp. 197–200.

Exercise 14—pp. 206–209.

Exercise 15—pp. 216–220.

C. Directions: Do Additional Practice 1 on this page and the next if you missed words from Exercise 13. Do Additional Practice 2 on pp. 241–242 if you missed words from Exercise 14. Do Additional Practice 3 on pp. 242–244 if you missed words from Exercise 15. Now go on to Part II.

Additional Practice 1 for Exercise 13

A. Directions: Following are the combining forms presented in Exercise 13. Match the combining form with its meaning.

_____ 1. tend, tens, tent   a. war

_____ 2. bello, belli   b. city

_____ 3. civ, civis   c. stretch; strain

_____ 4. polis   d. after

_____ 5. pac, pax   e. both

_____ 6. voc, vox   f. peace

_____ 7. post   g. voice; call

_____ 8. ambi   h. citizen

STOP. Check answers at the end of the chapter.

B. Directions: Following are the words presented in Exercise 13. Match the word with its meaning.

_____ 1. attention   a. aim

_____ 2. intention   b. person not in the military

_____ 3. tension   c. cultural development, as of a people

_____ 4. intense   d. mental concentration

_____ 5. belligerent

_____ 6. civilian   e. the science or art of government

_____ 7. civics   f. referring to a major city center and its surrounding area

_____ 8. civilization	g. warlike
_____ 9. civil	h. referring to the voice
_____ 10. politics	i. job; profession
_____ 11. politician	j. able to be taken two or more ways
_____ 12. metropolitan	
_____ 13. vocal	k. having extreme force
_____ 14. vocabulary	l. person engaged in the science or art of government
_____ 15. vocation	
_____ 16. ambiguous	m. the study of the rights and responsibilities of citizenship
_____ 17. postscript	n. to calm
_____ 18. pacify	o. something written after signature
	p. polite; relating to ordinary community life
	q. a list of words with definitions
	r. mental strain

STOP. Check answers at the end of the chapter.

Additional Practice 2 for Exercise 14

A. Directions: Following are the combining forms presented in Exercise 14. Match the combining form with its meaning.

_____ 1. luc, lum	a. wise
_____ 2. err	b. sleep
_____ 3. soph	c. stand
_____ 4. sist, sta	d. light; clear
_____ 5. nov	e. I; me; the self
_____ 6. dorm	f. over; above; excessive
_____ 7. peri	g. wander
_____ 8. hyper	h. around
_____ 9. ego	i. new

STOP. Check answers at the end of the chapter.

B. Directions: Following are the words presented in Exercise 14. Match the word with its meaning.

_____ 1. lucid		a.	second-year student
_____ 2. translucent		b.	to put in place of
_____ 3. error		c.	separated by time and/or space
_____ 4. sophisticated		d.	work of fiction of some length
_____ 5. sophomore		e.	clear
_____ 6. philosophy		f.	something newly introduced
_____ 7. circumstances		g.	inactive
_____ 8. substitute		h.	to continue in some course even when it is difficult
_____ 9. assist		i.	the study of human knowledge
_____ 10. consist		j.	mistake
_____ 11. distant		k.	to help
_____ 12. obstacle		l.	worldly-wise
_____ 13. persist		m.	something in the way of
_____ 14. innovation		n.	something connected with an act
_____ 15. novel		o.	portion of time
_____ 16. dormitory		p.	self-centered
_____ 17. dormant		q.	permitting light to go through but not allowing a clear view
_____ 18. period		r.	high blood pressure
_____ 19. hypertension		s.	a building providing sleeping quarters
_____ 20. egocentric		t.	to be made up of

STOP. Check answers at the end of the chapter.

Additional Practice 3 for Exercise 15

A. Directions: Following are the combining forms presented in Exercise 15. Match the combining form with its meaning.

_____ 1. mitt, miss   a. spirit; mind; soul

_____ 2. pos, pon   b. born

_____ 3. animus, anima   c. place; set

_____ 4. magna   d. people

_____ 5. hypn, hypno   e. trust; faith

_____ 6. feder, fid, fide   f. great; large

_____ 7. nasc, nat   g. equal

_____ 8. equi   h. sleep

_____ 9. pop   i. send

STOP. Check answers at the end of the chapter.

B. Directions: Following are the words presented in Exercise 15. Match the word with its meaning.

_____ 1. mission   a. place occupied by a thing

_____ 2. dismiss   b. sure of

_____ 3. admission   c. time between events

_____ 4. permission   d. the manner of carrying the body

_____ 5. submit   e. to enlarge

_____ 6. transmit   f. referring to agreement of two or more states to join into a union

_____ 7. intermission

_____ 8. position   g. the task or responsibility of a person

_____ 9. postpone

_____ 10. positive   h. sleeplike trance artificially brought on

_____ 11. posture

_____ 12. post   i. occurring after birth

_____ 13. proposal   j. necessary qualities of something or someone

_____ 14. magnanimous

_____ 15. animosity   k. to give in to

_____ 16. magnify   l. to tell to go

_____ 17. magnificent   m. splendid

_____ 18. hypnosis   n. total number of people in an area

_____ 19. federal   o. occurring before birth

_____20. confide

_____21. innate

_____22. postnatal

_____23. prenatal

_____24. nature

_____25. popular

_____26. population

_____27. equivalent

p. forgiving of insults

q. liked by many people

r. government job

s. act of allowing to enter

t. to send from one place to another

u. to tell in trust

v. hatred

w. equal to

x. a consent

y. born with

z. to delay

aa. an offer

STOP. Check answers at the end of the chapter.

ANSWERS

Exercise 13 (pp. 197-206)

Practice A

(1) attention, (2) intention, (3) tension, (4) intense, (5) pacify, (6) belligerent, (7) civics, (8) civilian, (9) politics, (10) politician, (11) ambiguous, (12) vocation, (13) civilization, (14) civil, (15) vocal, (16) vocabulary, (17) postscript, (18) metropolitan.

Practice B

(1) c, (2) d, (3) b, (4) d, (5) c, (6) c, (7) b, (8) d, (9) c, (10) a, (11) d, (12) b, (13) d (14) b, (15) a, (16) a, (17) c, (18) d.

Practice C

(1) mental concentration; (2) aims; (3) mental strain; (4) very strong; (5) warlike; (6) one not in the military; (7) the part of political science dealing with the rights and responsibilities of citizens; (8) cultural development of a people; (9) the science or art of government; (10) polite; (11) one who is in politics; (12) referring to a major city center and surrounding area; (13) freely expressive of opinions; (14) stock of words; (15) work; (16) having two or more meanings; (17) addition to a letter after signature; (18) calm.

Additional Words Derived from Combining Forms (pp. 204–205)

1. **postmortem.** Happening or performed after death; pertaining to an examination of a human body after death; a postmortem examination; autopsy.

2. **posterior.** Located behind; in the rear; later; following after; coming after in order; suceeeding; (*sometimes plural*) the buttocks.

3. **posterity.** Future generations; all of one's descendants (offsprings).

4. **posthumously.** After death.

5. **provoke.** To stir up anger or resentment; to irritate.

6. **pacifist.** One who is against war.

7. **megalopolis.** One very large city made up of a number of cities; a vast, populous, continuously urban area.

8. **ambidextrous.** Able to use both hands equally well.

9. **vociferous.** Of forceful, aggressive, and loud speech; marked by a loud outcry; clamorous.

10. **convocation.** A group of people called together; an assembly.

11. **avocation.** Something one does in addition to his or her regular work, usually for enjoyment; a hobby.

12. **detention.** A keeping or holding back; confinement; the state of being detained in jail.

13. **detente.** Easing of strained relations, especially between nations.

Practice for Additional Words Derived from Combining Forms (p. 206)

(1) d, (2) i, (3) g, (4) j, (5) e, (6) k, (7) a, (8) b, (9) m, (10) h, (11) f, (12) c, (13) l.

Exercise 14 (pp. 206–216)

Practice A

(1) error, (2) lucid, (3) translucent, (4) philosophy, (5) circumstance, (6) sophomore, (7) sophisticated, (8) substitute, (9) assist, (10) distant, (11) obstacle, (12) consist, (13) innovation, (14) novel, (15) dormant, (16) dormitory, (17) persist, (18) egocentric, (19) hypertension, (20) period, (21) periodical.

Practice B

(1) lucid, (2) translucent, (3) error, (4) none—sophisticated, (5) sophomore, (6) philosophy, (7) none—circumstances, (8) substitute, (9) consist, (10) assist, (11) distant, (12) obstacle, (13) persist, (14) innovation, (15) novel, (16) dor-

mitory, (17) dormant, (18) period, (19) periodical, (20) none–hypertension, (21) none–egocentric.

WORD SQUARE

I	N	N	O	V	A	T	I	O	N	P	T	S
I	S	P	E	R	S	I	S	T	O	H	R	Q
D	O	D	I	S	T	A	N	T	V	I	A	W
O	P	O	B	S	T	A	C	L	E	L	N	K
R	H	R	L	U	S	S	O	E	L	O	S	T
M	O	M	O	B	Y	S	N	R	I	S	L	D
A	M	I	O	S	N	I	S	R	N	O	U	L
N	O	T	M	T	O	S	I	O	G	P	C	Y
T	R	O	E	I	N	T	S	R	S	H	E	H
R	E	R	R	T	Y	O	T	E	E	Y	N	W
O	L	Y	R	U	L	U	C	I	D	E	T	N
P	M	Y	O	T	O	D	U	E	E	O	R	A
H	O	M	P	E	R	I	O	D	I	C	A	L

Practice C

(1) separated by distance; far away; (2) inactive; (3) conditions; (4) permitting light to go through; (5) mistake; (6) clear; (7) is made up of; (8) the study of human knowledge; (9) place that houses persons; (10) put in place of; (11) help; (12) obstruction; (13) new methods; (14) continue; (15) punctuation mark; (16) publication issued at fixed time intervals; (17) high blood pressure; (18) self-centered; (19) immature person; (20) cultured; (21) unusual.

Additional Words Derived from Combining Forms (pp. 214–215)

1. **perimeter.** A measure of the outer part or boundary of a closed plane figure; boundary line of a closed plane figure.

2. **periphery.** The outer part or boundary of something.

3. **periscope.** An instrument used by a submarine to see all around.

4. **hyperbole.** Great exaggeration or overstatement.

5. **illuminate.** To give light to; light up; make clear.

6. **egotistic.** Conceited; very concerned with oneself; selfish; vain.

7. **novice.** Someone new at something; a rookie; a beginner.

8. **stamina.** Staying power; resistance to fatigue, illness, and the like.

9. **obstinate.** Stubborn; tenacious.

10. **sophistry.** Faulty reasoning; unsound or misleading but clever and plausible (appearing real) argument or reasoning.

11. **erratic.** Wandering; not regular; not stable.

12. **periodic.** Occurring or appearing at regular intervals.

Practice for Additional Words Derived from Combining Forms (pp. 215-216)

(1) i, (2) e, (3) h, (4) g, (5) f, (6) a, (7) b, (8) j, (9) k, (10) c, (11) d, (12) l.

Exercise 15 (pp. 216-227)

Practice A

(1) submit, (2) population, (3) animosity, (4) mission, (5) equivalent, (6) popular, (7) admission, (8) dismiss, (9) transmit, (10) intermission, (11) postpone, (12) position or proposal, (13) posture, (14) positive, (15) post or position, (16) prenatal, (17) proposal, (18) postnatal, (19) magnanimous, (20) magnify, (21) magnificent, (22) hypnosis, (23) innate, (24) nature, (25) confide, (26) federal, (27) permission.

Practice B

(1) transmit, (2) positive, (3) post, (4) position, (5) magnanimous, (6) posture, (7) intermission, (8) hypnosis, (9) magnificent, (10) proposal, (11) prenatal, (12) innate, (13) postnatal, (14) nature, (15) federal, (16) confide, (17) magnify, (18) animosity, (19) population, (20) admission, (21) mission, (22) equivalent, (23) popular, (24) postpone, (25) dismiss, (26) submit, (27) permission.

Practice C

(1) admission, (2) submit, (3) dismissed, (4) positive, (5) magnificent, (6) postpone, (7) posture, (8) posts, (9) intermission, (10) transmit, (11) magnanimous, (12) magnify, (13) hypnosis, (14) proposal, (15) postnatal, (16) nature, (17) innate, (18) equivalent, (19) confide, (20) prenatal, (21) federal, (22) popular, (23) population, (24) permission, (25) mission, (26) position, (27) animosity.

1. **equivocate.** To use ambiguous language on purpose.

2. **missile.** An object, especially a weapon, intended to be thrown or discharged, as a bullet, an arrow, a stone, and so on.

3. **remission.** A temporary stopping or lessening of a disease; a pardon.

4. **emissary.** A person or an agent sent on a specific mission.

5. **intermittent.** Starting or stopping again at intervals; not continuous; coming and going at intervals.

6. **intercede.** To come between; to come between as an influencing force; to intervene.

7. **intervene.** To come between; to act as an influencing force; to intercede.

8. **proposition.** A plan or something put forth for consideration or acceptance.

9. **disposition.** One's usual frame of mind or one's usual way of reacting; a natural tendency.

10. **depose.** To remove from a throne or other high position; to let fall.

11. **expound.** To state in detail; to set forth; to explain.

12. **infidelity.** Breach of trust; lack of faith in a religion; unfaithfulness of a marriage partner; adultery.

13. **perfidious.** Violating good trust; treacherous; deceitful; deliberately faithless.

14. **magnate.** A very important or influential person.

15. **malediction.** A speaking badly of someone; slander; a curse.

16. **malefactor.** Someone who does something bad; one who commits a crime; a criminal.

17. **animate.** To make alive; to move to action.

Practice for Additional Words Derived from Combining Forms (p. 227)

(1) j, (2) p, (3) g, (4) l, (5) m, (6) o, (7) c, (8) b, (9) a, (10) d or i, (11) i or d, (12) e, (13) f, (14) q, (15) h, (16) n, (17) k.

Crossword Puzzle 5 (pp. 228–229)

Word Scramble 5 (pp. 229–231)

(1) attention, (2) tension, (3) belligerent, (4) civilian, (5) civil, (6) politics, (7) vocal, (8) vocation, (9) ambiguous, (10) pacify, (11) lucid, (12) error, (13) sophomore, (14) circumstance, (15) substitute, (16) assist, (17) obstacle, (18) persist, (19) novel, (20) dormant, (21) period, (22) egocentric, (23) mission, (24) dismiss, (25) admission, (26) submit, (27) intermission, (28) postpone, (29) positive, (30) post, (31) proposal, (32) magnify, (33) hypnosis, (34) confide, (35) innate, (36) nature, (37) popular, (38) equivalent, (39) animosity.

Analogies 5 (pp. 231–232)

(1) malediction, (2) malefactor, (3) lucid, (4) impolite, (5) novice, (6) convocation, (7) tense, (8) active, (9) stubborn, (10) infidelity, (11) peace, (12) animosity,

(13) vocation,[1] (14) civilian, (15) intense, (16) aid, (17) persist, (18) novel, (19) knowledge, (20) oral.

Multiple-Choice Vocabulary Test 5 (pp. 232-237)

Exercise 13

(1) c, (2) d, (3) a, (4) b, (5) d, (6) d, (7) d, (8) c, (9) b, (10) a, (11) d, (12) d, (13) b, (14) d, (15) a, (16) b, (17) d, (18) b.

Exercise 14

(19) b, (20) c, (21) c, (22) a, (23) b, (24) c, (25) a, (26) a, (27) d, (28) c, (29) a, (30) c, (31) d, (32) c, (33) b, (34) d, (35) b, (36) c, (37) d, (38) b.

Exercise 15

(39) a, (40) b, (41) c, (42) a, (43) c, (44) d, (45) d, (46) a, (47) b, (48) c, (49) c, (50) a, (51) d, (52) c, (53) d, (54) c, (55) c, (56) c, (57) d, (58) b, (59) d, (60) d, (61) c (62) c, (63) b, (64) b, (65) a.

True/False Test 5 (pp. 237-238)

(1) F, (2) F, (3) F, (4) F, (5) T, (6) T, (7) F, (8) F, (9) T, (10) F, (11) F, (12) F, (13) F, (14) F, (15) T, (16) F, (17) T, (18) T, (19) F, (20) T, (21) F, (22) T, (23) T, (24) F,[2] (25) T, (26) T, (27) F, (28) F, (29) F, (30) F.

STOP. Turn to page 238 for the scoring of the tests.

Additional Practice Sets (pp. 239-244)

Additional Practice 1

A. (1) c, (2) a, (3) h, (4) b, (5) f, (6) g, (7) d, (8) e.
B. (1) d, (2) a, (3) r, (4) k, (5) g, (6) b, (7) m, (8) c, (9) p, (10) e, (11) l, (12) f, (13) h, (14) q, (15) i, (16) j, (17) o, (18) n.

---

[1] *Vocation* is the answer because the relationship between *pine* and *tree* is one of *classification.*

[2] Persons can be active while under *hypnosis.* Also, *hypnosis* is a noun and *dormant* is an adjective.

Additional Practice 2

A. (1) d, (2) g, (3) a, (4) c, (5) i, (6) b, (7) h, (8) f, (9) e.

B. (1) e, (2) q, (3) j, (4) l, (5) a, (6) i, (7) n, (8) b, (9) k, (10) t, (11) c, (12) m, (13) h, (14) f, (15) d, (16) s, (17) g, (18) o, (19) r, (20) p.

Additional Practice 3

A. (1) i, (2) c, (3) a, (4) f, (5) h, (6) e, (7) b, (8) g, (9) d.

B. (1) g, (2) l, (3) s, (4) x, (5) k, (6) t, (7) c, (8) a, (9) z, (10) b, (11) d, (12) r, (13) aa, (14) p, (15) v, (16) e, (17) m, (18) h, (19) f, (20) u, (21) y, (22) i, (23) o, (24) j, (25) q, (26) n, (27) w.

© 1974 by NEA, Inc.

"YOU GOTTA SPEAK PLAIN ENGLISH TO MY MOM! YOU ASK FOR BREAD AND YOU GET BREAD ... ASK FOR MONEY!"

Part II
VOCABULARY WORDS

INTRODUCTION

In Part II most of the words are not as easily derived from a knowledge of combining forms as are those in Part I. However, the words in Part II are used often, and you will meet them in your subject matter courses, in newspapers, in magazines, and so on. Exercises 16–24 consist of general vocabulary words.

Because you will not have as much help from combining forms to unlock word meanings, you should be especially aware of other helpful clues. A most important clue is context (surrounding words in a sentence). Many times you gain the meaning of the word from the surrounding words. For example, in the following sentence see if you can figure out the meaning of *hippodrome*.

> In ancient times the Greek people would assemble in their seats to observe the chariot races being held in the *hippodrome*.

From the context of the sentence, you should realize that *hippodrome* refers to some arena (place) where races were held in ancient Greece.

Sometimes you can actually gain the definition of the word from the sentence or following sentences. For example:

> The house had a cheerful atmosphere. At any moment I expected *blithe* spirits to make their entrance and dance with joy throughout the house.

From the sentences, you can determine that *blithe* refers to something joyful, gay, or merry.

253

As you have already seen in Part I, context clues are especially important in determining meaning for words that have more than one meaning. For example, note the many uses of *capital* in the following sentences.

1. That is a *capital* idea.

2. Remember to begin each sentence with a *capital* letter.

3. The killing of a policeman is a *capital* offense in some states.

4. Albany is the *capital* of New York State.

5. In order to start a business, you need *capital*.

Each of the preceding sentences illustrates one meaning for *capital*.

In sentence 1 *capital* means "excellent."
In sentence 2 *capital* means "referring to a letter in writing that is an uppercase letter."
In sentence 3 *capital* means "punishable by death."
In sentence 4 *capital* means "the seat of government."
In sentence 5 *capital* means "money or wealth."

Alert readers can also use contrasts or comparisons to gain clues to meanings of words. For example, what do you think is the meaning of *ethereal* in the following sentence?

He was impressed by the *ethereal* grace of Jane's walk rather than Ellen's heavy-footed one.

If you guessed *light, airy* for the meaning of *ethereal*, you were correct. You know that *ethereal* is somehow the opposite of *heavy*. This is an example of contrasts.

In the next example, see how comparisons can help you.

Maria was as *fickle* as a politician's promises before election.

In this sentence *fickle* means "not firm in opinion" or "wavering." Because politicians try to court all their constituents (voters) before an election, they often are not firm in their opinions, make many promises, and are wavering. By understanding the comparison you can get an idea of the meaning of *fickle*.

Good readers use all these clues to help them to determine word meanings.

Note that Step I in Part II is different from Step I in Part I. In Step I of Part II, the vocabulary words for each exercise will be presented in sentences because no combining forms are being given. The sentences will contain many of the words presented in Part I. As a means of helping you unlock word meanings, context clues for each new word will be given in the sentences.

Steps II and III in Part II are similar to Steps II and III in Part I. You are now ready to continue *Gaining Word Power*.

CHAPTER SEVEN

EXERCISE 16

Step I. Vocabulary Words in Sentences

Directions: Following are sentences using the ten vocabulary words from Exercise 16. See whether you can figure out the meanings of the underlined words from the clues in the sentences. Sometimes the clue to help you figure out the word is in the next sentence or sentences. Blanks are provided for your estimates of the definitions. Check your meanings with those in Step II.

1. My associates say that I must be unsophisticated or childish because I am so <u>naive</u> as to believe that the board of directors will vote for such an innovative proposal as mine. _____

2. They feel that there is a <u>tacit</u> agreement among board members to vote down anything new, especially a plan to <u>integrate</u> the different research departments into one. Because none of the board members will come right out and say that he or she is against uniting the research departments, we never know for sure where the board members stand. _____ ; _____

3. Because I am a very <u>candid</u> person, people usually know exactly where I stand. _____

4. My associates told me that when I present my proposal to the board at our next conference, I'd better be <u>terse</u> and not <u>verbose</u>. The board members can't stand persons who are too wordy._____ ; _____

_____

5. Although there are some members who might be against <u>segregating</u> the different research departments, they would probably not be too vocal about their views._____

6. My associates told me not to be <u>frustrated</u> when my plan is defeated.

_____

7. Because the board members do not like to answer too many questions, they dislike <u>inquisitive</u> people. They feel that they are prying._____

8. It is difficult to believe that the stockholders would <u>sustain</u> the board's policies. But many stockholders seem to support the board's views.

_____

Step II. Vocabulary Words

1. **candid** (kan′ did) *adj.* Honest; outspoken; frank. *You know that Frank is* **candid** *about his political views because he is so outspoken and open about everything.*

2. **frustrate** (frus′ trāt¢) *v.* To defeat; to bring to nothing. *adj.* (frustrated) Filled with a sense of discouragement and dissatisfaction as a result of defeated efforts, inner conflicts, or unresolved problems. *After a great amount of effort, they were able to* **frustrate** *the politicians' plan, so that it was defeated.*

3. **inquisitive** (in ·quis · i · tive) (in · kwiz′ i · tiv¢) *adj.* Curious; given to asking many questions; unnecessarily or improperly curious; prying. *The* **inquisitive** *neighbor asked too many prying questions.*

4. **integrate** (in · te · grāt¢′) *v.* To unite; to make whole or complete by adding together parts. *When we* **integrated** *all the separate parts and saw the whole plan, we realized how good it was.*

5. **naive** (na · ive) (nī · ēv¢′) *adj.* Foolishly simple; childlike; unsophisticated. *He is so* **naive** *that, like a child, he will believe anything you tell him.*

6. **segregate** (seg′ re · gāt¢) *v.* To set apart from others; to separate. *In school some students tend to* **segregate** *themselves from others by forming special clubs that are not open for membership to everyone.*

7. **sustain** (sus · tā⁄n′) *v.* To maintain; to keep in existence; to keep going; to uphold; to support. *Because the judge* **sustained** *the defense lawyer's objections, the prosecuting attorney had to resort to a different line of questioning.*

258

8. **tacit** (tas' it) *adj.* Unspoken; not expressed openly but implied. *There seemed to be a **tacit** agreement because everybody knew how to behave even though no one said anything.*

9. **terse** (ters¢) *adj.* Brief; concise. *Remember to be **terse** because the audience doesn't like long answers.*

10. **verbose** (ver · bōs¢') *adj.* Wordy. *Her speech is so **verbose** that the audience is becoming restless from listening to her.*

Special Notes

You met the combining form *ten, tent, tain* meaning "hold" in Exercise 12. Did you recognize that *sustain* is derived from the combining form *ten, tent, tain*?

Step III. Practice

A. Directions: Each sentence has a missing word. Choose the word that *best* completes the sentence. Write the word in the blank. *All words fit in.*

Word List

verbose, terse, frustrate, tacit, candid, integrate, segregate, naive, inquisitive, sustain.

1. As Jane is so outspoken, we know that she will give us her _____ opinion on that matter.

2. We have a(n) _____ agreement on how to proceed from here, so no one has to say anything.

3. Can't we get someone less_____ for our fraternity dinner speaker? The one you are thinking of talks too much.

4. I know a good speaker who is _____ rather than wordy.

5. It's all right to be_____to a point, but not when you appear childlike.

6. If the children _____ their good conduct throughout the trip, that will be their longest period of good behavior.

7. To _____ a plan means "to bring it to nothing."

8. Some persons resent _____ reporters because they ask more questions than are necessary or even proper.

9. Some students in school always seem to_____themselves from others and have nothing to do with them.

10. In order to _____ the schools so that there were children of all races in each school, the school board had to develop a plan for combining students from various schools.

STOP. Check answers at the end of the chapter.

B. Directions: Following are ten sentences that contain the meanings of vocabulary presented in Exercise 16. Choose the word that *best* fits the word or phrase underlined in the sentence.

Word List

terse, verbose, tacit, frustrate, inquisitive, naive, candid, integrate, segregate, sustain.

1. I will do everything in my power to defeat your attempts to gain possession of these files. _____

2. Do you know how to unite the various factions? _____

3. Try not to behave in such an unsophisticated manner. _____

4. People don't like prying persons who try to find out too much about the affairs of others. _____

5. Don't be too outspoken at the party. _____

6. Try to mix with more people rather than always trying to separate yourself from others. _____

7. When there is an unspoken agreement among people, everyone knows what to do without anyone's saying a word. _____

8. It is difficult to listen to speakers who are too wordy. _____

9. I prefer speeches that are logical and brief. _____

10. The union members said that they would maintain their vote concerning their contract. _____

STOP. Check answers at the end of the chapter.

C. Directions: Following are the words from Exercise 16. Match the words with their meanings.

_____ 1. candid   a. curious

_____ 2. tacit   b. wordy

_____ 3. verbose   c. to unite

_____ 4. terse   d. honest; outspoken

_____ 5. integrate   e. to maintain; uphold

_____ 6. segregate   f. to defeat

_____ 7. inquisitive   g. unspoken; not expressed but implied

_____ 8. sustain   h. unsophisticated; childlike

_____ 9. frustrate   i. brief; concise

_____ 10. naive   j. to separate

STOP. Check answers at the end of the chapter.

EXTRA WORD
POWER

> **dom.** State or condition of being; rank; total area of. *Dom* is added to the end of many words. For example: *Christendom*—the Christian world; *dukedom*—the rank or title of a duke; the area governed by a duke; *freedom*—condition of being free; *kingdom*—area controlled by a king; *stardom*—the status of being a star; *wisdom*—the state of having knowledge. How many more words that end in *dom* can you supply?

Additional Words

From your ability to use context clues, can you figure out the meanings of the following words?

1. **listless** (list' less) *adj. Mrs. James was upset when her usually playful and energetic child behaved in such a **listless** and apathetic manner.*

_____

2. **ecstasy** (ec · sta · sy) (ek' sta · sē) *n. He was in a state of **ecstasy** when the homecoming queen said that she would go to the dance with him.*

_____

3. **peruse** (pe · rūze') *v. I will **peruse** the material at my leisure because I need time to go over it carefully.*

_____

4. **terminate** (ter' mi · nāte) *v. We decided to **terminate** our contract with that firm because it was always late in delivering our goods.*

_____

5. **tentative** (ten' ta · tiv¢) *adj.   The arrangements we have made are only **tenta-**
   tive ones because we want to see how well they work before we commit
   ourselves to something more permanent.*

_____

STOP. Check answers at the end of the chapter.

Practice for Additional Words

Directions: Match each word with the *best* definition.

_____	1. listless	a. done on trial
_____	2. peruse	b. great joy
_____	3. terminate	c. spiritless
_____	4. tentative	d. to read carefully
_____	5. ecstasy	e. to end

STOP. Check answers at the end of the chapter.

EXERCISE 17

Step I.   Vocabulary Words in Sentences

Directions: Following are sentences using the ten vocabulary words from Ex-
            ercise 17. See whether you can figure out the meanings of the
            underlined words from the clues in the sentences. Sometimes
            the clue to help you figure out the word is in the next sentence
            or sentences. Blanks are provided for your estimates of the def-
            initions. Check your meanings with those in Step II.

1. <u>Hostile</u> nations that are on unfriendly terms usually maintain very sophisticated spy systems. _____

2. Persons who read about spying operations feel that they are all <u>fictitious.</u>
   On the contrary, they are real. _____

3. The training that spies go through is as intense as that of astronauts because
   the consequences of an error could be <u>fatal.</u> Because their lives depend on
   making no mistakes, spies must be very careful. _____

4. One of the first things spies learn is to keep their spying activities <u>covert</u> and
   tell no one about them, not even their spouses. Some spies have kept their
   spying activities a secret for decades. No one except certain government officials knows who these spies are. _____

5. They could be <u>affluent</u> persons or persons without money. _____

6. They could be people with whom we deal all the time and who seem to do everything in an open or <u>overt</u> manner. _____

7. One thing that's sure is that when a spy is asked to do something, he or she must <u>curtail</u> everything else that he or she is involved in and carry out orders. _____

8. Many times what spies are asked to do may not seem <u>relevant</u> to them because it doesn't seem to relate or apply to anything else. However, they do not choose their assignments. _____

9. Did you know that spies carry a <u>lethal</u> dose of poison so that they can kill themselves if they are captured? _____

10. If a government discovers a spy in its midst, the chances for a pardon or <u>amnesty</u> are not very high. _____

Step II. Vocabulary Words

1. **affluent** (af′ flū · ent) *adj.* Having an abundance of goods or riches; wealthly; flowing freely. *Although Jane is very affluent, you would never know she has money from the way she acts.*

2. **amnesty** (am′ nes · tē) *n.* (*pl.* **ties**) A pardon from the government; act of letting someone off. *The government changed its policy on the granting of amnesties so that more persons would be able to receive pardons.*

3. **curtail** (kur · tāil′) *v.* To shorten; to lessen; to cut off the end or a part. *In order to curtail expenses, we are buying fewer clothes and not eating out as much as we did before.*

4. **covert** (cov · ert) (kō′ vert) *adj.* Secret; concealed; covered over; sheltered. *They behaved in such a covert manner that everyone knew that they were trying to hide something.*

5. **fatal** (fā′ tul) *adj.* Resulting in or capable of causing death; deadly; bringing ruin or disaster; having decisive importance. *When someone has a fatal accident, his insurance company pays money to the members of his family who survive him.*

6. **fictitious** (fic · ti · tious) (fik · ti′ shus) *adj.* Imaginary; not real; made up; fabricated. *Janet's story was completely fictitious with no basis in fact.*

7. **hostile** (hos′ tilɇ) *adj.* Unfriendly; referring to an enemy. *The hostile audience did not applaud the speaker and behaved in a very unfriendly manner.*

8. **lethal** (lē′ thul) *adj.* Causing death; deadly. *The lethal blow caused his death.*

9. **overt** (ō′ vert) *adj.* Open to view; public; apparent; able to be seen. *Because his actions were overt, nobody could accuse him of trying to hide anything.*

10. **relevant** (rel′ e · vant) *adj.* Applying to the matter in question; suitable; relating to. *Is what you are saying **relevant** to the issue, or does it apply to something else?*

Step III. Practice

A. Directions: Each sentence has a missing word. Choose the word that *best* completes the sentence. Write the word in the blank. *All words fit in.*

Word List

hostile, covert, fictitious, relevant, lethal, fatal, overt, amnesty, affluent, curtail.

1. The characters in this book are purely _____ , and any resemblance to real persons is merely due to chance.

2. Spies usually engage in _____ activities because they do not want other persons to learn about them.

3. We were told to _____ our coffee breaks because they were too long.

4. When the deserters heard that they were being forgiven and consequently being given a(n)_____ , they went wild with joy.

5. I like all my dealings to be _____ and aboveboard rather than secretive.

6. Because that is not a(n)_____ question and doesn't apply to the case, you do not have to answer it.

7. I do not like to be in the company of people who are _____ because I like people who are friendly.

8. The _____ dose of cleaning fluid that the child had drunk caused her death.

9. Although_____ people have a lot of money, it doesn't mean that they are all happy.

10. The _____ hour was drawing near, when everyone would learn whether he or she had been accepted into college.

STOP. Check answers at the end of the chapter.

B. Directions: Ten sentences follow. Define the underlined word. Put your answer in the blank.

1. If a course doesn't apply to my chosen vocation, it just isn't <u>relevant</u> for me. _____

264

2. In order to make the surprise party a real secret, we had to behave in a very covert manner. _____

3. Prizefighters cannot get into fights in bars because their hands are considered lethal weapons. _____

4. An amnesty for the revolutionaries was one of the demands of the hijackers. _____

5. When James became chairperson, he said that everything would be done in an overt manner. _____

6. After Dick's heart attack, he had to curtail a lot of activities he used to love. _____

7. The blow on the back of Mary's neck proved to be fatal. _____

8. The crops were so good this year that we became affluent. _____

9. From the hostile way that they are behaving to one another, you can tell they are enemies. _____

10. The people Jennifer had told us about were purely fictitious and didn't actually exist. _____

STOP. Check answers at the end of the chapter.

C. Directions: In the Word Square there are eight words from Exercise 17. Find the words in the square and match them with their correct meanings. Note that there are *more* meanings than words. If there is no word in the square for a meaning, write *none*, and give the word.

WORD SQUARE

F	I	C	F	A	T	A	L
H	O	S	T	I	L	F	C
L	E	T	H	A	L	F	O
C	U	R	T	A	I	L	V
O	L	O	M	O	S	U	E
M	E	S	E	R	T	E	R
R	E	L	E	V	A	N	T
S	A	M	N	E	S	T	Y

Meanings	Words
1. Wealthy	_____
2. A pardon	_____
3. Cut short	_____
4. Secret	_____
5. Resulting in or causing death; having decisive importance	_____
6. Imaginary	_____
7. Unfriendly	_____
8. Deadly	_____
9. Open to view	_____
10. Relating to	_____

STOP. Check answers at the end of the chapter.

EXTRA WORD POWER

> y. Having; full of; tending to; like; somewhat. When *y* is added to the end of a word, it changes the word to an adjective. For example: *dirt–dirty*—full of dirt; *health–healthy*—full of health; *stick–sticky*—tending to stick; *wave-wavy*—like a wave; *horse-horsy*—like a horse; *salt–salty*—full of salt. How many more words with *y* can you supply?

Additional Words

From your ability to use context clues, can you figure out the meanings of the following words?

1. **crafty** (craf · ty) (kraf′ tē) *adj. I like trustworthy people who are above-board in everything they do rather than crafty ones.*

_____

2. *versatile* (ver′ sa · tilȼ) *adj. The **versatile** actor was able to play many different types of roles with ease.*

_____

3. **tenure** (ten · ure) (ten′ yurȼ) *n. After persons receive job **tenure**, it is very difficult to dismiss them.*

_____

266

4. **temerity** (te · mer′ i · tē) *n.* *What **temerity** the driver had to pass four cars on a curve on a two-way road that had only one lane for each way.*

---

5. **tenet** (ten′ et) *n.* *One of my basic **tenets** is that hard work pays off.*

STOP. Check answers at the end of the chapter.

Practice for Additional Words

Directions: Match each word with the *best* definition.

_____ 1. tenure	a. turning with ease from one thing to another
_____ 2. tenet	
_____ 3. temerity	b. the right to possess something
_____ 4. versatile	c. sly
_____ 5. crafty	d. belief
	e. rash boldness

STOP. Check answers at the end of the chapter.

EXERCISE 18

Step I. Vocabulary Words in Sentences

Directions: Following are sentences using the ten vocabulary words from Exercise 18. See whether you can figure out the meanings of the underlined words from the clues in the sentences. Sometimes the clue to help you figure out the word is in the next sentence or sentences. Blanks are provided for your estimates of the definitions. Check your meanings with those in Step II.

1. Many times in life we do not have <u>alternatives </u>or choices. There are tasks that have to be done, and we must do them. _____

2. Sometimes these tasks may be such <u>formidable</u> ones that we are frightened by them. However, most of us usually persist and overcome our fears and accomplish our tasks. _____

3. Many times tasks seem more difficult to us because we are either <u>fatigued</u> or <u>famished.</u> Obviously, if we are overtired or starved, we will have difficulty in doing anything. _____ ; _____

267

4. Sometimes persons have difficulty in accomplishing some tasks because they are such <u>pessimists.</u> They are gloomy about the task before they begin.
   _____

5. I concede that it's difficult to be cheery about a difficult task, but I am an <u>optimist.</u> _____

6. Have you ever found that you can become <u>nostalgic</u> about some <u>mundane</u> or ordinary task you accomplished almost a decade ago? Looking at some pictures reminded me of some everyday job my mother had me do. The pictures made me feel very homesick._____;_____

7. Actually, the pictures also made me feel so <u>sentimental</u> that I was overcome with emotion. _____

8. As a result, I wrote my parents a long letter rather than my usual <u>concise</u> one. _____

Step II. Vocabulary Words

1. **alternative** (al · ter′ na · tiv∉) *n.* One or more things offered for choice; a choice between two or more things; a remaining choice; a choice. *adj.* Offering or providing a choice between two or more things. *As the **alternative** to paying a fine was to go to jail, I chose the first penalty.*

2. **concise** (con · cise) (kon · sīs∉) *adj.* Brief; terse. *The **concise** statement was brief and to the point.*

3. **famish** (fam′ ish) *v.* To make or be very hungry; starve. *adj.* (**famished**) Very hungry. *I am so **famished** that I could eat almost anything.*

4. **fatigue** (fa · tēgu∉′) *n.* Physical or mental tiredness; weariness. *v.* To tire out; to weary; to weaken from continued use. *I was so tired from working today that I was completely **fatigued**.*

5. **formidable** (for · mi · da · ble) (for′ mi · da · bul) *adj.* Dreaded; causing awe or fear; hard to handle; of discouraging or awesome strength, size, difficulty, and so on. *That is such a **formidable** task that it may be too hard to handle.*

6. **mundane** (mun′dān∉) *adj.* Referring to everyday things; referring to that which is routine or ordinary; referring to worldly things rather than more high-minded or spiritual things. *After listening to a lecture about the kinds of activities that the archaeologists engage in, my tasks sounded **mundane** and ordinary.*

7. **nostalgic** (nos · tal · gic) (nos · tal′ jik) *adj.* Homesick; longing to go back to one's home, hometown, and so on; longing for something far away or long ago. *When I saw some of my childhood things, I became very **nostalgic**.*

268

8. **optimist** (op′ ti · mist) *n.* One who is hopeful; a cheerful person; one who tends to take the most hopeful view or expects the best outcome. *Carol always looks at the bright side of things because she is such an* **optimist.**

9. **pessimist** (pes′ ṣi · mist) *n.* One who expects the worst to happen in any situation; one who looks on the dark side of things; a gloomy person. *George is such a* **pessimist** *that he seems to expect only bad things to happen.*

10. **sentimental** (sen · ti · men′ tul) *adj.* Marked by tenderness, emotion, feeling, and so on; influenced more by feeling or emotion than by reason; acting from feeling rather than from practical motives. *At my parents' fiftieth wedding anniversary I behaved like a* **sentimental** *fool because I was so overcome with emotion.*

Special Note

1. The word *sentimental* may also mean "having or showing exaggerated or superficial emotion." This meaning is often used in literature.

Step III. Practice

A. Directions: Each sentence has a missing word. Choose the word that best completes the sentence. Write the word in the blank. *All words fit in.*

Word List

alternative, concise, famished, fatigued, optimist, pessimist, mundane, sentimental, formidable, nostalgic.

1. We had no_____ but to concede to his demands.

2. After not eating all day, I was _____ .

3. I dreaded starting such a(n)_____task because I felt that I could not handle it.

4. Being a(n)_____ , I know that tomorrow everything will be great.

5. On the contrary, as a(n)_____, I feel that everything will not be very good tomorrow.

6. When certain things make me very_____, I am overcome with emotion.

7. Looking through my high school yearbook made me feel so_____ that I started to long for a reunion with my high school buddies.

8. I prefer to do something out of the ordinary rather than the same _____things I always do.

9. The campers were so _____ after their ten-mile hike that they said they had to rest or they would collapse.

10. I enjoy speakers who are _____ and to the point.

STOP. Check answers at the end of the chapter.

B. Directions: Following are ten sentences that contain the meanings of vocabulary presented in Exercise 18. Choose the word that *best* fits the word or phrase underlined in the sentence.

Word List

alternative, concise, famished, fatigued, formidable, mundane, nostalgic, pessimist, optimist, sentimental.

1. I become <u>overwhelmed with emotion</u> when I see things that relate to my early childhood. _____

2. After working all night on a paper, I was so <u>mentally and physically tired</u> that I collapsed. _____

3. Writing three themes in one week is <u>hard to handle</u>. _____

4. When I don't eat breakfast or lunch, I feel <u>starved</u> by dinner time.

   _____

5. Sharon is <u>a person who always looks on the bright side of things.</u>

   _____

6. Jack is <u>a person who always looks on the gloomy side of things.</u>

   _____

7. What is <u>routine or ordinary</u> to one person may not be for another.

   _____

8. We had no <u>choice</u> in the matter, so we let him go. _____

9. Answer the questions in a <u>brief</u> manner. _____

10. After being away from home, I started to have <u>homesick</u> feelings.

   _____

STOP. Check answers at the end of the chapter.

C. Directions: Following are the words from Exercise 18. Match the word with its meaning.

_____ 1. alternative   a. starved

_____ 2. famished   b. one who expects the most hopeful outcome

_____ 3. fatigued

_____ 4. formidable

_____ 5. optimist

_____ 6. pessimist

_____ 7. mundane

_____ 8. concise

_____ 9. sentimental

_____ 10. nostalgic

c. brief; terse

d. choice

e. ordinary; everyday

f. influenced more by emotion than reason

g. of discouraging difficulty

h. homesick

i. one who expects the worst

j. physically or mentally tired

STOP. Check answers at the end of the chapter.

EXTRA WORD
POWER

> **ful.** Full of. When *ful* is added to the end of a word, it means "full of" and is spelled with only one *l.* In words ending in *y* after a consonant, the *y* changes to an *i* when *ful* is added. For example: *beauty–beautiful*—full of beauty; *pity–pitiful*—full of pity; *tearful*—full of tears; *shameful*—full of shame. How many more words with *ful* can you supply?

Additional Words

From your ability to use context clues, can you figure out the meanings of the following words?

1. **tactful** (takt′ ful) *adj. Because Mary does not like to hurt anyone's feelings, she is trying to think of a **tactful** way to tell Mrs. Brown that her son has been arrested.*

_____

2. **expedite** (ex · pe · dite) (ek′ spe · dīte) *v. The buyer said that because he needs the order now, he wants the salesman to **expedite** the delivery of the goods.*

_____

3. **obfuscate** (ob · fus′ kāte) *v. Everytime he spoke, instead of clarifying the issue, he **obfuscated** it even more.*

_____

4. **constraint** (kon · straint′) *n. One of the **constraints** of the job was that I could not leave whenever I desired.*

_____

5. **variable** (var · i · a · ble) (var′ ē · a · bul) *adj. n. Because the weather has been so **variable**, it's difficult to know what to wear.*

STOP. Check answers at the end of the chapter.

Practice for Additional Words

Directions: Match each word with the *best* definition.

_____ 1. tactful   a. to hasten

_____ 2. obfuscate   b. changeable

_____ 3. constraint   c. to confuse

_____ 4. variable   d. skillful in dealing with people

_____ 5. expedite   e. restriction

STOP. Check answers at the end of the chapter.

CROSSWORD PUZZLE 6

Directions: The meanings of a number of the words from Exercises 16–18 follow. Your knowledge of these words, as well as the combining forms from Part I, will help you to solve this crossword puzzle.

1. Way of saying *mother*
3. Opposite of *stop*
5. Female pronoun
6. Brief
9. Third letter of the alphabet
10. Opposite of *happy*
11. Comb. f. for *one who*
12. Comb. f. for *not*
14. Same as # 12 Across
15. Wordy
18. Abbreviation for Civil Defense
19. Past tense of *to send*
20. A dog and cat are household ___s
21. Unspoken
22. Indefinite article
23. A long-tailed rodent
25. A girl's name
27. Ending for the past tense
    of regular verbs
28. Homonym of *two*
29. Meaning of *fatigued*
32. Slang for *to catch*
33. Unsophisticated
35. Imitated someone
36. Meaning of *alternative*
38. Plural of comb. f. for *ped*
41. A cover
42. Abbreviation for *pint*
44. To turn around
45. Betsy ___ made the first
    American flag.
46. In school you go through the ___ s
47. Comb. f. for *back*
48. Opposite of *go*
50. Imaginary
51. Mental strain
54. Same as # 47 Across
56. Same as # 22 Across
57. Separate
62. Two thousand pounds
63. Same as # 55 Down
64. On earth there are plants and ___s

1. Pronoun referring to *self*
2. Comb. f. for *one who*
3. Meaning of *theo*
4. Opposite of *off*
5. A plant used for seasoning in
   cooking
6. Outspoken; honest
7. Hidden; concealed
8. Arrange
9. Cut off
10. To accomplish what you want-
    ed to accomplish
12. Employ
13. Meshed fabric used to catch fish
16. Comb. f. for *in*
17. A person who always looks on
    the bright side of things
19. Nineteenth letter of the
    alphabet
22. Abbreviation for advertisement
23. Dried grape
24. First three letters of the alpha-
    bet
25. Unite
26. Infant makes this sound and
    parents think it means "father"
29. You leave this for the waiter
30. A tenant ___s an apartment
31. Same as # 27 Across
32. Homesick
34. ___ and vigor
35. Title used for both married
    and unmarried women
36. Fresh and firm: ___ vegetables
37. Latin for *this*
38. To defeat
39. Doing something with ___ is the
    opposite of doing something with
    difficulty
40. Same as # 27 Across
42. Comb. f. for *before*
43. You sleep in this on a camping trip

65. When a female conceives, an ___
    unites with sperm
67. Without this part, a plant would die
70. Same as # 54 Across
71. When you stop breathing, you ___
72. Girl's name
73. Same as # 16 Down
74. Comb. f. for *together*
75. Spelling of the letter *T*
76. Fifth letter of the alphabet

46. Same as # 3 Across
49. Same as # 42 Down
50. Sixth letter of the alphabet
51. Comb. f. for *from a distance*
52. Homonym of *sew*
53. Same as # 16 Down
55. Comb. f. for *one who*
58. Same as # 16 Down
59. Opposite of *take*
60. Rhymes with *ham*
61. To ___ and feather someone
65. Same as # 27 Across
66. Comb. f. for *earth*
68. Meaning of *mono, uni*
69. Same as # 68 Down

STOP. Check answers at the end of the chapter.

WORD SCRAMBLE 6

Directions: Word Scramble 6 is based on words from Exercises 16–18. The meanings are your clues to arranging the letters in correct order. Write the correct word in the blank.

Meanings

1. nidadc   _____ honest

2. treatsurf   _____ to defeat

3. rintatgee   _____ to unite

4. resgteega   _____ to set apart

5. catti   _____ unspoken

6. reets   _____ brief

7. snatsui   _____ to maintain

8. ulfantef   _____ wealthy

9. tocrev   _____ secret

10. yestman   _____ a pardon

11. claiurt   _____ to shorten

12. ehsolit   _____ unfriendly

13. nervealt   _____ relating to

14. nativealter   _____   a choice

15. maihfsde   _____   starved

16. moreifbald   _____   of discouraging difficulty

17. numenad   _____   ordinary

18. glonstica   _____   homesick

19. spessiimt   _____   one who expects the worst

20. stimiopt   _____   one who expects the best

STOP. Check answers at the end of the chapter.

ANALOGIES 6

Directions: Find the word from the following list that *best* completes each analogy. *There are more words in the list than you need.*

Word List

naive, defeat, temerity, curtail, mundane, posterior, concise, tacit, sustain, obfuscate, ecstasy, amnesty, optimist, tactful, verbose, vociferous, voiced, tenet, prying, covert, happiness, bad, good, pathetic, spiritless, tentative, clear, lucid, candid, terminate, commence, tenacious, changeable, termite, expedite, constraint, incredible, term, steady, famished, integrate.

1. Fictitious: real :: sophisticated :_____.

2. Covert : overt :: segregate :_____.

3. concede : surrender :: starved :_____.

4. Affluent : wealthy :: frustrate :_____.

5. Hostile : friendly :: clarify : _____.

6. Relevant : irrelevant :: unusual :_____.

7. Permanent : tentative :: variable :_____.

8. Lethal : deadly :: terse : _____.

9. Crafty : sly :: listless :_____.

10. Sentimental : unfeeling :: pessimist : _____.

11. Pat : strike :: joy :_____.

12. Dreaded : formidable :: foolhardiness : _____.

13. Positive : definite :: rear :_____.

14. Contemporary : ancient :: begin : _____ .

15. Post : position :: pardon : _____ .

16. Pacify : calm :: belief : _____ .

17. Species : kind :: inquisitive : _____ .

18. Archetype : model :: clamorous : _____ .

19. Dormant : active :: lengthen : _____ .

20. Animate : deaden :: spoken : _____ .

STOP. Check answers at the end of the chapter.

MULTIPLE-CHOICE VOCABULARY TEST 6

Directions: This is a test on words in Exercises 16–18. Words are presented according to exercises. *Do all exercises before checking answers.* Underline the meaning that *best* fits the word.

Exercise 16

1. candid
   - a. happy
   - b. frank
   - c. cheerful
   - d. to the point

2. frustrate
   - a. to defeat
   - b. anxious
   - c. to separate
   - d. foolish

3. integrate
   - a. to separate
   - b. to unite
   - c. force
   - d. race

4. inquisitive
   - a. prying
   - b. a quiz
   - c. wise
   - d. going before

5. naive
   - a. happy
   - b. sophisticated
   - c. childlike
   - d. apathetic

6. segregate
   - a. to unite
   - b. regulate
   - c. foolish
   - d. to separate

7. sustain
   - a. to help
   - b. to maintain
   - c. unnecessary
   - d. to go

8. tacit
   - a. to the point
   - b. open
   - c. unspoken
   - d. friendly

9. terse
   - a. unspoken
   - b. brief
   - c. frank
   - d. a pardon

10. verbose
   - a. quiet
   - b. brief
   - c. wordy
   - d. friendly

Exercise 17

11. affluent
    - a. result
    - b. wealthy
    - c. cause
    - d. secret

12. amnesty
    - a. short
    - b. wordy
    - c. a pardon
    - d. honest

13. curtail
    - a. curious
    - b. cheerful
    - c. to shorten
    - d. inactive

14. covert
    - a. open
    - b. concealed
    - c. prying
    - d. spy

15. fatal
    - a. poison
    - b. secret
    - c. open
    - d. causing death

16. fictitious
    - a. story
    - b. real
    - c. imaginary
    - d. unsophisticated

17. hostile
    - a. friendly
    - b. unfriendly
    - c. kill
    - d. hurt

18. lethal
    - a. poison
    - b. hurt
    - c. dangerous
    - d. deadly

19. overt
    - a. open
    - b. closed
    - c. secret
    - d. relating to

20. relevant
    - a. friendly
    - b. open
    - c. secret
    - d. relating to

Exercise 18

21. alternative
    - a. relating to
    - b. choice
    - c. imaginary
    - d. unfriendly

22. concise
    - a. wordy
    - b. long
    - c. to cut off
    - d. brief

23. famished
    - a. tired
    - b. long
    - c. starved
    - d. food

24. fatigued
    - a. hungry
    - b. starved
    - c. tired
    - d. asleep

25. formidable
    - a. of discouraging difficulty
    - b. inactive
    - c. apathetic
    - d. open

26. mundane
    - a. healthy
    - b. ordinary
    - c. uncaring
    - d. friendly

27. nostalgic
    - a. nosy
    - b. homesick
    - c. friendly
    - d. noticeable

28. pessimist   a. one who is a pest   c. one who is gloomy
                            b. one who is sad   d. one who is cheerful

29. optimist   a. one who is bad   c. relating to
                            b. one who is friendly   d. one who is cheerful

30. sentimental   a. lacking feeling   c. emotional
                            b. sentence   d. friendly

TRUE/FALSE TEST 6

Directions: This is a true/false test on Exercises 16–18. Read each sentence carefully. Decide whether it is true or false. Put a *T* for *true* or an *F* for *false* in the blank. The number after the sentence tells you if the word is from Exercise 16, 17, or 18.

_____ 1. *Integrate* and *segregate* are antonyms. 16

_____ 2. When you <u>frustrate</u> someone, you stop him or her from doing something he or she wants to do. 16

_____ 3. A <u>naive</u> person is sophisticated. 16

_____ 4. A biography would be <u>fictitious.</u> 17

_____ 5. An <u>inquisitive</u> person would be considered a curious person. 16

_____ 6. When someone <u>sustains</u> something, he or she wants to get rid of it. 16

_____ 7. Something <u>overt</u> would be out of view. 17

_____ 8. To <u>curtail</u> your allowance would be to increase it. 17

_____ 9. A <u>formidable</u> task would be easy to achieve. 18

_____ 10. Something <u>covert</u> would be open to all. 17

_____ 11. A <u>listless</u> person would be a spiritless person. 16

_____ 12. An <u>affluent</u> person would have an abundance of goods or riches. 17

_____ 13. *Optimist* and *pessimist* are antonyms. 18

_____ 14. <u>Mundane</u> things are spiritual or high-minded things. 18

_____ 15. Persons who are <u>nostalgic</u> look to the future. 18

_____ 16. A <u>sentimental</u> person would be apathetic. 18

_____ 17. A <u>pessimist</u> looks on the gloomy side of things. 18

_____ 18. When you have an <u>alternative</u>, you have no choice. 18

STOP. Check answers for both tests at the end of the chapter.

SCORING OF TESTS

Multiple-Choice Vocabulary Test   **True/False Test**

Number Wrong	Score	Number Wrong	Score
0–2	Excellent	0–1	Excellent
3–5	Good	2–3	Good
6–8	Weak	4–5	Weak
Above 8	Poor	Above 5	Poor
Score _____		Score _____	

1. If you scored in the excellent or good range on *both tests,* you are doing well. Go on to Chapter Eight.

2. If you scored in the weak or poor range on either test, look below and follow directions for Additional Practice. Note that the words on the tests are arranged so that you can tell in which exercise to find them. This will help you if you need additional practice.

ADDITIONAL PRACTICE SETS

A. Directions: Write the words you missed on the tests from the three exercises in the space provided. Note that the tests are presented so that you can tell to which exercises the words belong.

Exercise 16 Words Missed

1. _____   6. _____
2. _____   7. _____
3. _____   8. _____
4. _____   9. _____
5. _____   10. _____

Exercise 17 Words Missed

1. _____   6. _____
2. _____   7. _____
3. _____   8. _____
4. _____   9. _____
5. _____   10. _____

Exercise 18 Words Missed

1. _____   6. _____
2. _____   7. _____
3. _____   8. _____
4. _____   9. _____
5. _____   10. _____

B. Directions: Restudy the words that you have written down on p. 279 and this page. Step I and Step II for those you missed. Note that Step I and Step II are on the following pages:

Exercise 16—pp. 257–259.

Exercise 17—pp. 262–264.

Exercise 18—pp. 267–269.

C. Directions: Do Additional Practice 1 on this page and the next if you missed words from Exercise 16. Do Additional Practice 2 on p. 281 if you missed words from Exercise 17. Do Additional Practice 3 on pp. 281–282 if you missed words from Exercise 18. Now go on to Chapter Eight.

Additional Practice 1 for Exercise 16

Directions: Ten sentences follow. Define the underlined word. Put your answer in the blank.

1. Sometimes it's best not to be so <u>candid</u> because people often don't want to hear the truth. _____

2. Because I don't like nosy questions, I wish you wouldn't be so <u>inquisitive</u>. _____

3. How could you be so <u>naive</u> as to believe that he wanted you to go to his apartment to look at his pictures? _____

4. Many school districts are trying to <u>integrate</u> their schools by combining groups of students from different neighborhoods. _____

5. At the party, try not to go off in a corner and <u>segregate</u> yourself from everyone else. _____

6. I don't know how we will be able to <u>sustain</u> ourselves on the salary that we have. _____

7. No one said anything, but there was a <u>tacit</u> agreement on what to do. _____

8. Remember to be <u>terse</u> when you give the report so that we can leave early.
   _____

9. After working so hard on that plan, I am <u>frustrated</u> to learn that it has been defeated. _____

10. Some speakers are so <u>verbose</u> that they can go on for hours. _____

STOP. Check answers at the end of the chapter.

Additional Practice 2 for Exercise 17

Directions: Following are ten sentences that contain the meanings of vocabulary presented in Exercise 17. Choose the word that *best* fits the word or phrase underlined in the sentence. *All words fit in.*

Word List

overt; fatal; covert; affluent; relevant; lethal; hostile; fictitious; amnesty; curtail.

1. As John is so <u>wealthy</u>, money means nothing to him. _____

2. The <u>secret</u> activities of the government spies were finally uncovered.
   _____

3. All my business deals have to be <u>open and aboveboard.</u> _____

4. We knew that the <u>decisive</u> hour would arrive soon. _____

5. As children, my friend and I used to make up lots of <u>imaginary</u> stories to tell to each other. _____

6. <u>A pardon</u> was given to a former spy who helped the government capture other spies. _____

7. If you <u>cut off</u> any more of my funds, we won't have enough to live on.
   _____

8. Why are some people so <u>unfriendly</u>? _____

9. He accidentally drank a <u>deadly</u> dose of poison. _____

10. When you write your report, make sure that everything you put in it is <u>related</u> to your topic. _____

STOP. Check answers at the end of the chapter.

Additional Practice 3 for Exercise 18

Directions: Ten sentences follow. Define the underlined word. Put your answers in the blank.

1. We had no <u>alternative</u> but to concede that we were beaten. _____

2. When you give your answers on the final, be <u>concise</u> and to the point.
   _____

3. The task seemed so <u>formidable</u> to her that she didn't know whether she should undertake it. _____

4. I'm <u>famished</u> because I haven't eaten for almost twenty-four hours.
   _____

5. I'm so <u>fatigued</u> that I feel as though I could sleep for a week.
   _____

6. Everyday I have the same old <u>mundane</u> things to do. _____

7. When he saw his newborn child, he felt very <u>sentimental.</u>
   _____

8. Because I'm an <u>optimist</u>, I predict that we'll have a sunny day for our picnic tomorrow. _____

9. Because I'm a <u>pessimist</u>, I predict it will rain for our picnic tomorrow.
   _____

10. Every year during the spring I become <u>nostalgic</u> about my former home with its garden and large lawn. _____

STOP. Check answers at the end of the chapter.

ANSWERS

Exercise 16 (pp. 257–262)

Practice A

(1) candid, (2) tacit, (3) verbose, (4) terse, (5) naive, (6) sustain, (7) frustrate, (8) inquisitive, (9) segregate, (10) integrate.

Practice B

(1) frustrate, (2) integrate, (3) naive, (4) inquisitive, (5) candid, (6) segregate, (7) tacit, (8) verbose, (9) terse, (10) sustain.

Practice C

(1) d, (2) g, (3) b, (4) i, (5) c, (6) j, (7) a, (8) e, (9) f, (10) h.

Additional Words (pp. 261–262)

1. **listless.** Spiritless; indifferent; inactive; apathetic.

2. **ecstasy.** Great joy.

3. **peruse.** To read carefully; to inspect closely.

4. **terminate.** To end.

5. **tentative.** Done on trial or experimentally; not final; uncertain.

Practice for Additional Words (p. 262)

(1) c, (2) d, (3) e, (4) a, (5) b.

Exercise 17 (pp. 262-267)

Practice A

(1) fictitious, (2) covert, (3) curtail, (4) amnesty, (5) overt, (6) relevant,
(7) hostile, (8) lethal, (9) affluent, (10) fatal.

Practice B

(1) suitable, (2) secret, (3) deadly, (4) pardon, (5) open, (6) cut off, (7) deadly,
(8) wealthy, (9) unfriendly, (10) imaginary.

Practice C

(1) affluent, (2) amnesty, (3) curtail, (4) covert, (5) fatal, (6) none—fictitious,
(7) none—hostile, (8) lethal, (9) overt, (10) relevant.

Word Square

```
F  I  C  F  A  T  A  L
H  O  S  T  I  L  F  C
L  E  T  H  A  L  F  O
C  U  R  T  A  I  L  V
O  L  O  M  O  S  U  E
M  E  S  E  R  T  E  R
R  E  L  E  V  A  N  T
S  A  M  N  E  S  T  Y
```

Additional Words (pp. 266-267)

1. **crafty.** Sly; skillful in deceiving; cunning.

2. **versatile.** Changeable; turning with ease from one thing to another.

3. **tenure.** The right to hold or possess something; length of time something is held; status assuring an employee of permanence in his or her position or employment (tenure protects an employee such as a teacher from being dismissed except for serious misconduct or incompetence).

4. **temerity.** Rash boldness; foolhardiness.

5. **tenet.** Any opinion, doctrine, principle, dogma, and the like held as true; belief.

Practice for Additional Words (p. 267)

(1) b, (2) d, (3) e, (4) a, (5) c.

Exercise 18 (pp. 267-272)

Practice A

(1) alternative, (2) famished, (3) formidable, (4) optimist, (5) pessimist, (6) sentimental, (7) nostalgic, (8) mundane, (9) fatigued, (10) concise.

Practice B

(1) sentimental, (2) fatigued, (3) formidable, (4) famished, (5) optimist, (6) pessimist, (7) mundane, (8) alternative, (9) concise, (10) nostalgic.

Practice C

(1) d, (2) a, (3) j, (4) g, (5) b, (6) i, (7) e, (8) c, (9) f, (10) h.

Additional Words (pp. 271-272)

1. **tactful.** Considerate; conscientiously inoffensive; skillful in dealing with people or difficult situations.

2. **expedite.** To hasten; to speed up the progress of; to make easy the progress of.

3. **obfuscate.** To darken; to confuse; to obscure.

4. **constraint.** Confinement; the act of restricting; a restriction; the act of using force; force; compulsion; coercion.

5. **variable.** Changeable; something that may or does vary.

Practice for Additional Words (p. 272)

(1) d, (2) c, (3) e, (4) b, (5) a.

Crossword Puzzle 6 (pp. 272-274)

Word Scramble 6 (pp. 274-275)

(1) candid, (2) frustrate, (3) integrate, (4) segregate, (5) tacit, (6) terse, (7) sustain, (8) affluent, (9) covert, (10) amnesty, (11) curtail, (12) hostile, (13) relevant, (14) alternative, (15) famished, (16) formidable, (17) mundane, (18) nostalgic, (19) pessimist, (20) optimist.

Analogies 6 (pp. 275-276)

(1) naive, (2) integrate, (3) famished, (4) defeat, (5) obfuscate, (6) mundane, (7) steady, (8) concise, (9) spiritless, (10) optimist, (11) ecstasy, (12) temerity, (13) posterior, (14) terminate, (15) amnesty, (16) tenet, (17) prying, (18) vociferous, (19) curtail, (20) tacit.

Multiple-Choice Vocabulary Test 6 (pp. 276-278)

Exercise 16

(1) b, (2) a, (3) b, (4) a, (5) c, (6) d, (7) b, (8) c, (9) b, (10) c.

Exercise 17

(11) b, (12) c, (13) c, (14) b, (15) d, (16) c, (17) b,.(18) d, (19) a, (20) d.

Exercise 18

(21) b, (22) d, (23) c, (24) c, (25) a, (26) b, (27) b, (28) c, (29) d, (30) c.

True/False Test 6 (p. 278)

(1) T, (2) T, (3) F, (4) F, (5) T, (6) F, (7) F, (8) F, (9) F, (10) F, (11) T, (12) T, (13) T, (14) F, (15) F, (16) F,[1] (17) T, (18) F.

STOP. Turn to page 279 for the scoring of the tests.

Additional Practice Sets (pp. 279-282)

Additional Practice 1

(1) honest, (2) prying, (3) unsophisticated, (4) unite, (5) separate, (6) maintain, (7) unspoken, (8) brief, (9) filled with a sense of discouragement, (10) wordy.

Additional Practice 2

(1) affluent, (2) covert, (3) overt, (4) fatal, (5) fictitious, (6) amnesty, (7) curtail, (8) hostile, (9) lethal, (10) relevant.

Additional Practice 3

(1) choice; (2) brief; (3) discouragingly difficult; (4) starved; (5) tired; (6) ordinary; (7) filled with tenderness; emotional; (8) person who looks at the bright side of things; (9) person who looks at the bad or gloomy side of things; (10) homesick.

---

[1] As a sentimental person is filled with emotion, he or she would not be apathetic. An apathetic person is without feelings.

CHAPTER EIGHT

EXERCISE 19

Step I.   Vocabulary Words in Sentences

Directions: Following are sentences using the ten vocabulary words from Exercise 19. See whether you can figure out the meanings of the underlined words from the clues in the sentences. Sometimes the clue to help you figure out the word is in the next sentence or sentences. Blanks are provided for your estimates of the definitions. Check your meanings with those in Step II.

1. I have always been a very <u>diligent</u> worker. It makes no difference if it's a formidable task or not, because I will apply myself to it and persist until I have succeeded. _____

2. Last week, I met my friend in the library, and by <u>coincidence</u> we had both chosen equivalent topics to write on for our anthropology course. It seemed incredible that by chance we should both have chosen the same tribe of people about which to write. _____

3. It was a unique tribe, which centuries ago had <u>isolated</u> itself from all contact with civilization. It lived alone, never integrating with any other tribes.
_____

4. Although there were not many references about this tribe, I was able to find enough with <u>pertinent</u> information. The references were relevant and applied exactly to my topic. _____

5. Even though my report was rather long, I wouldn't <u>delete</u> one word. I left every word in. _____

6. However, I had a <u>dilemma</u>. Everyone was supposed to be writing on different topics, and the paper was due the next day; so I didn't have time to do another. _____

7. My friend said that he would <u>affirm</u> that we had not planned it together. After all, we were telling the truth. _____

8. Concerning the tribe, when the anthropologists discovered it, the tribespeople seemed to regard the scientists with <u>disdain</u>. Perhaps they looked upon them as unworthy because the scientists looked so different and might be a threat to them. _____

9. The tribespeople, who were a <u>haughty</u> group, took great pride in themselves. _____

10. They had been able to survive for so long by <u>eradicating</u> anyone that came upon their land. On the basis of these facts, why did this tribe allow these anthropologists to live? _____

Step II. Vocabulary Words

1. **affirm** (af · firm′) *v.* To declare or state positively; to say or maintain that something is true. *The auditor examined the bank accounts and **affirmed** that they were all in order with positively no problems.*

2. **coincidence** (co · in · ci · dence) (kō · in′ si · dens) *n.* The occurrence of things or events at the same time by chance. *What a **coincidence** to find Jim in Paris at the same time that I was there.*

3. **delete** (de · lēt′) *v.* To take out or remove a letter, word, and so on; to cross out; to erase. *After Ms. Jones had dictated the letter to her secretary, she asked her to **delete** the whole last paragraph because it was not worded properly.*

4. **dilemma** (di · lem′ma) *n.* Any situation that necessitates a choice between equally unfavorable or equally unpleasant alternatives; an argument that presents two equally unfavorable alternatives. *Mr. Morton's **dilemma** is a serious one because if he agrees to the transplant, he might die during the operation or from the effects of it; but if he doesn't have one, he might die also.*

5. **diligent** (dil′ i · jent) *adj.* Applying oneself in whatever is undertaken; working in a constant effort to accomplish something; industrious. *He*

*worked in such a **diligent** manner to complete his project that he didn't even stop for a break.*

6. **disdain** (dis · dāin') *v.* To regard as unworthy; to despise. *n.* The feeling of scorn or of despisal; expression of scorn (contempt). *Jane was looked at with great **disdain** by all her fellow workers when they found that she had been giving covert information about them to the boss.*

7. **eradicate** (e · rad' i · kāte) *v.* To destroy completely; to pull out by the roots; to wipe out; to exterminate. *The engineers wanted to **eradicate** all possible errors from their calculations before attempting to construct their new machine.*

8. **haughty** (haugh · ty) (haw' tē) *adj.* Having or showing great pride in one-self and contempt (disrespect) or scorn for others; overbearing; snobbish; arrogant. *Many **haughty** people are so egocentric and overbearing that they make others feel hostile toward them.*

9. **isolate** (ī' so · lāte) *v.* To set apart from others; to place alone; to separate. *In the hospital, doctors **isolate** patients with contagious (catching) diseases in rooms by themselves so that they will not spread their germs to others.*

10. **pertinent** (per' ti · nent) *adj.* Relevant; relating to or bearing upon the matter in hand; being to the point. *The witness said that he had **pertinent** information that was relevant to the case.*

Step III. Practice

A. Directions: Each sentence has a missing word. Choose the word that *best* completes the sentence. Write the word in the blank. *All words fit in.*

Word List

diligent, haughty, eradicate, coincidence, pertinent, isolate, dilemma, affirm, delete, disdain.

1. It was a remarkable _____ that two scientists working separately in different countries discovered a cure for a disease at the exact same time.

2. You face a terrible _____ because either choice you make will have unfortunate consequences.

3. Make sure you report only _____ information and leave out anything not relevant.

4. We can both _____ that the evidence you have given is truthful.

289

5. _____ people, who are filled with pride and show disrespect toward others, are not well liked.

6. Because I had a contagious disease, the hospital had to _____ me from the other patients.

7. In order to _____ all the rats in the building, the exterminator used toxic materials that were lethal only to rats and other rodents.

8. A number of times censors _____ words from television programs because they feel that the words should not be presented to a family audience.

9. He looked with _____ at the man who was responsible for so many deaths because of his reckless driving.

10. As a(n) _____ worker, I always apply myself to whatever I do.

STOP. Check answers at the end of the chapter.

B. Directions: Following are ten sentences containing the meanings of vocabulary presented in Exercise 19. Choose the word that *best* fits the meaning of the word or phrase underlined in the sentence.

Word List

diligent, haughty, eradicate, coincidence, pertinent, isolate, dilemma, affirm, delete, disdain.

1. The doctors said that they could completely wipe out certain diseases if they had enough money to support the scientific research. _____

2. People don't like an overbearing person. _____

3. The club members had feelings of scorn for Mike because he told nonmembers about their covert doings. _____

4. He is such a success because he is an industrious worker. _____

5. The material you collected for the report is all relevant. _____

6. Try not to set yourself apart from everyone at the gathering.
_____

7. I had to take out a number of words from my report because it was too long. _____

8. John and I couldn't get each other on the phone because by chance we were phoning each other at the same time. _____

9. "Let me state positively that I feel that my client is innocent," said the lawyer. _____

10. When we found ourselves with <u>an equally bad pair of alternatives</u>, we didn't know what to do. _____

STOP. Check answers at the end of the chapter.

C. Directions: Following are the words presented in Exercise 19. Match each word with the *best* definition.

_____ 1. coincidence

_____ 2. delete

_____ 3. affirm

_____ 4. dilemma

_____ 5. haughty

_____ 6. diligent

_____ 7. pertinent

_____ 8. disdain

_____ 9. eradicate

_____ 10. isolate

a. applying oneself in whatever is undertaken

b. to destroy completely

c. a choice between two equally unpleasant things

d. the feeling of scorn or despisal

e. to erase; to cross out

f. occurrence of events at the same time by chance

g. showing great pride in oneself; overbearing

h. to set apart from others

i. relevant

j. to declare positively

STOP. Check answers at the end of the chapter.

EXTRA WORD POWER

ante. Before. *Ante* is placed in front of many words and means "before." In Exercise 9 you had the combining form *anti,* meaning "against." Do not confuse *ante* with *anti.* Examples: *antebellum*—before the war; *anteroom*—waiting room, a lobby; *antedate*—to date before; *antemeridian*—before noon (the abbreviation is A.M.); *antecedent*—going before.

Additional Words

From your ability to use context clues, can you figure out the meanings of the following words?

1. **arrogant** (ar′ ro · gant) *adj.* *He is so **arrogant** that persons try to avoid being in his presence because it's no fun being with someone who thinks he's so great.*

_____

2. **thrifty** (thrif′ tē) *adj.* *When you have a limited amount of money and many expenses, you have to be **thrifty**.*

_____

3. **replete** (re · plēte′) *adj.* *His words were **replete** with praise for his colleague, whom he admired.*

_____

4. **replenish** (re · plen′ ish) *v.* *Unless they **replenished** their stock immediately, they would run out of everything.*

_____

5. **vestige** (ves′ tije) *n.* *There was no **vestige** of woodland in this area, which had once been replete with trees.*

_____

STOP. Check answers at the end of the chapter.

Practice for Additional Words

Directions: Match each word with the *best* definition.

_____ 1. arrogant   a. clever at managing money

_____ 2. thrifty   b. a trace

_____ 3. replete   c. to supply again

_____ 4. replenish   d. full of pride

_____ 5. vestige   e. well filled

STOP. Check answers at the end of the chapter.

EXERCISE 20

Step I. Vocabulary Words in Sentences

Directions: Following are sentences using the ten vocabulary words from Exercise 20. See whether you can figure out the meanings of the underlined words from the clues in the sentences. Sometimes the clue to help you figure out the word is in the next sentence or sentences. Blanks are provided for your estimates of the definitions. Check your meanings with those in Step II.

1. The saying "Turn the other cheek," which comes to us from the Scripture, is sometimes very difficult to follow. Let me tell you a tale for which I'm sure there are many precedents, that is, I'm sure you, too, can give similar examples. _____

2. At the end of last semester, right after finals, some of my colleagues and I decided to combine our efforts to try to get a research grant from the federal government. As my fellow workers are very diligent, I like to work with them. _____

3. Being reliable individuals, if they say that they will persevere until something is completed, they will persist until the task is done. That's how dependable they are. _____ ; _____

4. Well, we spent what seemed like an infinite amount of time and energy developing an intricate research design with which we finally were all pleased. _____

5. Antecedent to this complex research plan, we had been involved in a very sophisticated project concerning hypertension. _____

6. We felt that we had made a significant breakthrough in the area of high blood pressure, which is known as the "silent killer." Although we felt the breakthrough was important and meaningful, we felt that we needed to do some more research before we released our results to others. _____

7. We were reluctant to reveal our results because we felt that more study was needed. As we were unwilling to release our results, a man, whom I'll call Dr. X, decided to steal our findings and do his own research with them. _____

8. Dr. X made an adaptation of our plan, called it his own, and submitted it to Washington, D.C., for a grant. Actually, it wasn't even an adaptation, for so few changes were made. _____

9. You can imagine our surprise when a federal agency called us to Washington, D.C., and started to interrogate us about our research. When they questioned us, they acted as though we had done something illegal. It wasn't until much later that we learned about Dr. X and what he had done. _____

1. **adaptation** (ad · ap · ta · tion) (ad · ap · tā′ shun) *n.* The act of fitting or suiting one thing to another; an adjusting to fit new conditions; a modification (a partial or slight change) for a new use. *As the story was too long for the kindergarten children, the teacher made an **adaptation** of it to suit the children's attention span.*

2. **antecedent** (an · te · sēd′ ent) *adj.* Going before in time; prior; preceding; previous. *n.* The word, phrase, or clause to which a pronoun refers. *In writing you must be careful that your pronoun refers to a definite **antecedent**.*

3. **colleague** (col · league) (kol′ ēg) *n.* A fellow worker in the same profession. *My **colleagues** and I feel that our vocation needs more members who are diligent workers.*

4. **intricate** (in · tri · cate) (in′ tri · kit) *adj.* Complicated; difficult to follow or unerstand; complex. *The plan was so **intricate** that we needed many meetings in order to be able to understand it.*

5. **interrogate** (in · ter′ ɾo · gāt¢) *v.* To ask questions of formally; to examine by questioning. *The police said that they would **interrogate** everyone who was anywhere near the location of the homicide to try to get some answers.*

6. **persevere** (per · se · vēr¢′) *v.* To persist; to continue doing something in spite of difficulty. *Despite all hardships, some people are able to **persevere** and succeed in achieving their objectives.*

7. **precedent** (pres′ e · dent) *n.* Something done or said that may serve as an example; in law, a legal decision serving as an authoritative rule in future similar cases. *adj.* Preceding; anterior; going before. *By doing that, you may have set a **precedent** for other people to follow.*

8. **reliable** (re · li · a · ble) (re · lī′ a · bul) *adj.* Dependable; trustworthy. *As Arthur is so **reliable** I know that we can depend on his doing the job diligently and well.*

9. **reluctant** (re · luk′ tant) *adj.* Unwilling; opposed. *We were all **reluctant** to say that we would buy tickets to the show until we had more information about the cost.*

10. **significant** (sig · nif′ i · kant) *adj.* Having or expressing meaning; full of meaning; important. *The test results were so **significant** that the scientists knew that they had made a great breakthrough in medicine.*

Special Notes

1. **precedent** *n.* Something done or said that may serve as an example. In Part I, you met the verb *precede*, meaning "to go before." Note that the noun

precedent presented in this exercise comes from the same combining form *ced,* meaning "go" or "yield," and *pre,* meaning "before."

2. **antecedent** *adj.* Going before in time. *n.* Word, phrase, or clause to which a pronoun refers. Note that *antecedent* is derived from the combining form *ced,* meaning "go" or "yield," and *ante,* meaning "before." You have probably met the term *antecedent* in your English course. The word, phrase, or clause to which a pronoun refers is called the *antecedent.* For example, in the sentence "John Smith was the judge who made that important decision," *judge* is the antecedent of *who.* In other words, *who* refers to *judge.* In "Jack lost his hat," *Jack* is the antecedent of *his.*

Step III. Practice

A. Directions: Each sentence has a missing word. Choose the word that *best* completes the sentence. Write the word in the blank. *All words fit in.*

Word List

intricate, antecedent, adaptation, interrogate, significant, reliable, colleague, reluctant, precedent, persevere.

1. My_____ s and I held our biannual professional conference at the biologists' convention.

2. As there were no _____s to go by, the lawyers knew that they were dealing in a new legal area.

3. The mountain climbers said that they would allow nothing to get in the way of achieving their formidable task, and they would _____ at all costs.

4. Only the most_____ federal agents, who could be trusted, were used to guard former criminals who were giving evidence against top crime figures.

5. When we lost our passports in Europe, we were told by customs officials that they would have to_____us to determine if they had been stolen or lost.

6. I am always_____ to sign anything that I haven't first read.

7. The man in the commercial was trying to affirm that there was a(n) _____difference between his product and another similar product produced by another manufacturer.

8. The directions to get to the picnic grounds were so_____ that we all had difficulty following them.

9. _____to this exercise, you worked on Exercise 19.

10. Have you ever seen a(n)_____ of an old movie in which the main story line is kept the same, but the period in which the story takes place is changed?

STOP. Check answers at the end of the chapter.

B. Directions: Following are ten sentences. Define the underlined word. Put your answer in the blank.

1. The judge's decision will serve as a <u>precedent</u> in future similar cases.

   _____

2. That event was <u>antecedent</u> to the war and may have been the cause of it.

   _____

3. Only <u>reliable</u> men were chosen for the mission because they had to be trusted with very secret information. _____

4. The stockholders were <u>reluctant</u> to vote a pay increase for the company executives because the company was losing money. _____

5. Is the study you are working on so <u>significant</u> that it will make a difference in the way things will be done in the future? _____

6. Professor Jones said that he was meeting a number of his <u>colleagues</u> at their annual professional convention. _____

7. Some of the methods that are used to <u>interrogate</u> persons are quite cruel.

   _____

8. The <u>intricate</u> dress pattern was too complicated for me; so I asked my friend, a professional dressmaker, to help me. _____

9. A new television show, which is an <u>adaptation</u> of a former radio program, is well suited for a contemporary audience. _____

10. When persons became frustrated, they tend to give up rather than to <u>persevere</u>. _____

STOP. Check answers at the end of the chapter.

C. Directions: In the Word Square there are seven words from Exercise 20. Find the words in the square and match them with their correct meanings. Note that there are *more* meanings than words. If there is no word in the square for a meaning, write *none,* and give the word.

WORD SQUARE

```
  →
L  A  D  A  P  T  A  T  I  O  N
O  M  O  N  T  P  U  S  R  S  P
A  I  M  T  E  E  I  I  N  M  R
I  N  T  E  R  R  O  G  A  T  E
I  T  M  C  E  S  A  N  S  R  C
J  R  O  E  L  E  R  I  W  E  E
R  I  N  D  I  V  S  F  I  L  D
S  G  S  E  A  E  O  I  C  U  E
Q  U  R  N  B  R  M  C  O  C  N
U  E  A  T  L  E  U  A  I  R  T
S  F  A  R  E  S  E  N  L  E  O
C  O  L  L  E  A  G  T  U  L  M
```

Meanings	*Words*
1. Complicated	_____
2. Important	_____
3. Act of fitting one thing to another	_____
4. Going before	_____
5. Fellow worker	_____
6. To question	_____
7. To persist	_____
8. Example	_____
9. Dependable	_____
10. Unwilling	_____

STOP. Check answers at the end of the chapter.

> **ship.** State, condition, or quality of; office, rank, or
> dignity; art or skill. *Ship* is added to the end of many
> nouns. For example: *kingship*—dignity or rank of
> king; *governorship*—rank or office of governor; *lord-
> ship*—rank of a lord; *dictatorship*—office or rank of a
> head of government who has absolute control of the
> government; *citizenship*—state or quality of being a
> citizen; *friendship*—state of being a friend; *penman-
> ship*—art or skill of handwriting; *leadership*—skill as
> a leader. How many more words with *ship* can you
> supply?

Additional Words

From your ability to use context clues, can you figure out the meanings of the
following words?

1. **procrastinate** (prō · kras' ti · nāte) *v. If you **procrastinate** all the time, you
will never accomplish anything. You can put off doing things for just so long.*

   _____

2. **prudent** (prū' dent) *adj. On the contrary, John was always **prudent** rather
than rash in dealing with difficult matters.*

   _____

3. **virile** (vir' ile) *adj. **Virile** men usually don't have to prove their masculinity
to anyone.*

   _____

4. **vindictive** (vin · dik' tive) *adj. It's difficult not to want **vindictive** punishment for killers who have murdered your loved ones.*

   _____

5. **satiate** (sa · ti · ate) (sā' shē · āte) *v. Everyone was able to **satiate** his or
her appetite at the banquet.*

   _____

STOP. Check answers at the end of the chapter.

Practice for Additional Words

Directions: Match each word with the *best* definition.

_____ 1. procrastinate   a. revengeful

_____ 2. prudent   b. to overindulge

_____ 3. virile   c. sensible

_____ 4. vindictive   d. to put off doing

_____ 5. satiate   e. manly

STOP. Check answers at the end of the chapter.

EXERCISE 21

Step I. Vocabulary Words in Sentences

Directions: Following are sentences using the ten vocabulary words from Exercise 21. See whether you can figure out the meanings of the underlined words from the clues in the sentences. Sometimes the clue to help you figure out the word is in the next sentence or sentences. Blanks are provided for your estimates of the definitions. Check your meanings with those in Step II.

1. In my high school class there were a number of students who had many liabilities. These students had no fathers, no mothers, no one who took an interest in them, and no money. They had many disadvantages.

   _____

2. The only asset that some of these students had was their desire to persist, to persevere, to make something of themselves. This asset proved to be a very valuable thing to have. _____

3. A decade later I met one of these students at a high school reunion, but I didn't recognize him because not only had his appearance changed, but he had also modified his manner of speaking and way of acting.

   _____

4. When I learned about how successful he had become, I asked him how he had achieved it. He said that instead of coveting or desiring what others had, he went after what he wanted. _____

5. He said that he was very frugal. He spent money only for necessities.

   _____

6. He said that he had learned to economize. He didn't know what it was to have anything extra. _____

7. Throughout college, he said that he allotted himself a certain amount of time for study, a certain amount of time for work, and very little time for leisure. _____

8. Upon talking to some other former high school buddies whom I hadn't seen before the reunion, I found that they had greatly changed their views on life. Many <u>conservative</u> students, who didn't want change in anything, were now broad-minded. Many <u>liberal</u> students, who had been broad-minded, were now conservatives. _____; _____

9. From my high school reunion, I learned that people are not like <u>stagnant</u> water, which remains in one place, but are dynamic, active beings who can control their lives. _____

Step II. Vocabulary Words

1. **allot** (a⋅lot') *v.* To divide or distribute by lot; to distribute or parcel out in portions; to appoint. *The State Department of Education said that it would **allot** the money to school districts on the basis of a new formula, so that the money would be equally divided.*

2. **asset** (as'⋅set) *n.* Anything owned that has value; any valuable or desirable thing that serves as an advantage. *Instead of being a problem and undesirable, he turned out to be an enormous **asset** to us.*

3. **conservative** (kon⋅ser'⋅va⋅tive) *adj.* Tending to maintain established traditions and to resist or oppose any change in these; cautious; moderate; traditional in style or manner; avoiding showiness. *n.* One who clings to traditional or long-standing methods, views, ideas, and so on. *A **conservative** person is reluctant to see any change.*

4. **covet** (kov'et) *v.* To desire very much what another has; to crave; to long for. *In the Scriptures it says that you should not **covet** another's wife.*

5. **economize** (e⋅kon'o⋅mize) *v.* To use or manage with thrift or prudence; to avoid waste or needless spending; to reduce expenses. *With everything costing so much, we will have to **economize** and curtail our spending.*

6. **frugal** (frū'gal) *adj.* Thrifty; not spending freely; avoiding waste. *When you have a fixed and limited income and when the price of everything is high, you must be **frugal**.*

7. **liability** (lī⋅a⋅bil'i⋅tē) *n.* Something that is owed; a debt; legal obligation to make good any loss or damage that occurs in a transaction (a business deal); something that works to a person's disadvantage. *The officers of the corporation realized that the new company they had acquired was a **liability** to them because of its large losses.*

8. **liberal** (lib'er⋅al) *adj.* Giving freely; generous; large or plentiful; tolerant of views differing from one's own; broad-minded; favoring reform or progress; *n.* A person who is open-minded or broad-minded. *As a very **liberal**-minded person, he is for reform and a great amount of personal freedom for individuals.*

9. **modify** (mod$'$ i · fī) *v.* To change slightly or make minor changes in character, form, and so on; to change or alter; to limit or reduce; in grammar, to limit or restrict a meaning. *Persons usually* **modify** *their views as they get older because their ways of seeing things change.*

10. **stagnant** (stag$'$ nant) *adj.* Lacking motion or current; not flowing or moving; foul (dirty and bad-smelling) from lack of movement; lacking in activity; sluggish; dull. *The* **stagnant** *pond had a terribly bad odor because many of the aquatic plants in it were decaying.*

1. *Asset* has a special meaning when used in the plural, *assets.* The term *assets* is used in accounting to mean all the items on a balance sheet that show the property or resources (what an individual has) of a person or business, such as inventory (list of all goods in stock), cash, real estate, equipment, accounts and notes receivable, and so on.

2. When *liability* is used in the plural, it usually is referring to a debt such as accounts payable, capital stock, losses, and so on. Accounts payable, losses, and capital stock are *liabilities* of a corporation.

3. When *modify* is used in grammar, it means "to limit or restrict in meaning." In the sentence "That is a huge dormitory," *huge* modifies *dormitory.* Adding the word *huge* to *dormitory*, limits or restricts *dormitory.* You know that it is not a small dormitory. If *co-ed* is added to *huge dormitory,* you are limiting the meaning of *dormitory* even more. Words that limit or restrict another word are describing the word. That is, *huge* and *co-ed* are describing *dormitory.*

Step III. Practice

A. Directions: Each of the following sentences has a missing word. Choose the word that *best* completes the sentence. Write the word in the the blank. *All words fit in.*

Word List

allot, asset, liability, frugal, stagnant, modify, conservative, liberal, economize, covet.

1. The _____ pond was completely still.

2. We usually _____ our views in college because our experiences cause us to make some changes in the way we think or feel.

3. Because I'm paying my own way through school, I must be very _____ .

4. Fortunately, I don't have even one _____ , because at this moment I couldn't afford to owe anyone anything.

5. The_____group was opposed to the changes that were being proposed.

6. Rather than _____what affluent people have, why don't you try to do something with your own potential?

7. Make the most of your _____s, and play down your faults when you go on the job interview.

8. He is very_____with money because he is so affluent and generous.

9. Even though I am quite affluent now, I still _____because I can't stand waste.

10. Did you _____each person an equivalent portion?

STOP. Check answers at the end of the chapter.

B. Directions: Following are ten sentences. Define the underlined word. Put your answer in the blank.

1. If I don't start to <u>economize</u> now, I won't have any money left at the end of the week._____

2. My views are always contrary to my parents' views, and because they like everything to remain the same, I'm a <u>liberal</u>. _____

3. Mary is so <u>frugal</u> that absolutely nothing is ever wasted by her.

_____

4. As a young child, John was ridiculed about being so tall, but at college his height was an <u>asset</u> for the basketball team._____

5. I <u>allot</u> myself a certain amount of time each week to spend in reading books other than those assigned in class._____

6. One of the political parties in our township is so <u>conservative</u> that it won't even let you change a meeting time. _____

7. I saw a film in which you know that conflict is going to take place because in the opening scene a young cowhand wanders in, looks at the wife of the rancher, and immediately you know he <u>covets</u> her._____

8. The <u>stagnant</u> pond water smelled as bad as a sewer. _____

9. The city council members found that they would have to <u>modify</u> their plan if they wanted it to be accepted. _____

10. As a successful model, Jane found her height was an advantage to her rather then a <u>liability</u>. _____

STOP. Check answers at the end of the chapter.

C. Directions: In the Word Square there are seventeen words from Exercises 19, 20, 21, and some previous exercises. Find the words in the square and match them with their correct meanings. Note that there are *more* meanings than words. If there is no word in the square for a meaning, write *none*, and give the word.

WORD SQUARE

E	C	O	N	O	M	I	Z	E	S	E	R
A	L	L	O	T	P	R	E	D	U	A	L
R	I	F	R	U	G	A	L	E	P	M	U
E	A	S	S	E	T	C	I	L	E	N	A
L	B	I	T	M	A	A	B	E	R	E	L
U	I	S	A	O	C	N	E	T	V	S	A
C	L	O	G	D	I	D	R	E	I	T	U
T	I	L	N	I	T	I	A	C	T	Y	D
A	T	A	A	F	O	D	L	O	A	A	I
N	Y	T	N	Y	M	A	O	V	L	E	B
T	O	E	T	O	E	E	U	E	S	D	L
C	O	N	S	E	R	V	A	T	I	V	E

Meanings   *Words*

1. Frank   _____

2. Able to be heard   _____

3. A pardon   _____

4. The occurrence of events
   at the same time   _____

5. To divide or distribute   _____

6. Unspoken   _____

7. To separate from; to
   place apart from   _____

8. Thrifty   _____

9. Unwilling   _____

10. A valuable thing to have   _____

11. To take out   _____

303

12. To desire what others have   _____

13. To state positively   _____

14. Tending to maintain established
    traditions   _____

15. Giving freely; broad-minded   _____

16. To avoid waste   _____

17. A debt   _____

18. To change slightly   _____

19. Lacking motion   _____

20. Difficult choice because
    both are disagreeable   _____

STOP. Check answers at the end of the chapter.

EXTRA WORD
POWER

> **super.** Above in position; over; above or beyond; greater than or superior to; extra; in the highest degree; in excessive degree. *Super* is found at the beginning of many words. You have probably met *super* in words like *superior*, meaning "of higher degree"; *superb*, meaning "of the highest quality"; and *superlative*, meaning "of the highest degree." Following is a list of words in which *super* is added to the beginning of the word and changes the word meaning to include "in excessive degree" or "in the highest degree." *supercritical*—highly critical; *superbias*—excessive bias; *supersafe*—safe in the highest degree; *supersweet*—sweet in the highest degree; *superabundance*—abundance in excess; *superacid*—excessively acid. Following is a list of words in which *super* is found at the beginning of the word, and it is a necessary part of the word; that is, if *super* were deleted from the word, the word would lose its meaning. *supervision*—the act of overseeing others; *superintendent*—one who has charge of a department, building, institution, and the like; *superstitious*—having beliefs that are not consistent with the known laws of science. How many more words with *super* can you supply? Check your dictionary for a long list of *super* words.

Additional Words

From your ability to use context clues, can you figure out the meanings of the following words?

1. **vital** (vī' tul) *adj.* *The doctor said that the operation was so **vital** that not having it would be fatal.*

   _____

2. **laudable** (laud · a · ble) (laud' a · bul) *adj.* *What the group has done is highly **laudable**, and it should be praised for its efforts. Not many students would give up their free time to help others.*

   _____

3. **vindicate** (vin' di · kātɇ) *v.* *Although she was completely **vindicated** by the trial, some people treated her as though she were guilty.*

   _____

4. **sedate** (se · dātɇ') *adj. v.* *The sedative calmed him down so much that it was hard to believe that this **sedate** person had been belligerent a few moments ago.*

   _____

5. **castigate** (kas' ti · gātɇ) *v.* *The judge **castigated** the parents for their behavior toward their children and warned them that next time he would take the children away from them.*

   _____

STOP. Check answers at the end of the chapter.

Practice for Additional Words

Directions: Match each word with the *best* definition.

_____ 1. vital   a. worthy of praise

_____ 2. laudable   b. calm; composed

_____ 3. vindicate   c. necessary to life

_____ 4. sedate   d. to correct or subdue
                                by punishing
_____ 5. castigate
                             e. to clear from criticism

STOP. Check answers at the end of the chapter.

Some People Have Different Opinions on What Is *Vital*

Reprinted by permission of NEA, Inc.

CROSSWORD PUZZLE 7

Directions: The meanings of a number of the words from Exercises 19–21 follow. Your knowledge of these words, as well as the combining forms from Part I, will help you to solve this crossword puzzle.

Across

1. Way of saying *father*
3. Broad-minded
6. Sixth letter of the alphabet

Down

1. A friend
2. Comb. f. for *other*
3. Worthy of praise

7. Comb. f. for *without*
8. Dependable
13. Comb. f. for *before*
15. Opposite of *down* (pl.)
18. When your heart stops beating, you are ___
19. Thrifty
22. Same as # 1 Down
25. When your heart stops beating you have___
27. Homonym of *sew*
28. Comb. f. for *in*
29. Homonym of *two*
30. Same as # 23 Down
31. Comb. f. for *against*
32. Comb. f. for *laugh*
33. Comb. f. for *out of; from*
34. Abbreviation for *South Carolina*
35. Sound you make when you laugh
37. Comb. f. for *through*
38. Same as # 10 Down
39. Foul from not moving
43. Comb. f. for *measure*
46. Your dog or cat is your___
47. Same as # 9 Down
48. Part of your face
49. To wipe out completely
52. Choice between two equally bad alternatives
55. To question formally
58. Another way of referring to God
60. Same as # 23 Down
61. To give food to
62. Same as # 28 Across
63. Same as # 28 Across
64. Opposite of *gain*
65. Applying oneself to whatever is undertaken
68. Same as # 66 Down
69. Slang for *Communists*
71. Sound made when laughing
72. Comb. f. for *in*
73. Something that tastes good is ___
75. Same as # 7 Across

4. Comb. f. for *one who*
5. Comb. f. for *back*
6. Lots of water vapor on the ground causes ___, which makes it difficult to see
9. *Much___ About Nothing*
10. Homonym of *bee*
11. Musical syllable
12. Ending for the past tense of regular verbs
13. Example
14. A ___ in your stocking will ruin it
16. ___needles, which come from an evergreen tree
17. ___the table
19. Same as # 6 Across
20. Rhymes with *cat*
21. ___and behold; means *see*
22. A ___of paper
23. Same as # 2 Down
24. A debt; disadvantage
26. To despise; scorn
27. Important; full of meaning
32. Abbreviation for *rear admiral*
33. Christian holiday around March 21
34. California is a ___
35. Masculine pronoun
36. Same as # 20 Down
40. Same as # 29 Across
41. Without any; nothing left
42. Past tense of something necessary
43. Abbreviation of girl's name, *Margaret*
44. Time period
45. Same as # 32 Across
46. To persist
47. Rhymes with *ham*
50. To divide or portion off
51. Homonym of *two*
52. Way of saying *father* (pl.)
53. ___ of the valley; a flower

76. Comb. f. for *together; with*
78. You ___ your *i* and put this at the end of a sentence
79. Same as # 20 Down
80. Referring to *voice*
82. Same as # 77 Down
83. Unwilling
87. Opposite of *she*
88. Same as # 7 Across
89. Grows in ground, is eaten, and has a strong, sharp smell and taste
90. Opposite of *near*
91. Refers to a small child
92. To desire very much what others have
93. Form of the verb *to be*
94. Same as # 5 Down

54. ___ shot; slang for picture of face
56. You do this when you are fatigued
57. Opposite of *off*
59. Comb. f. for *people*
66. Pronoun referring to *me*
67. Unspoken
70. To carry out; to perform
71. Same as # 35 Across
73. Same as # 29 Across
74. Indefinite article
77. Opposite of *off*
81. Same as # 7 Across
83. Same as # 32 Down
84. Same as # 21 Down
85. Comb. f. for *not*
86. Same as # 51 Down
87. To own
90. Previous; former; earlier
92. You drive this

STOP. Check answers at the end of the chapter.

WORD SCRAMBLE 7

Directions: Word Scramble 7 is based on words from Exercises 19–21. The meanings are your clues to arranging the letters in correct order. Write the correct word in the blank.

Meanings

1. diiccnocene _____ the occurrence of things at the same time by chance

2. eeeltd _____ to take out

3. riffma _____ to state positively

4. melmaid _____ a situation that presents two equally disagreeable choices

5. gentilid _____ applying oneself

6. tentrepin _____ relevant

7. aaadoitnpt _____ act of fitting or suiting one thing to another

8. centdeanet _____ going before

9. nitiraetc   ————————— complicated

10. guelolaec   ————————— fellow worker

11. tingerorate   ————————— to question

12. servereep   ————————— to persist

13. eelblair   ————————— dependable

14. cansignfiti   ————————— important

15. tsase   ————————— something of value

16. tagstnna   ————————— without motion

17. altol   ————————— to divide or distribute by lot

18. gufrla   ————————— thrifty

19. toevc   ————————— to desire what others have

20. domyfi   ————————— to alter

STOP. Check answers at the end of the chapter.

ANALOGIES 7

Directions: Find the word from the following list that *best* completes each
analogy. *There are more words in the list than you need.*

Word List

*sensible, timid, fearful, blast, persevere, scorn, temerity, think, bold, eradicate,
manly, decisive, diligent, vital, save, frugal, replenish, replete, satiate, affirm,
associate, isolate, contagious, commendable, rebuke, build, alter, delete,
omission, reply, question, postpone, broad-minded, conservative, sophisticated,
covet, covert, overt, buy, intricate.*

1. Frank : candid :: virile : _____.

2. Positive : definite :: disdain : _____ .

3. Parade : procession :: interrogate : _____.

4. Hostile : friendly :: liberal : _____.

5. Haughty : arrogant :: resupply : _____.

6. Stale : fresh :: deny : _____.

7. Dependable : reliable :: persist : _____.

8. Synonym : antonym :: simple : _____.

9. Frustrated : defeated :: colleague : _____.

10. Castigate : rebuke :: segregate :: _____.

11. Thrifty : frugal :: laudable : _____ .

12. Inferior : superior :: insert : _____ .

13. Hate : animosity :: desire : _____ .

14. Provisions : supplies :: prudent : _____ .

15. Plump : corpulent :: modify : _____ .

16. Pertinent : relevant :: industrious : _____ .

17. Tepid : lukewarm :: essential : _____ .

18. Modest : shy :: procrastinate : _____ .

19. Alarm : warn :: bomb : _____ .

20. Blanket : cover :: economize : _____ .

STOP. Check answers at the end of the chapter.

MULTIPLE-CHOICE VOCABULARY TEST 7

Directions: This is a test on words in Exercises 19–21. Words are presented
according to exercises. *Do all exercises before checking answers.*
Underline the meaning that *best* fits the word.

Exercise 19

1. coincidence
   a. something that happens
   b. a chance happening
   c. occurrence of things at the same time by chance
   d. a happening

2. delete
   a. to put in
   b. to take out
   c. to write
   d. to allow

3. affirm
   a. to deny
   b. to ask
   c. to question
   d. to state positively

4. dilemma
   a. a problem
   b. an argument
   c. something unpleasant
   d. a choice between two equally disagreeable things

5. diligent
   a. a choice
   b. a choice between equally disagreeable things
   c. applying oneself
   d. an argument

6. disdain
   a. a disagreement
   b. unequal choices
   c. to regard as unworthy
   d. to apply oneself

310

7. eradicate
   a. to take a word away
   b. to wipe out completely
   c. to despise
   d. to disagree with

8. haughty
   a. having a lot of pride in oneself
   b. applying oneself
   c. disagreeable
   d. hostile

9. isolate
   a. to harm
   b. to help
   c. to set apart
   d. to stay together

10. pertinent
    a. unrelated
    b. not appropriate
    c. appropriate
    d. set apart

Exercise 20

11. adaptation
    a. act of adjusting to old situations
    b. a fitting outcome
    c. refers to adoption
    d. act of fitting one thing to another

12. antecedent
    a. going against
    b. going after
    c. going before
    d. going first

13. intricate
    a. complicated
    b. simple
    c. presenting a problem
    d. helpful

14. colleague
    a. a college buddy
    b. a friend
    c. an enemy
    d. a fellow worker in a profession

15. interrogate
    a. to speak
    b. to state
    c. to question
    d. to make a choice

16. persevere
    a. to help
    b. to persist
    c. to move
    d. to be active

17. precedent
    a. something that serves as an example
    b. an offense
    c. something unnecessary
    d. something that comes after

18. reliable
    a. helpful
    b. dependable
    c. hostile
    d. presenting an example

19. reluctant
    a. willing
    b. helping
    c. unwilling
    d. hostile

20. significant
    a. a sign
    b. a meaning
    c. helpful
    d. full of meaning

Exercise 21

21. allot
    a. to donate
    b. to state an opinion
    c. to sell a lot
    d. to divide

| 22. asset | a. to assess | c. a valuable thing |
| | b. happy | d. an opinion |

23. conservative	a. tending to like change	c. tending to be broad-minded
	b. tending to like differences	
		d. tending to like things to remain the same

24. covet	a. to like things	c. to desire greatly things that others have
	b. to dislike things	
		d. to hope

| 25. frugal | a. spending freely | c. spends often |
| | b. wise | d. thrifty |

| 26. liability | a. a gift | c. a debt |
| | b. legal | d. a feeling |

| 27. economize | a. to spend freely | c. refers to economics |
| | b. to spend money | d. to avoid waste |

| 28. liberal | a. big | c. remain the same |
| | b. broad-minded | d. helpful |

| 29. modify | a. to change slightly | c. to dress |
| | b. to move | d. to be mod |

| 30. stagnant | a. lacking movement | c. healthful |
| | b. moving | d. refers to running water |

TRUE/FALSE TEST 7

Directions: This is a true/false test on Exercises 19–21. Read each sentence carefully. Decide whether it is true or false. Put a *T* for *true* or an *F* for *false* in the blank. The number after the sentence tells you if the word is from Exercise 19, 20, or 21.

_____ 1. Someone who <u>economizes</u> would be a frugal person. 21

_____ 2. All <u>assets</u> are good to have. 21

_____ 3. *Frugal* and *thrifty* are antonyms. 21

_____ 4. When you <u>allot</u> something to someone, you give him a lot. 21

_____ 5. A <u>dilemma</u> is easy to solve. 19

_____ 6. When someone is held in <u>disdain</u>, he is scorned. 19

_____ 7. When something is <u>eradicated</u>, it is partially wiped out. 19

_____ 8. *Liability* and *asset* are antonyms. 21

_____ 9. When something is <u>stagnant</u>, it is still. 21

_____ 10. In the sentence "Mother is a wonderful woman, who is a great cook," *woman* is the <u>antecedent</u> of *who*. 20

_____ 11. A <u>precedent</u> comes to us from the past and serves as a guide or example. 20

_____ 12. A <u>diligent</u> worker is a lazy person. 19

_____ 13. <u>Pertinent</u> information is information that doesn't apply. 19

_____ 14. When something happens by <u>coincidence</u>, it is planned. 19

_____ 15. An <u>adaptation</u> of a plan is a plan that has been changed to suit the new situation. 20

_____ 16. A <u>significant</u> result in a study is a doubtful finding. 20

_____ 17. A <u>conservative</u> person resists change. 21

_____ 18. When you <u>delete</u> a sentence, you are <u>modifying</u> it. 19, 21

_____ 19. A <u>colleague</u> refers to a friendly fellow. 20

_____ 20. An <u>intricate</u> plan is a simple plan. 20

STOP. Check answers for both tests at the end of the chapter.

SCORING OF TESTS

Multiple-Choice Test

Number Wrong	Score
0–2	Excellent
3–5	Good
6–8	Weak
Above 8	Poor
Score _____	

True/False Test

Number Wrong	Score
0–1	Excellent
2–3	Good
4–5	Weak
Above 5	Poor
Score _____	

1. If you scored in the excellent or good range on *both tests,* you are doing well. Go on to Chapter Nine.

2. If you scored in the weak or poor range on either test, turn to the next page and follow directions for Additional Practice. Note that the words on the tests are arranged so that you can tell in which exercise to find them. This will help you if you need additional practice.

ADDITIONAL PRACTICE SETS

A. Directions: Write the words you missed on the tests from the three exercises in the space provided. Note that the tests are presented so that you can tell to which exercises the words belong.

Exercise 19 Words Missed

1. _____   6. _____
2. _____   7. _____
3. _____   8. _____
4. _____   9. _____
5. _____   10. _____

Exercise 20 Words Missed

1. _____   6. _____
2. _____   7. _____
3. _____   8. _____
4. _____   9. _____
5. _____   10. _____

Exercise 21 Words Missed

1. _____   6. _____
2. _____   7. _____
3. _____   8. _____
4. _____   9. _____
5. _____   10. _____

B. Directions: Restudy the words that you have written down on this page. Do Step I and Step II for those you missed. Note that Step I and Step II are on the following pages:

Exercise 19—pp. 287–289.

Exercise 20—pp. 292–295.

Exercise 21—pp. 299–301.

C. Directions: Do Additional Practice 1 on the next page if you missed words from Exercise 19. Do Additional Practice 2 on pp. 315–316 if you missed words from Exercise 20. Do Additional Practice 3 on pp. 316–317 if you missed words from Exercise 21. Now go on to Chapter Nine.

Directions: Following are ten sentences with missing words. Underline the word
that *best* fits the sentence. Two choices are given for each sentence.

1. Because he is such a (pertinent; diligent) worker, he will finish the job on
   time.

2. What a (dilemma; coincidence) to have to choose between two equally bad
   things.

3. My essay was too long; so I decided to (affirm; delete) some words.

4. Hitler tried to (eradicate; isolate) a whole group of people by murdering
   all of them.

5. This statement must be left in because it is (diligent; pertinent) to the report.

6. Because nations depend upon one another, it is difficult in contemporary
   times for nations to (affirm; isolate) themselves from others.

7. The witness said that he would again (affirm; delete) the statement he made
   before because it was correct and important.

8. What a (coincidence; dilemma) to have both of us doing the same thing at
   the same time.

9. I do not like to be with (diligent; haughty) people because they think that
   they are so great and they look down on others.

10. When they heard that Ms. Jones had betrayed their confidence, she was
    held in great (dilemma; disdain).

STOP. Check answers at the end of the chapter.

Additional Practice 2 for Exercise 20

Directions: Following are ten sentences containing the meanings of vocabulary
presented in Exercise 20. Choose the word that *best* fits the word
or phrase underlined in the sentence. *All words fit in.*

Word List

*intricate, interrogate, antecedent, adaptation, colleague, significant, reliable,
precedent, persevere, reluctant.*

1. This play, which is based on a famous novel, is a perfect <u>modification</u> suited
   to the contemporary scene. _____

2. The plan we developed is so <u>involved and complicated</u> that it will probably
   take some time for the others to understand it. _____

3. The findings from your research are so <u>important and full of meaning</u> that they should be shared with the world. _____

4. My <u>fellow professional associates</u> are joining me at a special convention. _____

5. I am <u>unwilling</u> to go along with the rest of you because the idea does not sound <u>workable</u> to me. _____

6. As he is a very <u>dependable and trustworthy</u> person, I will vote for him. _____

7. The judge used <u>a former case as an example</u> on which to make his decision. _____

8. As a policewoman, I must always tell persons of their rights before I can <u>formally question</u> them. _____

9. When I have a hard job to do, I <u>persist</u> until I have finished it. _____

10. The invention of the train was <u>prior</u> to that of the airplane. _____

STOP. Check answers at the end of the chapter.

Additional Practice 3 for Exercise 21

Directions: Following are ten sentences containing the meanings of vocabulary presented in Exercise 21. Choose the word that *best* fits the word or phrase underlined in the sentence. *All words fit in.*

Word List

conservative, stagnant, allot, frugal, covet, liberal, asset, liability, economize, modify.

1. Under the terms of the will, they will <u>divide</u> the money equally among the children. _____

2. A pleasant smile is <u>a valuable and desirable thing</u> to have. _____

3. We are <u>traditional</u> persons reluctant to have any change, and our group will oppose any changes that you attempt to make. _____

4. I am a <u>thrifty</u> person. _____

5. I <u>spend</u> my money <u>wisely</u> to avoid waste. _____

6. The major <u>debt</u> I have is my school loan. _____

7. Some people only <u>desire what other people have.</u> _____

8. When lake water is <u>without motion,</u> it can begin to have a bad smell. _____

9. My <u>broad-minded</u> friends are all very interested in reform and progress.
_____

10. I am going to <u>change</u> my speech <u>slightly</u> so that it will appeal to more people._____

STOP. Check answers at the end of the chapter.

ANSWERS

Exercise 19 (pp. 287–292)

Practice A

(1) coincidence, (2) dilemma, (3) pertinent, (4) affirm, (5) haughty, (6) isolate, (7) eradicate, (8) delete, (9) disdain, (10) diligent.

Practice B

(1) eradicate, (2) haughty, (3) disdain, (4) diligent, (5) pertinent, (6) isolate, (7) delete, (8) coincidence, (9) affirm, (10) dilemma.

Practice C

(1) f, (2) e, (3) j, (4) c, (5) g, (6) a, (7) i, (8) d, (9) b, (10) h.

Additional Words (pp. 291–292)

1. **arrogant.** Full of pride and self-importance; overbearing; haughty.
2. **thrifty.** Clever at managing one's money; economical; not spending money unnecessarily.
3. **replete.** Well filled or supplied.
4. **replenish.** To supply or fill again.
5. **vestige.** A trace, mark, or sign of something that once existed but doesn't anymore.

Practice for Additional Words (p. 292)

(1) d, (2) a, (3) e, (4) c, (5) b.

Exercise 20 (pp. 292–299)

Practice A

(1) colleague, (2) precedent, (3) persevere, (4) reliable, (5) interrogate, (6) reluctant, (7) significant, (8) intricate, (9) antecedent, (10) adaptation.

Practice B

(1) example, (2) prior, (3) dependable, (4) unwilling, (5) important, (6) fellow workers in a profession, (7) question, (8) complicated, (9) modification for a new use, (10) persist.

Practice C

(1) none—intricate, (2) significant, (3) adaptation, (4) antecedent, (5) none—colleague, (6) interrogate, (7) persevere, (8) precedent, (9) reliable, (10) none—reluctant.

WORD SQUARE

L	A	D	A	P	T	A	T	I	O	N
O	M	O	N	T	P	U	S	R	S	P
A	I	M	T	E	E	I	I	N	M	R
I	N	T	E	R	R	O	G	A	T	E
I	T	M	C	E	S	A	N	S	R	C
J	R	O	E	L	E	R	I	W	E	E
R	I	N	D	I	V	S	F	I	L	D
S	G	S	E	A	E	O	I	C	U	E
Q	U	R	N	B	R	M	C	O	C	N
U	E	A	T	L	E	U	A	I	R	T
S	F	A	R	E	S	E	N	L	E	O
C	O	L	L	E	A	G	T	U	L	M

Additional Words (p. 298)

1. **procrastinate.** To put off doing something until a future time; to postpone taking action.

2. **prudent.** Capable of using sound judgment in practical matters; wisely cautious; sensible; not rash.

3. **virile.** Manly; masculine; forceful; able to procreate (to produce or reproduce).

4. **vindictive.** Revengeful in spirit; spiteful.

5. **satiate.** To fill; to satisfy the appetite completely; to supply with anything to excess; to glut (overindulge). (*Satiate* used to mean only "to satisfy com-

pletely," but the term is now usually used to mean "to overindulge to the point that there is no longer any pleasure.")

Practice for Additional Words (pp. 298–299)

(1) d, (2) c, (3) e, (4) a, (5) b.

Exercise 21 (pp. 299–305)

Practice A

(1) stagnant, (2) modify, (3) frugal, (4) liability, (5) conservative, (6) covet, (7) asset, (8) liberal, (9) economize, (10) allot.

Practice B

(1) avoid waste, (2) a person who is open-minded, (3) thrifty, (4) something of value, (5) parcel out or set aside, (6) opposed to change, (7) longs for, (8) foul from not moving, (9) alter, (10) disadvantage.

Practice C

(1) candid, (2) audible, (3) amnesty, (4) none–coincidence, (5) allot, (6) tacit, (7) isolate, (8) frugal, (9) reluctant, (10) asset, (11) delete, (12) covet, (13) none–affirm, (14) conservative, (15) liberal, (16) economize, (17) liability, (18) modify, (19) stagnant, (20) none–dilemma.

WORD SQUARE

E	C	O	N	O	M	I	Z	E	S	E	R
A	L	L	O	T	P	R	E	D	U	A	L
R	I	F	R	U	G	A	L	E	P	M	U
E	A	S	S	E	T	C	I	L	E	N	A
L	B	I	T	M	A	A	B	E	R	E	L
U	I	S	A	O	C	N	E	T	V	S	A
C	L	O	G	D	I	D	R	E	I	T	U
T	I	L	N	I	T	I	A	C	T	Y	D
A	T	A	A	F	O	D	L	O	A	A	I
N	Y	T	N	Y	M	A	O	V	L	E	B
T	O	E	T	O	E	E	U	E	S	D	L
C	O	N	S	E	R	V	A	T	I	V	E

319

Additional Words (p. 305)

1. **vital.** Necessary to life; essential; energetic.

2. **laudable.** Worthy of praise; commendable.

3. **vindicate.** To clear from criticism, accusation, or suspicion.

4. **sedate.** Calm; composed; quiet; serene; sober; to put under sedation.

5. **castigate.** To correct or subdue by punishing; to criticize with drastic severity; to rebuke.

Practice for Additional Words (p. 305)

(1) c, (2) a, (3) e, (4) b, (5) d.

Crossword Puzzle 7 (pp. 306-308)

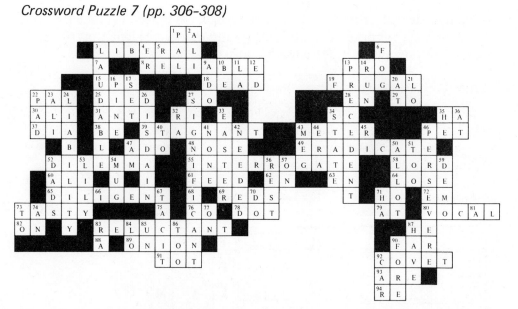

Word Scramble 7 (pp. 308-309)

(1) coincidence, (2) delete, (3) affirm, (4) dilemma, (5) diligent, (6) pertinent, (7) adaptation, (8) antecedent, (9) intricate, (10) colleague, (11) interrogate, (12) persevere, (13) reliable, (14) significant, (15) asset, (16) stagnant, (17) allot, (18) frugal, (19) covet, (20) modify.

Analogies 7 (pp. 309-310)

(1) manly, (2) scorn, (3) question, (4) conservative, (5) replenish, (6) affirm, (7) persevere, (8) intricate, (9) associate, (10) isolate, (11) commendable, (12) delete, (13) covet, (14) sensible, (15) alter, (16) diligent, (17) vital, (18) postpone, (19) eradicate, (20) save.

Multiple-Choice Vocabulary Test 7 (pp. 310–312)

Exercise 19

(1) c, (2) b, (3) d, (4) d, (5) c, (6) c, (7) b, (8) a, (9) c, (10) c.

Exercise 20

(11) d, (12) c, (13) a, (14) d, (15) c, (16) b, (17) a, (18) b, (19) c, (20) d.

Exercise 21

(21) d, (22) c, (23) d, (24) c, (25) d, (26) c, (27) d, (28) b, (29) a, (30) a.

True/False Test 7 (pp. 312–313)

(1) T, (2) T, (3) F, (4) F, (5) F, (6) T, (7) F, (8) T, (9) T, (10) T, (11) T, (12) F, (13) F, (14) F, (15) T, (16) F, (17) T, (18) F, (19) F, (20) F.

STOP. Turn to p. 313 for the scoring of the tests.

Additional Practice Sets (pp. 314–317)

Additional Practice 1

(1) diligent, (2) dilemma, (3) delete, (4) eradicate, (5) pertinent, (6) isolate, (7) affirm, (8) coincidence, (9) haughty, (10) disdain.

Additional Practice 2

(1) adaptation, (2) intricate, (3) significant, (4) colleagues, (5) reluctant, (6) reliable, (7) precedent, (8) interrogate, (9) persevere, (10) antecedent.

Additional Practice 3

(1) allot, (2) asset, (3) conservative, (4) frugal, (5) economize, (6) liability, (7) covet, (8) stagnant, (9) liberal, (10) modify.

CHAPTER NINE

EXERCISE 22

Step I. Vocabulary Words in Sentences

Directions: Following are sentences using the ten vocabulary words from Exercise 22. See whether you can figure out the meanings of the underlined words from the clues in the sentences. Sometimes the clue to help you figure out the word is in the next sentence or sentences. Blanks are provided for your estimates of the definitions. Check your meanings with those in Step II.

1. Jeffrey James was a young man who had strong artistic <u>inclinations</u>. As a young child, he used to isolate himself from others and spend all his time drawing and painting. _____

2. While at school, he didn't pay attention to anything except what he considered <u>aesthetic</u> things, such as art and beauty. _____

3. His teachers didn't understand his feelings or <u>attitudes</u> toward art. _____

4. His behavior and opinions <u>antagonized</u> them. Rather than help him to develop his artistic potential, they frustrated his efforts to paint. _____

323

5. The teachers had felt that it was an <u>affront</u> to them that Jeffrey wouldn't do anything but draw. They were insulted because they felt that what they were presenting in school was more important for Jeffrey than his drawing.

_____

6. As a result, they sometimes made <u>derogatory</u> remarks about his paintings. Soon Jeffrey was ridiculed by students also. _____

7. Fortunately for Jeffrey, one of his special <u>characteristics</u> was being able to survive despite formidable odds. _____

8. He was not easily <u>intimidated</u>. The more the students made fun of him, the more he drew. He was not afraid. _____

9. It's interesting to note what <u>hypocrites</u> many of Jeffrey James's former classmates are. When Jeffrey became famous, they said that they knew all along how good he was. _____

10. However, while in school, they didn't even use any <u>euphemisms</u> to tell Jeffrey how they felt. They just came right out and said <u>distasteful</u> things to him. _____

Step II. Vocabulary Words

1. **aesthetic** (æs · thet′ ik) *adj.* Referring to beauty; sensitive to art and beauty; showing good taste; artistic. *Sharon has a highly developed **aesthetic** sense because she is so sensitive to art and beauty.*

2. **affront** (af · front′) *v.* To insult. *n.* An insult; an open and intentional insult. *That was a definite **affront** to me because I was the only one in the class not invited.*

3. **antagonize** (an · tag′ o · nīzę) *v.* To make unfriendly; to make an enemy of; to oppose; to act against. *If you persist in behaving in this way, you will **antagonize** your boss and make him hostile toward you.*

4. **attitude** (at′ ţi · tūdę) *n.* A way of feeling, acting, or thinking that shows one's disposition (one's frame of mind) or opinion; the feeling itself; posture. *It is very difficult to change **attitudes** because the way we feel about things comes to us from our past experiences and has been with us for some time.*

5. **characteristic** (char · ac · ter · is ·tic) (kar · ak · ter · is′ tik) *adj.* Marking the peculiar quality or qualities of a person or thing; distinctive; special. *n.* A special trait, feature, or quality; individuality. *All mammals have certain **characteristics** in common.*

6. **derogatory** (de · rog · a · to · ry) (de · rog′ a · tor · ē) *adj.* Tending to make less well regarded; tending to belittle someone or something; disparag-

ing; belittling. *The **derogatory** remarks were supposed to make us think less of Mr. Jones, but on the contrary, they made us think less of the person who made them.*

7. **euphemism** (eu · phe · mism) (ŧū′ fe · miz · um) *n.* The substitution of a word or phrase that is less direct, milder, or vaguer for one thought to be harsh, offensive, or blunt; a word or phrase considered less distasteful or less offensive than another. *"They are in their final resting place" is a **euphemism** for "They are dead."*

8. **hypocrite** (hyp · o · crite) (hip′ o · krīt∉) *n.* A person who pretends to be what he or she is not; one who pretends to be better than he or she really is. *He is a **hypocrite** because he made us all feel guilty about asking for our share of the profits when he had already pocketed his share a long time ago.*

9. **inclination** (in · cli · na · tion) (in · kli · nā′ shun) *n.* A personal leaning or bent; a liking; a bending, slanting, or sloping surface; a slope. *Whatever your **inclinations** are in this matter, you must try to be fair and not allow your personal leanings to get in the way of your decision.*

10. **intimidate** (in · tim′ i · dāt∉) *v.* To make timid; to cause fear; to scare; to discourage by threats or violence. *The reason many big crime figures are not convicted is that they **intimidate** witnesses so that the witnesses are afraid to say anything against them.*

Special Notes

1. You met the word *posture* in Chapter 15. Note that *posture* and *attitude* are synonyms. Posture can mean "a mental position or frame of mind." Also, the way that one carries himself or herself or the position of the body can show an individual's attitude.

2. The phrase *strike an attitude* means "to assume a posture or pose for effect."

Step III. Practice

A. Directions: Each sentence has a missing word. Choose the word that *best* completes the sentence. Write the word in the blank. *All words fit in.*

Word List

affront, aesthetic, attitude, characteristic, inclination, hypocrite, derogatory, euphemism, intimidate, antagonize.

1. You can usually tell what a person's _____ toward something is by the way he or she behaves.

2. Because some people have a more developed _____ sense than others, they are more sensitive to art and beauty.

3. When you are insulted by someone you count as a friend, the _____ is even more painful.

4. The doctor asked the mother of the child if she noticed any special _____ s that the child had.

5. As I don't like to have people hostile toward me, I try not to _____ others.

6. The hill's _____ was so steep that I had difficulty walking up the slope.

7. "She is pleasingly plump" is a(n) _____ for "she is fat."

8. Mary is a(n) _____ because she had us believing that she was going to help us when all along she had no intention of doing this.

9. They tried to _____ us by using threats and insults, but we wouldn't change our story.

10. Politicians usually make _____ remarks about their opponents because they want to belittle them.

STOP. Check answers at the end of the chapter.

B. Directions: Following are ten sentences. Define the underlined word. Put your answer in the blank.

1. I like his characteristic way of greeting one and feel that it makes him more distinctive. _____

2. We were very upset by the derogatory statements made about our friend by someone trying to belittle her. _____

3. When a visiting diplomat was not invited to a state dinner recently, it was regarded as a direct affront to the diplomat and the country he represented. _____

4. Presidents' wives seem to be interested in art and become involved in aesthetic functions. _____

5. I always use a euphemism when I don't want to come right out and say something that might be distasteful. _____

6. He is a hypocrite to act so moral when he has been more immoral than anyone else. _____

7. She seems to have an inclination to help persons who are in trouble. _____

326

8. From the way he behaved, it was difficult to tell what his <u>attitude</u> toward the speaker's comments was. _____

9. When the judge learned that an attempt to <u>intimidate</u> jurors had been made, he asked the police to arrest the persons who were trying to frighten the jurors. _____

10. The insulting remarks did <u>antagonize</u> the witness, so that he became hostile to the lawyer. _____

STOP. Check answers at the end of the chapter.

C. Directions: Following are the words presented in Exercise 22. Match the word with the meaning that *best* fits.

Words		*Meanings*
_____	1. antagonize	a. an insult
_____	2. attitude	b. tending to belittle; belittling
_____	3. aesthetic	c. one's feeling
_____	4. affront	d. to make an enemy of
_____	5. characteristic	e. a less distasteful word or phrase to describe something
_____	6. derogatory	
_____	7. euphemism	f. referring to beauty
_____	8. hypocrite	g. a personal leaning or bent
_____	9. intimidate	h. to make timid
_____	10. inclination	i. one who pretends to be what he or she is not
		j. peculiar quality

STOP. Check answers at the end of the chapter.

EXTRA WORD
POWER

> **age.** Condition; state of; action; collection of; place for. When *age* is added to the end of a word, it can mean "condition," "state of," "act of," "collection of," or "place for." For example: *outrage*—act of shocking violence or cruelty; *damage*—condition of loss; *marriage*—state of being wed; *passage*—act of passing; *wastage*—amount wasted; *salvage*—the act of saving; *acreage*—collection of acres; *orphanage*—place

for orphans or collection of orphans; *advantage*—any condition, state, or circumstance favorable to success; *outage*—state of being interrupted; *wattage*—amount of electric power; total number of watts needed; *shrinkage*—act of shrinking; amount of decrease; *spillage*—amount spilled; the act of spilling; *courage*—state of being fearless or brave. How many more words can you supply that end in *age*?

ure. Act; result of an action; agent of action; state of. *Ure* is found at the end of many nouns. For example: *legislature*—body of lawmakers; *exposure*—state of being exposed or laid open; *posture*—state of carriage (how one carries oneself); *rupture*—the act of something breaking apart; *torture*—act of causing severe pain; *temperature*—degree of hotness or coldness of something. How many more words that end in *ure* can you supply?

Additional Words

From your ability to use context clues, can you figure out the meanings of the following words?

1. **exonerate** (ex · on · er · ate) (ig · zon′ e · rāte) *v. He was granted an amnesty by the government and **exonerated** of all charges made against him.*

   _____

2. **jeopardy** (jeøp′ ar · dē) *n. (pl. **ies**) When the witness testified against a major crime figure, he knew that he was putting his life in **jeopardy**.*

   _____

3. **temperate** (tem · per · ate) (tem′ per · it) *adj. As Arthur is **temperate** in everything he does, you would not expect him to overeat or overdrink.*

   _____

4. **corroborate** (koŕ · rob′ o · rāte) *v. He **corroborated** our suspicions concerning her guilt when he testified that she tried to sell him the stolen goods.*

   _____

5. **repent** (re • pent') *v.* *He **repented** the fact that he had not been kinder to his mother while she was still alive.*

___

STOP. Check answers at the end of the chapter.

Practice for Additional Words

Directions: Match each word with the *best* definition.

_____ 1. exonerate   a. danger

_____ 2. jeopardy   b. to feel regret

_____ 3. temperate   c. to confirm

_____ 4. corroborate   d. to clear of guilt

_____ 5. repent   e. moderate

STOP. Check answers at the end of the chapter.

EXERCISE 23

Step I. Vocabulary Words in Sentences

Directions; Following are sentences using the ten vocabulary words from Exercise 23. See whether you can figure out the meanings of the underlined words from the clues in the sentences. Sometimes the clue to help you figure out the word is in the next sentence or sentences. Blanks are provided for your estimates of the definitions. Check your meanings with those in Step II.

1. By the time he was twenty, John ("Baby Face") Malloy was infamous. Baby Face was known throughout the country for his bank robberies.

___

2. All bank presidents and employees were apprehensive about their banks being robbed by Baby Face. They feared that they would be next.

___

3. In discussing Baby Face, some persons claimed that he was bland and mild-mannered. Others claimed he was violent and vicious._____

4. Some said that as long as the people being robbed were docile, they were not harmed. Others stated that even if persons in the bank were obedient, Baby Face would beat them. _____

5. Some claimed he took a <u>miscellaneous</u> collection of bills from the banks. Others said that he took only large bills, not several kinds. _____

6. It was obvious from the contradictory statements that there was no <u>unanimous</u> agreement on Baby Face's characteristics. _____

7. In order to capture Baby Face, a new operation was <u>initiated</u> called Operation Baby Face. _____

8. Everyone on this mission was very <u>discreet</u> or careful in what he or she said or did. _____

9. The members of the mission were all sure that their plan was foolproof and that no <u>omissions</u> had been made. Nothing was left to chance or left out. _____

10. They had <u>scrutinized</u> every possible problem that could arise. At no time in the police chiefs' memories could they remember such a careful investigation. _____

Step II. Vocabulary Words

1. **apprehensive** (ap · p̸re · hen′ sive) *adj.* Fearful; expecting evil, danger, or harm; anxious. *The frightened witness was so **apprehensive** about his life that he refused to give evidence.*

2. **bland** (bland) *adj.* Mild; soft; gentle; balmy; kindly; soothing. *You should eat only **bland** foods after you have had an upset stomach because they are very gentle.*

3. **discreet** (dis · krē̸t′) *adj.* Careful about what one says or does; prudent; cautious. *The president's relatives should be **discreet** because if they are not careful about what they do or say, it can embarrass the president.*

4. **docile** (doc · ile) (dos′ ul) *adj.* Easy to teach; easy to discipline; obedient. *Teachers like to have **docile** students in their classes because they are easy to teach.*

5. **infamous** (in′ fa · m̸ous) *adj.* Having a bad reputation; notorious. *Al Capone was **infamous** because he was well known for his bad actions.*

6. **initiate** (in · i · ti · ate) (i · nish′ ē · at̸) *v.* To introduce by doing or using first; to bring into use or practice; to admit as a member into a fraternity, sorority, club, and so on, especially through the use of a secret ceremony. *I will **initiate** the program by having everyone introduce himself or herself to everyone else.*

7. **miscellaneous** (mis · cel · la · ne · ous) (mis · u̸ · lā′ nē · ous) *adj.* Mixed; consisting of several kinds; various. *The box contained a number of **mis-**

cellaneous items, which were different things I had collected through the
years.

8. **omission** (o · mis · sion) (o · mish′ un) *n.* Anything left out or not done;
failure to include. *When it was discovered that the main speaker's name was
left out of the program, an investigation was started to determine who was
responsible for the **omission.***

9. **scrutinize** (skrū′ ti · nīz∅) *v.* To observe closely; to examine or inquire into
critically; to investigate. *The police said that they would **scrutinize** the evidence very carefully to make sure that nothing escaped investigation.*

10. **unanimous** (ū · nan′ i · m∅us) *adj.* Agreeing completely; united in opinion;
being of one mind; being in complete agreement. *As everyone was in
agreement, the vote was **unanimous.***

Step III. Practice

A. Directions: Each sentence has a missing word. Choose the word that *best*
completes the sentence. Write the word in the blank. *All words
fit in.*

Word List

*infamous, bland, discreet, docile, apprehensive, unanimous, scrutinize, omission,
miscellaneous, initiate.*

1. Spies must be _____ about what they do because they never
know who is watching or listening to them.

2. People are _____ about walking alone late at night because
it is so dangerous.

3. Not every school has students who are so _____ and obedient.

4. Although you are well known when you are _____, you are
known because of the bad things that you have done.

5. I am on a(n) _____ diet because of my ulcer.

6. I am going to _____ that situation very carefully because it
looks to me as if something is wrong.

7. Whenever a(n) _____ is made, we try to determine whether
the item was left out on purpose or not.

8. At our meetings it's almost impossible to get everyone to agree on anything,
so we never have _____ agreements.

9. The _____ items were put on sale because the several things
that were left were all one of a kind.

10. The fraternity decided not to _____ any members this year because of the fatal accident that occurred last year.

STOP. Check answers at the end of the chapter.

B. Directions: Following are ten sentences containing the meanings of vocabulary presented in Exercise 23. Choose the word that *best* fits the word or phrase underlined in the sentence.

Word List

infamous, discreet, initiate, bland, unanimous, scrutinize, miscellaneous, docile, apprehensive, omission.

1. His kindly personality is a relief after going with Jeff, who was always ready to explode. _____

2. Please be careful about what you say and do because we are being watched.
   _____

3. I am so fearful about the exam results. _____

4. All of us were in complete agreement that we go to the shore for our class picnic. _____.

5. Hitler was notorious. _____

6. After the auction, only a few different items were left for sale.
   _____

7. The leaving out of my name from the report was merely a mistake.
   _____

8. At our college we decided to start a class on the art of cooking and choosing wines. _____

9. In our biology class, we had to observe carefully cells under the microscope to determine whether they were moving or not. _____

10. The children were so obedient that they were very easy to teach.
    _____

STOP. Check answers at the end of the chapter.

C. Directions: In the Word Square there are eleven words that you have met. Find the words in the square and match them with their correct meanings. Note that there are *more* meanings than words. If there is no word in the square for a meaning, write *none*, and give the word. Some words in the square are from preceding exercises.

WORD SQUARE

I	N	I	T	I	A	T	E	O
A	D	I	S	C	R	E	E	T
C	O	D	E	L	E	T	E	A
I	C	O	V	E	T	R	T	S
M	I	N	F	A	M	O	U	S
B	L	A	N	D	U	O	S	E
O	E	F	R	U	G	A	L	T
U	N	A	N	I	M	O	U	S
O	M	I	S	S	I	O	N	E

Meanings   *Words*

1. To desire what others have   _____

2. To introduce by doing or
    using first   _____

3. Anything left out   _____

4. Agreeing completely   _____

5. Mixed; consisting of several kinds   _____

6. To take out   _____

7. To observe closely   _____

8. Thrifty   _____

9. Careful about what one does   _____

10. Something valuable   _____

11. Mild   _____

12. Fearful   _____

13. Easy to teach   _____

14. Having a bad reputation   _____

STOP. Check answers at the end of the chapter.

EXTRA WORD
POWER

ism. Act of, practice of, or result of; condition of
being; action or quality of. *Ism* is used at the end

of a great number of words. For example: *terrorism*—practice of terror; the use of fear to frighten or intimidate; *barbarism*—the condition of being primitive or brutal; *pauperism*—the condition of being very poor; *patriotism*—quality of being a patriot; *Americanism*—practice of values characteristic of Americans; *socialism*—the principle whereby the ownership and operation of the means of production are by society or the community rather than by private individuals, with all members of the community sharing in the work and products; *nationalism*—devotion to one's nation. How many other words with *ism* can you supply?

ive. of; relating to; belonging to; having the nature or quality of; tending to. *Ive* is added to the end of many words. For example: *legislative*—relating to the body of lawmakers; *affirmative*—having the quality of a positive statement; *derogative*—tending to belittle; *native*—belonging to a country by birth; *creative*—tending to be able to create; *destructive*—tending to cause destruction or the tearing down of things; *massive*—having the quality of being very large. How many more words with *ive* can you supply?

Additional Words

From your ability to use context clues, can you figure out the meanings of the following words?

1. **futile** (fu · tile) (fū′ tul) *adj.* *The doctor's efforts to save the child who had consumed the toxic liquid were **futile**, because the dose consumed was a lethal one.*

2. **criterion** (cri · te · ri · on) (krī · tir′ ē · un) *n.* (*pl.* **criteria**) (krī · tir′ ē · an) *The journal's staff decided on the **criteria** they would use to judge whether papers were acceptable for publication in their journal.*

3. **valid** (val′ id) *adj.* *After the judge ruled that the will was **valid**, the lawyer for the estate called all the beneficiaries together for a reading of it.*

4. **datum** (dā′ tum) *n.* (*pl.* **data**) (dā′ ta). (Usually used in the plural.) *Because of insufficient **data**, the problem could not be solved.*

---

5. **invincible** (in · vin · ci · ble) (in · vin′ si · bul) *adj.* *The **invincible** army won every battle.*

© 1966 United Feature Syndicate, Inc.

STOP. Check answers at the end of the chapter.

Practice for Additional Words

Directions: Match each word with the *best* definition.

_____ 1. futile   a. not able to be conquered

_____ 2. invincible   b. information given

_____ 3. criterion   c. a standard of judging

_____ 4. valid   d. useless

_____ 5. data   e. sound in principle

STOP. Check answers at the end of the chapter.

EXERCISE 24

Step I. Vocabulary Words in Sentences

Directions: Following are sentences using the ten vocabulary words from Exercise 24. See whether you can figure out the meanings of the underlined words from the clues in the sentences. Sometimes the clue to help you figure out the word is in the next sentence or sentences. Blanks are provided for your estimates of the definitions. Check your meanings with those in Step II.

1. The <u>acquisition</u> of vocabulary is the objective of this book. If you have acquired knowledge of words and their meanings, this intention has been realized. _____

2. By this time you should be more <u>adept</u> at figuring out words, using context clues. As you have seen, to become an expert at something, you have to work diligently and persevere. _____

3. The words that have been presented in this book are neither <u>exotic</u> nor <u>trite</u>; that is, the words are neither so strange that you will hardly meet them nor so commonplace that they are used with almost no meaning. _____ ; _____

4. If you are a <u>gregarious</u> person who likes to be with a lot of people, you will find that being adept in vocabulary will help you in telling <u>anecdotes</u>. The more skilled you are in vocabulary, the more able you will be to make your stories exciting, interesting, and entertaining. _____; _____

5. You will find also that you will become more active rather than <u>passive</u> in discussions. _____

6. With your skill in words, you would probably be able to overcome your <u>opponent</u> in a debate. Persons would be reluctant to oppose you because of your verbal ability. _____

7. No more would your stomach be in a <u>turmoil</u> because you had to give a speech in a particular class. There is no need for feeling disturbed when you have "word power."_____

8. It is hoped that learning new vocabulary words will become a <u>contagious</u> "disease" from which you will not be cured. Not only will you continue acquiring new words, but you will spread this enthusiasm for words to others. _____

Step II. Vocabulary Words

1. **acquisition** (ac · qui · si · tion) (ak · wi · zish′ un) *n.* The act of obtaining or acquiring; something obtained or gained as property, knowledge, and so on. *When the school population increased, the **acquisition** of another building was necessary to house all the students.*

2. **adept** (a · dept′) *adj.* Highly skilled; proficient; expert. *I would call him an expert golfer because he is so **adept** at it.*

3. **anecdote** (an′ ek · dōte) *n.* A short, entertaining account of some happening, usually personal or biographical. *The sailor told us many interesting **anecdotes** about his sea adventures.*

4. **contagious** (con · ta · gious) (kon · tā′ jus) *adj.* Spreading by contact; spreading or tending to spread from person to person. *Some diseases are very* **contagious**, *and you can catch them from persons if they sneeze or cough near you.*

5. **exotic** (ex · ot · ic) (ig · zot′ ik) *adj.* Foreign; not native; introduced from a foreign country; having the charm of the unfamiliar; strangely beautiful. *The florist imported some* **exotic** *plants from another country for one of his special customers.*

6. **gregarious** (gre · gar′ ē · ∅us) *adj.* Fond of the company of others; sociable; characteristic of a flock, herd, or crowd. **Gregarious** *people usually enjoy being in the company of other people.*

7. **opponent** (o∅ · pō′ nent) *n.* One who opposes another, as in battle or debate; one who acts against something or another; adversary; antagonist. *When you play a game, the person whom you are playing against is your* **opponent***.*

8. **passive** (pa∅′ siv∅) *adj.* Not acting; acted upon; unresisting; not opposing; unenthusiastic; inactive. *When you have no interest in something, you behave in a very* **passive** *manner.*

9. **trite** (trīt∅) *adj.* Used so often as to be too common; made commonplace by repetition; lacking freshness or originality. *It is easier to use* **trite** *phrases, which are ready-made and common, than to think of a more original way to say something.*

10. **turmoil** (tur′ moil) *n.* Confused motion or state; disturbance; tumult. *There was so much* **turmoil** *in the stores during the Christmas rush, with everyone rushing around in all different directions, that I became confused.*

Special Notes

1. The word *contagious* usually refers to the spreading of disease, but it can also refer to the spreading of other things, such as laughter, sadness, and so on. For example:
   a. The *contagious* laughter spread throughout the whole class, and before long everyone was aching from laughing so much.
   b. The child's crying was so *contagious* that soon all the children in the kindergarten were crying.

2. The term *opponent*, meaning "one who opposes another," is derived from the combining form *pos, pon,* meaning "place" or "set." You met this combining form in Exercise 15.

A. Directions: Each sentence has a missing word. Choose the word that *best* completes the sentence. Write the word in the blank. *All words fit in.*

Word List

contagious, adept, turmoil, acquisition, trite, anecdote, exotic, opponent, passive, gregarious.

1. The_____of knowledge is necessary for anyone who wishes to enter some profession or trade.

2. The_____ laughter spread throughout the room.

3. There was such a(n)_____after the robbery that no one knew what anyone was doing.

4. As that is such a(n)_____ saying, can't you come up with something more original?

5. He is so_____at so many things that we call him Mr. General Expert.

6. If you continue to be so_____, we will have to ask you to go, because we want more active people on this job.

7. Opposites must attract, because George is so shy and his girl friend, Karen, is so _____ .

8. Do you know who your _____will be in the chess game?

9. Every night she tells her children a delightful _____about something that happened to her during the day.

10. We are going on a trip to a(n)_____country that is far away and strangely beautiful.

STOP. Check answers at the end of the chapter.

B. Directions: Following are ten sentences. Define the underlined word. Put your answer in the blank.

1. The heavyweight champion's <u>opponent</u> was a very strong man who would give the champion a good fight. _____

2. Why don't you play a more active role in the convention elections rather than such a <u>passive</u> one? _____

3. As my brother can't stand any disturbances, we avoid any <u>turmoil</u>.
   _____

4. *Gross* is a <u>trite</u> word because it is used too often. _____

5. A Southern politician was known for the <u>anecdotes</u> he would tell concerning funny things that had happened to him. _____

6. When a number of people had a <u>contagious</u> disease, the doctors isolated these patients in a special wing of the hospital. _____

7. I like <u>exotic</u> things because they are rare. _____

8. As Jack and Herb are very <u>gregarious</u>, they shine when they are with lots of people. _____

9. When the store ran out of necessary supplies, the manager was upset to learn that his order for the <u>acquisition</u> of new supplies had not yet been sent out. _____

10. A good secretary should be <u>adept</u> at typing and shorthand. _____

STOP. Check answers at the end of the chapter.

C. Directions: Following are the words presented in Exercise 24. Match each word with the *best* definition.

Words	*Meanings*
_____ 1. acquisition	a. foreign; not native
_____ 2. adept	b. act of obtaining something
_____ 3. anecdote	c. one who acts against something or another
_____ 4. contagious	
_____ 5. exotic	d. highly skilled
_____ 6. gregarious	e. confused motion
_____ 7. opponent	f. used so often as to be commonplace
_____ 8. passive	
_____ 9. trite	g. fond of the company of others
_____ 10. turmoil	h. spreading by contact
	i. not acting
	j. a short, entertaining account of some happening

STOP. Check answers at the end of the chapter.

EXTRA WORD
POWER

> **ish.** Belonging to; like or characteristic of; tending to; somewhat or rather; about. Many words end in *ish.*

For example: *Spanish*—belonging to Spain; *Irish*—belonging to Ireland; *Danish*—belonging to Denmark; *devilish*—like or characteristic of a devil; *boyish*—like or characteristic of a boy; *bookish*—inclined to books; involved with books; *tallish*—rather tall; *bluish*—rather blue; *thirtyish*—about thirty. How many words with *ish* can you supply?

ic. Relating to; like. *Ic* is added to the end of a great number of words. For example: *hyperbolic*—relating to a hyperbole or a great exaggeration; *heroic*—like a hero; *poetic*—like poetry; *tragic*—like a tragedy, in which something is very sad or there is disaster; *public*—relating to the public or people at large; *euphemistic*—relating to euphemism or a milder way of saying something; *enthusiastic*—relating to enthusiasm or a lively interest in something; *toxic*—relating to poison; *epidemic*—relating to the rapid spread of a disease or something; *scientific*—relating to science; *historic*—relating to history, which is an account of what has happened; famous in history. How many words with *ic* can you supply?

Additional Words

From your ability to use context clues, can you figure out the meanings of the following words?

1. **attrition** (at · tri · tion) (a · trish′ un) *n.* *When employees retired or quit their jobs, no new persons were hired to take their places. The employers were not firing anyone; they were just letting the work force become smaller through* **attrition.**

   _____

2. **abridge** (a · bridge) (a · brij′) *v.* *The kindergarten teachers decided to* **abridge** *some of the longer stories so that they would suit the younger children's attention spans.*

   _____

3. **imminent** (im′ mi · nent) *adj.* *The people were warned that an earthquake was* **imminent***, so that they would have to leave their homes immediately.*

   _____

4. **paradox** (par · a · dox) (par' a · doks) *n.* *It is a **paradox** to say that you are here and not here at the same time.*

_____

5. **phenomenon** (fe · nom' e · non) *n.* (*pl.* **phenomena**) *An eclipse is a **phenomenon** of astronomy that has been observed and scientifically described.*

_____

STOP. Check answers at the end of the chapter.

Practice for Additional Words

Directions: Match each word with the *best* definition.

_____ 1. attrition   a. a scientifically described fact

_____ 2. abridge   b. contradiction

_____ 3. imminent   c. a gradual wearing down

_____ 4. paradox   d. about to happen

_____ 5. phenomenon   e. to curtail

STOP. Check words at the end of the chapter.

CROSSWORD PUZZLE 8

Directions: The meanings of a number of the words from Exercises 22–24
follow. Your knowledge of these words, as well as the combining
forms from Part I, will help you to solve this crossword puzzle.

1. Sound of surprise
4. You ___ the bell
6. Respectful address to men
7. Comb. f. for *away from; apart; not*
10. Meaning of *ego*
11. Same as # 8 Down
12. To stay or fall behind
13. He ___ with his eyes
15. Holds back water
18. Texas is a ___
21. Abbreviation of *South Carolina*
22. Able to be taught
24. Belittling; disparaging
27. Opposite of *he*
28. Meaning of *ego*
29. Comb. f. for *one who*
30. A ___ of film
32. Comb. f. for *without*
33. Rhymes with *cat*
34. Same as # 14 Down
36. Exam
37. Faster than *walk*
39. To make an opening with a knife
40. Opposite of *present*
42. Past tense of *is*
43. A game called ___ ball
44. Same as # 33 Down
45. You roll these in games of chance
46. Abbreviation of *period*
47. Something of value
50. Slang for *is not*
51. Comb. f. for *condition; state of*
52. Mixed; variety
55. Girl's name
56. Comb. f. for *one who*
57. Opposite of *yes*
58. Referring to *voice*
60. Comb. f. for *laugh*
61. Sound made when you laugh
63. Abbreviation of *Elizabeth*
64. Same as # 32 Across
65. A person involved in covert activities

1. Comb. f. for *one who*
2. Opposite of *hers*
3. To make lively; to make alive
5. Sociable
7. Careful about what you say or do
8. Anger
9. You plant this
12. A drug that makes you erratic
14. Code signal for *help*
15. When your heart stops, you ___
16. Comb. f. for *relating to*
17. Homonym of *meat*
19. Homonym of *two*
20. Comb. f. for *me; I*
21. Feeling out of ___
23. Special trait
25. Same as # 1 Down
26. Opposite of *no*
31. Abbreviation of *lieutenant*
33. Indefinite article—rhymes with *man*
34. Synonym of *intimidate*
35. What you get when something is boiling
38. Employ
40. Opposite of *active*
41. A short, entertaining story
42. Opposite of *loser*
43. To ask for charity in a humble way
45. Comb. f. for *through*
46. Way of saying *father*
48. *Yes* in Spanish
49. *Docile* means "easy to ___ "
50. Same as # 16 Down
53. Comb. f. for *not*
54. Homonym of *sew*
59. Opposite of *early*
61. Opposite of *she*
62. Same as # 33 Across
66. You write with this
67. Comb. f. for *having; full of*
68. Soft; mild; kindly

68. In games of chance you place ___
70. Too commonplace
73. Flower ___
76. Same as # 28 Across
77. Meaning of *vid, vis*
78. Known for bad actions
82. Referring to beauty
87. Comb. f. for *other*
88. Same as # 57 Across
89. A girl's name
90. Same as # 83 Down
91. Iron ___ is found in a mine
93. Meaning of *derm*
94. Opposite of *subtract*
95. A woman devoted to the religious life
96. Same as # 2 Down
99. She is ___ good ___ he
101. You commit a ___ when you break a religious law
103. To scare
107. Opposite of *woman*
108. Comb. f. for *through*
110. Slang for *go away*
111. Same as # 95 Across
112. An insult
113. Same as # 31 Down
114. Same as # 83 Down
115. To attempt
116. Same as # 61 Down
118. An aquanaut travels under the ___
119. A man wears this on his shirt
120. Same as # 15 Down
121. Same as # 32 Across
122. A precious stone is called a ___
123. Skillful
126. Same as # 10 Across
128. Opposite of *off*
129. Meaning of *astro*
131. Girl's name
132. A waitress takes your ___
134. A word for what you call yourself

69. Opposite of *stand*
71. Comb. f. for *again; back*
72. Same as # 28 Across
73. A friend is a ___
74. The act of leaving out
75. Same as # 19 Down
77. To observe carefully
79. Musical sound
80. Comb. f. for *one*
81. Male child
83. Comb. f. for *in; into*
84. Same as # 61 Down
85. Same as # 83 Down
86. Comb. f. for *state of; act of*
89. Abbreviation of *advertisement*
92. Same as # 83 Down
94. Same as # 32 Across
96. Same as # 2 Down
97. A leaning
98. Same as # 18 Across
99. Rhymes with *ham*
100. To state something is not true
101. Opposite of *dangerous*
102. Same as # 78 Across
104. Rhymes with *sit*
105. Comb. f. for *before*
106. Disturbance; confused motion
107. Used to support sails on a ship
108. You ___ your *i*
109. When you were famished, you ___
114. You ___ when you are hungry
116. To own
117. The garden where Adam and Eve first lived
120. Contraction for *do not*
122. To welcome
124. Same as # 56 Across
125. Same as # 46 Down
127. Comb. f. for *wander*
129. Meaning of *pos, pon*
130. Same as # 32 Across
133. The hiding place of a wild animal; lair

136. A long poem telling a tale of some deed
138. Same as # 83 Down
139. You go to a doctor to help____you of an illness
140. Manner of feeling
143. ____ and behold; look
144. Same as # 14 Down
145. Neither this____that
148. Rhymes with *sit*
149. Meaning of *non*
150. Same as # 128 Across
151. Same as # 71 Down
152. You build a house on a____
153. Same as # 33 Down

135. Slang for a *baseball glove*
137. Comb. f. for *together*
139. Comb. f. for *together*
140. Same as # 32 Across
141. Comb. f. for *not*
142. Homonym of *due*
144. Same as # 54 Down
146. Same as # 29 Across
147. Same as # 71 Down
152. Musical syllable

STOP. Check answers at the end of the chapter.

WORD SCRAMBLE 8

Directions: Word Scramble 8 is based on words from Exercises 22–24. The meanings are your clues to arranging the letters in correct order. Write the correct word in the blank.

Meanings

1. goanitanez _____ to make unfriendly

2. roffant _____ insult

3. actactherisicr _____ peculiar quality

4. meehpumsi _____ a milder word or phrase

5. datinimite _____ to frighten

6. tioninainlc _____ a leaning or bent

7. adnlb _____ mild; soft

8. seetcird _____ careful about what one does or says

9. clodie _____ easy to teach

10. nofamuis _____ known for bad actions

11. itinatei _____ to begin; to bring into practice

12. imissono _____ anything left out

345

13. initscurez   _____   to observe closely

14. minonusua   _____   being in complete agreement

15. petad   _____   skillful

16. gatnocsuoi   _____   spreading by contact

17. coeitx   _____   foreign; strangely beautiful

18. veissap   _____   not acting

19. reitt   _____   used so often as to be
                                            commonplace

20. oilturm   _____   disturbance

STOP. Check answers at the end of the chapter.

ANALOGIES 8

Directions: Find the word from the following list that *best* completes each
analogy. *There are more words in the list than you need.*

Word List

*exonerate, risk, insult, careful, compliment, bland, feeling, gregarious, inclina-
tion, commonplace, exotic, active, scrutinize, passive, common, commence,
notorious, overindulgent, standard, characteristic, ally, expert, euphemism,
spreading, undisputed, fearful, imminent, aesthetic, jeopardy, unskilled, skilled
unmanageable, terminate, disturbance.*

1. Convenient : unsuitable :: affront : _____ .

2. Error : mistake :: apprehensive : _____ .

3. Isolate : integrate :: initiate : _____ .

4. Tenacious : stubborn :: trite : _____ .

5. Corroborate : deny :: adept : _____ .

6. Inanimate : alive :: opponent : _____ .

7. Conceited : egotistical :: criterion : _____ .

8. Custom : habit :: leaning : _____ .

9. Boundary : limit :: contagious : _____ .

10. Concede : resist :: docile : _____ .

11. Attitude : feeling :: turmoil : _____ .

12. Innate : inborn :: vindicate : _____ .

13. Confuse : obfuscate :: mild : _____ .

14. Abridge : curtail :: infamous : _____ .

15. Temerity : discreet :: domestic : _____ .

16. Repentant : remorseful :: inactive : _____ .

17. Lush : barren :: indiscreet : _____ .

18. Inward : shy :: outgoing : _____ .

19. Rain : torrent :: observe : _____ .

20. Simmer : boil :: temperate : _____ .

STOP. Check answers at the end of the chapter.

MULTIPLE-CHOICE VOCABULARY TEST 8

Directions: This is a test on words in Exercises 22-24. Words are presented according to exercises. *Do all exercises before checking answers.* Underline the meaning that *best* fits the word.

Exercise 22

1. aesthetic
   a. referring to being poor
   b. likes food
   c. referring to beauty
   d. a feeling

2. affront
   a. an insult
   b. a front
   c. friendly
   d. not friendly

3. antagonize
   a. helpful
   b. friendly
   c. to make an enemy of
   d. feeling

4. attitude
   a. manner of feeling
   b. unfriendly feeling
   c. friendly feeling
   d. happy feeling

5. characteristic
   a. person
   b. play
   c. special trait
   d. feeling

6. derogatory
   a. a lot of
   b. tending to belittle
   c. helpful
   d. talkative

7. euphemism
   a. a wise saying
   b. hold back
   c. a saying
   d. a less distasteful description of something

8. hypocrite
   a. to frighten
   b. to be friendly
   c. to lean
   d. one who pretends to be what he or she is not

9. inclination
   a. insult
   b. a leaning
   c. frighten
   d. a saying

10. intimidate
   a. to scare
   b. to lean
   c. to insult
   d. to make unfriendly

Exercise 23

11. apprehensive
   a. mild
   b. fearful
   c. helpful
   d. cheerful

12. bland
   a. refers to sadness
   b. friendly
   c. mild
   d. evil

13. discreet
   a. fearful
   b. friendly
   c. evil
   d. careful

14. docile
   a. active
   b. easy to teach
   c. noisy
   d. frightened

15. infamous
   a. well known
   b. happy
   c. a crook
   d. having a bad reputation

16. initiate
   a. to party
   b. to start
   c. to insult
   d. to frighten

17. miscellaneous
   a. mixed
   b. most
   c. one
   d. wrong

18. omission
   a. task
   b. skill
   c. trip
   d. anything left out

19. scrutinize
   a. able to see
   b. to watch someone
   c. to observe very closely
   d. to help

20. unanimous
   a. agreeing completely
   b. some
   c. several
   d. not any

Exercise 24

21. acquisition
   a. curious
   b. inquisitive
   c. quiet
   d. the obtaining of something

22. adept
   a. helpful
   b. friendly
   c. skillful
   d. changing

23. anecdote
   a. something funny
   b. a note
   c. a joke
   d. a short, entertaining account of a happening

24. contagious	a. germs b. referring to contact	c. spreading from person to person d. unhealthy
25. exotic	a. native b. foreign	c. far away d. pretty
26. gregarious	a. hostile b. helpful	c. sociable d. strange
27. opponent	a. friend b. enemy	c. one who opposes another d. hostile
28. passive	a. enthusiastic b. lively	c. unresisting d. active
29. trite	a. important b. meaningful	c. different d. commonplace
30. turmoil	a. movement b. confused motion	c. spirit d. lively

TRUE/FALSE TEST 8

Directions: This is a true/false test on Exercises 22–24. Read each sentence carefully. Decide whether it is true or false. Put a *T* for *true* or an *F* for *false* in the blank. The number after the sentence tells you if the word is from Exercise 22, 23, or 24.

_____ 1. A characteristic would be a special individual trait of a person. 22

_____ 2. To affront someone is to insult him or her intentionally. 22

_____ 3. An artistic person would not have any aesthetic sense. 22

_____ 4. When you have a miscellaneous group of things, you have an assortment of things. 23

_____ 5. Persons who are apprehensive are not fearful or anxious about something. 23

_____ 6. Someone with bland manners is usually very rude. 23

_____ 7. When detectives scrutinize evidence, they examine it very carefully. 23

_____ 8. Something exotic is usually something mundane. 24

_____ 9. Gregarious people like to isolate themselves. 24

_____ 10. An <u>omission</u> is never an error. 23

_____ 11. In a <u>unanimous</u> decision, not everyone must agree. 23

_____ 12. "He is underprivileged" is a <u>euphemism</u> for "He is poor." 22

_____ 13. When someone says something in a <u>derogatory</u> manner, he or she is being kind. 22

_____ 14. _Passive_ and _dormant_ are antonyms. 24

_____ 15. An <u>acquisition</u> of something means the selling of something. 24

_____ 16. An <u>anecdote</u> is a biography. 24

_____ 17. "He is mature" can be a <u>euphemism</u> for "He is old." 22

_____ 18. To be <u>adept</u> at something is to be skillful at it. 24

_____ 19. An <u>infamous</u> person is a famous celebrity known for good deeds. 23

_____ 20. A <u>discreet</u> person tells his or her secrets to anyone who will listen. 23

STOP. Check answers for both tests at the end of the chapter.

SCORING OF TESTS

Multiple-Choice Test		True/False Test	
Number Wrong	_Score_	_Number Wrong_	_Score_
0–2	Excellent	0–1	Excellent
3–5	Good	2–3	Good
6–8	Weak	4–5	Weak
Above 8	Poor	Above 5	Poor
Score _____		Score _____	

1. If you scored in the excellent or good range on _both tests,_ you are doing well. _You have now completed the work in this text._

2. If you scored in the weak or poor range on either test, turn to the next page and follow directions for Additional Practice. Note that the words on the tests are arranged so that you can tell in which exercise to find them. This will help you if you need additional practice.

ADDITIONAL PRACTICE SETS

A. Directions: Write the words you missed on the tests from the three exercises in the space provided. Note that the tests are presented so that you can tell to which exercises the words belong.

Exercise 22 Words Missed

1. _____   6. _____
2. _____   7. _____
3. _____   8. _____
4. _____   9. _____
5. _____   10. _____

Exercise 23 Words Missed

1. _____   6. _____
2. _____   7. _____
3. _____   8. _____
4. _____   9. _____
5. _____   10. _____

Exercise 24 Words Missed

1. _____   6. _____
2. _____   7. _____
3. _____   8. _____
4. _____   9. _____
5. _____   10. _____

B. Directions: Restudy the words that you have written down on this page. Do Step I and Step II for those you missed. Note that Step I and Step II are on the following pages:

Exercise 22—pp. 323–325.

Exercise 23—pp. 329–331.

Exercise 24—pp. 335–337.

C. Directions: Do Additional Practice 1 on the next page if you missed words from Exercise 22. Do Additional Practice 2 on pp. 352–353 if you missed words from Exercise 23. Do Additional Practice 3 on pp. 353–354 if you missed words from Exercise 24.

Directions: Following are ten sentences containing the meanings of vocabulary presented in Exercise 22. Choose the word that *best* fits the meaning of the word or phrase underlined in the sentence.

Word List

characteristic, inclination, attitude, affront, derogatory, hypocrites, euphemism, antagonize, intimidate, aesthetic.

1. What <u>an insult</u> it was not to shake my hand in front of all my friends.
   _____

2. A person's <u>way of feeling</u> is very difficult to change. _____

3. Can you think of <u>a milder phrase</u> for "the economy is terrible"?
   _____

4. If anyone tries to <u>frighten</u> you so that you will not tell your story, go to the police. _____

5. Jennifer has a certain <u>leaning</u> toward music. _____

6. Every person should have at least one good <u>trait</u>. _____

7. I dislike <u>those who pretend to be virtuous but who are not</u>. _____

8. John doesn't like to <u>make an enemy of</u> anyone. _____

9. You have an <u>artistic</u> appreciation of nature. _____

10. No one is allowed to make <u>belittling</u> remarks about my friends in my presence.
    _____

STOP. Check answers at the end of the chapter.

Directions: Following are ten sentences containing the meanings of vocabulary presented in Exercise 23. Choose the word that *best* fits the meaning of the word or phrase underlined in the sentence.

Word List

apprehensive, discreet, bland, unanimous, scrutinize, docile, miscellaneous, omission, infamous, initiate.

1. <u>The act of leaving out</u> his name from the guest list caused us a lot of embarrassment. _____

2. Seth is such a <u>mild and kindly</u> gentleman. _____

3. There were <u>various</u> items from which I could choose what I wanted.

   _____

4. Our art teacher taught us to <u>observe very carefully</u> the subjects that we were painting. _____

5. Everyone was <u>in complete agreement</u> that the meeting should have convened an hour ago. _____

6. Throughout the land, he is <u>known for his bad actions.</u>

   _____

7. I enjoy having <u>obedient</u> children in my class. _____

8. He decided to <u>introduce</u> a new game among his friends. _____

9. Try to be <u>careful about what you say</u> because I don't want anyone to know that I'm seeing you. _____

10. I am rather <u>fearful</u> about telling my parents about what happened in school today. _____

STOP. Check answers at the end of the chapter.

Additional Practice 3 for Exercise 24

Directions: Following are ten sentences containing the meanings of vocabulary presented in Exercise 24. Choose the word that *best* fits the meaning of the word or phrase underlined in the sentence.

Word List

passive, acquisition, trite, anecdote, opponent, turmoil, contagious, adept, exotic, gregarious.

1. You always seem to use <u>commonplace</u> phrases rather than original ones.

   _____

2. The <u>disturbance</u> at the factory was due to the strike. _____

3. His <u>adversary</u> was very skillful._____

4. Why are you always so <u>unenthusiastic</u>? _____

5. The disease was <u>spreading from person to person</u> so rapidly that the doctors feared there would soon be an epidemic. _____

6. Carol is a <u>very sociable</u> person. _____

7. Arthur is <u>very skillful</u> in fixing anything in the house. _____

8. <u>The act of obtaining</u> knowledge is not easy. _____

9. Some of the birds I saw in Africa were <u>strangely beautiful.</u>_____

10. <u>The short, entertaining story</u> told by Sharon was very funny.

_____

STOP. Check answers at the end of the chapter.

ANSWERS

Exercise 22 (pp. 323–329)

Practice A

(1) attitude, (2) aesthetic, (3) affront, (4) characteristic, (5) antagonize, (6) inclination, (7) euphemism, (8) hypocrite, (9) intimidate, (10) derogatory.

Practice B

(1) distinctive; (2) belittling or disparaging; (3) insult; (4) artistic; (5) a less direct way of saying something; (6) one who pretends to be better or other than he or she is; (7) leaning, liking; (8) opinion; (9) scare; (10) make unfriendly.

Practice C

(1) d, (2) c, (3) f, (4) a, (5) j, (6) b, (7) e, (8) i, (9) h, (10) g.

Additional Words (pp. 328–329)

1. **exonerate.** To relieve, as of a charge or blame resting on one; to clear of a charge of guilt; to declare or prove blameless; to relieve of a debt or duty.

2. **jeopardy.** Risk; danger; peril.

3. **temperate.** Moderate in everything; avoiding extremes or excesses.

4. **corroborate.** To confirm (to strengthen; to make firm; to affirm); to make more certain.

5. **repent.** To feel pain, sorrow, or regret for something left undone or done; to feel remorse.

Practice for Additional Words (p. 329)

(1) d, (2) a, (3) e, (4) c, (5) b.

Exercise 23 (pp. 329–335)

Practice A

(1) discreet, (2) apprehensive, (3) docile, (4) infamous, (5) bland, (6) scrutinize, (7) omission, (8) unanimous, (9) miscellaneous, (10) initiate.

Practice B

(1) bland, (2) discreet, (3) apprehensive, (4) unanimous, (5) infamous, (6) miscellaneous, (7) omission, (8) initiate, (9) scrutinize, (10) docile.

Practice C

(1) covet, (2) initiate, (3) omission, (4) unanimous, (5) none—miscellaneous, (6) delete, (7) none—scrutinize, (8) frugal, (9) discreet, (10) asset, (11) bland, (12) none—apprehensive, (13) docile, (14) infamous.

WORD SQUARE

I	N	I	T	I	A	T	E	O
A	D	I	S	C	R	E	E	T
C	O	D	E	L	E	T	E	A
I	C	O	V	E	T	R	T	S
M	I	N	F	A	M	O	U	S
B	L	A	N	D	U	O	S	E
O	E	F	R	U	G	A	L	T
U	N	A	N	I	M	O	U	S
O	M	I	S	S	I	O	N	E

Additional Words (pp. 334–335)

1. **futile.** Useless; vain; ineffectual; trifling; unimportant.

2. **criterion.** A standard of judging; any established law, rule, or principle by which a correct judgment may be formed.

3. **valid.** Sound; well grounded on principles or evidence; having legal force.

4. **datum.** Information given; a premise upon which something can be argued; material used as a basis for calculations. (*Data* is often used for the singular.)

5. **invincible.** Impossible to overcome; not able to be conquered.

Practice for Additional Words (p. 335)

(1) d, (2) a, (3) c, (4) e, (5) b.

Exercise 24 (pp. 335-341)

Practice A

(1) acquisition, (2) contagious, (3) turmoil, (4) trite, (5) adept, (6) passive, (7) gregarious, (8) opponent, (9) anecdote, (10) exotic.

Practice B

(1) adversary; (2) unenthusiastic or inactive; (3) disturbance; (4) commonplace; (5) short, entertaining accounts of some happenings; (6) spreading by contact; (7) foreign or strange; (8) fond of the company of others; (9) act of obtaining something; (10) highly skilled.

Practice C

(1) b, (2) d, (3) j, (4) h, (5) a, (6) g, (7) c, (8) i, (9) f, (10) e.

Additional Words (pp. 340-341)

1. **attrition.** A gradual wearing down or weakening; a rubbing out or grinding down.

2. **abridge.** To shorten; to curtail; to give the substance of in fewer words.

3. **imminent.** About to happen; threatening (said especially of danger).

4. **paradox.** Contradiction; a self-contradictory statement that is false; a statement that seems absurd, contradictory, or unbelievable but may be true.

5. **phenomenon.** Any fact, circumstance, or experience that is apparent to the senses and that can be scientifically described; something extremely unusual.

Practice for Additional Words (p. 341)

(1) c, (2) e, (3) d, (4) b, (5) a.

Grid entries (numbered cells):

1 A, 2 H, 3 A
4 R, I, N, 5 G
6 S, I, R
7 D, 8 I, 9 S
10 M, E
11 I, R, E
12 L, A, G
13 S, E, E, 14 S
15 D, 16 A, 17 M
18 S, T, A, 19/20 T E
21 S, C
22 D, 23 O, C, I, L, E
24 D, E, R, O, 25 G, A, T, O, R, 26 Y
27 S, H, E
28 I
29 O, R
30 R, E, E, 31 L
32 A
33 A, T
34 S, O, 35 S
36 T, E, S, T
37 R, 38 U, N
39 C, U, T
40 P, 41 A, S, T
42 W, A, S
43 B, A, S, E
44 A, N
45 D, I, C, E
46 P, E, R
47 A, 48 S, S, E, 49 T
50 A, I, N, T
51 A, G, E
52 M, I, S, C, E, L, L, A, N, E, O, U, 53 S, 54 S
55 I, D, A
56 E, R
57 N, O
58 V, O, C, A, L, 59 L
60 R, I
61 H, 62 A
63 B, E, T, H
64 A
65 S, 66 P, 67 Y
68 B, E, T, 69 S
70 T, 71 R, 72 I, T, E
73 P, 74 O, 75 T
76 I
77 S, E, E
78 I, N, 79 F, A, M, O, U, 80 U, 81 S
82 A, 83 E, S, T, 84 H, 85 E, T, 86 I, C
87 A, L, I
88 N, O
89 A, N, N
90 E, N
91 O, R, 92 E
93 S, K, I, N
94 A, D, D
95 N, U, N
96 H, 97 I, 98 S
99 A, S
100 D
101 S, 102 I, N
103 I, N, T, 104 I, M, I, D, A, 105 T, 106 E
107 M, A, N
108 D, I, 109 A
110 S, C, A, T
111 N, U, N
112 A, F, F, R, O, N, T
113 L, T
114 E, N
115 T, R, Y
116 H, 117 E
118 S, E, A
119 T, I, E
120 D, I, E
121 A
122 G, E, M
123 A, D, 124/125 E P, T
126 M, 127 E, Z
128 O, N
129 S, 130 T, A, R
131 V, E, R, A
132 O, R, 133 D, E, R
134 N, A, 135 M, E
136 E, P, I, C, 137 C
138 E, N
139 C, U, R, E
140 A, T, T, I, T, U, D, E
141 U, 142 D, E
143 L, O
144 S, O, S
145 N, 146 O, 147 R
148 I, T
149 N, O, T
150 O, N
151 R, E
152 L, O, T
153 A, N

Word Scramble 8 (pp. 345–346)

(1) antagonize, (2) affront, (3) characteristic, (4) euphemism, (5) intimidate, (6) inclination, (7) bland, (8) discreet, (9) docile, (10) infamous, (11) initiate, (12) omission, (13) scrutinize, (14) unanimous, (15) adept, (16) contagious, (17) exotic, (18) passive, (19) trite, (20) turmoil.

Analogies 8 (pp. 346–347)

(1) compliment, (2) fearful, (3) terminate, (4) commonplace, (5) unskilled, (6) ally, (7) standard, (8) inclination, (9) spreading, (10) unmanageable, (11) disturbance, (12) exonerate, (13) bland, (14) notorious, (15) exotic, (16) passive, (17) careful, (18) gregarious, (19) scrutinize, (20) overindulgent.

Multiple-Choice Vocabulary Test 8 (pp. 347–349)

Exercise 22

(1) c, (2) a, (3) c, (4) a, (5) c, (6) b, (7) d, (8) d, (9) b, (10) a.

Exercise 23

(11) b, (12) c, (13) d, (14) b, (15) d, (16) b, (17) a, (18) d, (19) c, (20) a.

Exercise 24

(21) d, (22) c, (23) d, (24) c, (25) b, (26) c, (27) c,[1] (28) c, (29) d, (30) b.

True/False Test 8 (pp. 349–350)

(1) T, (2) T, (3) F, (4) T, (5) F, (6) F, (7) T, (8) F, (9) F, (10) F, (11) F, (12) T, (13) F, (14) F, (15) F, (16) F, (17) T, (18) T, (19) F, (20) F.

STOP. Turn to p. 350 for the scoring of the tests.

---

[1] Choice *c* is a better answer than *b* because not all opponents are enemies. Your opponent in a game would not be your enemy.

Additional Practice Sets (pp. 351–354)

Additional Practice 1

(1) affront, (2) attitude, (3) euphemism, (4) intimidate, (5) inclination, (6) characteristic, (7) hypocrites, (8) antagonize, (9) aesthetic, (10) derogatory.

Additional Practice 2

(1) omission, (2) bland, (3) miscellaneous, (4) scrutinize, (5) unanimous, (6) infamous, (7) docile, (8) initiate, (9) discreet, (10) apprehensive.

Additional Practice 3

(1) trite, (2) turmoil, (3) opponent, (4) passive, (5) contagious, (6) gregarious, (7) adept, (8) acquisition, (9) exotic, (10) anecdote.

APPENDIXES

APPENDIX A: THE DICTIONARY

The dictionary, which is an important reference book for all persons, is filled with information about individual words, as well as other useful information. Even though the dictionary is a necessary tool, with which all students should be familiar, it should not be used as a crutch; that is, every time you meet a word whose meaning is unknown to you, you should first try to use your knowledge of combining forms and context clues to unlock the meaning. If these techniques do not help, and the word is essential for understanding the passage, then you should look up the meaning.

To use the dictionary effectively, you should know that the purpose of dictionaries is not to prescribe or make rules about word meanings and pronunciations, but only to describe. Lexicographers use various methods to compile the words in the dictionary. One important method is based on citations of usage and research consulting older dictionaries. Another method involves choosing a group of people and recording the ways in which these subjects pronounce and use words. These then are recorded as the accepted standard spellings, definitions, and word usage.

Difficulties exist concerning pronunciation because persons in different parts of the country often pronounce words differently. Pronunciation in the East is often different from that in the South or Midwest. As a result, pronunciation of a word as given in the dictionary may not be in accord with your region's pronunciation of it.

Also, to compound this problem, different dictionaries may use different pronunciation keys. The pronunciation key is composed of words with diacritical marks. To know how to pronounce a word in a particular dictionary, you must familiarize yourself with the pronunciation key in that dictionary. For example, look at the way that five different dictionaries present a few similar words.

Word	Webster's New Twentieth Century Dictionary	Webster's Third New International Dictionary	Random House Dictionary of the English Language	The American Heritage Dictionary of the English Language	Funk & Wagnalls Standard College Dictionary
1. coupon	cou′pon	′k(y)ü, pän	ko͞o′pon	ko͞o′pŏn′	ko͞o′pon
2. courage	cour′age	′kər · ij	kûr′ij	kûr′ĭj	kûr′ij
3. covet	cov′ĕt	′kəvət	kuv′it	kŭv′ĭt	kuv′it

If you had no knowledge of the pronunciation key of the specific dictionary, you would have difficulty in pronouncing the word. (See p. 365 for the Guide to Pronunciation in *Webster's New Twentieth Century Dictionary*.) Pronunciation guides are generally found in the beginning of dictionaries. Many dictionaries also have a simplified pronunciation key at the bottom of every page. (See pp. 366–367 for two pages from *Webster's New Twentieth Century Dictionary*.)

In this vocabulary book an adaptation of *Webster's New Twentieth Century Dictionary's* style is being used because the phonetic spelling (the way a word sounds) is most closely related to the actual spelling of the word. Also, the diacritical system—that is, the marks that are used with a letter to distinguish it from another and to help in pronunciation—is a simplified one. Some examples of diacritical marks are: ă, ā, à.

Because this text will be used in various parts of the country, this book uses an even more simplified pronunciation key, which is presented in Chapter One.

Before reading any further, list in the following space all the uses that you can think of for the dictionary.

USES OF THE DICTIONARY

Now compare your list with the following:

I. *Uses of the Dictionary*

    A. *Information Concerning a Word*

        1. Spelling.

        2. Definitions.

        3. Correct usage.

        4. Pronunciation.

        5. Syllabication.

        6. Antonyms.

        7. Synonyms.

        8. Parts of speech.

9. Idiomatic phrases.

10. Etymology —the history of the word.

11. Semantics —the analysis of the word's meanings.

B. *Other Useful Information*

1. Biographical entries.

2. Lists of foreign countries, provinces, and cities with their population figures.

3. Charts of other geographical data.

4. Air distances between principal cities.

5. Listing of foreign words and phrases.

6. Complete listing of abbreviations in common use.

7. Tables of weights and measures.

8. Signs and symbols.

9. Forms of address.

Most persons do not realize what an abundance of information can be gained from the dictionary. (The kind of information presented varies according to the dictionary.)

Using your dictionary, answer the following questions:

1. In what countries do centaurs live? _____

2. Where is Mount Everest? _____

3. Was Prometheus the goddess of fire? _____

4. Is a songstress a man who writes songs? _____

5. Is *Miss.* an abbreviation for *Missus*? _____

6. Is haiku a Hawaiian mountain? _____

7. Did Andrew Jackson fight in the Civil War? _____

8. Is a statute a work of art? _____

9. Is a quadruped an extinct animal? _____

10. Is a centipede a unit of measurement in the metric system? _____

Using the given dictionary page (see p. 366), see how well you can answer the following questions. Answers are on the next page.

1. Would the word *Porphyrio* be found on this page? _____

2. Between what two words would you find *porose*? _____

3. How many definitions are given for *pore*? _____

4. What parts of speech can *pore* be? _____

5. In what seas do you find porcupine fish? _____

6. What was *pork* originally? _____

7. What is the slang meaning of *pork barrel*? _____

8. Is there such a thing as porcupine grass? _____

9. What is the Latin for *pore*? _____

10. What is *populus alba?* _____

11. How many syllables does the word *poriferous* have? _____

12. Which syllable is accented in *porism*? _____

13. Which syllable is accented in *porismatic*? _____

14. According to the pronunciation key at the bottom of the page, $\bar{a}$ sounds like *a* in what word? _____

15. The *c* in the word *porotic* sounds like _____ in the word _____ in the pronunciation key at the bottom of the page.

16. The *c* in the word *porcelain* sounds like _____ in the word _____ in the pronunciation key.

ANSWERS

1. no, *porphyrine* is the last word—*rio* would be after *rine*
2. *Porosa* and *porosity*
3. six
4. noun and verb
5. tropical
6. pig or hog
7. government appropriations for political patronage
8. yes
9. *porus*
10. the European white poplar
11. four
12. first
13. third
14. fate
15. c; cat or chord
16. *c*; ace

GUIDE TO PRONUNCIATION

PRONUNCIATION in this dictionary is indicated directly on the entry word by a system of symbols, or diacritical marks. Thus, the symbol c is used to indicate the sound of the hard c in cat, and the word is entered in the vocabulary as cat. The Key to Pronunciation printed below gives a complete description of the symbols used and the sounds they represent. The modified sounds are unmarked, as the e in cent, the a in apply, the i in pin, the u in tub, the o in on, and the y in myth.

When two vowels stand together, only the one which indicates the sound of the word is marked, as in strĕak, brăin, mōat. The clusters ae and oe ending a syllable are pronounced as ē; when followed by a consonant in the same syllable they are pronounced as e in met.

In a few instances it is impossible to indicate the pronunciation on the word itself; in such cases the word, or part of it, is respelled in parentheses immediately following the entry. The word is respelled phonetically, that is, according to its sound, regardless of the letters that compose it. Examples of respelling are eight (āt); guide (gīd); heir (âr); and här′le-quin (-kin or -kwin).

The accents are indicated thus: primary ′, secondary ″. The secondary accent or subordinate stress is normally indicated only when it falls at an irregular interval from the primary or main stress, that is, at an interval other than two syllables.

Although full vowel quality is indicated in all syllables, it should be understood that in totally unstressed syllables the vowel quality is variously reduced, or weakened, in colloquial speech to a more or less neutral sound. To avoid the confusion of excessive diacritical marks, sounds in non-English words are indicated by the English sounds most nearly approximating these.

KEY TO PRONUNCIATION

ā	as in	fāte, āle, ā′corn, be-rāte′, nat″u-ral-i-zā′tion.
ä	" "	fär, fä′ther, ärch, mär′shal, cär-toon′; also as in whät, wänt.
à	" "	fàst, glàss, a-làs′; also as in so′dà, à-dapt′à-ble.
ạ	" "	fạll, pạw, ạw′ful, ap-plạud′.
ă	" "	fĭ′năl, sea′măn, tol′er-ănt, men′ăce.
â	" "	câre, âir, mil′i-târ-y, de-clâre′.
a	" "	at, ac-cord′, com-par′i-son, car′ry.
ē	" "	ēve, mēte, hē, Ē′den, in-ter-vēne′; also as in hēre, drēar′y.
ẹ	" "	prẹy, ẹight, o-bẹy′.
ē̆	" "	hē̆r, vē̆rse, sē̆r′vice, in-tē̆r′.
e	" "	met, ebb, en-dorse′, mon′e-tar-y, dis-tend′.
ee	" "	feed, pro-ceed′, lee′way.
ī	" "	pīne, I-de′a, īce′berg, de-cīde′, al-lī′ance.
ĭ	" "	clĭque, ma-rĭne′; also as in Mar-tĭ′ni.
î	" "	bîrd, stîr, ex′tîr-pate, fîrm′a-ment.
i	" "	it, hit, re-mit′, cit′y; also as in pos′si-ble, grav′i-ty, pu′pil.
ō	" "	nōte, ōat, sō, ō′pen, hel-lō′; also as in ren′ō-vate, prō-pel′.
ŏ	" "	mŏve, prŏve, tŏmb.
ọ	" "	lọng, crọss, ọff, ọrb, fọr-bid′, dọr′mer.
ô	" "	at′ôm, plôv′er; also as in ac′tôr, wôrd, wôrk.
o	" "	not, for′est, non′sense; also as in dog, broth, cost; also as in con-fess′, con-cur′.
ọọ	" "	mọọn, cọọ, fọọd, brọọd′er.
oo	" "	book, hood, foot, look, cook′y.
ū	" "	ūse, fūse, ū-til′i-ty, fū′tile, im-mūne′.
ụ	" "	bụll, pụt, fụl-fil′, boun′ti-fụl.
ú	" "	brúte, jú′ry; also used for the German ü.
û	" "	tûrn, fûr, bûr-lesque′, de-mûr′.
u	" "	up, rub, sun′set, in-sult′.
ȳ	" "	crȳ, eȳe.
y	" "	myth, cit′y.
ç	" "	çat, to-baç′ço.
ç	" "	ma-çhine′.
c	" "	ace, ce′dar.
ch	" "	church.
çh	" "	çhord.

ġ	as in	ġem.
ñ	" "	añ′ger, sphiñx.
ṅ	" "	French boṅ.
ng	" "	ring.
ş	" "	mi′şer, aş.
th	" "	this.
th	" "	thin.
ẓ	" "	aẓure.
au	" "	umlaut.
aw	" "	straw.
ou	" "	out.
oi	" "	oil.
oy	" "	boy.
ew	" "	new, few.
ow	" "	now.
-tūre	as -chēr (in picture).	
-tion -sion	}as -shun (in nation, tension).	
-ciăn -tiăn -siăn	}as -shun (in Martian, Melanesian, mortician).	
-şiăn -şion	}as -zhun (in Persian, fusion).	
-liŏn	as -lyun or -yun (in million).	
-ceous -(s)cious	}as -shus (in cretaceous, delicious, conscious).	
qu	as kw (in queen).	
-ous	as -us (in porous).	
ph-	as f- (in phone, etc.).	
-le	as -l (at end of syllable, as in able, cycle, etc.).	
-iá	as -yá (in pharmacopoeia).	
wh-	as hw- in whale, etc.	
kh	as in German doch (dokh).	

xii

pop'u·late, v.t.; populated, pt., pp.; populating, ppr. [from ML. populatus, pp. of populare, to populate, from L. populus, the people.]
1. to be or become the inhabitants of; to inhabit.
2. to people; to furnish with people or inhabitants, either by natural increase or by immigration or colonization.

pop'u·late, v.i. to propagate; to increase. [Obs.]

pop·u·la'tion, n. [LL. populatio.]
1. all the people in a country, region, etc.
2. the number of these.
3. a (specified) part of the people in a given area; as, the Japanese population of Hawaii.
4. a populating or being populated.
5. in biology, all the organisms living in a given area.
6. in statistics, a group of items or individuals.
population explosion; the very great and continuing increase in human population in modern times.

pop'u·lā·tŏr, n. one who populates or peoples.

pop'u·lin, n. [L. populus, poplar, and -in.] a crystallizable substance found in the bark, root, and leaves of the Populus tremula, or aspen, along with salicin.

Pop'u·lism, n. [from L. populus, the people; and -ism.]
1. the theory and policies of Populists.
2. the Populistic movement.

Pop'u·list, n. one belonging to the People's party.

Pop'u·list, a. same as Populistic.

Pop·u·list'ic, a.
1. of Populists or their views.
2. having to do with the People's party.

pop'u·lous, a. [L. populosus.] full of people; thickly populated.

pop'u·lous·ly, adv. with many inhabitants in proportion to the extent of country.

pop'u·lous·ness, n. the state of being populous.

Pop'u·lus, n. [L., poplar.] a genus of trees which includes the common poplar. Populus alba is the European white poplar.

por'bēa″gle, n. [from Corn. dial.] any shark of the genus Lamna, especially Lamna cornubica, found in northern seas: it is large and fierce and brings forth living young rather than eggs.

por'cāte, por'çā·ted, a. [L. porca, a ridge.] ridged; formed in ridges.

pŏr'cē·lain (-lin), n. [so called from its resemblance to the Venus shell, which is, in It., porcellana, from porcella, a little pig, the upper surface of the shell resembling the curve of a pig's back.]
1. a fine, white, translucent, hard earthenware with a transparent glaze; china.
2. porcelain dishes or ornaments, collectively.

pŏr'cē·lain, a. made of porcelain.

pŏr'cē·lain crab, a crab having a very smooth, polished shell, as Porcellana platycheles, the broad-clawed species.

pŏr'cē·lain·ized, a. altered by heating so as to resemble porcelain; in geology, metamorphosed so as to resemble white earthenware, as clays, shales, etc.

pŏr'ce·lain jas'pĕr, porcelanite.

pŏr·cē·lā'nē·ous, pŏr·cel·lā'nē·ous, a. of or resembling porcelain.

pŏr'ce·lā·nite, pŏr'cel·lā·nīte, n. a semivitrified clay or shale, somewhat resembling jasper.

pŏr'ce·lā·nous, pŏr'cel·lā·nous, a. same as porcelaneous.

pŏrch, n. [ME. and OFr. porche, from L. porticus, from porta, a gate, entrance, or passage.]
1. a covered entrance to a building, usually projecting from the wall and having a separate roof.
2. an open or enclosed gallery or room on the outside of a building; a veranda.
3. a portico; a covered walk. [Obs.]
the Porch; a portico in Athens where the Stoic philosopher Zeno taught his disciples.

pŏrch clĭmb'ĕr (klĭm'), a burglar who gains entrance to a house by climbing the porch. [Slang.]

pŏr'cine, a. [L. porcinus, from porcus, hog.] of or like pigs or hogs.

por'cū·pine, n.; pl. por'cū·pines or por'cū·pine, [ME. porkepyn, pork despyne; OFr. porc espin, the spinous hog, or spine hog; L. porcus, and spina, a spine or thorn.] any of a number of related gnawing animals; specifically, (a) the old-world porcupine,

Hystrix cristata, of the family Hystricidæ, bearing long, stiff, erectile spines sometimes a foot in length; (b) the North American porcupine, of the family Erethizontidæ, which is armed with short, sharp quills or spines that may be easily detached from the body. The two species of this porcupine are Erethizon dorsatus of the eastern part of the United States and Canada, and Erethizon epixanthus of the West.

PORCUPINE

por'cū·pine ant'ēat·ĕr, an echidna, an ant-eating mammal resembling a porcupine.

por'cū·pine crab, a Japanese crab having long spines on its carapace and limbs; the Lithodes hystrix.

por'cū·pine fish, a fish of the tropical seas, Diodon hystrix, which is covered with spines or prickles capable of being erected by its inflating the body; also, any fish with similarly erectile spines.

por'cū·pine grass, the common prairie grass, Stipa spartea, of the United States.

por'cū·pine wood, the outer wood of the cocoanut palm, which, when cut horizontally, presents markings resembling porcupine quills.

pōre, n. [ME. pore, poor; L. porus; Gr. poros, a passage, a pore, from peran, to pierce.]
1. originally, a passage; a channel.
2. a tiny opening, usually microscopic, as in plant leaves, skin, etc., through which fluids may be absorbed or discharged.
3. a similar opening in rock or other substances.

pōre, v.i.; pored, pt., pp.; poring, ppr. [ME. poren, pouren.]
1. to gaze intently or steadily.
2. to look searchingly; to read carefully; to study minutely (with over); as, he pored over the book.
3. to think deeply and thoroughly; to ponder; meditate (with on, upon, or over); as, he pored on the wonders of science.

pōr'ĕr, n. one who pores.

por'gee, n. same as porgy.

por'gy (or -ji), n.; pl. por'gies or por'gy, [prob. var. of pogy.] any of a large number of salt-water food fishes having spiny fins and a wide body covered with large scales.

Pō·rif'e·rà, n.pl. [pore, and L. ferre, to bear.] in zoology, a phylum of invertebrates which includes sponges.

pō·rif'ĕr·an, a. any of the Porifera.

pō·rif'ĕr·ous, a.
1. having pores.
2. in zoology, of or related to the Porifera.

pō'ri·form, a. [L. porus, pore, and form.] resembling a pore.

pōr'i·ness, n. the state of being porous, or having numerous pores.

pō'rism, n. [ME. porysme; ML. porisma; Gr. porisma, lit., a thing brought, from porizein, to bring.] in ancient mathematics, a geometrical proposition variously defined; specifically, (a) a proposition deduced from some other demonstrated proposition; a corollary; (b) a proposition that uncovers the possibility of finding such conditions as to make a specific problem capable of innumerable solutions.

pō·ris·mat'ic, a. pertaining to a porism; seeking to determine by what means and in how many ways a problem may be solved.

pō·ris·mat'ic·ăl, a. porismatic.

pō'rīte, n. a coral of the family Poritidæ, or of the genus Porites.

Pō·rī'teş, n. [LL., from L. porus, pore.]
1. in zoology, a genus of perforate madreporarian corals, having small twelve-rayed calices and a very porous structure.
2. a genus of millepores.

Pō·rit'i·dæ, n.pl. a family of corals of which Porites is the type genus.

pŏrk, n. [ME. and OFr. porc; L. porcus, a pig.]
1. originally, a pig or hog.

2. the flesh of a pig or hog, used, fresh or cured, as food.

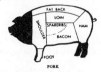

PORK

3. money, position, etc. received from the government through political patronage. [Slang.]

pŏrk bar'rel, government appropriations for political patronage, as for local improvements to please legislators' constituents. [Slang.]

pŏrk'ĕr, n. a hog, especially a young one, fattened for use as food.

pŏrk'et, n. a young hog. [Rare.]

pŏrk'fish, n.; pl. pŏrk'fish·es or pŏrk'fish, a black grunt, Anisotremus virginicus, with yellow stripes, of the West Indies.

pŏrk'ling, n. a young pig.

pŏrk pīe, 1. a meat pie made of chopped pork, usually eaten cold.
2. a soft hat with a round, flat crown, worn by men; now often porkpie.

pŏrk'pīe, n. same as pork pie, sense 2.

pŏrk'y, a.; comp. porkier; superl. porkiest.
1. of or like pork.
2. fat, as though overfed.
3. saucy, cocky, presumptuous, impertinent, or the like. [Slang.]

por'nŏ, n. pornography. [Slang.]

por'nŏ, a. pornographic. [Slang.]

por·noc'ra·cy, n. [Gr. pornē, prostitute, and kratein, to rule.] government by prostitutes; domination, sway, or influence of profligate women; specifically, the government of Rome in the early part of the tenth century.

por·nō·graph'ic, a. of, or having the nature of, pornography; obscene.

por·nog'ra·phy, n. [Gr. pornē, prostitute, and graphein, to write.]
1. originally, a description of prostitutes and their trade.
2. writings, pictures, etc. intended to arouse sexual desire.
3. the production of such writings, pictures, etc.

por·o·mēr'ic, n. [arbitrary coinage, prob. from porous, and polymeric.] a synthetic, leather-like, porous material, often coated or impregnated with a polymer.

pō·rō·phyl'lous, a. [Gr. poros, pore, and phyllon, leaf.] in botany, having leaves covered with transparent points or dots.

Pō·rō'sà, n.pl. same as Perforata.

pō·rōse', a. [LL. porosus, full of pores.]
1. porous.
2. of or pertaining to the Porosa.

pō·ros'i·ty, n.; pl. pō·ros'i·ties, [ME. porosite; ML. porositas, from porosus, from L. porus, a pore.]
1. the quality or state of being porous.
2. the ratio of the volume of a material's pores to that of its solid content.
3. anything porous.
4. a pore.

pō·rot'ic, n. [Gr. pōros, a callus.] any medicine which assists in the formation of callus.

pō'rous, a. [from pore.] full of pores, or tiny holes through which fluids, air, or light may pass; as, a porous skin; porous wood; porous earth.

pō'rous·ly, adv. in a porous manner.

pō'rous·ness, n. the quality or state of having pores; porosity; as, the porousness of the skin of an animal, or of wood.

por'pen·tīne, n. porcupine. [Obs.]

por·phy·rāc'eous, a. same as porphyritic.

por'phyre, n. porphyry. [Obs.]

por'phy·rin, n. [from hematoporphyrin, from hemato-, and Gr. porphyra, purple, purple product of hemoglobin decomposition.] any of a group of pyrrole derivatives of hemoglobin and chlorophyll, containing no iron or magnesium.

por'phy·rine (-rēn), n. a chemical substance, colorless and uncrystallized, obtained from the bark of an Australian tree, Alstonia constricta.

1402   fāte, fär, fàst, fall, finăl, cāre, at; mēte, prey, hẽr, met; pīne, marine, bĭrd, pin; nōte, mŏve, fŏr, atŏm, not; mŏŏn, book;

366

Pọr·phyr′i·ō, *n.* [Gr. *porphyriōn*, the purple gallinule, from *por-phyra*, purple.]
1. a genus of birds of the rail family, including *Porphyrio hyacinthinus*, the purple or hyacin-thine gallinule, a bird found in Eur-ope, Asia, and Africa, having a strong beak and long legs.
2. [p-] a bird of this genus.

PORPHYRIO

pọr′phy·rīte, *n.* any rock of a porphyritic nature.

pọr·phy·rit′iç, *a.* [ME. *porphiritike*; ML. *porphyriticus*; L. *porphyrites*; Gr. *porphy-rītēs*, porphyry.]
1. composed of or pertaining to porphyry.
2. resembling porphyry; containing dis-tinct crystals embedded in a fine-grained mass.

pọr′phy·ri·zā′tion, *n.* the act or process of porphyrizing, or the condition or quality of being porphyrized.

pọr′phy·rize, *v.t.* to cause to resemble por-phyry.

pọr′phy·rō·ġēne″, *a.* [Gr. *porphyra*, purple, and *gennān*, to beget.] born to the purple or of royal descent.

pọr″phy·rō·ġē·net′iç, *a.* [Gr. *porphyrītēs*, por-phyry, and *gennān*, to beget.] of or relating to porphyrogenitism.

pọr″phy·rō·ġĕn′i·tişm, *n.* the mode of suc-cession in some royal families, notably the Byzantine, whereby a younger son, if born in the purple, that is, after the accession of his parents to the throne, was preferred to an older son, who was born before the parents' accession.

pọr″phy·rō·ġĕn′i·tus, *n.* [Gr. *porphyra*, pur-ple, and *gennētos*, from *gennān*, to beget.] a son born to a sovereign, especially in the Byzan-tine Empire.

pọr′phy·roid, *n.* a rock that resembles, or has the structure of, porphyry.

pọr′phy·ry, *n.*; *pl.* **pọr′phy·rieş**, [ME. *pur-fire, porfirie*; OFr. *porfire*; ML. *porphyreus*, from Gr. *porphyros*, purple.]
1. originally, a hard Egyptian rock having red and white feldspar crystals embedded in a fine-grained, dark-red or purplish ground-mass.
2. any igneous rock of similar texture.

pọr′phy·ry shell, a univalve shell of the genus *Murex*; also, a seashell, *Oliva porphyria*, that is spotted like porphyry.

Pọr′pi·tà, *n.* [Gr. *porpē*, brooch.] a genus of bright-colored, disk-shaped marine siphono-phores.

pọr′poise (-pus), *n.*; *pl.* **pọr′pois·eş** or **pọr′poise**, [ME. *porcpisce, porpesse, porpese, porpus*, lit., swine fish, from L. *porcus*, a pig or swine, and *piscis*, a fish.]
1. any of a number of small, related ceta-ceans of the genus *Phocæna*, dark above and white below, with a triangle-shaped fin on the back, a blunt snout, and many teeth.

PORPOISE

2. a dolphin or any of several other small cetaceans.

pọr′pọ·rāte, *a.* arrayed in purple or royal raiment.

pọr′pus, *n.* a porpoise. [Dial.]

por·rā′ceous, *a.* [L. *porraceus*, from *porrum*, a leek or onion.] greenish; resembling the leek in color.

por·reçt′, *a.* in zoology, denoting a part which extends forth horizontally.

por·reçt′, *v.t.* [L. *porrectus*, pp. of *porrigere*, to extend.] to extend horizontally.

por·reç′tion, *n.* [L. *porrectio*, from *porrigere*; *por*, for *pro*, forward, and *regere*, to direct.] the act of stretching forth.

por′ret, *n.* [It. *porretta*; L. *porrum*, a leek.] a scallion; a leek or small onion. [Now Dial.]

por′ridġe, *n.* [altered from *pottage* by confusion with ME. *porrey*; OFr. *poree*; LL. *porrata*, leek broth, from L. *porrum*, leek.]
1. originally, pottage.
2. a soft food made of cereal or meal boiled in water or milk until thick. [Chiefly Brit.]

por′rin·ġer, *n.* [earlier *pottanger, pottage*, from Fr. *potager*, soup dish: altered by association with *porridge*.]
1. a small metal vessel for porridge, etc., especially one from which children are fed.
2. a headdress in the shape of a porringer. [Rare.]

port, *n.* [ME. *porte, port*; OFr. *porte*; L. *porta*, a door.]
1. a gateway; a portal. [Obs. except Scot.]
2. (a) a porthole; (b) the covering for this.
3. an opening, as in a cylinder face or valve face, for the passage of steam, gas, water, etc.
4. a mouthpiece of curved metal used in some bridle bits.

port, *v.t.* [ME. *porten*; OFr. *porter*; L. *portare* to carry.]
1. originally, to carry.
2. to carry, hold, or place (a rifle or sword) diagonally in front of one, crossing the left shoulder, as for inspection.

port, *n.* [ME. *porte*; OFr., from the v.]
1. the manner in which one carries oneself; carriage; deportment; demeanor.
2. the position of porting a weapon.
3. purport; meaning.
4. state; splendid or stately manner of liv-ing. [Obs.]
5. a piece of iron, somewhat in the shape of a horseshoe, fixed to the saddle or stirrup, and used to carry the lance when held upright. [Obs.]

port, *n.* [ME., from OFr. and AS. *port*, port, haven, harbor, from L. *portus*, a haven; akin to L. *porta*, gate; Gr. *poros*, a passage.]
1. a harbor; a haven; any bay, cove, inlet, or recess of the sea or of a lake, or the mouth of a river, which ships or vessels can enter, and where they can lie safe from injury by storms.
2. a city or town with a harbor where ships arrive and depart, and load or unload cargoes.
3. a port of entry.

port, *n.* [from *port* (harbor), with reference to the side opposite the steering oar.] the left-hand side of a ship or airplane as one faces forward, toward the bow; larboard: opposed to *starboard*.

port, *a.* of or on the port, or left-hand side.

port, *v.t.* and *v.i.* to move or turn (the helm) to the left.

port, *n.* [from *Oporto*, Portugal.] a fortified sweet wine, usually dark-red, originally from Portugal.

pọr·tà, *n.*; *pl.* **pọr′tae**, [L.] the entrance for nerves and ducts into an organ.

port·à·bil′i·ty, *n.* the condition or quality of being portable.

port′à·ble, *a.* [L. *portabilis*.]
1. that can be carried.
2. easily carried.
3. bearable; endurable. [Obs.]

port′à·ble, *n.* anything portable.

port′à·ble·ness, *n.* the quality or state of being portable.

port′āġe, *n.* [ME.; OFr.; ML. *portaticum*, from *portare*, to carry.]
1. the act of transporting or carrying.
2. the cost or price of transporting or carrying.
3. capacity for carriage; tonnage; burden. [Obs.]
4. a carrying or transporting of boats and supplies overland between navigable rivers, lakes, etc., as during a canoe trip.
5. any place or route over which this is done.
6. a sailor's wages.

pọr′tāġe, *v.t.* and *v.i.*; portaged, *pt., pp.*; por-taging, *ppr.* to carry or transport (boats, etc.) over a portage.

Pọr′tāġe fọr·mā′tion, a geological subdivi-sion of the Upper Devonian of the United States. It is named after Portage township in New York State.

pọr′tà·ġŭe, *n.* an obsolete Portuguese coin.

pọr′tàl, *n.* [ME.; OFr.; ML. *portale*, orig. neut. of *portalis*, of a door, from L. *porta*, gate.]
1. a doorway or entrance, especially a large and imposing one.
2. in architecture, the lesser gate, where there are two gates of different dimensions.

3. formerly, a little square corner of a room, separated from the rest by a wainscot, and forming a short passage into a room.
4. any entrance: often figurative, as, the *portal* of wisdom. [Poetic.]
5. the portal vein.

pọr′tàl, *a.* [ML. *portalis*.] designating, of, or like the vein carrying blood from the in-testines, stomach, etc. to the liver.

pọr′tàl-tö-pọr′tàl pāy, wages for workers based on the total time spent from the mo-ment of entering the mine, factory, etc. until the moment of leaving it.

pọr·tà·men′tō, *n.*; *pl.* **pọr·tà·men′tī**, [It., from *portare*, to carry; L. *portare*.] in music, a continuous gliding from one note to another, sounding all intervening tones; a glide.

pọr′tànce, *n.* [Early Mod. Eng., from Fr. *portance*, from *porter*, to bear.] air; mein; carriage; port. [Archaic.]

pọr′tass, *n.* [OFr. *porte-hors*; *porter*, to carry, and *hors*, out of doors.] so called from being easily portable.] a breviary; a prayer book.

pọr′tāte, *a.* [L. *portatus*, pp. of *portare*, to carry.] in heraldry, placed bend-wise in an escutcheon; that is, lying as if carried on a person's shoulder, as a cross.

pọr′tà·tive, *a.* [ME. and OFr. *portatif*, lit., that is carried, from L. *portatus*, pp. of *portare*, to carry, and OFr. *-if*.]
1. of or having the power of carrying a load, charge, etc.
2. that can be carried; portable. [Obs.]

CROSS PORTATE

port au·thor′i·ty, a governmental commission in charge of the traffic, regulations, etc. of a port.

port çap′tain (-tin), an official of a steamship company who assumes charge of vessels dur-ing their stay in port.

port chärġe, in commerce, a fee or duty charged for the privilege of keeping a ship or its cargo in a port.

port′çlūse, *n.* a portcullis. [Obs.]

port″crăy′ŏn, *n.* [Fr. *porte-crayon*; *porter*, to carry, and *crayon*, pencil.] a small metallic handle with a clasp for holding a crayon, etc. when used in drawing.

port′cul′lis, *n.* [ME. *portcoles*; OFr. *porte coleice*; *porte*, a gate, and *coleice*, f. of *coleis*, sliding, from L. *colare*, to strain, filter.]
1. in fortification, a heavy grating or lattice-work of timber or iron with the lower ends pointed like the teeth of a harrow, suspended by chains over the gateway of a castle, fort, etc., to be let down to prevent the entrance of an enemy.
2. a coin used by the East India Company in the reign of Queen Elizabeth I: it had a design of a portcullis on one side. [Obs.]

PORTCULLIS

port′cul′lis, *v.t.* to shut; to bar. [Rare.]

Pọrte, *n.* [Fr., the chief office of the Ottoman Em-pire was styled *Babi Ali*, lit., the High Gate, from the gate (*bâb*) of the palace at which jus-tice was administered. The French transla-tion of this term is *la Sublime Porte*: hence the use of this word.] the Ottoman Turkish government.

pọrte′-cō·chere′ (-shär′), *n.* [Fr. *porte*, gate, and *cochère*, coach.]
1. a large porch outside the entrance of a building, under which vehicles may be driven.
2. a large entrance gateway through which vehicles are driven into a square or courtyard.

pọrt′ed, *a.* having gates. [Obs.]

pọrte′feuille′ (-fē′y), *n.* [Fr., from *porter*, to carry, and *feuille*, L. *folium*, leaf.] a portfolio.

pọrte′-lu·miere″ (-myär″), *n.* [Fr., from *porter*, to carry, and *lumière*, light.] a mirror that can be adjusted so as to cast rays of light in any required direction; a simple form of heliostat.

pọrte′mŏn·nāie″ (-nä″), *n.* [Fr., from *porter* to carry, and *monnaie*, money.] a pocketbook for carrying money; a purse.

pọr·tend′, *v.t.*; portended, *pt., pp.*; portending, *ppr.* [L. *portendere, protendere*; *pro*, forth, and *tendere*, to stretch.]
1. to be an omen or warning of; to fore-

APPENDIX B: GLOSSARY

COMBINING FORMS PRESENTED IN *GAINING WORD POWER*

The number after the meaning refers to the exercise in which the combining form is presented.

A. Without. 5
Able. Can do; able. 4
Age. Condition, state of; action; collection of; place for. 22
Agog. Leading; directing; inciting. 5
Agogue. Leading; directing; inciting. 5
Al. Relating to. 13
Ali. Other. 5
Ambi. Both. 13
Ance. Act of; state of; quality of. 13
Anima. Spirit; mind; soul. 15
Animus. Spirit; mind; soul. 15
Anni. Year. 1
Annu. Year. 1
Ante. Before. 19
Anthrop. Mankind; man; human. 6
Anthropo. Mankind; man; human. 6
Anti. Against. 9
Aqua. Water. 7
Aqui. Water. 7
Ar. One who; that which. 1
Arch. Rule; chief. 5
Archae. Ancient. 12
Archaeo. Ancient. 12
Astro. Star. 7
Aud. Hear. 9
Audi. Hear. 9
Aut. Self. 1
Auto. Self. 1
Belli. War. 13
Bello. War. 13
Bene. Good. 9
Bi. Two. 1
Biblio. Book. 10
Bio. Life. 1
Brevi. Short; brief. 12
Cap. Take; receive. 11
Capit. Head. 8

Cata. Down. 10
Cede. Go; give in; yield. 12
Ceed. Go; give in; yield. 12
Cent. Hundred; hundredth part. 4
Centi. Hundred; hundredth part. 4
Cep. Take; receive. 11
Chron. Time. 12
Chrono. Time. 12
Cide. Murder; kill. 8
Civ. Citizen. 13
Civis. Citizen. 13
Co. With. 7
Col. With. 7
Com. With 7
Con. With 7
Contra. Against; opposite. 3
Cor. With. 7
Corp. Body. 8
Corpor. Body. 8
Cred. Believe. 4
Crypt. Secret; hidden. 12
Crypto. Secret; hidden. 12
Cura. Care. 9
Cycl. Circle; wheel. 12
Cyclo. Circle; wheel. 12
De. Away; from; off; completely. 11
Dec. Ten. 4
Deca. Ten. 4
Deci. Tenth part. 4
Dem. People. 5
Demo. People. 5
Derm. Skin. 11
Dermo. Skin. 11
Dia. Through. 10
Dic. Say; speak. 3
Dict. Say; speak. 3
Dis. Away from; apart; not. 12
Dom. State or condition of being; rank; total area of. 16
Dorm. Sleep. 14
Duc. Lead. 12
E. Out of; from; lacking. 11
Ego. I; me; the self. 14
Em. In; into. 8
En. In; into. 8

Ence. Act of; state of; quality of. 13

Enni. Year. 1

Epi. Upon; beside; among. 10

Equi. Equal. 15

Er. One who; that which. 1

Err. Wander. 14

Ex. Out of; from; lacking; former. 11

Fac. Make; do. 9

Fect. Make; do. 9

Feder. Trust; faith. 15

Fer. Bring; bear; yield. 10

Fic. Make; do. 9

Fid. Trust; faith. 15

Fide. Trust; faith. 15

Fin. End. 10

Frater. Brother. 8

Fratr. Brother. 8

Ful. Full of. 18

Gamy. Marriage. 6

Gen. Kind; race; descent. 6

Geno. Kind; race; descent. 6

Geo. Earth. 2

Gnosi. Knowledge. 11

Gnosis. Knowledge. 11

Gram. Something written or drawn; a record. 3

Graph. Something written; machine. 1

Gyn. Woman. 11

Gyno. Woman. 11

Hom. Same; man; human. 6

Homo. Same; man; human. 6

Hyper. Over; above; excessive. 14

Hypn. Sleep. 15

Hypno. Sleep. 15

Hypo. Under. 11

Ible. Can do; able. 4

Ic. Relating to; like. 24

Il. Not. 10

Im. Into; not. 10

In. Into, not. 10

Inter. Between; among. 14

Intra. Within; inside of. 14

Ion. State of; act of; result of. 3

Ir. Not. 10

Ish. Belonging to; like or characteristic of; tending to; somewhat or rather; about. 24

Ism. Act of, practice of, or result of, condition of being; action or quality of. 23

Ist. One who. 6

Ive. Of; relating to; belonging to; having the nature or quality of; tending to. 23

Kilo. Thousand. 4

leg. Law. 6

Legis. Law. 6

Less. Without. 7

Lex. Law. 6

Loc. Place. 9

Loco. Place. 9

Log. Speech; word 10

Logo. Speech; word 10

Luc. Light; clear. 14

Lum. Light; clear. 14

Magna. Great; large. 15

Mal. Bad; ill; evil; wrong; not perfect. 15

Man. Hand. 9

Manu. Hand. 9

Meter. Measure. 2

Micro. Very small. 2

Milli. Thousand; thousandth part. 4

Mis. Wrong; hate. 6

Miso. Wrong; hate. 6

Miss. Send. 15

Mitt. Send. 15

Mon. One. 5

Mono. One. 5

Mors. Death. 8

Mort. Death. 8

Nasc. Born. 15

Nat. Born. 15

Naut. Sailor. 7

Nomin. Name. 9

Non. Not. 9

Nov. New. 14

Ology. Study of; science of. 1

Omni. All. 7

Onym. Name. 9

Or. One who; that which. 1

Pac. Peace. 13

Pathy. Feeling; suffering. 8

Pax. Peace. 13
Ped. Foot; child. 1, 11
Pedo. Child. 11
Peri. Around. 14
Phob. Fear. 3
Phobo. Fear. 3
Phon. Sound. 2
Phono. Sound. 2
Pod. Foot. 1
Polis. City. 13
Poly. Many. 6
Pon. Place; set. 15
Pop. People. 15.
Port. Carry. 4
Pos. Place; set. 15
Post. After. 13
Poten. Powerful. 7
Pre. Before. 8
Pro. Before; forward. 10
Pseudo. False. 9
Re. Again; back. 2
Ri. Laughter. 11
Ridi. Laughter. 11
Risi. Laughter. 11
Sci. Know. 7
Scio. Know. 7
Scope. A means for seeing; watching or viewing. 2
Scrib. Write. 2
Scrip. Write. 2
Semi. Half; not fully; partly; occurring twice in a period. 15
Sequi. Follow. 12
Ship. State; condition or quality of; office, rank, or dignity; art or skill. 20
Sion. State of; act of; result of. 3
Sist. Stand. 4
Soph. Wise. 14
Spect. See; view; observe. 3
Sta. Stand. 14
Sub. Under; beneath; below; lower in rank. 12
Super. Above in position, over; above or beyond; greater than or superior to; extra; in the highest degree; in excessive degree. 21
Syl. Same; with; together; along with. 8
Sym. Same; with; together; along with. 8
Syn. Same; with; together; along with. 8
Tain. Hold. 12
Tele. From a distance. 2

Temp. Time. 11
Tempo. Time. 11
Tempor. Time. 11
Ten. Hold. 12
Tend. Stretch; strain. 13
Tens. Stretch; strain. 13
Tent. Hold; stretch; strain. 12, 13
Theo. God. 5
Tion. Act of; state of; result of. 3
Tox. Poison. 11
Toxo. Poison. 11
Trans. Across; beyond; through; on the other side of; over. 10
Un. Not. 8
Uni. One. 3
Ure. Act; result of an action; agent of action; state of. 22
Ven. Come. 7
Veni. Come. 7
Vent. Come. 7
Vid. See. 7
Vis. See. 7
Voc. Voice; call. 13
Vox. Voice; call. 13
Y. Having; full of; tending to; like; somewhat. 17

VOCABULARY WORDS PRESENTED IN *GAINING WORD POWER*[1]

The number after the meaning refers to the exercise in which the vocabulary word is presented. If there is more than one number, it means the word has also appeared in "Extra Word Power."

Abbreviation. A shortened form of a word or phrase. 12
Acquisition. The act of obtaining or acquiring; something obtained or gained, as property, knowledge, and so on. 24
Acreage. Collection of acres. 22.
Adaptation. The act of fitting or suiting one thing to another; an adjusting to fit new conditions; a change for a new use. 20
Adept. Highly skilled; proficient; expert. 24
Admission. Act of allowing to enter; entrance fee; a price charged or paid to be admitted; acknowledgment; a confession, as to a crime. 15
Advantage. Any condition, state, or circumstance favorable to success. 22
Aesthetic. Referring to beauty; sensitive to art and beauty; showing good taste; artistic. 22
Affect. To act upon or to cause something; to influence; to produce an effect or change in. 9

---

[1] Additional Words are presented separately.

Affirm. To declare or state positively; to say or maintain that something is true. 19

Affirmative. Having the quality of a positive statement. 23

Affluent. Having an abundance of goods or riches; wealthy; flowing freely. 17

Affront. To insult; an insult; an open and intentional insult. 22

Alias. Another name taken by a person, often a criminal. 5

Alien. A foreigner; a person from another country; foreign. 5

Alienate. To make others unfriendly to one; to estrange (to remove or keep at a distance). 5

Allocate. To set apart for a special purpose; to divide up something; to divide and distribute something. 9

Allot. To divide or distribute by lot; to distribute or parcel out in portions; to appoint. 21

Alternative. A choice between two or more things; a remaining choice; a choice. 18

Ambiguous. Having two or more meanings. 13

Americanism. Practice of values characteristic of Americans. 23

Amnesty. A pardon from the government; act of letting someone off. 17.

Amoral. Without morals; without a sense of right or wrong. 5

Anarchist. One who believes that there should be no government. 6

Anarchy. The absence of government; no rule; a state of disorder; chaos. 5

Anecdote. A short, entertaining account of some happening, usually personal or biographical. 24

Animosity. Hatred; resentment. 15

Anniversary. Yearly return of a date marking an event or an occurrence of some importance; returning or recurring each year. 1

Annual. Every year. 1, 13

Anonymous. Lacking a name; of unknown authorship. 9

Antacid. Something that acts against acid. 9

Antagonize. To make unfriendly; to make an enemy of; to oppose; to act against. 22

Antebellum. Before the war. 19

Antecedent. Going before in time; prior; preceding; previous; the word, phrase, or clause to which a pronoun refers. 19, 20

Antedate. To date before. 19

Antemeridian. Before noon (the abbreviation is A.M.). 19

Anteroom. Waiting room; a lobby. 19

Anthropologist. One who is in the field of anthropology. 6

Anthropology. Study of mankind; study of the cultures and customs of people. 6

Antigambling, Against gambling. 9

Antilabor. Against labor. 9

Antimachine. Against machines. 9

Antimen. Against men. 9

Antiwar. Against war. 9

Antiwomen. Against women. 9

Antonym. A word opposite in meaning to some other word. 9

Apathy. Lack of feeling; indifference. 8

Apodal. Relating to being without feet. 13

Apprehensive. Fearful, expecting evil, danger, or harm; anxious. 23

Aquanaut. One who travels undersea; a person trained to work in an underwater chamber. 7

Aquarium. A pond, a glass bowl, a tank, or the like, in which aquatic animals and/or plants are kept; a place in which aquatic collections are shown. 7

Aquatic. Living or growing in or near water; performed on or in water. 7

Archaeology. The study of the life and culture of ancient people, as by the digging up of old settlements, ruins from the past, and old man-made or other objects. 12

Archaic. Belonging to an earlier peirod; ancient; old-fashioned; no longer used. 12

Asset. Anything owned that has value; any valuable or desirable thing that serves as an advantage. 21

Assist. To give help to; an act of helping. 14

Assistance. Act of helping. 13

Astrology. The art or practice that claims to tell the future and interpret the influence of the heavenly bodies on the fate of people; a reading of the stars. 7

Astronaut. One who travels in space; a person trained to travel in outer space. 7

Astronomy. The science that deals with stars, planets, and space. 7

Atheist. One who does not believe in the existence of God. 5

Attention. Mental concentration; care; a position of readiness; acts of courtesy. 13

Attitude. A way of acting, thinking, or feeling that shows one's disposition (one's frame of mind) or opinion; the feeling itself; posture. 22

Audible. Capable of being heard. 9

Audience. An assembly of listeners or spectators at a concert, play, speech, and so on. 9

Audiovisual. Of, pertaining to, involving, or directed at both hearing and sight. 9

Audit. To examine or check such things as accounts; to attend class as a listener; an examination of accounts to report the financial state of a business. 9

Audition. A trial hearing, as of an actor or singer; the act of hearing; to try out for a part in an audition. 9

Auditorium. A building or hall for speeches, concerts, public meetings, and so on; the room in a building occupied by an audience. 9

Author. One who writes. 1

Autobiography. Life story written by oneself. 1

Autocracy. A form of government in which one person rules absolutely. 5

Autocrat. A ruler who has absolute control of a country. 5

Autograph. Signature; written by a person's own hand: an *autograph* letter; containing autographs: an *autograph* album; to write one's name on or in. 1

Barbarism. The condition of being primitive or brutal. 23

Beautiful. Full of beauty. 18

Beggar. One who begs. 1

Belligerent. Warlike; any nation, person, or group engaged in fighting war. 13

Benefactor. One who gives help or confers a benefit; a patron. 9

Beneficiary. One who receives benefits or advantages; the one to whom an insurance policy is payable. 9

Benefit. That which is helpful; advantage; a payment; a performance given to raise funds for a worthy cause; to aid. 9

Biannual. Twice a year; (loosely) accurring every two years. 1

Bibliography. A listing of books on a subject by an author (the description includes author's name, title, publisher, date of publication, and so on). 10

Bicentennial. Pertaining to or in honor of a two hundredth anniversary; consisting of or lasting two hundred years; occurring once in two hundred years; a two hundredth anniversary. 4

Bicycle. A vehicle having two wheels. 1

Biennial. Once every two years; lasting for two years. 1

Bigamist. One who is married to two spouses at the same time. 6

Bigamy. Marriage to two spouses at the same time. 6

Bimonthly. Every two months; twice a month. 1

Biographer. A person who writes biographies. 1

Biography. Person's life story. 1

Biologist. One who is in the field of biology. 6

Biology. Science of life. 1

Biped. Two-footed animal. 1

Biweekly. Every two weeks; twice a week. 1

Blameless. Without blame; without fault. 7

Bland. Mild; soft; gentle; balmy; kindly; soothing. 23

Bluish. Rather blue. 24

Bookish. Inclined to books; involved with books. 24

Boyish. Like or characteristic of a boy. 24

Candid. Honest; outspoken; frank. 16

Capable. Able to be affected; able to understand; having ability; having qualities that are able to be developed. 11

Capital. City or town that is the official seat of government; money or wealth; first letter of a word at the beginning of a sentence; excellent. 8

Capitalism. The economic system in which all or most of the means of production, such as land, factories, and railroads, are privately owned and operated for profit. 8

Capital punishment. The death penalty. 8

Capsule. A small container made of gelatin (or other material that melts) that holds a dose of medicine; a special removable part of an airplane or rocket. 11

Captive. One who is taken prisoner; one who is dominated. 11

Captor. One who holds someone a prisoner. 1

Catalog. A listing of names, titles, and so on in some order; a book containing such a list; to make a catalog. 10

Centennial. Pertaining to a period of one hundred years; lasting one hundred years; a one-hundredth anniversary. 4

Century. Period of one hundred years. 4

Characteristic. Marking the peculiar quality or qualities of a person or thing; distinctive; special; a special trait, feature, or quality; individuality. 22

Christendom. The Christian world. 16

Chronic. Continuing for a long time; prolonged; recurring. 12

Chronological. Arranged in time order (earlier things or events precede later ones). 12

Circumference. The distance around a circle; a boundary line of any rounded area. 10

Circumstance. Something connected with an act, event, or condition; (often pl.) the conditions, influences, and so on surrounding and influencing persons or actions; formal display, as in *pomp and circumstance*. 14

Citizenship. State or quality of being a citizen. 20

Civics. (Used in the singular.) The part of political science dealing with the study of civic affairs and the rights and responsibilities of citizenship. 13

Civil. Of a citizen or citizens; relating to citizens and their government; relating to ordinary community life as distinguished from military or church affairs; polite. 13

Civilian. One who is not in the military; of civilians; nonmilitary. 13

Civilization. A state of human society that has a high level of intellectual, social, and cultural development; the cultural development of a specific people, country, or region. 13

Coincidence. The occurrence of things or events at the same time by chance. 19

Colleague. A fellow worker in the same profession. 20

Collect. To gather together. 7

Combine. To join together; unite. 7

Concede. To give in; surrender; yield; grant; admit. 12

Conceive. To become pregnant with; to form in the mind; to understand; to think; to believe; to imagine; to develop mentally. 11

Concise. Brief; terse. 18

Conductor. One who guides or leads; a guide or director; one who has charge of a railroad train; the director of an orchestra or a chorus; any substance that conducts electricity, heat, and so on. 12

Conference. A discussion or meeting on some important matter. 10, 13

Confide. To tell in trust; to tell secrets trustingly.   15

Consequence. That which follows from any act; a result; an effect.   12

Conservative. Tending to maintain established traditions and to resist or oppose any change in these; cautious; moderate; traditional in style or manner; avoiding showiness; one who clings to traditional or long-standing methods, beliefs, and so on.   21

Consist. To be made up of.   14

Contagious. Spreading by contact; spreading or tending to spread from person to person.   24

Contemporary. Belonging to the same age; living or occurring at the same time; current; one living in the same period as another or others; a person or thing of about the same age or date of origin.   11

Content.[2] Satisfied; not complaining; not desiring something else.   12

Content.[2] What something holds (usually plural in this sense); subject matter; the material that something is made up of; the main substance or meaning.12

Contradiction. Something (such as a statement) consisting of opposing parts.   3

Contrary. Opposite.   3

Contrast. Difference between things; use of opposites for a certain result.   3

Convene. To come together; to assemble.   7

Convenient. Well suited to one's purpose, personal comfort, or ease.   7

Convention. A formal meeting of members for political or professional purposes; accepted custom, rule, or opinion.   7

Corporal punishment. Bodily punishment; a beating.   8

Corporation. A group of people who get a charter granting them as a body certain of the powers, rights, privileges, and liabilities (legal responsibilities) of an individual, separate from those of the individuals making up the group.   8

Corpse. Dead body.   8

Correspond. To be equivalent; to write letters to one another.   7

Courage. State of being fearless or brave.   22

Covert. Secret; concealed; covered over; sheltered.   17

Covet. To desire very much what another has; to crave; to long for.   21

Co-workers. Someone working with you.   7

Creative. Tending to be able to create.   23

Credential. Something that entitles one to credit or confidence; something that makes others believe in a person; (pl.) testimonials entitling a person to credit or to exercise official power.   4

Credible. Believable.   4

Credit. Belief in something; trust; faith; good name; in an account, the balance in one's favor; a unit of academic study; to supply something on credit to.   4

Crypt. An underground vault.   12

Cryptic. Having a hidden or secret meaning; mysterious.   12

Curtail. To shorten; to lessen; to cut off the end or a part.   17

---

[2]*Content* and *content* are presented separately because they are pronounced differently.

Cycle. A period that keeps coming back, in which certain events take place and complete themselves in some definite order; a round of years or ages; a pattern of regularly occurring events; a series that repeats itself. 12

Cyclone. A system of violent and destructive whirlwinds. 12

Damage. Condition of loss. 22

Danish. Belonging to Denmark. 24

Decade. Period of ten years. 4

Decapitate. To take off the head; to kill. 11

Deceive. To mislead by lying; to lead into error. 11

Decode. To change from code to simple language. 11

Decolor. To take color away. 11

Deduction. The act of drawing a conclusion by reasoning or reasoning that goes from the general to the particular; the taking away or subtraction of something; an inference or a conclusion. 12

Deflea. To take off fleas. 11

Delete. To take out or remove a letter, word, and so on; to cross out; to erase. 19

Delouse. To free from lice. 11

Demagogue. A person who stirs up the emotions of people in order to become a leader and achieve selfish ends. 5

Democracy. A form of government in which there is rule by the people either directly or through elected representatives. 5

Denude. To strip the covering from completely. 11

Dependence. Act of trusting; act of relying on someone for support. 13

Deport. To send someone away. 11

Deprive. To take something away from. 11

Dermatologist. A doctor who deals with skin disorders. 11

Derogative. Tending to belittle. 23

Derogatory. Tending to make less well regarded; tending to belittle someone or something; disparaging; belittling. 22

Description. An account that gives a picture of something in words. 2, 3

Destructive. Tending to cause destruction or the tearing down of things. 23

Detoxify. To take away poison; to destroy the poison. 11

Devilish. Like or characteristic of a devil. 24

Diagnose. To determine what is wrong with someone after an examination. 11

Diagram. An outline figure that shows the relationship between parts or places; a graph or chart. 10

Dialogue. A conversation in which two or more take part; the conversation in a play. 10

Diameter. A straight line passing through the center of a circle. 10

Dictation. The act of speaking or reading aloud to someone who takes down the words. 3

Dictator. A ruler who has absolute power. 3

Dictatorship. Office or rank of a head of government who has absolute control of the government. 20

Diction. Manner of speaking; choice of words. 3

Dictionary. A book for alphabetically listed words in a language, giving information about their meanings, pronunciations, and so forth. 3

Dilemma. Any situation that necessitates a choice between equally unfavorable or equally unpleasant alternatives; an argument that presents two equally unfavorable alternatives. 19

Diligent. Applying oneself in whatever is undertaken; working in a constant effort to accomplish something; industrious. 19

Dirty. Full of dirt. 17

Disable. To make an object or someone not able to do something. 12

Disapprove. Not to approve of; not to regard as worthy. 12

Disband. To break up (a group). 12

Discreet. Careful about what one says or does; prudent; cautious. 23

Disdain. To regard as unworthy; the feeling of scorn or despisal; expression of scorn (contempt). 19

Dishonest. Not honest; not to be trusted. 12

Disloyal. Not loyal. 12

Dismiss. To tell or allow to go; to discharge, as from a job; to get rid of; to have done with quickly; to reject. 15

Disrobe. To take off clothes. 12

Distant. Separated or apart by space and/or time; away from; far apart; not closely related. 14

Docile. Easy to teach; easy to discipline; obedient. 23

Dormant. Asleep or as if asleep; not active. 14

Dormitory. A large room in which many persons sleep; a building providing sleeping and living quarters, especially at a school, college, or resort (summer or winter hotel). 14

Dukedom. The rank of a duke. 16

Economize. To use or manage with thrift or prudence; to avoid waste or needless spending; to reduce expenses. 21

Effect. Something brought about by some cause; the result; consequence. 9

Effective. Producing or having the power to bring about an intended result; producing results with the least amount of wasted effort. 9

Egocentric. Self-centered; relating everything to oneself. 14

Empathy. The imaginative putting of oneself into another person's personality or skin; ability to understand how another feels because one has experienced it firsthand or otherwise. 8

Enjoyable. Able to be enjoyed. 4

Enthusiastic. Relating to enthusiasm or a lively interest in something. 24

Epidemic. Relating to the rapid spread of a disease or something else that spreads like an epidemic disease. 24

Epilogue. A short section added at the end to a book, poem, and so on; a short speech added to a play and given at the end. 10

Equivalent. Equal in value, meaning, force, and so on. 15

Eradicate. To destroy completely; to pull out by the roots; to wipe out; to exterminate. 19

Error. A mistake; something done, said, or believed incorrectly; a wandering from what is correct. 14

Euphemism. The substitution of a word or phrase that is less direct, milder, or vaguer for one thought to be harsh, offensive, or blunt; a word or phrase considered less distasteful or less offensive than another. 22

Euphemistic. Relating to euphemism or a milder way to say something. 24

Evidence. That which serves to prove or disprove something. 7

Evident. Obvious; clearly seen; plain. 7

Exception. The act of taking out; something or one that is taken out or left out; an objection. 11

Exclude. To keep from. 11

Excuse. To forgive. 11

Exhale. To breathe out. 11

Exit. To go out of. 11

Exotic. Foreign, charmingly unfamiliar; not native; strangely beautiful. 24

Expect. To look out for. 11

Export. To carry away; to carry or send some product to some other country or place; something that is exported. 4

Exposure. State of being exposed. 22

Ex-president. Former president. 11

Ex-wife. Former wife. 11

Factory. A building or buildings in which things are manufactured. 9

Famish. To make or be very hungry; starve. 18

Famished. Very hungry. 18

Fatal. Resulting in or capable of causing death; deadly; bringing ruin or disaster; having decisive importance. 17

Fatherless. Without a father. 7

Fatigue. Physical or mental tiredness; weariness; to tire out. 18

Federal. Of or formed by a compact; relating to or formed by an agreement between two or more states, groups, and so on; relating to a union of states, groups, and so on, in which central authority in common affairs is established by consent of its members. 15

Fertile. Able to produce a large crop; able to produce; capable of bearing offspring, seeds, fruit, and so on; productive in mental achievements; inventive; having abundant resources. 10

Fertilization. The act of making something able to produce; in biology, the union of a male and female germ cell; impregnation. 10

Fictitious. Imaginary; not real; made up; fabricated. 17

Final. Last; coming at the end; conclusive. 10

Finite. Having a limit or end; able to be measured. 10

Formidable. Dreaded; causing awe or fear; hard to handle; of discouraging or awesome strength, size, difficulty, and so on. 18

Fraternity. A group of men joined together by common interests for fellowship; a brotherhood; a Greek letter college organization. 8

Freedom. Condition of being free. 16

Friendship. State of being a friend. 20

Frugal. Thrifty; not spending freely; avoiding waste. 21

Frustrate. To defeat; to bring to nothing. 16

Frustrated. Filled with a sense of discouragement and dissatisfaction as a result of defeated efforts, inner conflicts, or unresolved problems. 16

General. Referring to all; in the U.S. Army and Air Force, an officer of the same rank as an admiral in the U.S. Navy. 6

Generic. Referring to all in a group or class. 6

Genocide. The systematic and deliberate killing of a whole group or a group of people bound together by customs, language, politics, and so on. 8

Geography. Study of the earth's surface and life. 2

Geologist. One who is in the field of geology. 6

Geology. Study of earth's physical history and makeup. 2

Geometry. Branch of mathematics dealing with the measurement of points, lines, planes, and so on. 2

Governorship. Rank or office of governor. 20

Gregarious. Fond of the company of others; sociable; characteristic of a flock, herd, or crowd. 24

Gynecologist. A doctor dealing with women's diseases, especially in reference to reproductive organs. 11

Harmless. Without harm; without hurting. 7

Haughty. Having or showing great pride in oneself and contempt (disrespect) or scorn for others; overbearing; snobbish; arrogant. 19

Healthy. Full of health. 17

Heroic. Like a hero. 24

Historic. Relating to history, which is an account of what has happened; famous in history. 24

Homicide. Any killing of one human being by another. 8

Homogeneous. Being the same throughout; being uniform. 6

Homograph. A word spelled the same way as another but having a different meaning. 6

Homonym. A word that agrees in pronunciation with some other word but differs in spelling and meaning. 9

Homosexual. Refering to the same sex or to sexual desire for those of the same sex; a homosexual individual. 6

Horsy. Like a horse. 17

Hostile. Unfriendly; referring to an enemy. 17

Hyperactive. Overactive. 14

Hyperbolic. Relating to a hyperbole or a great exaggeration. 24

Hyperproductive. Overproductive. 14

Hypersensitive. Oversensitive. 14

Hypertension. High blood pressure. 14

Hypnosis. A sleeplike trance that is artificially brought about. 15

Hypocrite. A person who pretends to be what he or she is not; one who pretends to be better than he or she really is. 22

Hypodermic. Referring to the area under the skin; used for injecting under the skin; a hypodermic injection; a hypodermic syringe or needle. 11

Hypothesis. An unproved scientific conclusion drawn from known facts; something assumed as a basis for argument; a possible answer to a problem that requires further investigation. 11

Illegal. Not legal; not lawful. 10

Immoral. Not moral; knows difference between right and wrong but chooses to do wrong. 5

Immortal. Referring to a being who never dies; undying; one who never dies. 8

Imperfect. Not perfect; having a fault. 10

Import. To carry in; bring in goods from another country; something that is imported. 4, 10

Important. Deserving of notice. 10

Impotent. Without power to act; physically weak; incapable of sexual intercourse (said of males). 7

Inclination. A personal leaning or bent; a liking; a bending, slanting, or sloping; a slope. 22

Incorporate. To unite; combine. 8

Incredible. Not believable. 4

Ineffectual. Not being able to bring about results. 10

Infamous. Having a bad reputation; notorious. 23

Infinite. Having no limit or end; not able to be measured. 10

Initiate. To introduce by doing or using first; to bring into practice or use; to admit as a member into a fraternity, sorority, club, and so on, especially through use of a secret ceremony. 23

Innate. Inborn; born with; not acquired from the environment; belonging to the fundamental nature of something. 15

Innovation. Something newly introduced; a new method, something new. 14

Inquisitive. Given to asking many questions; prying; curious. 16

Inspection. The act of looking into something. 10

Integrate. To unite; to make whole or complete by adding together parts. 16

Intense. Having great or extreme force; very strong; existing or occurring to a high or extreme degree. 13

Intention. Aim; goal; purpose. 13

Intercollegiate. Between colleges. 14

Interdepartmental. Between departments. 14

Interdependent. Dependent upon one another. 14

Intermission. Time between events; recess. 15

Interrogate. To ask questions of formally; to examine by questioning. 20

Interstate. Between states. 14

Intimidate. To make timid; to cause fear; to scare; to discourage by threats or violence. 22

Intracollegiate. Within the college. 14

Intradepartmental. Within the department. 14

Intramural. Within a school or an institution. 14

Intricate. Complicated; difficult to follow or understand; complex. 20

Invisible. Not able to be seen. 7

Irregular. Not uniform; not the same. 10

Irish. Belonging to Ireland. 24

Isolate. To set apart from others; to place alone; to separate. 19

Killer. One who kills. 1

Kingdom. Area controlled by a king. 16

Kingship. Dignity or rank of a king. 20

Laughable. Able to be laughed at. 4

Leadership. Skill as a leader. 20

Legal. Referring to law; lawful. 6, 13

Legislative. Relating to the body of lawmakers. 23

Legislature. Body of persons responsible for lawmaking. 6, 22

Lethal. Causing death; deadly. 17

Liability. A debt; legal obligation to make good any loss or damage that occurs in a transaction (a business deal); something that works to one's disadvantage. 21

Liberal. Giving freely; generous; large or plentiful; tolerant of views differing from one's own; broad-minded; favoring reform or progress. 21

Local. Referring to a relatively small area, region, or neighborhood; limited. 9, 13

Location. A place or site; exact position or place occupied; a place used for filming a motion picture or a television program. 9

Logical. Relating to the science concerned with correct reasoning. 10

Lordship. Rank of a lord. 20

Lucid. Clear; easily understood; bright; shining. 14

Magnanimous. Forgiving of insults or injuries; high-minded; great of soul. 15

Magnificent. Splendid; beautiful; superb. 15

Magnify. To increase the size of; to make larger. 15

Maintain. To carry on or continue; to keep up; to keep in good condition. 12, 13

Maintenance. The act of keeping up. 13

Malformed. Abnormally formed. 15

Malfunction. To function badly. 15

Malnourished. Badly nourished. 15

Maltreated. Treated badly. 15

Manageable. Able to be managed. 4

Manicure. Care of the hands and fingernails; to care for the hands; to cut evenly. 9

Manual. Referring to the hand; made, done, or used by the hands; a handy book used as a guide or source of information. 9, 13

Manufacture. To make goods or articles by hand or by machinery; to make something from raw materials by hand or machinery; the act of manufacturing. 9

Manuscript. Written by hand or typed; not printed; a document written by hand; a book written by hand and usually sent in for publication; style of penmanship in which letters are not joined together. 9

Marriage. State of being wed. 22

Massive. Having the quality of being very large. 23

Metropolitan. Referring to a major city center and its surrounding area; a person who inhabits a metropolis or one who has the manners and tastes associated with a metropolis. 13

Microscope. Instrument used to make very small objects appear larger so that they can be seen. 2

Millennium. Period of one thousand years; a one thousandth anniversary; a period of great happiness (the millennium). 4

Million. A thousand thousands (1,000,000); a very large or indefinitely large number; being one million in number. 4

Misanthrope. Hater of mankind. 6

Miscellaneous. Mixed; consisting of several kinds; various. 23

Misnomer. A name wrongly applied to someone or something; an error in the naming of a person or place in a legal document. 9

Mission. Group or team of persons sent somewhere to perform some work; the task, business, or responsibility that a person is assigned; the place where missionaries carry out their work; a place where poor people may go for assistance. 15

Modify. To change slightly or make minor changes in character, form, and so on; to change or alter; to limit or reduce; in grammar, to limit or restrict a meaning. 21

Monarchy. A government or state headed by a king, a queen, or an emperor: called absolute (or despotic) when there is no limitation on the monarch's power and constitutional (or limited) when there is such limitation. 5

Monogamist. One who believes in or practices monogamy. 6

Monogamy. Marriage to one spouse at one time. 6

Morgue. Place where dead bodies (corpses) of accident victims and unknown persons found dead are kept; for reporters, it refers to the reference library of old newspaper articles, pictures, and so on. 8

Mortal. Referring to a being who must eventually die; causing death; ending in death; a human being. 8

Mortality. The state of having to die eventually; proportion of deaths to the population of the region; death rate; death on a large scale, as from disease or war. 8

Mortgage. The pledging of property to a creditor (one to whom a sum of money is owed) as security for payment; to pledge. 8

Mortician. A funeral director; undertaker. 8

Motherless. Without a mother. 7

Mundane. Referring to everyday things; referring to that which is routine or ordinary; referring to wordly things rather than more high-minded or spiritual things. 18

Naive. Foolishly simple; childlike; unsophisticated. 16

Nationalism. Devotion to one's nation. 23

Native. Belonging to a country by birth. 23

Nature. The necessary quality or qualities of something; sort; kind; wild state of existence; uncivilized way of life; overall pattern or system; basic characteristic of a person; inborn quality; the sum total of all creation. 15

Nautical. Relating to sailing. (See Additional Words Glossary.) 13

Non-Arab. Not an Arab. 9

Nonbeliever. Not a believer. 9

Noncapitalist. One who is not a capitalist. 9

Non-Catholic. Not a Catholic. 9

Non-Communist. One who is not a Communist. 9

Noncriminal. Not criminal. 9

Nonefficient. Not efficient. 9

Non-English. Not English. 9

Nostalgic. Homesick; longing to go back to one's home, hometown, and so on; longing for something far away or long ago. 18

Novel. A work of fiction of some length; new; strange; unusual. 14

Obstacle. Something that stands in the way or opposes; an obstruction. 14

Omission. Anything left out or not done; failure to include. 23

Omnipresent. Being present everywhere at all times. 7

Opponent. One who opposes another, as in battle or debate; one who acts against something or another; adversary; antagonist. 24

Optimist. One who is hopeful; a cheerful person; one who tends to take the most hopeful view or expects the best outcome. 18

Orphanage. Place for orphans or collection of orphans. 22

Outage. State of being interrupted. 22

Outrage. Act of shocking violence or cruelty. 22

Overt. Open to view; public; apparent; able to be seen. 17

Pacify. To bring peace to; to calm; to quiet. 13

Passage. Act of passing. 22

Passive. Not acting; acted upon; unresisting; not opposing; unenthusiastic. 24

Patriotism. Quality of being a patriot. 23

Pauperism. Condition of being very poor. 23

Pedestrian. One who goes on foot. 1

Pediatrician. A doctor who specializes in children's diseases. 11

Penmanship. Art or skill of handwriting. 20

Perception. The act of becoming aware of something through the senses of seeing, hearing, feeling, tasting, and/or smelling. 11

Period. A portion of time; a portion of time into which something is divided; a punctuation mark that signals a full stop at the end of a sentence; used after abbreviations. 14

Periodical. Referring to publications, such as magazines, that appear at fixed time intervals; a periodical publication. 14

Permission. Act of allowing the doing of something; a consent. 15

Persevere. To persist; to continue doing something in spite of difficulty. 20

Persist. To continue in some course or action even though it is difficult. 14

Pertinent. Relevant; relating to or bearing upon the matter in hand; being to the point. 19

Pessimist. One who expects the worst to happen in any situation; one who looks on the dark side of things; a gloomy person. 18

Philosophy. The study of human knowledge; the love of wisdom and the search for it; a search for the general laws that give a reasonable explanation of something. 14

Phobia. Extreme fear. 3

Pitiful. Full of pity. 18

Player. One who plays. 1

Poetic. Like poetry. 24

Politician. A person engaged in politics; a person involved in the science or art of government; a person who seeks advancement or power within an organization by dubious (doubtful) means. 13

Politics. (Although plural, it is usually looked upon as singular.) The science or art of government or of the direction and management of public or state affairs. 13

Polygamist. One who is married to many spouses at the same time. 6

Polygamy. Marriage to many spouses at the same time. 6

Popular. Approved of; admired; liked by most people; referring to the common people or the general public. 15

Population. Total number of people living in a country, city, or any area. 15

Port. Place to or from which ships carry things; place where ships may wait. 4

Portable. Can be carried; easily or conveniently transported. 4

Porter. A person who carries things; one who is employed to carry baggage at a hotel or transportation terminal. 4

Position. An act of placing or arranging; the manner in which a thing is placed; the way the body is placed; the place occupied by a person or thing; the proper or appropriate place; job; a feeling or stand; social standing. 15

Positive. Being directly found to be so or true; real; actual; sure of something; definitely set; confident. 15

Post. A position or employment, usually in government service; an assigned beat; a piece of wood or other material to be used as a support; a place occupied by troops; to inform; to put up (as on a wall); to mail (as a letter). 15

Postnatal. Occurring after birth. 15

Postpone. To put off to a future time; to delay. 15

Postscript. Something added to a letter after the writer's signature; something added to written or printed legal papers. 13

Posture. The placing or carriage of the body or parts of the body; a mental position or frame of mind. 15, 22

Potent. Physically powerful; having great authority; able to influence; strong in chemical effects. 7

Potential. The possible ability or power one may have; having force or power to develop. 7

Precede. To go or come before. 12

Precedent. Something done or said that may serve as an example; in law, a legal decision serving as an authoritative rule in future similar cases; preceding; anterior; going before. 20

Pre-Christian. Referring to the time before there were Christians. 8

Predict. To say before; to foretell; to forecast; to tell what will happen. 8

Preference. The choosing of one person or thing over another; the valuing of one over another; a liking better. 10

Preheat. To heat before. 8

Prehistoric. Referring to the time before history was recorded. 8

Prejudge. To judge or decide before. 8

Prejudice. An opinion or judgment made beforehand. 8

Premature. Ripened before. 8

Prenatal. Being or taking place before birth. 15

Prerevolutionary. Referring to time before a revolution. 8

Preset. To set before. 8

Preunite. To join together before. 8

Prisoner. One who is kept in prison. 1

Proceed. To go on; to go forward; to carry on an action. 12

Prognosis. A prediction or conclusion regarding the course of a disease and the chances of recovery; a prediction. 11

Prologue. An introduction, often in verse (poetry), spoken or snug before a play or opera; any introductory or preceding event; a preface. 10

Proposal. An offer put forth to be accepted or adopted; an offer of marriage; a plan. 15

Provision. The act of being prepared beforehand; something made ready in advance; a part of an agreement referring to a specific thing. 7

Pseudonym. False name, used by an author to conceal his or her identity; pen name; false name. 9

Public. Relating to the public or people at large. 24

Question. The act of asking. 3

Reception. The act of receiving or being received; a formal social entertainment; the manner of receiving someone. 11

Recomb. To comb again. 2

Redo. To do again. 2

Reference. A referring or being referred; the giving of a problem to a person, committee, or authority for settlement; a note in a book that sends the reader for information to another book; the name of another person who can offer information or recommendation; the mark or sign, as a number or letter, directing the reader to a footnote and so on; a written statement of character, qualification, or ability; testimonial. 10

Relevant. Applying to the matter in question; suitable; relating to. 17

Reliable. Dependable; trustworthy. 20

Reluctant. Unwilling; opposed. 20

Repay. To pay back. 2

Reporter. A person who gathers information and writes reports for newspapers, magazines, and so on. 4

Rerun. To run again. 2

Return. To go back. 2

Rework. To work again. 2

Rewrite. To write again. 2

Ridicule. Language or actions that make a person the object of mockery or cause one to be laughed at or scorned; to mock or view someone in a scornful way; to hold someone up as a laughingstock; to make fun of. 11

Ridiculous. Unworthy of consideration; absurd (senseless); preposterous. 11

Rupture. The act of something breaking apart. 22

Salty. Full of salt. 17

Salvage. Act of saving. 22

Science. Any area of knowledge in which the facts have been investigated and presented in an orderly manner. 7

Scientific. Relating to science. 24

Script. Writing that is either cursive, printed, or engraved; a piece of writing; a prepared copy of a play for the use of actors. 2

Scripture. Books of the Old and New Testaments; a text or passage from the Bible. 2

Scrutinize. To observe closely; to examine or inquire into critically; to investigate. 23

Segregate. To set apart from others; to separate. 16

Semiannual. Twice in a year; every half year. 15

Semiblind. Partly blind. 15

Semicircle. Half circle. 15

Semistarved. Partly starved. 15

Semiwild. Partly wild. 15

Sentimental. Having or showing tenderness, emotion, feeling, and so on; influenced more by feeling or emotion than by reason; having or showing exaggerated or superficial emotion. 18

Sequence. The following of one thing after another; order; a continuous or related series, with one thing following another. 12, 13

Shameful. Full of shame. 18

Shrinkage. Act of shrinking; amount of decrease. 22

Significant. Having or expressing meaning; full of meaning; important. 20

Socialism. The principle whereby the ownership and operation of the means of production are by society or the community rather than by private individuals, with all members of the community sharing in the work and the products. 23

Sophisticated. Not in a simple, natural, or pure state; worldly-wise; not naive; cultured; highly complicated; complex; experienced. 14

Sophomore. A second-year student in American high schools or colleges; an immature person; one who thinks he or she knows more than he or she does. 14

Spanish. Belonging to Spain. 24

Spectacle. Something showy that is seen by many (the public); an unwelcome or sad sight. 3

Spectacles. Eyeglasses. 3

Spectacular. Relating to something unusual, impressive, exciting, or unexpected. 3

Spectator. An onlooker; one who views something. 3

Spillage. The act of spilling; amount spilled. 22

Stagnant. Lacking motion or current; not flowing or moving; foul (dirty and bad-smelling) from lack of movement; lacking in activitity; sluggish; dull. 21

Stardom. Status of being a star. 16

Sticky. Tending to stick. 17

Subcommittee. A committee under the original committee. 12

Subfloor. Floor beneath. 12

Submarine. Ship undersea. 12

Submit. To give in to another; to surrender; to concede; to present for consideration or approval; to present as one's opinion. 15

Subsequent. Following soon after; following in time, place, or order; resulting. 12

Subset. Something that is under the larger set. 12

Substitute. To put in place of another person or thing; one who takes the place of another person; something that is put in place of something else or is available for use instead of something else. 14

Subtraction. The act of taking something away. 12

Succeed. To accomplish what is attempted; to come next in order; to come next after or replace another in an office or position. 12

Suffer. To feel pain or distress. 10

Suicide. Killing of oneself. 8

Superabundance. Abundance in excess. 21

Superacid. Excessively acid. 21

Superb. Very fine. 21

Superbias. Excessive bias. 21

Supercritical. Highly critical. 21

Superintendent. One who has charge of a building, office, institution, and so on. 21

Superior. Of higher degree. 21

Superlative. Of the highest degree. 21

Supersafe. Safe in the highest degree. 21

Superstitious. Having beliefs that are not consistent with the known laws of science. 21

Supersweet. Sweet in the highest degree. 21

Supervision. The act of overseeing others. 21

Sustain. To maintain; to keep in existence; to keep going; to uphold; to support. 16

Sympathy. Sameness of feeling with another; ability to feel pity for another. 8

Synonym. A word having the same meaning as some other word. 9

Tacit. Unspoken; not expressed openly but implied. 16

Tallish. Rather tall. 24

Tearful. Full of tears. 18

Telegram. Message sent from a distance. 3

Telegraph. Instrument for sending a message in code at a distance; to send a message from a distance. 2

Telephone. Instrument that sends and receives sound, such as the spoken word, over distance; to send a message by telephone. 2

Telescope. Instrument used to view distant objects. 2

Television. An electronic system for the transmission of visual images from a distance; a television receiving set. 7

Temperature. Degree of hotness or coldness of something. 22

Temporary. Lasting for a short period of time. 11

Tenant. A person who holds property; one who lives on property belonging to another; one who rents or leases from a landlord; one who lives in a place. 12

Tension. The act of stretching or the condition of being stretched tight; mental strain. 13

Terrorism. Practice of terror; use of fear to frighten or intimidate. 23

Terse. Brief; concise. 16

Theocracy. A form of government in which there is rule by a religious group. 5

Theologist. One who is in the field of theology. 6

Theology. The study of religion. 5

Thirtyish. About thirty. 24

Torture. Act of causing severe pain. 22

Toxic. Relating to poison. 11, 24

Tragic. Like a tragedy, in which something is very sad or there is disaster. 24

Transatlantic. Across the Atlantic Ocean. 10

Transfer. To carry or send from one person or place to another; to cause to pass from one person or place to another; an act of transferring or being transferred. 10

Transhuman. Beyond human limits. 10

Translucent. Permitting light to go through but not permitting a clear view of any object. 14

Transmit. To send from one place to another; to pass on by heredity; to transfer; to pass or communicate news, information, and so on. 15

Transparent. Able to be seen through. 10

Transport. To carry from one place to another. 10

Trite. Used so often as to be too common; made commonplace by repetition; lacking freshness or originality. 24

Turmoil. Confused motion or state; disturbance; tumult. 24

Unable. Not able. 8

Unaided. Not helped. 8

Unanimous. Agreeing completely; united in opinion; being in complete agreement; being of one mind. 23

Uncarpeted. Not carpeted. 8

Uncaught. Not caught. 8

Unclaimed. Not claimed. 8

Uncooked. Not cooked. 8

Uniform. Being always the same; a special form of clothing. 3

Union. A joining; a putting together. 3

Unique. Being the only one of its kind. 3

Unison. A harmonious agreement; a saying of something together. 3

Universal. Applying to all. 3, 13,

Universe. Everything that exists. 3

Unloved. Not loved. 8

Unwed. Not married. 8

Verbose. Wordy. 16·

Visible. Able to be seen; evident; apparent; on hand. 7

Vision. The sense of sight. 7

Vocabulary. A list of words and phrases, usually arranged alphabetically, that are defined or translated from another language; a stock of words possessed by an individual or group. 13

Vocal. Referring to the voice; having voice; oral; freely expressing oneself in speech, usually with force; speaking out. 13

Vocation. A calling; a person's work or profession. 13

Wastage. Amount wasted. 22

Wattage. Amount of electric power; total number of watts needed. 22

Wavy. Like a wave. 17

Wisdom. The state of having knowledge. 16

ADDITIONAL WORDS PRESENTED IN *GAINING WORD POWER*

The number after the meaning refers to the exercise in which the vocabulary word is presented.

Abridge. To shorten; to curtail; to give the substance of in fewer words. 24

Accreditation. Act of bringing into favor; a vouching for; a giving authority to. 4

Acrophobia. An abnormal fear of high places. 3

Affinity. Close relationship; attraction to another. 10

Agnostic. Professing uncertainty; one who is not for or against; one who doubts that the ultimate cause (God) and the essential nature of things are knowable. 11

Ambidextrous. Able to use both hands equally well. 13

Amortize. The gradual extinction of a debt such as a mortgage or a bond issue by payment of a part of the principal at the time of each periodic interest payment. 8

Anachronism. Something out of time order; an error in chronology in which a person, an object, or an event is assigned an incorrect date or period. 12

Animate. To make alive; to move to action. 15

Annuity. An investment yielding a fixed sum of money, payable yearly. 1

Anthropoid. A person resembling an ape either in stature, walk, or intellect; resembling man, used especially of apes such as the gorilla, chimpanzee, and orangutan; resembling an ape. 6

Anthropomorphic. Giving human shape or characteristics to gods, objects, animals, and so on. 6

Antipathy. A dislike for someone. 9

Antitoxin. Something used against bacterial poison; a substance formed in the body that counteracts a specific toxin; the antibody formed in immunization with a given toxin, used in treating certain infectious diseases or in immunizing against them 11

Apodal. Having no feet. 5

Archetype. The original pattern or model of a work from which something is made or developed. 5

Arrogant. Full of pride and self-importance; overbearing; haughty. 19

Attrition. A gradual wearing down or weakening; a rubbing out or grinding down. 24

Audiology. The study of hearing. 9

Audiometer. An instrument used to measure hearing. 9

Automatic. Moving by itself; performed without thinking about it. 1

Automaton. A person or an animal acting in an automatic or mechanical way. 1

Autonomous. Self-governing; functioning independently of other parts. 1

Avocation. Something a person does in addition to his or her regular work, usually for enjoyment; a hobby. 13

Benediction. A blessing; the expression of good wishes. 9

Bifocals. Pair of glasses with two-part lenses. 1

Bilateral. Involving two sides. 1

Bilingual. Able to use two languages equally well; a bilingual person. 1

Binary. Made up of two parts; twofold; relating to base two. 1

Biopsy. In medicine, the cutting out of a piece of living tissue for examination. 1

Bisexual. Of both sexes; having both male and female organs, as is true of some plants and animals; a person who is sexually attracted by both sexes. 6

Capitulate. To give up; surrender. 8

Caption. The heading of a chapter, section, or page in a book; the title or subtitle of a picture. 8

Castigate. To correct or subdue by punishing; criticize with drastic severity; to rebuke. 21

Centimeter. In the metric system, a unit of measure equal to 1/100 meter (.3937 inch). 4

Centipede. Wormlike animal with many legs. 4

Chronometer. A very accurate clock or watch; an instrument used to measure time. 12

Claustrophobia. An abnormal fear of being confined, as in a room or a small place. 3

Concession. An act of giving in; a right granted by the government or other authority for a specific purpose. 12

Constraint. Confinement; the act of restricting; the act of using force; compulsion; coercion; restriction. 18

Convocation. A group of people called together; an assembly. 13

Corpulent. Fat; fleshy; obese. 8

Corroborate. To confirm (to strengthen; to make firm; to affirm); to make more certain. 22

Crafty. Sly; skillful in deceiving; cunning. 17

Creditor. One to whom a sum of money or other thing is due. 4

Creed. A statement of religious belief; a statement of belief; principles. 4

Criterion. A standard of judging; any established law, rule, or principle by which a correct judgment may be formed. 23

Curator. Head of a department of a museum; one in charge. 9

Datum. (*Data*, the plural of *datum* is usually used.) Information given, granted, or admitted; a premise upon which something can be argued; material used as a basis for calculations. 23

Decameter. In the metric system, a measure of length containing ten meters, equal to 393.70 inches or 32.81 feet. 4

Decimal. Numbered by tens; based on ten; pertaining to tenths or the number 10; a decimal fraction. 4

Decimate. To take or destroy a tenth part of; to destroy but not completely; to destroy a great number or proportion of. 4

Decimeter. In the metric system, a unit of length equal to 1/10 meter. 4

Defer. To leave to another's opinion or judgment; to delay; to postpone. 10

Deference. Respect; a giving in to another's opinion or judgment. 10

Definitive. Conclusive; final; most nearly complete or accurate. 10

Demography. The statistical study of human populations, including births, deaths, marriages, population movements, and so on. 5

Deportment. Manner of conducting or carrying oneself; behavior; conduct. 4

Depose. To remove from a throne or other high position; to let fall. 15

Derisive. Mocking; jeering. 11

Detain. To stop; to hold; to keep from proceeding; to delay. 12

Detente. Easing of strained relations, especially between nations. 13

Detention. A keeping or holding back; confinement. 13

Dialect. A variety of speech; a regional form of a standard language. 10

Dictaphone. A machine for recording and reproducing words spoken into its mouthpiece (differs from a tape recorder because it has controls that fit it to use in transcription). 3

Dictum. An authoritative statement; a saying. 3

Disposition. One's usual frame of mind or one's usual way of reacting; a natural tendency. 15

Ecstasy. Great joy. 16

Egotistic. Conceited; very concerned with oneself; selfish; vain. 14

Emancipate. To set free from servitude or slavery; to set free. 9

Emissary. A person or agent sent on a specific mission. 15

Envision. To imagine something; to picture in the mind. 7

Epidermis. Outermost layer of skin. 11

Equivocate. To use ambiguous language on purpose. 15

Erratic. Wandering; not regular; not stable. 14

Exonerate. To relieve, as of a charge or blame resting on one; to clear of a charge of guilt; to relieve of a debt or duty. 22

Expedite. To hasten; to speed up the progress of. 18

Expound. To state in detail; to set forth; to explain. 15

Extemporaneous. Done or spoken without special preparation; makeshift. 11

Facsimile. An exact copy; to make an exact copy of. 9

Faction. A number of persons in an organization, group, government, party, and so on, having a common goal, often self-seeking. 9

Finale. The last part; end; the concluding movement of a musical composition the last scene of an entertainment. 10

Fratricide. Killing of a brother; may also refer to the killing of a sister. 8

Futile. Useless; ineffectual; trifling; unimportant. 23

Genealogy. The science or study of one's descent; a tracing of one's ancestors. 6

Generate. To produce; to cause to be; to bring into existence. 6

Genus. A class, kind, or group marked by shared characteristics or by one shared characteristic. 6

Geocentric. Relating to the earth as the center. 2

Grammar. That part of the study of language that deals with the forms and structure of words (morphology) and their arrangement in phrases and sentences (syntax); the study or description of the way language is used. 3

Graphic. Marked by realistic and vivid detail. 1

Graphology. The study of handwriting. 1

Hydrophobia. An abnormal fear of water; an inability to swallow water when rabies is present. 3

Hyperbole. Great exaggeration; an overstatement. 14

Illuminate. To give light to; make clear. 14

Imminent. About to happen; threatening (said especially of danger). 24

Indictment. A charge; an accusation. 3

Inference. Something derived by reasoning; something that is not directly stated but suggested in the statement; a logical conclusion that is drawn from statements; deduction. 10

Infidelity. Breach of trust; lack of faith in a religion; unfaithfulness of a marriage partner; adultery. 15

Infinitesimal. Too small to be measured; very minute. 10

Inscription. Something written or engraved on a surface; a brief or informal dedication in a book to a friend. 2

Intercede. To come between; to come between as an influencing force; to intervene. 15

Intercept. To stop or interrupt the course of. 11

Intermittent. Starting or stopping again at intervals; not continuous; coming and going at intervals. 15

Intervene. To come between; to act as an influencing force; to intercede. 15

Invincible. Impossible to overcome; not able to be conquered. 23

Jeopardy. Risk; danger; peril. 22

Kilometer. In the metric system, a unit of length equal to one thousand meters.

Laudable. Worthy of praise; commendable. 21

Listless. Spiritless; indifferent; inactive; apathetic. 16

Magnate. A very important or influential person. 15

Malediction. A speaking badly of someone; slander; a curse. 15

Malefactor. Someone who does something bad; a criminal. 15

Manipulation. The act of handling or operating; the act of managing or controlling skillfully or by shrewd use of influence; the act of changing or falsification for one's own purposes or profit. 9

Megalopolis. One very large city made up of a number of cities; a vast, populous, continuously urban area. 13

Meter. In the metric system, a unit of length equal to approximately 39.37 inches; an instrument for measuring the amount of something (as water, gas, electricity); an instrument for measuring distance, time, weight, speed, and so forth; a measure of verse. 2

Microbe. A very small living thing; a microorganism. 2

Microfilm. Film on which documents are photographed in a reduced size for storage convenience. 2

Micrometer. An instrument used to measure accurately very small distances, angles, and diameters. 2

Microorganism. An organism so small that it can be seen only under a microscope. 2

Microphone. A device that magnifies weak sounds. 2

Millimeter. In the metric system, a unit of length equal to 1/1000 meter (.03937 inch). 4

Misogamist. Hater of marriage. 6

Misogynist. Hater of women. 11

Missile. An object, especially a weapon, intended to be thrown or discharged, as a bullet, arrow, stone, and so on. 15

Monoglot. Person who knows, speaks, or writes only one language; speaking and writing only one language. 5

Monologue. A long speech by one person; a dramatic sketch performed by one actor. 10

Monophobia. Abnormal fear of being alone. 5

Monopoly. Exclusive control of a commodity or service in a given market; control that makes possible the fixing of prices and the elimination of free competition. 5

Monorail. A single rail serving as a track for trucks or cars suspended from it or balanced on it. 5

Monosyllable. A word consisting of one syllable. 8

Monotone. Speech not having any change in pitch; to speak in an unvaried tone. 5

Monotonous. Changeless; dull; uniform; having no variety. 5

Mortify. To cause to feel shame; to punish (one's body) or control (one's physical desires or passions) by self-denial, fasting, and the like, as a means of religious or ascetic (severe) discipline. 8

Nautical. Pertaining to seamen, ships, or navigation. 7

Novice. Someone new at something; a rookie; a beginner. 14

Obfuscate. To darken; to confuse; to obscure. 18

Obstinate. Stubborn; tenacious. 14

Oligarchy. A form of government in which there is rule by a few (usually a privileged few). 5

Omnibus. A large bus; an *omnibus* bill is a legislative bill that carries a mixture of provisions. 7

Omnipotent. All-powerful. 7

Omniscient. All-knowing. 7

Orthography. The part of language study that deals with correct spelling. 1

Pacifist. One who is against war. 13

Paradox. Contradiction; a self-contradictory statement that is false; a statement that seems absurd, contradictory, or unbelievable but may be true. 24

Pedagogue. A teacher. 11

Pedestal. A base or bottom support. 1

Pedicure. Care of the feet, toes, and nails. 9

Perceptive. Being aware; having insight, understanding, or intuition, as a *perceptive* analysis of the problems involved. 11

Perfidious. Violating good trust; treacherous; deceitful; dilberately faithless. 15

Perimeter. A measure of the outer part or boundary of a closed plane figure; boundary line of a closed plane figure. 14

Periodic. Taking place, occurring, or appearing at regular intervals. 14

Periphery. The outer part or boundary of something. 14

Periscope. An instrument used by a submarine to see all around. 14

Personification. A figure of speech in which a nonliving thing or idea is made to appear as having the qualities of a person. 9

Peruse. To read carefully; to inspect closely. 16

Phenomenon. Any fact, circumstance, or experience that is apparent to the senses and that can be scientifically described; something extremely unusual. 24

Phonetics. A study dealing with speech sounds and their production. 2

Phonics. Study of the relationship between letter symbols of a written language and the sounds they represent. 2

Podiatrist. Foot doctor. 6

Podium. A raised platform for the conductor of an orchestra; a dais. 1

Polyglot. A person who knows, speaks, or writes many languages; speaking or writing many languages. 6

Polygon. A closed plane figure with several angles and sides. 6

Posterior. In the rear; later; following after; coming after in order; succeeding; located behind; the buttocks. 13

Posterity. Future generations; all of one's descendants (offspring). 13

Posthumously. After death. 13

Postmortem. Happening or performed after death; referring to an examination of a human body after death; autopsy. 13

Potentate. A person possessing great power: a ruler; a monarch. 7

Prescription. A doctor's written directions for the preparation and use of medicine; an order; direction; rule. 2

Procession. A parade, as a funeral *procession*; any continuous course. 12

Procrastinate. To put off doing something until a future time; to postpone taking action. 20

Proficient. Knowing something very well; able to do something very well. 10

Proposition. A plan or something put forth for consideration or acceptance. 15

Provoke. To stir up anger or resentment; to irritate. 13

Prudent. Capable of using sound judgment in practical matters; wisely cautious; sensible; not rash. 20

Pseudopodium. False foot. 9

Pseudoscience. A false science. 9

Recession. The act of going back; in economics, the decline of business activity. 12

Remission. A temporary stopping or lessening of a disease; a pardon. 15

Repent. To feel pain, sorrow, or regret for something left undone or done; to feel remorse. 22

Replenish. To supply or fill again. 19

Replete. Well filled or supplied. 19

Retentive. Having the ability to retain or keep in things; tenacious, as a *retentive* memory; having a good memory. 12

Satiate. To fill; to satisfy the appetite completely; to supply with anything to excess; to glut (overindulge). 20

Scribe. A writer, author; a public writer or secretary; in Scripture and Jewish history, a man of learning. 2

Secede. To withdraw from. 12

Sedate. Calm; composed; quiet; serene; sober; to put under sedation. 21

Sophistry. Faulty reasoning; unsound or misleading but clever and plausible (appearing real) argument or reasoning. 14

Speculate. To think about something by viewing it from all sides; to take part in any risky business venture. 3

Stamina. Staying power; resistance to fatigue, illness, and the like. 14

Stethoscope. A hearing instrument used in examining the heart, lungs, and so on. 2

Subscription. An agreement; a promise in writing to pay some money; an agreement to receive something and pay for it. 12

Susceptible. Easily influenced by or affected with; especially liable to. 11

Syllable. A letter or a group of letters with one vowel sound. 8

Symbol. Something that stands for or represents another thing; an object used to represent something abstract. 8

Symmetry. Balanced form or arrangement; balance on both sides. 8

Symphony. Harmony of sound; harmony of any kind. 8

Symptom. In medicine, a condition that results from a disease and serves as an aid in diagnosis; a sign or token that indicates the existence of something else. 8

Synchronize. To cause to agree in rate or speed; to occur at the same time. 12

Synthesis. A putting together of two or more things to form a whole. 8

Tactful. Considerate; conscientiously inoffensive; skillful in dealing with people or difficult situations. 18

Telemeter. An instrument that measures distance; instrument that sends information to a distant point. 2

Temerity. Rash boldness; foolhardiness. 17

Temperate. Moderate in everything; avoiding extremes or excesses. 22

Tempo. The rate of speed at which a musical composition is supposed to be played; rate of activity. 11

Tenacious. Stubborn; tough; holding or tending to hold strongly to one's views, opinions, rights, and so on; retentive, as a *tenacious* memory. 12

Tenet. Any opinion, doctrine, principle, dogma, and the like held as true; belief. 17

Tentative. Done on trial or experimentally; not final; uncertain. 16

Tenure. The right to hold or possess something; length of time something is held; status assuring an employee of permanence in his or her position or employment (tenure protects employees such as teachers from being dismissed except for serious misconduct or incompetence). 17

Terminate. To end. 16

Thrifty. Clever at managing one's money; economical; not spending money unnecessarily. 19

Toxicologist. One who specializes in the study of poisons. 11

Transcript. A written or typewritten copy of an original; a copy or reproduction of any kind. 2

Unify. To make or form into one. 3

Unilateral. Occurring on one side only; done by one only; one-sided. 3

Untenable. Not able to be held or defended. 12

Valid. Sound; well grounded on principles or evidence; having legal force. 23

Variable. Changeable; something that may or does vary. 18

Venture. A risky or dangerous undertaking. 7

Versatile. Changeable; turning with ease from one thing to another. 17

Vestige. A trace, mark, or sign of something that once existed but doesn't anymore. 19

Vindicate. To clear from criticism, accusation, or suspicion. 21

Vindictive. Revengeful in spirit; spiteful. 20

Virile. Manly; masculine; forceful; able to procreate (to produce or reproduce). 20

Visa. Something stamped or written on a passport that grants an individual entry to a country. 7

Visage. The face; the appearance of the face or its expression. 7

Visionary. A person who sees visions. 7

Visor. The projecting front brim of a cap for shading the eyes. 7

Vital. Necessary to life; essential; energetic. 21

Vociferous. Of forceful, aggressive, and loud speech; clamorous. 13